FI

An Outline of Social Psychology

An Outline of Social Psychology

by
MUZAFER SHERIF

with an introduction by
GARDNER MURPHY

Harper & Brothers, Publishers, New York

Contents

Editor's Introduction

TO THOSE WHO HAVE FOLLOWED THE EXTRAORDINARY TRANS-
formation of social psychology in recent years, it will seem a
trifle absurd that I should write an introduction to Muzafer
Sherif. To him, more than to any other single person, is at-
tributable the whole manner of approaching social psychology
which characterizes the present period. Nevertheless, he has
asked me to say a word, and as a friend who has looked on with
admiration I cannot do otherwise.

It seems appropriate to refer to Sherif's contribution to social
psychology under three heads. First, he has taught us that
social behavior springs largely from the way in which the individual perceives his world; that behavior analysis without an
analysis of individual frames of reference, individual habits of
social perception, is a study of shadows whose deeper substance
is likely to be lost; that the dynamic, integrating principles
from which coherent social behavior springs are in the first instance principles regarding social perception. What a society
does when it molds the individual into membership in the group
is first of all to insist upon his learning to see the world in one
way rather than another. From the systematic study of social
perception—the ways of viewing the world in terms of one's
group memberships—follow the behavioral principles and all
the other principles with which the analysis of group life is concerned. This much was made clear in Sherif's *Psychology of
Social Norms*, published over a decade ago. It remained, however, to systematize and extend these conceptions, and to show
their adequacy to supply the whole broad basis for a systematic
social psychology. This task the present volume undertakes.

The role of wants, needs, deprivations, imperious biological
demands, was noted in his earlier work but subordinated to the
analysis of perceptual fields. In the present volume, the de-

termining role of the life of feeling and striving is much more
systematically considered, with intensive use made of those
studies of hunger, fear, affection, and other compelling forces
which drive the individual forcibly into this or that type of interpretation of his own social situation. The volume, while
making no use of traditional instinct theories, lays a firm dynamic foundation for the study of cognitive phenomena.

From this conception of the nature of social perception
follows the need to study intensively the role of group membership—class membership, national membership, etc.—in historical and in contemporary social trends; to find how the fact
of group membership gives structure to individual points of
view, and what the objective characteristics of the resulting
group behavior patterns are. We find ourselves confronting
the larger social aggregates, and the factors which today are
whirling them into ever more confused, violent, and unpre-
dictable forms. In a crisis situation, Sherif tells us, we may
begin to understand these factors which, at the "choice point,"
may make all the difference between one and another type of
social evolution. One begins, in fact, to realize that the study
of history becomes largely a study of crisis points, or choice
points, the interpretation of which may well lie largely in the
direction defined by Sherif's analysis. If so, this kind of a social
psychology might be the ticket of admission into a valid historical perspective for the understanding of our present world
predicament.

A third principle which was boldly enunciated in *The Psychology of Social Norms*, but left for the reader to develop in
his own way, was the unity of experimental and of "real life"
phenomena—the fact that a sound psychological analysis will
discover in laboratory situations and in life situations the same
fundamental dynamics of human life and conduct, because,
being human, one cannot *ever* function without displaying those
basic principles from which every sound interpretation proceeds. It is the task of the laboratory to discover the essentials
of the "real life" situations, and to throw light upon them,
just as it is the task of the study of life situations to see where
a given principle may be systematically explored in laboratory
terms.

This conception of the imperative need to base social psychology upon a sound and systematic general psychology, and to utilize the more exact approaches wherever they are appropriate, is expanded here and becomes perhaps the primary point of method which the book develops. In this context, it becomes reasonable to treat Ernie Pyle's study of the experience of the GI's of World War II, and the experience of Turkish peasants who as yet know nothing of industrialism, side by side with the experimental studies of the starving conscientious objectors of the Minnesota laboratory. Get the psychological principle clear, says Sherif, and you will find that it is sound in whatever individual or social situation you need to apply it. The moral of this for the development of an experimental social psychology is unavoidable and terrific. For it is the task of the experimentalist to find what is important and fundamental in life, and to find a way to develop valid and pertinent approaches to it, no longer selecting for laboratory work what merely happens to be convenient, but finding, as has the astronomer, that the task of experiment is to observe under controlled conditions those important phenomena which, in the "natural" situation, admit of no such control.

This is an attempt, then, to arrange all the fundamentals of social psychology in terms of one cardinal principle and the various corollaries and secondary principles which follow from it. In a sense this is too much for a textbook, and in a sense it is too little. It is, however, Sherif's belief that one big vista, one great glimpse of the integral meaning of participation in a social group, with dozens of supporting illustrations, may warrant the exclusion of much that is ordinarily included in social psychology texts. It may be, for example, that the study of attitudes and of prejudice is clarified more by the simple, unitary principle developed here than by the survey of the hundreds of generalizations from attitude studies and public opinion researches which characterize the present period. On this point our data are far from clear. He *may* be oversimplifying. No longer, however, can anyone say that social psychology is chaotic or undisciplined, that it is a rag-bag collection of uncoordinated facts, that it waits to determine its own method. Sherif's volume categorically removes any basis for such assertions. Whatever the strengths and weaknesses of this work may ultimately prove to be, it offers a clear, simple, elementary, fundamental, dynamic system for the interpretations of those types of social participation upon which group formation, group behavior, and historical change depend.

GARDNER MURPHY

Preface

THE MAIN FEATURES OF THIS OUTLINE OF SOCIAL PSYCHOLOGY
are derived from my earlier work—particularly from *A Study of
Some Social Factors in Perception* (1935) and *The Psychology of
Social Norms* (1936). On the whole, Part II is an attempt to
give an up-to-date account of the latter integrated into the
larger fabric of social psychology as I see it. I believe that a
number of loose ends have been pulled together here. Some
material from *The Psychology of Social Norms* has been used
with modifications in the chapters on group psychology (5 and
7) and on attitudes (9 and 10).

The treatment of ego-involvements (Chapters 11 and 12) is
essentially that developed in Chapters 8 and 9 of *The Psychology of Social Norms*. This early treatment was expanded in a
joint work (with H. Cantril), *The Psychology of Ego-Involvements* (1947), in which I was responsible for the first brief outline summarizing the main points and for the writing of
Chapters 1, 2, 3, 7, 8, 9, and 10. Since the problem of ego-involvements was not considered in relation to a general picture
of social psychology and particularly to the central topic of
motivation, a certain one-sided emphasis was inevitable in
that volume. An attempt is made here to give a more balanced
account of ego-involvements. "An Experimental Approach to
the Study of Attitudes" (*Sociometry*, 1937) is incorporated in
Chapter 10. Chapter 16 is based, in the main, on "The Psychology of Slogans" (*J. Abn. & Soc. Psychol.*, 1937).

This scheme of social psychology was first outlined for my
class in Ankara University in 1942–1943. In its elaboration I
owe much to my colleague, Professor Behice Boran of Ankara
University, and to the members of my class and seminar.

The time and means to work on the book were afforded
through a two-year State Department fellowship granted at

the end of 1944 and two Rockefeller grants (1947–1948), for which I am grateful.

Professor T. M. Newcomb of the University of Michigan has kindly contributed the systematic account of attitude change in the last section of Chapter 6. In developing the theme of the chapter on adolescence, I profited greatly from unpublished material made available to me by Drs. Harold and Mary Cover Jones during my visit to the University of California in 1945. Dr. Eugene Hartley wrote a summary of prejudice material for my use which, along with our discussions, made the writing of Chapter 14 smooth sailing. Without his authoritative aid on this topic, I would have struggled in pushing through the scattered material.

Professor Carl I. Hovland of Yale University made it possible for me to continue and complete this work by extending library and other facilities of the university and by arranging a research fellowship for the academic year 1947–1948. Without his effective help, this work would have never been completed.

It will be a felicitous experience for me if Professor Gordon Allport detects in this book some effect of his provocative suggestions and criticisms in the early thirties in the direction of giving greater weight to problems of individual characteristics and variations. I owe much to his encouragement and help in various ways while I was his student.

I cannot imagine being able to commit this outline or its forerunner, *The Psychology of Social Norms*, into writing without the unfailing and tolerant encouragement which I was fortunate to receive from Gardner Murphy. He spared much time to go over this work in various stages—in outline and in manuscript form. All the limitations and shortcomings are, of course, mine. The degree of indebtedness to his *Personality* book in the writing of Chapter 17 is far greater than formally acknowledged there. If his influence is reflected through an incorrigibly crude medium, it is not his fault.

My wife, Carolyn Sherif, contributed so much in the collection of new material as well as in the writing that I asked her to join me in signing this work. In spite of the fact that she declined my invitation with an attitude characteristic in our work, I consider this book a product of our joint effort.

I extend my thanks to various authors for permission to use passages and figures from their work, which are acknowledged in appropriate places throughout the book; and to Miss Dorothy Thompson of Harper & Brothers, who undertook the tedious task of editing and preparing the manuscript for publication.

M. S.

December 12, 1947
Saugatuck, Connecticut

An Outline of Social Psychology

1.

Introduction

Social Psychology

SOCIAL PSYCHOLOGY DEALS WITH THE EXPERIENCE AND behavior of the individual in relation to social stimulus situations. Interpersonal relationships, group interactions and their products, values or norms, language, art forms, institutions, and technology are certainly among the major social stimuli or stimulus situations. Since in the case of the newborn child all of these appear *first* as stimuli acting on him before they appear as responses made by him, an adequate account of their impact on him will ultimately give us the picture of his socialization—the central theme of social psychology.

But the individual is not a passive mechanism merely registering the imprints of the outside stimulus field. From birth on, he is an organism with certain needs to be satisfied which determine the goal-directed and hence the major *selective* feature of his behavior. This brings the psychology of motivation to the foreground at the very beginning. As he grows, he acquires new tastes and motives and new modes of behavior, the character and range of which vary from culture to culture. This being the case, generalizations in social psychology should be formulated on the basis of checking and cross-checking against the findings in related fields—biology and social science (sociology, ethnology, etc.).

As the receptivity of the individual in relation to any situation is circumscribed by his perception and discrimination, and as the acquisition of new modes of behavior is dependent on maturation and learning, the psychology of perception, judgment, maturation, and learning is basic in reaching general formulations in social psychology. The social psychology of these basic topics is essentially the same as their general psy-

1

chology. In other words, social psychology derives the designation *social* not from the use of a different set of concepts, but from the fact that it extends concepts valid in general psychology to the social field. By the same token, since individual differences are revealed in man's social reactions as well as in his other reactions, the social psychologist keeps a close eye on the findings of differential psychology.

It seems that the more profitable way of presenting the methods used in social psychology is in relation to concrete studies. Therefore, besides reporting in brief the results of research findings related to various topics treated in this book, we have made a point of presenting some representative studies more fully. In each case, it becomes evident that the methods and procedures followed are determined largely by the nature of the problem at hand. Of course, the final crucible for testing the validity of a hypothesis is *experimentation*, whenever it is feasible without destroying the main features of the problem.

The facts of variations of experience and behavior due to cultural variations have imposed themselves on social psychologists time and again. The perspective necessary to overcome the shortcomings of our own cultural biases—"ethnocentrisms"—can be effectively achieved by cross-checking our findings against those from different cultures and times.

Current issues, such as prejudice and the impact of technological developments on human relationships, are forcing themselves to the attention of the social psychologist. The most successful scientific way of dealing with such issues is to study them as part of the persistent problems to which they are organically related. It is only by dealing with them in this comprehensive manner that theory and practice concerning them can be effectively combined.

A Word on Perspective

The variations of values and psychological manifestations reported by sociologists and ethnologists studying different cultures, and the same culture at different periods, have forced a new perspective in the outlook of psychologists. As a consequence, social psychologists have now become more aware of

the danger that their established notions, formed in their particular culture, may creep in to distort the validity of their
generalizations, and that results obtained from the subjects of a
particular culture and of a particular economic-social class must
be checked against their counterparts in other cultures and social
classes. This has contributed to their emancipation, in the
capacity of social psychologists, from the absolutism of the
values and norms they have picked up as members of a given
social group. One concrete line of development in this field will
make the point clear. During the decades 1910–1930 many experimenters in social psychology reported results which seemed
to prove that individual competitiveness was an essential part
of human psychology and that there was almost a uniform
tendency toward mediocrity in collective behavior. A good
illustration of the point is the experimental research of the
sociologist Sorokin and his collaborators.[1] These investigators
did not intend even to bother themselves with the effect of group
situations in setting standards and goals for the individual in
group interaction and the subsequent effect of such standards and
goals as determining factors later when the individual is alone.

The above instance of experimental approach by a sociologist
forcefully drives home *the paradox that mere knowledge of comparative data, and even actually seeing and living in different cultures, are not enough if one is to achieve the necessary perspective.*
He has at the same time to emancipate himself from advocating
certain narrow socio-political tendencies. In the physical
sciences, research men may succeed, perhaps, in keeping separate their work in the laboratory, which is on a scientific level,
and their outlook as a member of a social class, of a church, and
the like. This compartmentalization does not hold if our scientific work is related to any field of social life. Then our scientific
field is so close to our outlook on social and political matters
that they inevitably become confused. As members of an ethnic or social group we have our appropriate duties. If we deliberately do not exclude their possible negative effects on our
research, if we allow our deep enthusiasms for the aspirations and

---

[1] P. A. Sorokin, with M. Tanquist, M. Parten, Mrs. C. C. Zimmerman, An experimental study of efficiency of work under various specified conditions, *Amer. J. Sociol.*,
1930, 35, 765–782.

rights of our social group or class to creep in, they will influence our approach and our formulation of research projects at the very outset.

Nowadays many a psychologist is making a humane plea to social psychologists to participate actively in a new world of democracy. If the social psychologist does participate without first getting rid of his personal involvement as a consciously or unconsciously identified member of a socio-economic class, as a member of a majority group or a minority group or a religious group, or as a representative of some particular "laboratory atmosphere," with their more or less well-established directions and values, he may (as experiments indicate) be contributing his bit to the already existing muddle of ideologies and not to democracy. (See Chapter 12.)

New contributions to social psychology, strongly tinged explicitly or implicitly with religious, national, and economic aspirations of particular groups, will fall short of achieving a discipline universally valid for all units of humanity, no matter how sophisticated and well worked out they appear to be in their formulation.

Current Social Issues and Social Psychology

Magic never succeeded in finding the principles and laws that govern natural and human processes. As has been said so many times during the past centuries, only by man's achieving the outlook and the techniques of yielding to the run-of-things-in-nature has nature yielded to man, in so many fields, the secrets of its working. The first step in yielding to nature is to be able to put appropriate questions to it, i.e., to formulate problems to which it will respond. It is deaf and dumb to questions that do not touch it, no matter how impressive our techniques may be. The use of experimental techniques and procedures becomes effective only after we achieve the correct orientation in formulating the problems in line with the run-of-things-in-nature.

But this does not mean that the scientist moves in a world of "bare existence." The supercilious attitude of the strict divorce of pure and applied science is nothing more than a self-conceited exhibition of aloofness by certain scholars. As aptly pointed

Introduction 5

out by Julian Huxley,[2] one of the outstanding biologists of our time, sometimes it is not easy to separate what is pure and what is applied even in the physical sciences. Was research on the atomic bomb, for example, pure or applied science? To begin with, topics of research do not drop down from the heavens on a few exceptional souls. They lie in the trend of the times. For example, the wonderful development of the physical sciences during the past centuries was prompted to a great extent by the demands of a rising business class. The really great men of science, like Galileo and Darwin, were men who responded effectively to the call of their respective times. Nor are altogether heavenly sounding philosophers any exception in this respect. Even Plato, with his ideal eternal Ideas as the essence of things, was theorizing on the basis of certain socio-economic and intellectual trends of his time, as Winspear recently pointed out.[3]

The social sciences, which are lagging almost helplessly behind the natural sciences, chiefly because of the resistance of things as they are, are today being forced to meet the challenge of our time. "Our time" may be characterized in this respect as a period of almost hodgepodge and crisis in human relationships, mainly because of the terrific impact of the socially uncontrolled, unplanned applications of technological advance. Naturally social psychologists, as well as other students of social relationships today, are dealing with the urgent problem of peace, with the problems of prejudice, public opinion, mass mediums of communication, with the persistent problems of "human nature" and the social order. Tons of literature on these and other problems of human concern are pouring out from once aloof universities, institutes, and commercial enterprises dealing with public opinion. Our evaluation of all such studies on current problems and topics should be made in terms of the criteria which have helped to extend the frontiers of science further. Among these criteria, we mention only two.

1. Is the investigation formulated in such a way that it will further our understanding of a scientific concept, principle, or law, aside from its possible practical value at the moment?

[2] J. Huxley, Science and its relation to social needs, in *Scientific Progress* (Sir Halley Stewart Lecture, 1935), London: Allen and Unwin, 1935, chap. 6.

[3] A. D. Winspear, *The Genesis of Plato's Thought*, New York: Dryden Press, 1940.

2. Is the investigation undertaken with the aim of finding out the truth about the topic, no matter whether the sponsors (or those who made the research possible) will be pleased with the results or not?

The reader who is interested in the methodological problems of social psychology today should consult the following:

ALLPORT, F. H. Methods in the study of collective action phenomena. *J. Soc. Psychol.*, *SPSSI Bull.*, 1942, 15, 165–185.

COTTRELL, L. S., JR., and R. GALLAGHER. Developments in social psychology, 1930–1940. *Sociometry Monogr.* No. 1, New York: Beacon House, Inc., 1941.

LEWIN, K. Field theory and experiment in social psychology: concepts and methods. *Amer. J. Sociol.*, 1936, 44, 868–896.

MURPHY, G., L. B. MURPHY, and T. M. NEWCOMB. *Experimental Social Psychology*, New York: Harper, 1937, chap. 1, The Field and the Methods of Social Psychology, pp. 3–26.

SHERIF, M. Some methodological remarks related to experimentation in social psychology. *Intern. J. Opin. and Attit. Res.*, 1947, 1, 71–93.

TOLMAN, E. Physiology, psychology, and sociology. *Psychol. Rev.*, 1938, 45, No. 3.

PART ONE

Motives

2.

The General Problem of Motives in Relation to Social Psychology

BEFORE APPROACHING RELEVANT CONCEPTS, FINDINGS, AND conclusions in the psychology of motivation, it will be worth while in the long run to get our first orientation from concrete instances of human motives as any person experiences them in his daily contacts. After all, the acid test of the validity of scientific work and conclusions in the field of motivation, as in any field, lies in their promise to clarify adequately and, ultimately, to manipulate our motives in the all-important process of living as human beings. In spite of the promising beginnings of some excellent research material, there is as yet no established psychology of motivation—motivation, especially on the human level, being one of the most difficult problems of the whole discipline. The complexity of the problem becomes even more intricate when motivation is considered in social psychology, for here it necessarily involves the impact of diverse groups (small and large) and culture on the individual. We have therefore to proceed cautiously, using only the steppingstones that appear to us most reliable, and guided by certain methodological considerations (Chapter 1) and by lessons taken to heart from some well-known vicious circles of the past.

That this is not a note of false alarm or an unduly provocative proclamation of confusion at the outset will become evident if one merely skims through the pages of the books of some contending "schools" in recent psychological literature. Take the accounts of motivation in any two books published in the 'thirties, for example, representing the individual as opposed to the "cultural" or collective approach in social psychology; or the lists of "needs" or drives drawn up by psychologists in general. One usually ends with more confusion than he started with.

9

It is hard to keep one's feet on the ground when some one or two instincts and frustrations thereof, or some "dynamic" personal "traits" are advanced to explain whole trends of radicalism or conservatism, or war, or an entire system of social organization such as capitalism.

When one observes himself and his fellow human beings in different cultures, as the author of this book has done, and then goes on to read about them (beyond a few abstractions deduced about their culture), he finds individuals everywhere directed toward certain ends or goals—goals that require shorter or longer time ranges for their fulfillment within a comparatively narrower or expanded radius of activities. He sees individuals invariably tending to obtain and prepare food for the next meal, or making sure that it will be ready for them. Of course the time, the kind and amount, the place, the atmosphere, and the trimmings of the meal are determined (usually) by an individual's culture and his social status and economic position in the social organization. Likewise, one sees him directed toward securing shelter and clothing—the kind, the amount, the size, the location, etc., in each case being, within limits, socially determined. One sees him in search of or longing for a mate (temporary or lasting), going along the channels of passive or active, roundabout or direct approaches, using all the possible devices for increasing his appeal value—masculine or feminine charm, position, power, riches, niceties, and the loopholes of etiquette—as prescribed by the norms of his particular milieu.

One sees him striving *to be a member in good standing* of his group, whatever his particular group may be. Subject to individual variations, he strives *to excel in his group,* whatever the hierarchical arrangement for excelling may be in his particular group. Of course, different behavior characteristics may be at a premium in different social settings. In one, the degree of competitiveness or individualism or outsmarting others may be the established rule for excelling in the order of things; in another, cooperativeness and solidarity, etc. One college student may aim at getting a C in his course; his classmate may feel frustrated unless he gets an A. A rich man may not feel satisfied unless his riches are second to none in his community, whereas a poor man who has had difficulty making both ends meet on a subsistence level may have a feeling of achievement if he is able to make a steady living for his family. The vice-president of a company may feel miserable until he becomes the full-fledged president.

One sees women who are miserable until they, like their friends, are able to appear in a new dress at every party. An adolescent girl may feel equally unhappy unless she is able to go to the movies twice a week with her friends and wear her blue jeans.

We have cited the instances in the above paragraphs to make our meaning clear. *Whether directed toward food, clothing, shelter, the opposite sex, or toward status, power, social distinction, recognition, trifles concerning dress, decoration, and etiquette, these are all cases of motivated behavior—motives.* We shall use the term *motives as a generic term to cover all the different cases and kinds of goal-directed (motivated) behavior.* We need such a collective term to cover the different kinds of motivated behavior—needs (drives) originating and embedded in the functioning of the organism of the individual, "derived drives" based on them, socially acquired desires, wishes, aspirations, ambitions, directed toward certain goals or values, etc.

However, distinguishing between universal motives (needs or drives) and acquired motives of various sorts ("derived drives," tastes, aspirations, ambitions) becomes imperative, especially in social psychology whose central problem is, perhaps, the process of socialization of the individual in various cultures and the profound effects of this socialization on his experience and behavior. The aim of the social psychologist is to achieve concepts and principles that are equally valid in different cultures, with their enormous diversity of norms and values relating to various phases of life—from the most intimate kinship relationships to the trifles of social etiquette. Since these variations give rise in turn to an enormous diversity of goal objects or situations, we must keep the distinction between motives based on their origin in mind throughout our work. This is not an idle verbal preoccupation. For, in trying times of economic depression, poverty, and crises such as the many countries of Europe and Asia are going through at present, people are dispensing with the pursuit of many goal objects and values which in better times they hold indispensable; they are striving to keep barely alive. We shall tentatively venture to generalize that, on the whole, in periods of scarcity and privation the motives of individuals become more and more directed toward the goal objects and situations that are closest to their organic needs. Later we shall present concrete illustrations of this tendency. (See Chapter 4, pages 84–90.) The tendency also holds true, in general, in certain cases of individual breakdown.

With such considerations in mind, it becomes necessary to distinguish motives as follows:

1. *Unlearned or biogenic motives.* These motives originate and are embedded in the functioning of the organic needs of the body. We shall restrict the use of the terms needs, basic drives, and instincts to unlearned or biogenic motives, and shall use these terms (need, basic drive, or instinct) interchangeably.

2. *Learned or sociogenic motives.* As the term implies, these motives are acquired in the course of the genetic development of the individual. Since at least most of these acquired motives are learned in connection with interpersonal relationships or with established social values or norms and institutions, they are sociogenic motives. Whether biogenic or sociogenic, whatever its origin may be, once a motive is aroused it has psychological consequences. For example, a person who is in the throes of seeking status or a person committed to a social ideal may go hungry *for one meal or longer* under pressing conditions, even though biogenic motives are *usually* more basic and pressing. Since all motives thus have psychological consequences, it seems preferable to use the term *sociogenic* to indicate the origin of acquired motives rather than "psychogenic" which is used by some authors. Learned motives that may be strictly personally acquired (if there are such things) need not concern us in social psychology. Specific kinds or types of sociogenic motives— such as tastes and desires for certain value objects, aspirations for a certain social position, ambitions to attain a certain status—are so numerous that appropriate terms will be used in each connection. Behavior revealing an

established attitude is to be taken as sociogenically motivated behavior inasmuch as attitudes are directed toward certain values or goal objects.

After making the distinction between biogenic and sociogenic motives, we must hasten to emphasize a fact which is relevant in this connection. Whether of biological (biogenic) or social origin (sociogenic), motives have consequential effects in the experience and behavior of the individual as long as they operate effectively. Take the case of an ambitious politician who lives far above the subsistence level and who has definitely set himself to obtain some office. He certainly will turn heaven and earth to get it. His major elations or frustrations will be a function of his experienced proximity to the goal (the office). Or take the case of a young person who is all set to attend a big football game or a commencement week-end which will be the high point of the year. If for some reason he is deprived of going, he will feel utterly miserable and terribly betrayed by circumstances or people. In short, whether of biological (biogenic) or social origin (sociogenic), once a motive is aroused, the individual experiences a sense of *urgency* in carrying it through to the goal; this urgency is of course proportional to the intensity of the motive.[1] We shall have some more to say on this point later. (See Chapter 11.)

Before we close these general introductory remarks, a word about the place of motives in social relationships may be in order. It is a truism of everyday life situations that individuals enter into interpersonal relationships and participate in group interaction to achieve certain ends. These ends may be to secure a livelihood, as in the case of labor unions; to find a mate, as in the case of various types of social functions; or to achieve social status or distinction, as in the case of clubs, etc. Any account of interpersonal relationships or group interaction will miss some major variables if motivational factors are left out. On the other hand, once groups start to function, there emerge supra-individual products which in turn become significant factors in determining or modifying the experience and behavior of the individuals that constitute the group, even in

[1] G. Murphy, L. B. Murphy, and T. M. Newcomb, *Experimental Social Psychology*, New York: Harper, rev. ed., 1937, p. 198.

relation to the motives which were first responsible for bringing
them together. For example, a group of boys in a slum area,
deprived of adequate food, clothing, and social ties, may meet
together as a gang to satisfy these deprivations, perhaps by
stealing. But once the group begins to function, once a "code"
of conduct (norms, values) appears in the group, the members
may willingly undergo hunger, deprivation, and temporary
separation from the gang in accordance with its code, in order
to preserve or enhance their status or to maintain the solidarity
of the group. We shall consider some examples of motives in
group situations later in more detail. (See Chapters 5, 6, and 7.)

The Importance of Motives in Controversies over Human Nature

No doubt because of the impact of the momentous events of
recent years—war, social and economic upheavals, and the
growing functional interdependence of people in a world that is
shrinking geographically as a result of such technological developments as the radio, airplanes, etc.—problems related to
the merits or defects of social orders have come forcefully to the
foreground. Friendly or antagonistic groups and individuals are
engaged in controversies—not to mention open conflicts—over
them. As typical illustrations of these currently flourishing
controversies, we shall mention in passing only two lines of
arguments used by the contending parties.

1. One line of argument centers around the relative effectiveness of incentives in competitive and in cooperative social
systems. The implications of such arguments have to be considered seriously in social psychology because they have a direct
bearing on the individual-society relationship. The advocate of
the individually competitive system argues that if you take
away individual competition, the incentive for excellence and
hence progress will disappear and our western civilization will
stagnate. And to prove his point, he cites the development of
the highly competitive capitalist system during the past few
centuries. His opponent argues with equal enthusiasm that this
contention is not true and cites the Soviet Union as an example.
Is individual competition—the passion to outdo others in busi-

ness, in work, in social life—the only possible incentive that can set a high pace for achievement? Since this question of motives involves the whole problem of socialization, we shall deal with this and related problems in Chapters 11 and 12, where the social motives are considered in more detail.

2. The second line of argument is more comprehensive and goes to the core of the problem of the inherent compatibility or incompatibility of this or that social system with the basic tendencies of what the contenders take to be "human nature." The party to the controversy who is dissatisfied with the existing order of human relationships, with its division of people into owners of the means of production on one side and their hired workers on the other side, argues for a change in human relationships that are based on the private ownership of capital. He points out that the major ills plaguing people today, such as imperialism, war, economic crises, periodic scarcity, labor-owner strife, ruthless and disastrous competition, are caused mainly by the private ownership system. His opponent, in turn, points to the wonderful progress achieved in industry under this system, and the blessings of modern technology. He goes on to attribute this progress to the motives of profit and competition, arguing again that without profit and competition progress will come to a standstill. Sooner or later in the course of his argument, he ends up with a conclusion that seems to him unanswerable: It is desirable to do away with economic crises, worker-owner conflicts, wars, etc., all of which cause hardships and misery to a great many people. But it is impossible to do away with the ownership system and individual competition because it is against "human nature" to do so. His opponent may venture to state with equal finality that, on the contrary, "human nature" is fundamentally opposed to such a system. In any case, the argument has reached a stalemate.

These are among the major persistent topics of controversy in the critical world of today. They constitute a challenge to the social psychologist in particular because they also involve some of the major problems in his field of research. Professor Dunham rendered a great service to those of us in whose life-work a systematic study of these problems holds an important place by bringing up for discussion these and related topics in his book, *Man Against Myth*.[2] He discusses in a broad philosophical perspective such rather widely used value judgments or "myths" as: "You Can't Change Human Nature," "The Rich Are Fit and the Poor Unfit," "There Are Superior and Inferior Races," "You Have to Look Out for Yourself," etc. One of the points he raises effectively is that there are interested groups who are consciously and actively, through various propaganda devices, perpetuating such value judgments for the masses of people.

These controversies over "human nature" are old problems which have been heatedly debated for centuries without any success. For example, Hobbes gave a picture of the cruelty and selfishness of human beings on the one hand; Rousseau gave a picture of the innocence and spontaneous goodness of original "human nature" on the other. There have been variations and offshoots of these main stands since then, usually couched in the currently fashionable intellectual expressions of their time. Thus Kropotkin, with his social inclinations, looked at the living creatures around him and proclaimed a world of sympathy and cooperation. His contemporary, Herbert Spencer, who lived at the peak of the British Empire's power at the end of the nineteenth century, painted a grim picture. Using the language of biological evolution current in his time, he sought to justify the might of the mighty, the fortunes of the wealthy, the misfortune of the downtrodden, on the basis of the rule of the jungle. Starting with such current evolutionary expressions as "struggle for existence," "survival of the fittest," and "natural selection," he arrived at the conclusion that the trend of human society too was working for the best interests of humanity as exemplified by the empires of his time. Of course, such systematizations are looked upon today with only historical interest.

However, even now we are not very far advanced from that stage of "scientific" justification for "human nature" in harmony with the picture of human relationships or society we fundamentally uphold. Of course, in pace with the more "scientifically-minded" temper of modern times, more scientific data are presented in the current controversies over original "human nature." One field of argument directed us to look at

---

[2] Barrows Dunham, *Men Against Myth*, Boston: Little, Brown, 1947.

more primitive peoples, the assumption being that the less developed a society is the closer its members are to original "human nature." And what were the results of such inquiries? Sure enough, both sides of the argument were selective in the choice of their facts; both found "facts" to prove the great argument in their favor. Methodologically, the vicious circle starts with the assumption that technically less-developed peoples are closer to original "human nature." It is safe to say, in general, that the members of less-developed groups usually cling more closely, conform more religiously to the values or norms of their society—no matter how strange or unnatural they may appear to outsiders—than do the members of societies at a higher level of technological development with their relatively more rapid changes and greater variations.

In spite of their more refined methods and techniques, psychologists, even in recent times, have not been exceptions in this tendency to start with certain assumptions and then present elaborate facts in their favor. For example, not so long ago certain psychologists reported results which virtually meant that the rich were rich because, without being appreciably affected by the life circumstances of their upbringing, they were congenitally more intelligent. Other psychologists came to opposite conclusions based on equally elaborate results. Similarly, one cannot help noticing the influence of certain fundamental human views ("austere" or "humane") in the lists of basic human instincts or drives presented by various psychologists.

All of this points to the inevitable conclusion that we must put more rigorous checks on our methodological grounds and keep abreast of new findings in the biological sciences, psychology, and the social sciences such as ethnology and sociology, in order to avoid such pitfalls.

Leaving more detailed accounts to the chapters that follow, we can safely state in passing that the picture of "human nature" prevalent in any society at any time corresponds rather closely to the established norms regarding human nature and the practice of human relationships sanctioned by these norms.[3] That this is the case can be gleaned from even a superficial

[3] R. S. and H. M. Lynd, *Middletown in Transition*, New York: Harcourt, Brace, 1937, pp. 176 ff.; R. S. Lynd, *Knowledge for What? The Place of Social Science in American Culture*, Princeton: Princeton University Press, 1939, especially chaps. 3 and 4.

glance at and comparison of the conceptions of "human nature" held by the French, Germans, or English in the ecclesiastically tinged feudal organizations and by the same peoples today. It is particularly the superstructure of social norms and "social techniques which lend to a particular society a large part of its characteristic flavor, its 'myth,' as to the Nature of Man." [4]

If this is true, it becomes a superfluous preoccupation to indulge in futile controversies over whether or not "human nature" can be changed. All the above considerations and those in the pages to follow force us *first* to raise the question: What *is* this "human nature" about which argument rages? When we start the argument with the question of whether or not human nature can be changed, we assume that we already know what it is. As yet, nowhere, including all the books on psychology, do we find an adequate picture of "human nature." Therefore, the first essential task is the study of it. And it becomes necessarily the study of the biological endowment (congenitally given organic needs, actual or potential plasticity or learning capacity, etc.) of the species. Whatever else may be included in the biological endowment of the species (ready at birth or coming to function eventually through maturation), biological needs (such as respiration, sleep, hunger, etc.) are certainly among the constituents of the organism which should be included in such a study. These organic needs constitute genetically the first motives of the individual (see Chapter 3, pp. 51–60).

Perhaps now the necessity for distinguishing the origin of motives is clearer. These endless controversies over "human nature" impose on us this necessity of distinguishing between the unlearned or *biogenic* motives and the learned or *sociogenic* motives at the outset. Real advance in this direction will help to clarify our study of the socialization process and our understanding of certain functional relationships in the individual's psychological make-up in the socialized state of later life. We shall see, for example, how keeping this distinction as to the origin of motives in mind helps us to understand certain behavior manifestations that arise under conditions of severe deprivation, in individual and collective crisis situations, and in at least some cases of ego-breakdown.

[4] E. C. Tolman, *Drives Toward War*, New York: Appleton-Century, 1942, p. 23.

Basic Motives (Drives or Instincts) Are Biogenic Needs

No matter what the social setting or "culture pattern" may be—imperial or colonial, western or oriental, highly industrial or primitive, leisure-class or poverty-stricken, Christian or heathen—man eats, drinks, breathes, sleeps, and tries to keep warm in order to carry forward the most essential complex of his preoccupations, living—that is, just keeping alive as a biological organism. No matter what other prosaic or refined, mean or noble, humble or distinguished activities and strivings he may be engaged in (which may not be related to the above preoccupations), he has first to achieve at least a subsistence level of living. And achieving a subsistence level means attending to the demands of such organic needs as hunger, thirst, sleep, etc. These biological functions he has in common not only with all the members of his own species, Homo sapiens, but also with many other animals. In Tolman's words: "Finally, taken together, it is the appetites plus aversions which, I declare, provide the ultimate and basic needs for all animals, human and subhuman. In the last analysis, it can be said that all the things we human beings do and want are ultimately to be evaluated with respect to the degree to which they tend to satisfy hunger, thirst, sex, and the rest, or to prevent pain, frustration. . . . " [5]

Of course, the forms, the particular objects, the circumstances and the manner of satisfying these basic needs are subject to cultural variations. This will be the concern of Part II of this book. However, in spite of cultural variations and the emergence of altogether new practices and strivings in different societies, the fact remains that if there is a common substratum of human strivings which may be labeled "human nature," it is these organic needs plus the almost infinite plasticity in learning, i.e., the capacity to acquire new reaction patterns, new tastes and values, to acquire and manipulate a host of symbols, concepts, and tools. Therefore, it is a task of the utmost significance to be able to single out these basic needs or drives.

Ever since the impact of the evolutionary teaching of Darwin began to be really felt in formal academic psychology (which was preoccupied at the time almost exclusively with efforts to sift out "sensations"), many attempts have been made to

[5] *Ibid.*, p. 23.

achieve a classification or list of basic drives or instincts in psychology itself. For example, William James made such a list. Psychology owes a great deal to the influence of the work of McDougall and Freud for the beginning of the current concern with problems of motivation. Both men drew up lists of instincts which they changed as they elaborated their systems further. McDougall's classification, which exerted a great influence at the time, especially on social psychology, now has only historical value. The instincts he listed are linked closely with his vitalistic speculation, and such instincts as ascendance and submission have not survived the test of evidence.[6] Such dramatic-sounding instincts as the instincts of death or destruction cannot be subjected to the check of controlled investigation.[7] And, alluring though they are, the various and diverse central concepts (such as the sexual libido of Freud, the "inferiority complex" of Adler, and the "collective unconscious" of Jung, not to mention the variations added by their disciples) which are used as magic keys to explain everything from the personal troubles of one individual to the rise of social systems like capitalism, blind us to the need for making room for other factors. These other factors stand out, at times blatantly, as stubborn facts which cannot be assimilated by the magic principles. More recently, Murray and his associates [8] have offered classificatory schemes which contain literally dozens of items. Even a glance at their lists is enough to convince one that such a scheme is not valid in the light of a few well-known facts of both physiology and ethnology. In short, it seems that there is not as yet a generally accepted classification of basic needs or drives. In this connection the point raised by Lashley [9] may serve as a realistic corrective: "The current trend in social psychology and psychopathology is to elevate the drive to the position formerly occupied by instinct, as some general motivating force apart from specific sensorimotor systems. Actually the term [instinct, drive, or need] is nothing more than a general designation of reactions to deficit, and its

---

[6] William McDougall, *Outline of Psychology*, New York: Scribner, 1923.

[7] S. Freud, *The Ego and the Id*, London: Hogarth, 1927.

[8] H. A. Murray, *et al.*, *Explorations in Personality*, New York: Oxford, 1938.

[9] K. S. Lashley, Experimental analysis of instinctive behavior, *Psych. Rev.*, 1938, 45, 445–469.

hypostatization as a real force can only blind us to the fact that each such reaction constitutes a special problem involving, perhaps, a unique mechanism" (p. 469).

A noteworthy list of innate biological drives has been suggested by Tolman.[10] He subdivides them into (1) appetites and (2) aversions, as follows:

The Appetites (p. 544)	The Aversions (p. 547)
A maternal (or suckling of the young) drive	Cold—avoidance
A nest-building drive	Heat—avoidance
Thirst	Danger—avoidance (*i.e.*, Fright)
Hunger	Obstruction—avoidance (*i.e.*, Aggression)
Sex	
A general activity drive	
An exploratory drive	
A rest or sleep drive	
A urination and defecation (in specific type of locale) drive	
A play drive	
An aesthetic drive	

In regard to the appetites, Tolman generalizes: "... Each is set in motion by some peculiar internal metabolic condition (state of the breasts, hunger, thirst, sex, need for exercise, and the like). This metabolic condition occurs in apparently more or less regular cycles due to combinations of internal and external conditions. And when it is in force the animal is *driven* until an appropriate consummatory object is found in the presence of which latter a corresponding consummatory response occurs. This consummatory response then relieves the internal metabolic condition and produces, at least temporarily, a final complementary state of internal *satiation*" (p. 547). Concerning aversions, he says: "Each of these aversions is set off, not by an internal metabolic condition (as is an appetite), but by an *evoking environmental object* (or situation), *i.e.*, cold, heat, danger, or obstruction. Further, whereas an appetite was seen primarily as a *getting-to* a final state of '*satiation*,' each of these aversions is, rather, a *getting-from* an internal state of

[10] E. C. Tolman, Motivation, learning and adjustment, *Proc. Amer. Philos. Soc.*, 1941, 84, 543–563.

'*sufferance.*' For cold, heat, danger, obstruction tend to produce internal sufferances. And it is such internal sufferances which are the terminal situations ultimately being got from in each case" (p. 547).

Tolman then lists the "social drives," which include among others such items as "loyalty to group," "sharing," etc. We shall not present this list here. At least most if not all of these "social drives" develop in the process of socialization of the individual (see Chapters 11, 12). Tolman himself cautions that his list of social drives is "very tentative."

Singling out these basic needs or drives is not an academic pastime, even though there have been inclinations in this direction. Knowledge of an exact inventory of the basic drives will contribute in a decisive way to resolving the futile controversies over "human nature" which have implications of the utmost significance for the whole range of social relationships. Furthermore, more exact knowledge in this field will necessarily indicate the realistic range of stimulus objects and situations which are of *biological significance* to the organism before the complications of new acquisitions enter the picture. It is becoming a recognized fact that the first objects and situations of *value* (positive or negative) to the individual are those which have *biological significance* to him as an organism, and that numerous other values are acquired as related or not related to them. The problem so forcefully raised by Watson in this regard is still urgent, no matter what the fate of his special findings and conclusions may be.[11]

The contradictory lists of needs (drives, instincts) and, in fact, the confusion in regard to the concept of needs (drives, instincts) that prevails today impose the necessity of strict observance of at least two methodological considerations: (1) certain minimum criteria for including any motive in the list of primary needs (drives, instincts), and (2) clear delineation of the essential problems of primary needs (drives, instincts) that give them their distinctive character. We shall consider them briefly.

[11] J. B. Watson, *Behaviorism*, New York: People's Institute Publishing Company, 1925. See also his chapter in C. Murchison (ed.), *Psychologies of 1925*, Worcester: Clark University Press, 1925.

1. Minimum criteria for including any motive in the list of primary needs (drives, instincts) are explicitly or implicitly accepted by almost everyone, but the requirements of such criteria are neglected somewhere along the way. These criteria include at least the *universality* of the instinctive reaction in the species, and the *unlearned* (innate) character of the reaction in relation to a more or less definite range of stimulus objects or situations. Certainly eating, drinking, breathing, sleeping, mating, etc., are universal human needs for all individuals in any social setting, no matter in what forms these needs are set forth in each case. Such universality cannot be claimed for motives like sharing, cooperation, competition, submission, domination, or wealth hoarding. The comparative studies of sociologists and ethnologists contain quantities of convincing evidence that the direction of such interpersonal and inter-group relationships is determined largely by the established practices and standards of the particular group at a particular period in its history. On the other hand, no matter whether competition or cooperation, dominance or submission, individual-ism or solidarity is preponderantly required from the members of any society, consequently making this required characteristic dominant in the individual members, we *universally* find human beings (after they reach a certain age) doing certain things in order to *belong* to the group and to acquire a *status*, whatever the status may be in any particular case.

Then, because of the *universality* of the activities connected with *belongingness* and *status*, which psychologically may be called ego problems, shall we say that individualism or solidar-ity, competition or cooperation, and the like, are instinctive in the sense that primary needs like hunger or thirst are? No. This brings us to the criterion of the *unlearned* nature of reactions. As we shall see in Chapter 11, the status or ego-attitudes are formed (learned) in the course of the genetic development of the individual and are shaped (in the particular direction they will take and in their varieties) by the particular values or norms and practices of his particular society. Of course, this social determination of status or ego-attitudes varies because of individual differences and the peculiar case history of the par-ticular individual. If there is an innate basis for these ego-attitudes other than that which is due to the humoral factors, capacities, and general conditions of the organism, and to the by-products of the functioning of innate needs, it is to be found in the human species' capacity for conceptual functioning on the highest cortical level. For it is only in the human species that we find *belongingness* and *status* arrangements in the sense that they involve lasting reciprocal identifications, loyalties, and responsibilities. The infant has none of these in the early years of his life; he learns them through social contacts and impositions after he achieves the great feat of regulating his experience and behavior according to *any rules or norms*. When he achieves this ability to grasp a set of rules or norms, thus enabling him to see himself in a reciprocal role in relation to those around him, *then* the status arrangements and norms of his family, his play group, his social setting become his own. Hence whatever pattern of interpersonal and intergroup relationships prevails in his particular social setting becomes his prevailing pattern, too. And these patterns vary from society to society; some patterns include matters related to the most intimate kinship arrangements. In short, behavior related to the individual's status and ego problems is *learned* and therefore cannot be included among the primary needs. These facts will be elaborated in Chapters 11 and 12, when we consider sociogenic motives in more detail.

2. A clear delineation of the essential problems of basic needs (instincts) has been made by Lashley.[12] Such a forceful demarcation clarifies our approach to the "psychology of instincts [which] was a dynamics of imaginary forces... " (p. 447). Lashley singles out two problems as basic in relation to innate instincts (needs or drives):

a. The problem of "the more or less precise reactions to definite objects.... These are reactions to specific stimuli. The problems which they suggest are those of neural integration: the nature of the stimulus which elicits the response, the pattern of motor activities by which a given result is achieved and, ultimately, the neurophysiology of the behavior" (p. 448).

b. The problem of the "reaction to a deficit.... *This reaction to deprivation of some stimulus presents the typical problem of motivation*" (p. 448; italics mine).

[12] K. S. Lashley, *op. cit.*

"*Only in cases of reaction to a deficit is there any justification for introducing the notion of a drive as a source of facilitation.* An increase in general activity or in exploratory behavior indicates an increased responsiveness to stimuli not obviously related to the specific sensori-motor patterns of the instinctive behavior. There is also inhibition of reactions to other stimuli ... " (p. 467; italics mine).

Once an instinctive activity is aroused as the result of a specific bodily deficit (such as food or water) or a specific bodily demand (such as that aroused by an accumulation of sex hormones), the whole organism becomes restless and sensitized to the search for the stimulus objects that are biologically significant for the particular need prevailing at the moment. "There is good evidence that animals without previous experience may give specific reactions to biologically significant objects and that the recognition or discrimination of these objects may be quite precise" (p. 452). " ... The exciting stimulus in instinctive recognition of mate or young is not mediated exclusively by any one sense modality" (p. 454). Yet the precision of the recognition or discrimination of the biologically significant objects is not a fixed entity. The properties of the stimulus objects can "be varied within limits without disrupting the reaction" (p. 455).

In his *Physiological Psychology*,[13] Morgan presents in four chapters a concise and integrated condensation of the facts relating to biogenic needs (instincts or drives). In the following chapter he gives a survey of the general characteristics of biogenic needs. Morgan's characterization of biogenic needs, which follows, sums up their main features and is much in line with Lashley's formulation of the problem:

Motivation must be thought of in terms of patterns of nervous activity which arise not merely from receptor stimulation but also, and perhaps even more important, from the direct influences of chemical conditions in the blood. *This pattern of nervous activity differs according to the factors giving rise to it, whether these are lack of food, water, or the presence of sex hormones.* Each pattern of activity may produce more or less general activity, *but also specific forms of behavior.* In addition, the pattern involves the *set or predisposition to perceive en-*

[13] C. T. Morgan, *Physiological Psychology*, New York: McGraw-Hill, 1943.

vironmental stimuli in certain ways and to give certain responses to these stimuli. Such perceptions and responses may be said to be the goals of the motivated organism and contribute in part to the reduction of the pattern of nervous activity that, physiologically speaking, is the motive (p. 458; italics mine).

Such a clarifying delineation of the essential earmarks of the basic needs (drives or instincts) and careful observance of the criteria (of universality and the unlearned nature of instinctive reactions) may pave the way to establishing an adequate list of basic needs. On the basis of such considerations, such items as ascendance, submission, acquisitiveness, competitiveness, sharing, and the like, naturally drop from the list of primary needs. Even a glance at ethnological facts makes this necessary.

Another relevant point about which we have to be careful before listing an observed reaction with instinctive activities is to make sure that the reaction is not elicited by a peculiar set of circumstances. For example, Fernberger [14] observed that when groups of from 250 to 400 albino rats were placed in a cage 2 feet by 6 feet by 3 feet, many of them jumped to the wire screen at the top of the cage and clung there, apparently dead. Actually they were asleep. Probably, under such pressing conditions most of the other rats would react in the same way without previous training. Shall we say, then, that rats have an instinct to jump up and cling to the ceiling? The reaction certainly was caused by the peculiar circumstances of the situation—overcrowding in a narrow place, etc. Nissen and Crawford's study of food-sharing behavior in young chimpanzees [15] is another illustration of the point. An examination of their data seems to show that the food-sharing behavior which they observed diminished considerably, almost to the vanishing point, as the amount of available food decreased. Sharing was observed especially in animals whose available food supply was several times larger than the animal would ordinarily eat at one time. In connection with these studies, attention should be called to the fact that it is not safe to attribute a drive or need to one species on the basis of observations made on another

[14] S. W. Fernberger, Unlearned behavior of the albino rat, *Amer. J. Psychol.*, 1929, 41, 343–344.

[15] H. W. Nissen and M. P. Crawford, A preliminary study of food-sharing behavior in young chimpanzees, *J. Comp. Psychol.*, 1936, 22, 383–419.

species, particularly in the case of a controversial need or drive. For example, migration and hibernation, which are seen as seasonal types of instinctive behavior in certain species because of the specific morphology and functioning of their organisms, are not observed in other subhuman species. Likewise, it has time and again been shown fallacious to posit social drives in man on the basis of analogies with social activities and social organizations of other animals such as ants, bees, wasps, and even subhuman primates. Before advancing generalizations based on analogies in other species, it may be worth while to remember that the continuity of social organization and culture in human societies is not transmitted through the genes of succeeding generations. Therefore, every generalization concerning a social characteristic observed in members of a subhuman species (including chimpanzees) should be checked by comparative ethnological studies before it is advanced as valid for the human species as well.

Approach to and Necessity for a List of Basic Needs

All the preceding considerations lead to the conclusion that an adequate inventory of basic needs can be achieved only by keeping the basic problems and criteria of instinctive behavior clearly in mind. The essential earmarks of instinctive behavior, we repeat, are: (1) that it constitutes a reaction to an innate organic demand such as a chemical deficit (e.g., of food, water, etc.) or other chemical state (e.g., accumulation of sex hormones), and (2) that it ultimately ends with "more or less precise reactions to definite objects," these reactions usually being referred to as consummatory behavior.

The minimum criteria for determining instinctive behavior in any animal species—again we repeat—are: (1) universality of the behavior in the members of the species, and (2) the unlearned character of such behavior. With this delineation of the essential problems of instinctive behavior and their minimum criteria clearly in mind, it may be safe to state that the following should be included among the basic biogenic needs (drives or instincts), subject, of course, to corrections made by investigators working in the biological sciences, for biological needs they are:

Hunger
Thirst
Activity-sleep (rest) cycle
Breathing [16]
Sex
Temperature regulation (avoidance of cold and heat
    differentials)
Suckling of young
Evacuation (urination and defecation)
Avoidance of organic injury (?)

An outline of social psychology is not the most appropriate place to present details of the findings concerning the functioning of each of these needs. In Morgan's *Physiological Psychology* the reader will find a level-headed presentation of the facts and specific problems connected with each of them. These needs, and probably others that biological research will teach us about, are the basic human needs which irrespective of the cultural setting and times, have to be attended to at least to a minimum degree in the carrying out and perpetuation of the urgent occupation of living. They all are essential, in various degrees, to the functioning of the organism. For example, the disruption of the periodic function of breathing during a very short period, on the order of a few minutes, will be fatal, whereas the disruption of drinking, eating, and mating may be endured for much longer periods—differing of course in each individual. Any considerable degree of deprivation of or inattendance to these needs, as everyone who has experienced it or studied them knows, has corresponding psychological consequences. No matter what place each occupies relative to being essential to the organism, when each need suffers various degrees of deprivation or enjoys various degrees of satisfaction it comes to dominate the individual's experience and behavior to the exclusion or inhibition of other needs. After a long and hectic day, the

[16] We include breathing here in accordance with the following remarks of Morgan (*op. cit.*, p. 438): "To be sure, respiratory behavior is not very relevant to most phases of psychology, for it probably plays an exceedingly minor role in learning and seldom enters into conscious experience. Respiration is, nevertheless, motivated behavior. Indeed, it is a model of such behavior in that it is relatively simple behavior whose mechanism is much better understood than other mechanisms of motivation; and its study offers some suggestions for the interpretation of other facts of motivation."

need for sleep and rest usually dominates other needs and otherwise fascinating activities. If a normal person misses a meal or two for some reason, hunger dominates his whole experience and behavior. Goldstein,[17] who took a definite stand against specific drives (the "so-called drives" in his terminology) in his efforts to establish the single general drive—i.e., the drive for self-actualization—remarks nevertheless, "If a human being is forced to live in a state of hunger for a long time, or if there are conditions in his body which produce a strong hunger feeling, so that he is urged to relieve this feeling, it disturbs the self-actualization of his whole personality" (p. 202). After stating this fact, he goes on in the interests of his systematic position: "Then he appears *as if* under a hunger drive. The same may be the case with sex" (p. 202; italics mine). The extensive hunger studies made on conscientious objectors during World War II which we will review briefly, and the profound socio-political consequences of there being hundreds of millions of hungry people in Europe and Asia today render theorizing in terms of "*as if under a hunger drive*" a little less attractive. In our opinion, we do not have to resort to such attenuations in defending the perfectly defensible organismic position, which holds that typical reactions of the organism are not fragmentary and that the conceptual or abstract level of psychological functioning is the level of human functioning in the normal conditions of civilized life.

A survey of the various biogenic needs, such as that presented by Morgan,[18] is sufficient to convince the reader that, besides broad generalizations which may be valid on the whole concerning motivation, there are specific functional problems in each case which have their psychological implications as well. It will not carry us far just to learn general facts concerning sense modalities; we have to understand the functioning of specific sense organs and their particular place in the whole nervous system before we can know anything about seeing, hearing, and the like. We have to know at least something about the rods and cones in the retina and the basilar membrane in the inner ear to have any understanding of seeing and hearing respec-

[17] Kurt Goldstein, *The Organism*, New York: American Book, 1939.
[18] C. T. Morgan, *op. cit.*

tively. Likewise we have to learn, from the current work in physiology, as much as possible about the functioning of biogenic needs, their activation and adequate stimuli in each case, before we can acquire more precise knowledge about biologically significant stimulus objects. After all, objects are biologically significant only in relation to definite biological needs. Of course, our main concern is motivation-environment correlations and their modifications on the psychological level. The more precise findings on the physiological level can contribute greatly to the solution of our psychological problems. The psychology of motivation cannot be entirely alien or contradictory to the facts of motivation on the physiological level.

Before we close this section, it will be pertinent to call attention to a generally known fact which is fundamental in socio-economic relationships. It is noteworthy for social psychology, in particular, that the degree of biological usefulness of adequate stimuli does not in all cases determine the degree of social complications they create. As Cannon pointed out in his classic, *The Wisdom of the Body*,[19] "Some of the needs are satisfied gratuitously. Oxygen and sometimes water also, we may have at will, without cost. It is noteworthy that in cities a supply of water is obtained only by community action and at public expense. There are other needs, however, which in the long run are quite as urgent as the needs for water and oxygen, and which at times cannot be satisfied because of the lack of social stability. These are the elementary requirements of food and shelter (clothing, housing and warmth) and the benefits of medical care" (p. 295). Needs which depend greatly on the whole socio-economic scheme for their satisfaction (e.g., food, shelter, and sex) are of urgent concern as internal factors in the field of social psychology.

The inability of individuals, because of personal or socio-economic circumstances, to meet the demands of biogenic needs has psychological consequences that produce major effects, in corresponding degrees, on the total personality of the individual. We shall present a few examples of the effects of such deprivations in Chapter 4. The far-reaching effects, on the whole established socio-economic structure, of widespread deprivation suffered by masses of people will be the major concern of Chap-

[19] W. B. Cannon, *The Wisdom of the Body*, New York: Norton, 1932.

ter 16. The consequences of such widespread deprivation of biogenic needs constitute one of the major areas of fruitful research for social psychology today. Here the social psychologist has one of the most suitable fields for the study of genuine group formation and of various aspects of collective phenomena and collective emergence. At the present time, it is rather the politicians who are realistically treating these grim problems as they force themselves on our attention. These problems have not yet succeeded in acquiring a focal place in the genteel tradition of academic social psychology.

Emotional Motivation

A consideration of motives necessitates at least a brief characterization of the almost baffling subject of emotions. The well-known human emotions (fear, anger, startle, etc.) are elicited primarily by external stimuli or stimulus situations. The external stimulating conditions that arouse emotions (at least on the adult human level in any society) are frequently social situations—other persons or groups, danger situations, excited meetings, mass situations, etc. Therefore any treatment of emotions necessarily becomes *social* psychology.

There may be a substantial grain of truth in the position taken by McDougall [20] and others that instinctive strivings (e.g., hunger, sex) and acts are accompanied by appropriate emotions. This seems to be a fact of everyday life experience, especially when instinctive strivings and activities take place after a period of deprivation. But aside from being parts of instinctive activities, there are unmistakable facts of emotion which may or may not be related to the grip of a biogenic need, in some degree, on the organism. Fear and rage, for example, are among the emotional reactions which, no matter by what diverse situations they are aroused and no matter how their expression is regulated in various cultures, seem to appear universally in all human groups. They are universal and unlearned in infants of the human species, of course subject to diverse regulations regarding the manner and the degree in which they are expressed in various cultures; they are thus regulated perhaps even more than the basic needs are.

[20] As formulated especially in his *Outline of Psychology*.

As pointed out by Morgan,[21] these fundamental biogenic emotions (e.g., fear and anger) have the same general properties as the biogenic needs; hence the necessity of including them under the topic of motivation. To be specific: (1) They tend to persist at least until the stimulus situation that arouses them is perceived to be removed (anger) or escaped (fear). (2) The emotional state grips the entire organism, especially through the involvement of autonomic functions. (3) Yet, "there are also specific forms of behavior called out by emotional stimuli" (p. 464). Examples of these specific forms of behavior are getting away from the danger situation in the case of fear, and striving to remove the obstacle in the case of anger. (4) These emotional states also mobilize and prime the organism for certain *ends* in relation to the situation. In other words, these "emotional states supply a set or preparation for reactions to stimulus situations" (p. 464).

The great difference between the two kinds of motivated state is that *the stimulus condition in the emotional state is external* (e.g., danger situation or obstacle), whereas it is mainly internal or organic (e.g., "depletion of food reserves, loss of water, and the accumulation of sex hormones") in the case of needs or drives (pp. 463–464).

The fact that the stimulus condition is external (at least at the outset) makes social factors much more important in the case of emotional motivation, for many of the situations arousing fear or anger that the individual faces throughout his life are social.

We are not yet in a position to list the universal and unlearned emotions in man and the original stimulus conditions ("unconditioned stimuli") that arouse them. Ever since Watson made his classical but rather short list (fear, anger, and love), several authors have made attempts in this direction. We think that fear, rage, disgust, and startle will be included in the final list of basic human emotions.[22]

As the functioning of biogenic needs is regulated culturally, so the functioning, form, expression, and the very arousal of

[21] C. T. Morgan, *op. cit.*

[22] We think that other emotionally tinged phenomena such as shame and anxiety, which are so important in human relationships, are dependent on the development of the ego. We shall touch on this problem later, in chap. 11.

the fundamental emotions are socially determined. The fact that the stimulus condition that arouses emotion is external to start with makes it more liable to social regulation and determination. No wonder, then, that "the explorer and the anthropologist sometimes have difficulty in 'reading' native faces."[23] So much so that even the shedding of tears, which is *usually* elicited *involuntarily* under conditions of considerable grief and misfortune, may become *voluntarily* controlled and socially regulated. "Thus the Andaman Islander learns how and when to cry (without feeling sad). When an important man returns after a long absence, one weeps copious tears; the fountains are under control, can be released for exhibition to the ethnologist even when the normal occasion is lacking" (p. 154). Even intense emotions expressed in instinctive activities become socially regulated in the manner in which they are expressed. The different types of actions for carrying out sexual behavior in various cultures may be mentioned as one of the striking illustrations of the point. The social determination of emotions is even more striking when we look at the manifestation of emotions in social situations which take place in culturally prescribed channels. To cite one example—in America, it is customary to open a gift in the presence of the giver, to express appreciation of it in superlative terms, and to exhibit great joy over it whether you like it or not. In the Near East, *until recently* the established behavior under similar conditions was to thank the donor in rather humiliated terms and then to put the gift inconspicuously away until the giver had left.

Not only are the forms of expressing emotions and the situations calling them forth socially regulated, but the degree of expression and even the amount of general expressiveness also run along prescribed social channels. The example of an English gentleman in England and his highly expressive American grandson illustrates the point clearly.[24]

In spite of all these variations, the social psychology of emotional motivation should be the same for all cultures. In short, this means that there are established social norms in regard to

---

[23] G. Murphy, L. B. Murphy, and T. M. Newcomb, *op. cit.*, p. 152.

[24] Klineberg's survey presents fascinating examples of cultural variations in emotional expression and control. See O. Klineberg, *Social Psychology*, New York, Henry Holt, 1940, pp. 166–202.

emotions as well as other psychological functions and that certain situations are standardized as particular stimulus situations to elicit certain standardized emotional reactions. An adequate psychology of the formation and functioning of attitudes should present essentially valid principles for the regulation of emotions and for the manifestations of sociogenic emotional reactions. No amount of evidence concerning cultural variations in the expression of emotions (or in anything else, for that matter) will be sufficient to enable us to formulate a social psychology of emotion and feeling. We must first have a more rounded psychology of the baffling topics of feeling and emotion.

Learned or Sociogenic Motives

We, as grownups, do not eat, mate, and sleep in any old way, but in certain definite ways, with certain objects and in certain places which are mainly prescribed by our social setting, whatever this particular setting may be. If we are Chinese in China (under ordinary conditions) we may not be quite satisfied with our meal if rice is not included in it. If we are good Catholics, we will not indulge in steaks on Fridays, but will look for smelts, lobster, or other delicacies from the ocean. Under ordinary conditions, any old bed will not do. We want to live and sleep in a certain locality where the people are "nice," or in a hotel on the level with our standards. Similarly with our mates. The steady girl or boy friend, or lasting mate, has to be a person who will not constitute a threat to our social standing in our group, and who has certain socially and personally approved features that go with our values of masculinity or femininity. We may feel utterly frustrated if we do not succeed in joining a certain organization or club, or going to a certain college. We may feel left out if we are not able to wear a certain fraternity or sorority pin. Likewise, our enjoyment of playing golf on a beautiful links may not be so complete if we realize that our next-door neighbor pays a thousand dollars more a year to belong to his golf club.

These are only a few examples of the way that the tastes, goals, or motives we acquire as we grow up in a social setting affect us. There are hundreds of such tastes and motives that

we acquire as we see nice things around us and achieve belongingness to various groups in society. These acquired tastes and
motives increase in number as the social organization becomes
more highly developed and more highly differentiated. They
are infinitely more numerous if we belong to the upper stratum
of the leisure class of a highly developed and wealthy society.
We have to keep up with our exclusive set in hundreds of ways.
It may become of major concern to us if we cannot entertain
members of our set, whose nationality may differ from our own,
in our exclusive yacht club or private swimming pool. Likewise, we derive special satisfaction in describing our eventful
vacation on the letterheads of internationally approved hotels
or resorts.

None of these tastes and motives are present at birth, nor do
they develop spontaneously as a consequence of maturation.
They are acquired through learning as the result of training on
the part of grownups and by membership in play, church,
school, and other groups within the reach of the individual. To
be sure, not all individuals brought up in contact with the same
groups develop exactly the same tastes and motives. There are
individual differences within limits. At birth and through the
process of maturation, only the basic motives—the biogenic
needs—are present. And they are satisfied by a well-defined
range of biologically significant stimuli or objects—milk, water,
food, etc. Beyond the necessary caloric requirement, at this
level we do not require food at a particular restaurant with a
special atmosphere. Nor is a bed in a certain desirable part of
the city, or water or drink served by a butler necessary for biological satisfaction. Of course, a certain baby may prefer mother's milk to a formula recommended by the doctor, or vice
versa. A certain crib may be more comfortable for the baby
than another one. But, as pointed out by Lashley, the range of
biologically significant stimuli and objects is well defined within
certain limits. This range does not include the *practice* of consummatory behavior in a million-dollar mansion, with silver
plates for the baby, special maids or nurses for various tasks,
or a butler to receive the doctor.

These facts lead us to say that the learned or sociogenic motives are derived from the social setting in which the individual

is reared, as determined by the practices, values, or norms prevailing in that setting at the time. As we shall bring out at greater length in the next chapter, the objects and stimuli which *first* have *value* for the child are those which satisfy his biogenic needs; then the objects, stimuli, persons, and situations which are instrumental to attaining or related to these biologically significant ones acquire *value* for him.[25] All these acquired values can be included in the general problem of attitude formation.

Acquired motives whose beginnings can be directly traced to the biogenic needs, i.e., "derived drives," are not coextensive with the whole range of acquired motives. There are acquired motives connected with the genetically developing ego values, for example, which, on the contrary, oppose—in fact, inhibit— the uncontrolled satisfaction of biogenic needs or of acquired motives that are derivations of biogenic needs ("derived drives"). These ego values, which collectively may be referred to as *conscience*, are incorporated from the prevailing values or norms of one's group; they are imposed by parents, school, church, play group, clique, etc. These ego values, thus derived from the prevailing social values that come to regulate behavior and social relationships in a major way, are not, in many cases, conducive to the satisfaction of biogenic needs or the "derived drives" traceable to them. Grownups first demand that Johnny be a good boy; only later does Johnny himself want to be a good boy. In order to be a good boy, he may be required not to—and later he will not—eat before the others are served at dinner, even if he feels very hungry. A member who is temporarily in sole possession of the loot from a foray by his gang, the other members being ignorant of the amount, will not, as a good gang member, take part of it for himself before it is divided, even though taking it may mean satisfaction of his needs for a longer period. A Catholic priest or nun, once dedicated to the service of the Church, may not indulge in sex activity, in spite of a strong urge to do so. A good Hindu whose food supply is very scarce does not consider shooting and eating certain "sacred" animals that may be running around loose in the village. Ethnological literature contains much material which shows that entire groups

[25] See G. Murphy, L. B. Murphy, and T. M. Newcomb, *op. cit.*, chaps. 3, 4; E. C. Tolman, Motivation, learning and adjustment.

will not even touch many plants or animals which constitute perfectly good foods.

We cite these illustrations in order to touch upon one of the crucial topics of controversy. According to the psychoanalytic approach, all the social values and ego values (conscience = superego) are derivatives of basic drives (primarily sex in the orthodox Freudian brand of psychoanalysis). This is an utter denial of the stubborn fact of *emergences* in group interaction (see Chapters 5–7). To be sure, people associate and interact primarily to secure satisfaction of their basic biogenic needs. But once interaction occurs and continues, there emerge products (standards, values, or norms) which in turn acquire a reality of their own and act as real factors, in their own right, in the determination of individual or group behavior. Once such a superstructure of norms comes into existence, it tends to continue even after the people who took part in the original interaction are no longer present. The conditions which brought about the original contact and interaction may change, but the products (values or norms) keep on regulating the experience and behavior of new members and even new generations, with perhaps certain modifications. Grownups are effective in dealing with their offspring rather as carriers of this superstructure of norms or values, nor is such a superstructure generated anew by each generation or by the particular father-mother-child relationship. Hence the social values incorporated in the individual may or may not be in harmony with the satisfaction of his basic needs. In short, not all the acquired motives of the individual are derivatives of basic needs.

But whether they are such derivatives or not, all the acquired values and motives directed toward acquired values come under the general heading of attitude formation and the psychology of attitudes. The ego or status motives, which are so crucially important in interpersonal and group relationships, certainly constitute one of the central areas of acquired motives. We shall deal with them in Part II, when we give a more detailed account of sociogenic motives.

The learned or acquired character of these motives does not make them unreal. They affect individuals and mobilize them to strive for the fulfillment of their desired goals with various degrees of intensity and absorption as long as they last. The person who is motivated by them does not stop to think that he can easily dispense with them; as long as he is in their grip, they are real and absolute to him.[26] Thus a socialite will strive earnestly to keep slender and to be seen in fashionable spots wearing the latest styles, even if it means sacrificing food and sleep, up to a certain point. A college student whose mind is set on belonging to a certain group or club on the campus will move heaven and earth to become a member, even though membership provides no satisfaction other than distinction. Persons who have been in solitary confinement report that they would willingly have sacrificed food and sleep (up to a certain point) to be able to chat with a human being for an hour.

However, we have to keep in mind that no matter how real and how absolute acquired motives are felt to be, they constitute the superstructure of human motivation. As the deprivation of biogenic needs (sleep, food, or water) begins to grow intense, the individual returns or regresses to the level which is dominated by the biogenic needs, and the superstructure of the acquired motives is subject to collapse in various degrees. Eyewitnesses in the areas now under the stress of hunger give grim reports of such collapse. In conflicts between strong urges arising from hunger or sex deprivation and conscience (ego values), it is *usually* the conscience that loses out. The hundreds of cases of petty stealing and of man's ungentlemanly conduct toward woman are illustrations of the point.

Of course there are men and women who so intensely become symbols of a social ideal, a movement, or a doctrine that they achieve the supreme feat of *forcing themselves* to deprive themselves to the bitter end, even to death. The lives of such persons are the highest models of personality integration and are very illuminating as such. Except for periods of great transitions, crises, war, and revolution, such people constitute the few at the extreme end of the normal distribution.

Resistance to or vacillation between the strong instinctive urges of sex or hunger on the one side and the dictates of maintaining values on the other may result in all sorts of abnormalities. These abnormal consequences fall rather in the field of

[26] See G. Murphy, L. B. Murphy, and T. M. Newcomb, *op. cit.*, p. 198.

abnormal psychologists, although we must of course learn as much from them as possible. However, exclusive preoccupation with individual abnormalities usually leads to the neglect of the central problems of social psychology.

General Orientation in the Psychology of Motivation

In the next two chapters we shall deal briefly with the dominant place of biological needs in the human infant, some recent experimental studies of human motivation, and the effects of relatively prolonged deprivation of biogenic needs. Before considering this evidence, it will help in giving us some vantage points if we seek at least a minimum general orientation in the psychology of motivation.

During the past few decades, there has been a rapidly accumulating body of research on various phases of the psychology of motivation. Notable among these studies are the brilliant investigations of Köhler, Tolman and his associates—Blodgett, Elliot, Honzik, Krechevsky, and others—and Warden and his associates.[27] Thanks to these and other investigations, it may be safe to state that a major line of orientation has been taking shape. More recently the experimental work by Murphy and his associates, Sanford, and Bruner substantiates at least certain aspects of this general orientation *on the human level*.[28]

Behavior that is motivated by a need (instinct or drive) may be characterized as behavior which is at first innate (unlearned) and common to all members of the species. This innate behavior may appear at birth or later through maturation.

[27] For example, W. Köhler, *The Mentality of Apes*, New York: Harcourt, Brace, 1925; E. C. Tolman, *Purposive Behavior in Animals and Men*, New York: Appleton-Century, 1932; E. C. Tolman, Motivation, learning and adjustment; E. C. Tolman, *Drives Toward War;* C. J. Warden, *Animal Motivation*, New York: Columbia University Press, 1931.

[28] R. Levine, I. Chein, and G. Murphy, The relation of the intensity of a need to the amount of perceptual distortion: a preliminary report, *J. Psychol.*, 1942, 13, 283–293; H. Proshansky and G. Murphy, The effects of reward and punishment on perception, *J. Psychol.*, 1942, 13, 295–305; R. Schafer and G. Murphy, The role of autism in a visual figure-ground relationship, *J. Exper. Psychol.*, 1943, 32, 335–343; R. N. Sanford, The effects of abstinence from food upon imaginal processes: a preliminary experiment, *J. Psychol.*, 1936, 2, 129–136; R. N. Sanford, The effects of abstinence from food upon imaginal processes: a further experiment, *J. Psychol.*, 1937, 3, 145–159; J. S. Bruner and C. C. Goodman, Value and need as organizing factors in perception, *J. Abn. & Soc. Psychol.*, 1947, 42, 33–44.

It is aroused (in most cases) by some periodically recurring organic need (such as hunger for food, thirst for water) which activates and heightens the motor, sensory, and central (perceptual-symbolic) functions of the individual and renders him highly selective in the direction of the goal object or situation. If the need continues and grows more intense, such motivated behavior persists until the goal object or situation is reached, and it ends in a specific pattern of consummatory behavior, thereby satisfying the need.

We have already said in this chapter that biogenic needs are common to all members of the species and that they are unlearned. They may be present at birth, as in the case of sleeping, breathing, evacuation, and suckling (though the last in particular may be crude at birth), or they may appear later, like sex, through maturation. For example, Stone observed sexual behavior in an animal brought up in isolation and with almost all the receptor organs eliminated.[29]

Most of the biogenic needs (hunger, thirst, sleep, breathing, probably sex desire) recur periodically, or cyclically with shorter or longer intervals of periodicity. Of course, this holds true only before such physiological rhythms are modified or regulated by social and other factors. We see such periodicity, at least in a general way, in the recurrent needs of the human infant, subject within limits to individual variations and to modifications as the child grows up under varying circumstances. Taking the hunger cycle as an illustration of the point, Stone [30] gave a concise formulation of the periodic arousal of biogenic needs: "It starts with hunger contractions, which by many physiologists are thought to be the instigators of the search for raw foodstuffs. Then the locomotor apparatus comes into action, the sense organs are utilized to differentiate objects, and past experience plays a determining role in the choice of hunting grounds, the discovery of prey, the chase, the kill, and the consummatory act" (pp. 75–76). (See Fig. 1.) Of course, "searching for prey," "chase," and "destruction of prey" in the figure should be expressed in terms of the various degrees

[29] C. P. Stone, Further study of sensory functions in the activation of sexual behavior in the young albino rat, *J. Comp. Psychol.*, 1923, 3, 469–473.

[30] C. P. Stone, "Motivation," chap. 4 in F. A. Moss (ed.), *Comparative Psychology*, New York: Prentice-Hall, rev. ed., 1942.

of refinement resulting from social regulations at different age levels and in different social settings. Sleep cycles and "the change from polyphasic to monophasic sleep from birth to

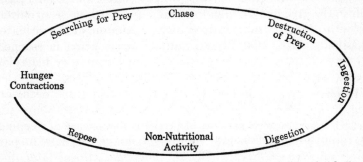

FIG. 1. Schematic representation of the hunger cycle in animals.[31]

adulthood" are represented in Fig. 2. Modifications due to the individual's environmental setting hold for the sleep cycle also.

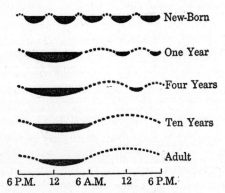

FIG. 2. The change from polyphasic to monophasic sleep as the individual grows up. (From N. Kleitman, *Sleep and Wakefulness*, Chicago: University of Chicago Press, 1939.)

But whatever the social variations may be, under ordinary conditions there will be some degree of periodicity in each setting which can vary only within certain limits. For example,

[31] Figs. 1, 3, and 4 are reproduced by permission of Prentice-Hall, Inc., from Chapter 4 by Calvin P. Stone of *Comparative Psychology* edited by F. A. Moss. Copyright, 1934, 1942, by Prentice-Hall, Inc.

except for days of fasting, there will be more or less regular mealtimes during the day. "Although individual cycles may vary in detail from species to species, and in the same individual from day to day, their broader outlines are repeated over and over in the lifetime of the individual" (p. 76). This recurrence is shown in Fig. 3 as schematized by Stone. Some of the needs are "mutually antagonistic" and inhibit each other; consequently

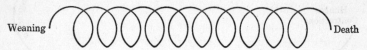

FIG. 3. Schematic representation of periodic recurrence of an instinctive activity in broad outline without modifications due to cultural regulation or the age level of the organism.

they operate successively and the cycles of the various needs differ in duration. These interrelationships are represented in Fig. 4. We repeat again, these are merely schematizations of purely physiological, biogenic need cycles without the modifications and complications arising from cultural factors; we are fully aware of the social regulation of the functioning of the basic needs. Nevertheless, these simple diagrams will serve to develop various points when we discuss the social effects of

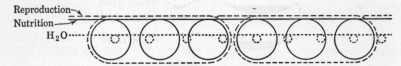

FIG. 4. Schematic representation of the differential periodicity of various needs in the organism. Modifications due to cultural factors are not represented.

deprivations in Part III. For, if the social regulation of basic needs or a scarcity of objects that satisfy them disrupts their periodic recurrence beyond certain points, these needs "backfire," so to speak, and lead individuals to new pursuits for their satisfaction, and, in turn, the superstructure of culture suffers.

Heightened motor activity, the restless state of the organism under the spell of an aroused need is best represented by the admirable findings of Richter, one of the outstanding investigators in the field of motivation. As his figures are self-explanatory, it will suffice simply to reproduce one of them (Fig. 5). Such bodily activity related to hunger contractions was observed on the human level by Wada.[32] Anyone can easily observe such activity in a hungry human infant. But as Lashley [33] cautions, this relationship between hunger contractions and heightened

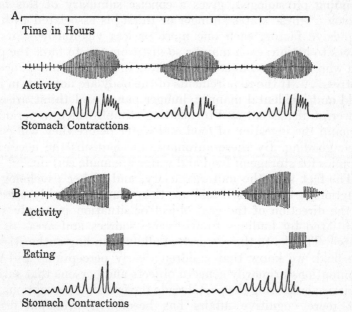

A

Time in Hours

Activity

Stomach Contractions

B

Activity

Eating

Stomach Contractions

FIG. 5. Schematic representation of the relation between periods of gross bodily activity and stomach contractions.

A, Simple activity cage without food. B, Double cage with food. (From C. P. Richter, Animal behavior and internal drives, *Quart. Rev. Biol.*, 1927, 2, 312.)

bodily activity should not be taken too literally. The activity does not stop abruptly with the cessation of stomach contractions.

The fact that motivated behavior persists in a state of restlessness, with the motor, sensory, and central (perceptual-

[32] T. Wada, Experimental study of hunger in its relation to activity, *Arch. Psychol.*, 1922, no. 57.
[33] K. Lashley. *op. cit.*

symbolic) functions sensitized in the direction of the goal object or situation, has been observed by almost all investigators in the field of motivation—and by anyone who has experienced it, for that matter. One simply cannot canalize or sublimate hunger, thirst, or sleeplessness into other channels beyond a certain point. In the following general formulation Cannon, an outstanding physiologist, gives a concise summary of this fact: "Each of these states [hunger or thirst] is associated with an impulsive factor; each one more or less vigorously spurs or drives to action; each may be so disturbing as to force the person who is afflicted to seek relief from intolerable annoyance or distress. . . . If the requirements of the body are not met, in this mild and incidental manner, hunger pangs and thirst arise as powerful, persistent and tormenting stimuli which imperiously demand the ingestion of food and water before they will cease their goading. By these automatic mechanisms the necessary supplies for storage of food and water are made certain." [34]

The fact that the motor, sensory, and higher psychological functions are mobilized and are thus rendered highly *selective* in the direction of the goal object or situation is amply substantiated by findings from diverse sources and areas of research. Thanks to the research of all outstanding authorities in the field, we know that children's early perceptions and discriminations primarily concern objects and persons that satisfy their needs. During the past decade the fact that perceptions are not mere cognitive affairs has become a principle firmly grounded on fact and it is being substantiated almost from day to day by new facts. Perceptions are highly selective, their very organization [35] being determined not solely by the properties of the external stimuli but, at times, preponderantly by internal factors that are operating currently. Motivating states of the individual, such as lust and hunger, as well as attitudes formed during the course of his development are among the major examples of these internal factors.

We especially emphasize the selectivity of perceptions as determined by motivated states of the individual. The selectivity

[34] W. B. Cannon, *op. cit.*, pp. 75–76.
[35] In the sense used by W. Köhler in *Gestalt Psychology*, New York: Liveright, 1929.

of perception is coming more and more to be taken as the pro- *D, B,*
totype of the selective nature of all "higher" psychological
functions. To cite just a few examples, Bartlett demonstrated
this in the field of remembering; Köhler and his associates and
Tolman and his students, in the field of learning; Murphy and
others, in various processes.[36] We shall present some of these
findings in the next two chapters.

The selectivity of psychological functions due to motivational ✓
and emotional factors is a fact of everyday experience. Only
psychologists of the Wundt and Titchener type tried hard, and
made their students and textbooks try hard, to get rid of these
factors in their forced abstracted analyses. The factors and
meanings affected by such factors nevertheless intruded on
them no matter how hard they tried to throw them into the
wastebasket as useless nuisances. Ask a young man strolling
restlessly in a park on a spring Sunday, ask a hungry man sitting on a park bench, ask an elegantly dressed lady what each
noticed in the park. You will almost invariably get perceptions,
discriminations, and memories clearly tinged by the individual's
appropriate motives.

Psychologists who were studying conditioning and stressing
only the aspects of their results most directly related to learning
were certainly studying motivation at the same time, even
though at least some of them soft-pedaled that aspect of their
experimental conditions. As Lashley put it,[37] "Motivation of
the hungry animal in the maze is really effective only after the
maze has been associated with the getting of food" (pp. 467–468).
Even in the case of Pavlov's dogs, the degree of conditioning,
the number of trials necessary, etc., were at least partly due
to the condition of slight hunger; the animals were brought to
the experimental room a precise number of hours after their
last feeding.[38] We know now as an established fact that the
number of trials necessary to learn or to eliminate errors is in

---

[36] See F. C. Bartlett, *Remembering: A Study in Experimental and Social Psychology,*
Cambridge: University Press, 1932; W. Köhler, *The Mentality of Apes;* F. C. Tolman,
Purposive Behavior in Animals and Men; R. Levine, I. Chein, and G. Murphy, *op. cit.;*
H. Proshansky and G. Murphy, *op. cit.;* R. Schafer and G. Murphy, *op. cit.*

[37] K. Lashley, *op. cit.*

[38] I. P. Pavlov, *Lectures on Conditioned Reflexes,* New York: International Publishers, 1928.

part a function of the time interval between the experimental session and the last feeding. All in all, *cognition and motivation and action are not discrete functions operating in separate compartments. They are functionally inseparably interrelated in the psychological product of any given moment.* In Tolman's words,[39] "... Purposiveness and cognitiveness seem to go together" (p. 13). And again, changes in performance (for better or worse) due to different types of goal objects take place "only by virtue of some sort of accompanying 'cognitive expectations' as to the character of such coming goal objects" (p. 71).

Methodological Remarks Suggested by the Foregoing and by Morgan's General Survey of Motivation

The foregoing material suggests that motivational and cognitive (perceptual and symbolic) factors do not operate in separate areas; they all become organized to produce the psychological product that appears at any time. Consequently, the best research of recent years has come from those who have not placed motivational and cognitive factors in dichotomous departments of psychology, but have tried to study the contribution of the various factors in a unified scheme. We shall present further concrete evidence to this effect. In spite of this realistic orientation, there are still some, who from their sect-like confinement or preconceptions, write and talk in terms of surface fragments of the conscious phenomena of "academic" psychology in contrast with the urges and complexes of "depth" psychology—libido, dramatic-sounding complexes (Oedipus, Electra, etc.), collective unconscious, dozens of needs and urges, etc. We shall not digress here to question the scientific validity of these concepts, which frequently are not verified in different social settings. We shall only suggest that all these depth phenomena are derived through free association, slips of memory, dream analysis, distortions of perception, memories, diverse kinds of rationalizations, and other manifestations of experience and behavior which are themselves not infrequently cognitive phenomena. It is usually by relating these to the whole picture of the individual that they acquire their meaning as symptoms of perhaps deeply rooted motivational urges.

[39] E. C. Tolman, *Purposive Behavior in Animals and Men.*

Our concern as psychologists is not with bits of muscle twitches, isolated bits of behavior items as such. We are mainly concerned with the experience and behavior of individuals as these reveal something about the whole individual. Such behavior is integrated or "molar" behavior as contrasted with "molecular" behavior and isolated items. On the basis of this perfectly defensible conception of psychology, there is a tendency to treat needs, drives, and tensions as if they were not related to an organism having a definite place in the scale of organisms. Our conceptualizations of integrated experience and behavior in psychology may not have benefited fully from the dominant nineteenth-century type of physiological knowledge about reflexes and "mental chemistry." But this does not justify our ignoring the necessity of checking our conclusions in psychology against the conclusions arrived at in the current physiology. Checking the conclusions arrived at on different levels of research will help us to work on firmer and better-verified ground. In the same way, sociologists who still consider psychology as an academic pursuit of the abstract and artificial elements of human experience are, in our opinion, overlooking more precise testing grounds for their theorizing. For in psychology today, they will find certain of their own problems and their own conclusions (e.g., structural properties generated in group situations) being worked out in terms of more precise variables.

Recently Morgan made a general formulation of the place and function of the central nervous system in motivated behavior.[40] His formulation, which is full of direct implications regarding the role of perception, learning, and other "higher" processes in motivation, is based on the extensive examination of a great bulk of direct physiological findings related to the field of motivation. In Morgan's own words: "The facts of motivation reviewed in the last four chapters are greatly in need of being drawn together into a general conception of the nature of motivation in order that their fullest significance for psychology can be perceived, and also in order that they may be fitted into the picture of learning and related functions which will emerge in the chapters to follow" (p. 457). After discussing the essen-

[40] C. T. Morgan, *op. cit.*

tial humoral basis ("humoral motive factor") of motivation, he draws a general picture of the function of "neural integrative" activity which he designates as the *central motive state* (c.m.s.). His summary account of the "central motive state" has a striking bearing on the methodological problem raised in this section. The following slightly abbreviated passage on the properties of the central motive state is significant for our problem:

1. The c.m.s. appears to be partly self-perpetuating. That is to say, there is some reverberatory activity . . . in the neurons involved in the c.m.s., such that neural activity, once it has been initiated, tends to continue. . . . Some of the reverberation maintaining the c.m.s. may be a purely central affair accounted for in terms of recurrent neural circuits; some of it, on the other hand, may be caused by circular, reflexive activity—*i.e.*, the c.m.s. may lead to gastric contractions, to changes in the sexual organs, or the like, and these may, in turn, send in afferent stimulation which builds up the c.m.s.

2. In addition to reverberation, we must postulate three behavioral properties of the c.m.s. One of these is general activity. As we have already seen in previous chapters, an increase in body activity goes along with the need for food and water and, in female animals, is dramatically correlated with sexual drive. Although some have argued that such activity arises from local tissue conditions associated with the drive in question, the facts may be interpreted as indicating that both local behavioral changes (*e.g.*, stomach contractions) and general activity are the outcome of a c.m.s.

3. Another property of the c.m.s. is that it evokes specific forms of behavior. . . . These specific forms of behavior do not depend upon any especial environmental conditions and appear to be the expression of the c.m.s.

4. A further aspect of the c.m.s. is what may be called a *set* or potentiality for presenting various patterns of behavior when the appropriate stimulus conditions in the external environment are available. This is the priming property of the c.m.s. . . . Thus there are forms of behavior that depend not only upon the presence of the c.m.s. but also upon external stimulus conditions, and in the absence of these, the c.m.s. can be said to prepare, prime, or set the organism for these forms of behavior when they become possible.

These three behavioral aspects of the c.m.s.—general activity, specific behavior, and the readiness to perceive and react to stimulus situations in particular ways—are obviously intimately related to each other in such a way as to form an effective means of eventually remedying the condition which motivated the animal. In many ways, however, the priming aspect of the c.m.s. is the most important feature for the psychologist. It is this which makes motivated behavior appear so purposive, for it is the set to perceive and react in certain ways which defines the goal.[41]

[41] *Ibid.*, pp. 460–461.

3.

The Place and Effects of Biogenic Needs in the Life of the Individual

THE LIFE OF THE ADULT HUMAN IS ORDINARILY REGULATED chiefly by the prevailing schedules, standards, values, or norms of his particular social setting. And these vary from culture to culture. In his daily life he is driven by various motives, some of which stem directly from biogenic needs or derivatives thereof through learning, and others of which are acquired through his contacts with the established standards, values, or norms of his special social surroundings. Even the number of these acquired motives varies from society to society; they are relatively fewer in less developed, less differentiated social units, and almost innumerable in highly developed and differentiated societies, especially in the leisure class. (No matter how the biogenic needs are regulated; no matter what the kind, the number, etc., of the "derived drives" or acquired motives may be; no matter how the individual may at times be driven by sociogenic motives so that he is almost consciously oblivious of the biogenic needs (in cases where these needs are satisfied to the point of being taken for granted), the demands of the biogenic needs continue until death. The individual keeps on eating, drinking, sleeping, keeping himself reasonably warm, etc. Ever-recurrent cycles of the biogenic needs continue to motivate him. They are subject within limits to regulation in various of their aspects (timing, kind of stimulus objects, places, etc.) and are liable to certain detours and deviations ("substitutive activities"). In early infancy his behavior is motivated chiefly by these needs. Up to a certain stage of development his psychology is dominated almost completely by their satisfaction ("pleasure principle"). His earliest perceptions and discriminations, as well as actions, appear chiefly in

50

relation to biologically significant objects and are then "canal-ized" to objects and persons instrumental to such satisfactions. As he grows to adulthood, his perceiving, remembering, learning, thinking, etc., continue to be selective in the direction of biologically significant goals as well as the goals and ends which become socially desirable to him. He keeps on perceiving, at times distorting, and interpreting his physical and social surroundings *selectively*, primarily as motivated by his biogenic and sociogenic motives. Especially in the *deprivation* of biogenic needs, his *selectivity* becomes heightened at times to morbid degrees, with various psychological consequences for him. Under stringent conditions of prolonged and intense *deprivation* he becomes almost a different person; he may then recast his surroundings anew psychologically.

In Part II, we shall consider the formation and functioning of sociogenic motives in more detail. In this and the next chapter we shall present samples of the concrete findings and observations that demonstrate the facts pointed out in the above paragraphs. We consider them representative of the accumulating evidence from scientific research and everyday life situations. Unfortunately, in an outline such as this, only a few illustrations can be presented.

The Child's Behavior First Dominated by Biogenic Needs

The activity of a baby in the first weeks of his life is determined chiefly by the biogenic needs with which he is born. From the standpoint of a socialized adult, his behavior may seem utterly chaotic and haphazard. But as Gesell put it so colorfully: "From the standpoint of 4-week-oldness his behavior is patterned, meaningful, significant."[1] And the determiners of this "standpoint of 4-week-oldness" are the physiological states of his organism. This general fact can be substantiated by anyone who carefully observes or cares for an infant. It stands out clearly in K. C. Pratt's summary of research on the baby from birth to about one month of age. The characteristics of the hunger cycle before social regulation becomes effective, and the

[1] A. Gesell and F. L. Ilg, *Infant and Child in the Culture of Today*, New York: Harper, 1943, p. 93.

relative effectiveness of the biogenic motives and external stimuli in evoking activity at various phases of the cycle are described dramatically:

The alimentary canal plays a dominant role in the activity of the neonate. When "hunger" contractions of the stomach begin, the irritability of the child increases; with the mounting vigor of each successive period of stomach contraction the general activity spreads so that almost all of the musculature of the body is in action. Initially intermittent, feeble crying becomes continuous and intense. *At this extreme height of activity very few stimuli act to inhibit or quiet the child.* In a very small percentage of the cases auditory stimuli are momentarily effective. Swinging or rocking is much more efficient, but when such stimulation ceases the general activity is not long in reappearing. If the cheek or lip areas are now stimulated, the head quickly turns toward the source of stimulation. . . .

The child, put to breast or bottle, shows some disorganization of sucking but soon performs with regularity and precision. The general activity disappears. If one now stimulates the organism the ordinary consequence is some modification of the sucking act. *Potent stimuli are required to cause the child to cease feeding if the food substance be mother's milk or an accepted substitute.* As the stomach fills, the sucking becomes irregular, less vigorous, with long periods of quiescence. During such a period of quiescence almost all types of stimuli such as dropping, a flash of light, pulling hair, etc., lead to renewed sucking.

The feeding act over, the infant lies quiescent and asleep. *At this time, although irritability is not as great, it is possible to observe the effects of different stimulus modalities.* . . .

During the quiescent period regurgitation, excretory activities, etc., may be accompanied by short periods of activity.[2]

At this stage of development, the baby does not respond in a discriminatory way to objects or persons around him except as they satisfy or prevent satisfaction of the dominant need at the moment. Gesell observed that the newborn infant is "socially deaf and blind to the approach of another person who bends over him and gives him every social provocation to respond."[3] This seems to hold true in the early weeks of life, even though

[2] K. C. Pratt, "The Neonate," in C. Murchison (ed.), *A Handbook of Child Psychology,* Worcester: Clark University Press, 2nd ed., 1933, pp. 200–201 (italics mine).

[3] A. Gesell and H. Thompson, *Infant Behavior, Its Genesis and Growth,* New York: McGraw-Hill, 1934, p. 287.

there is every indication that infants are not, as the statement might lead one to believe, deaf and blind in a literal sense.

As the baby grows and develops, the opportunities for varied stimulation and contact with persons and objects in his environment increase. In many respects, the most important of these contacts arise in connection with feeding, sleep, elimination, and other physiological functions. It is not surprising, in view of what is known about the effects of the biogenic needs on the learning process, to find that the earliest discriminatory responses are preponderantly directed toward persons and objects related to the satisfaction of these needs. These are the persons and objects which first acquire *value* for the child. According to Gesell, most children respond positively to their mothers by about the age of 4 months.[4] On the other hand, it is not until several months later, according to one study, that babies are observed to respond with relative frequency to another child.[5] It is through the observation of such discriminative responses that we are able to learn something about the motives that direct the formation and organization of children's perceptions and attitudes. This area of study in child psychology, as Proshansky and Murphy suggest in a study to be reviewed in the next chapter, may yield valuable evidence for social psychology concerning the basic problem of the formation (learning) of attitudes.

As difficult as it has been for child psychologists to investigate the formation and organization of children's perceptions, the evidence indicates the major importance of biogenic needs in the process. In a survey of the visual perception of children, Vernon concludes that children are particularly likely to perceive their surroundings in terms of "a series of undifferentiated meaningful wholes." She notes that the structural properties of the stimuli are perhaps "less important than those of biological utility, interest and affective value" in determining what a child perceives.[6] As a result, the child responds most readily to the patterns which are familiar and meaningful to him. And these are the faces of the mother, father, or whoever

---

[4] *Ibid.*, p. 262.

[5] M. Mandry and M. Nekula, Social relations between children of the same age during the first two years of life, *J. Genet. Psychol.*, 1939, 54, 193–215.

[6] M. D. Vernon, *Visual Perception*, Cambridge: University Press, 1937, p. 178.

may happen to care for him for any length of time, and objects similarly associated with the daily satisfaction of his biogenic needs, such as a bottle.

This tendency for children's early perceptions to be concerned with persons or objects related to the satisfaction of biogenic needs is illustrated in a study by Beaumont and Hetzer.[7] They observed children's reactions to cards, some of which were plain, some of which had colored geometric figures, and some of which had pictures of a woman or a cup. On the basis of this observation, they concluded that until about 18 months of age these children showed little or no discrimination among the various cards. Their reactions to all the cards and patterns might be described simply as "receptive manipulation." But around the 18th month these children began to respond differently to the pictures of the woman and the cup—stimuli which by this time had acquired value to them as instrumental in satisfying their needs.

The dominant role which biogenic needs play in the formation and organization of children's early perceptions may be demonstrated conversely by observing reactions to patterns which have not been related to the satisfaction of their basic drives. Thus it has been found that children even 3 or 5 years old ordinarily tend *not* to perceive fine and minute details in abstract patterns or to notice irregularities in geometrical forms.[8] A common reaction of children placed in an experimental situation which calls for them to deal with abstract sensory qualities (such as length, color, form) is to make repetitive or superfluous responses. Such perseverative responses were reported, for example, by Brian and Goodenough in 2-year-olds matching colored geometrical solids and forms.[9]

However, saying that young children usually do not make fine discriminations between patterns and forms does not mean that they *cannot* do so. On the contrary, experiments have shown that, when *properly motivated*, young children are able

[7] H. Beaumont and H. Hetzer, Spontane Zuwendung zu Licht und Farben in ersten Lebensjahr, *Ztsch. f. Psych. u. Physiol. d. Sinnesorg*, 1929, 113, 239–267.

[8] W. Line, The development of visual perception, *Brit. J. Psychol. Monogr.*, 1931, No. 15.

[9] C. R. Brian and F. L. Goodenough, The relative potency of color and form perception at various ages, *J. Exper. Psychol.*, 1929, 12, 197–213.

Fɪɢ. 6. A suggestive photographic representation of the selectivity of the child's perceptions. (By *Life* photographer Herbert Gehr. © *Time*, Inc.)

to discern quite fine differences. In the case of young children, the effective motivation is that of biogenic needs. In a study by Munn and Steining,[10] a 15-month-old child learned to discriminate between two boxes on the basis of small black and white geometrical designs on the cover. He found a piece of chocolate in the "correct" box at each trial. When he had learned the discrimination, he continued to choose correctly even when the figure on the "correct" box was rotated 45 degrees, when the background of the "correct" design was changed, and when a different form was used on the cover of the empty box. Even finer discriminations were made by the two fairly hungry 2-year-olds that Gellerman used in a similar study.[11] A comparison of these results with those obtained in studies in which no reward related to a biogenic need was given suggests vividly the primacy of biogenic needs in regulating the behavior of young children, and their importance in the learning process.

Another line of evidence leading to the above conclusion lies in the development of language behavior. As we shall see later (Chapter 8, pages 196–201), there seems to be a significant tendency for the development of children's perceptions and concepts to have a similar course. Here, however, we shall merely cite a few illustrations of language behavior to show the importance of biogenic motives in the learning process. It is commonly observed in everyday life that children's early generalizations, like their early perceptions, may be extremely broad and flexible. For example, a child may learn "juice" in connection with his daily orange juice and proceed to apply it to any and all liquids which he drinks or wants to drink. A 2-year-old child with whom we leafed through a magazine called all the women in the pictures "mamma." A year-old-child, Cindy, used "mama" to designate anyone who waited on or cared for her; even her 3-year-old brother and her 5-year-old sister were called "mamma." Such an early generalization may be "general and so flexible that it is often practically without meaning to an

[10] N. L. Munn and B. R. Steining, The relative efficacy of form and background in a child's discrimination of visual patterns, *J. Genet. Psychol.*, 1931, 39, 73–90.

[11] L. W. Gellerman, Form discrimination in chimpanzees and two-year-old children. I. Discrimination of form *per se*. II. Form versus background, *J. Genet. Psychol.*, 1933, 42, 1–50.

adult." [12] In contrast, children even 3 years of age may show an apparent inability to generalize or extend an equivalent reaction to stimuli of a more abstract class of objects or relations such as "roundness" [13] or "middle-sizedness." [14] One of the clues to an explanation of such differential results seems to be the connection between the class of objects or relations and the satisfaction of biological needs. Children's first words, like their early perceptions, tend to relate to persons and objects more or less closely concerned in such satisfaction. For example, Gesell found that the most frequent early words of the children he observed at 52 weeks of age were for "things to eat." [15] He also noted that for a time a child may say "bye-bye" to his father but apparently be unable to say it to another person.

Although this and other evidence from child study points to the conclusion that the objects and persons which first acquire value for the child are related to the satisfaction of his biogenic needs (drives), this does not mean that his attitudes toward these objects and persons are formed once and for all in a stable and lasting way. On the contrary, because his actions are so strongly under the grip of these needs (hunger, thirst, sleep, temperature regulation, etc.), the baby's or young child's behavior is not, in an adult sense, *consistent*. For example, Lewin observed that even after an infant recognizes his mother and other persons in his environment, the relationship with them does not for some time "become a stable constituent of the child's pyschological environment." The bond between mother or nurse and infant is one "in which, functionally, the [biologically important] needs of the baby have primacy." [16] A child may customarily react positively to his mother; but let her deprive him of his meal or delay it, and you will see him turn on her with all the explosive intensity of which he is capable. Even during the course of a child's hunger and rest cycles (as modified by the schedules prevailing for his age group and the

---

[12] L. Long, Conceptual relationships in children: The concept of roundness, *J. Genet. Psychol.*, 1940, 57, 289–315.

[13] *Ibid.*

[14] J. D. Hicks and F. D. Stewart, The learning of abstract concepts of size, *Child Develop.*, 1930, 1, 195–203.

[15] A. Gesell and H. Thompson, *op. cit.*, p. 255.

[16] K. Lewin, "Environmental Forces," in C. Murchison (ed.), *A Handbook of Child Psychology*, Worcester: Clark University Press, 2nd ed., 1933, p. 595.

medical practice current in his social setting), the usual run of things may be upset as the needs in question become more and more dominant. Mary Cover Jones reported that the most frequent crying episodes in a group of children from 16 months to 3 years of age occurred at the end of the morning when they were tired and hungry.[17] That these episodes were related to the needs in question is shown by the fact that when the feeding and rest schedules were adjusted to meet these needs, "the total amount of crying was considerably lessened."

Of course, as a baby grows older, motives other than the biogenic ones come into the picture. Then it may be possible for a short time to distract him from the immediate satisfaction of a biogenic need. Lewin concludes that this comes about only as the result of a certain development and the child's acquisition of values from the social world around him. After observing that the objects of value (positive or negative "valences") in the infant's environment "depend essentially upon his own needs and their momentary condition," Lewin points out that the possibility of influencing older children by "psychological means" is disproportionately greater. He concludes that "the possibility of direct influence is correlated with the increasing psychological reality for the child of social facts, especially the powers of others."[18] This important fact—the acquisition of sociogenic motives in the course of the child's development—will be our concern in Chapters 11 and 12.

Piaget and his associates studied extensively the language and reasoning, conception of the world around them, judgment, and socialized behavior of children from the early years until preadolescence. The same general trend in psychological development is visible in all these aspects. Thus, in the early years of childhood, the "pleasure principle" dominates all phases of the child's psychology as regulated chiefly by the urges and temporal shifts of biogenic needs (autism). Hence the whims and mercurial changes in direction manifested, at times, almost from moment to moment. Let us illustrate this general trend by one specific phase of development studied by Piaget and his associates. The summary of their research on language and

---

[17] M. C. Jones, "Emotional Development," in *ibid.*, p. 290.
[18] K. Lewin, *op. cit.*, p. 612.

reasoning brings together tendencies found in different areas of child study and gives a more comprehensive picture of the motivation of the developing child and of his mentality as revealed in language behavior.[19] Piaget observed that the infant's behavior is governed chiefly by the organic needs. At this stage of development "reality may be said to be simply and solely what is desired" (p. 246). The world is fashioned in accordance with the "pleasure principle," to use Freud's term. The infant's behavior may therefore be characterized as "autistic," and "autism knows of no adaptation to reality, because pleasure is its only spring of action" (p. 244). There is a corresponding "absence of social needs" (p. 213).

As the child meets obstacles, rewards, and differences in his environment, he must begin to adapt to the world of persons and objects as it exists. But even though he is forced to this adaptation and strives to make it, he is as yet unable to act on the basis of any point of view other than that of his own satisfactions. He does not yet differentiate between his wishes and desires and the external world. Since an understanding of reciprocity with other persons as well as with one's own desires is necessary for socialized behavior, the child passes through a stage in which his behavior, though revealing play and other desires not aimed at "organic or 'ludistic'" satisfaction, is still autistic in form ("egocentric" stage) (p. 205); ". . . in a word, he is conscious of nothing but his own subjectivity" (p. 249). Consequently, even though he may begin to perceive social realities and relationships as they exist, he cannot yet function as a socialized being (with all the various desires for recognition and status, etc., which accompany a grasp of the hierarchical arrangements of reciprocal action).

In this section we have had to restrict ourselves to these representative conclusions to draw attention to the fact that the behavior of the infant consists chiefly of reactions motivated by biogenic needs. Hence, it follows that the first objects, persons, and situations that are of *value* to the child are those which are related to the satisfaction of these needs. In the course of his development he acquires other *values*, either built up on

[19] J. Piaget, *Judgment and Reasoning in the Child*, London: Kegan Paul, Trench, Trubner, 1928, pp. 199–256.

these first values or formed through contact with the prevailing practices, values, or norms of his social setting. These latter values, incorporated in him through contact with persons, situations, groups, and institutions around him, constitute the basis of his *sociogenic motives.* The psychology of the formation of these motives and their effect on his behavior and experience will be our concern in Part II, especially Chapters 11 and 12.

For purposes of clarification, just one concrete comparison of the *values* directly linked to the satisfaction of biogenic needs and the acquired values or preferences as determined by social contacts will suffice at present. In several interesting studies, Davis reported the results of the self-selection of food by newly weaned babies and older children in hospital wards.[20] The children were provided at each meal with a fairly large selection of food and were allowed to choose and eat whatever they pleased, without any suggestions from grownups. To adults in almost any society, at least some of the resulting choices would be somewhat startling. Thus, salt was taken only occasionally. The children seldom mixed their foods—for example, putting milk on cereal—but preferred to eat them pure. On occasion, they would eat a meal consisting entirely of one food. (One child 2½ years old ate ten eggs at one meal.) Although the children occasionally indulged in large amounts of the same food for several successive days, no disgust or signs of overeating followed such sprees. And special foods were not demanded or rejected to an extent injurious to health.

These findings are in contrast to the food tastes of most children in the United States today after a certain age. Furthermore, as is well known, some children develop definite likes and dislikes for certain foods which makes their eating something of a problem. When McCarthy compared the eating habits of a group of children from 2 to 7½ years of age with those of their parents, she found that many of the children's food likes and dislikes were shared by other members of the family. For example, 47 per cent of the food dislikes of the children who were

[20] See the following by C. M. Davis: Self-selection of diets: an experiment with infants, *Trained Nurse and Hosp. Rev.*, 1931, 86, 5; Self-selection of diet by newly weaned infants, *Amer. J. Diseases of Children*, 1928, 36, 651–679; A practical application of some lessons of the self-selection diet study to the feeding of children in hospitals, *Amer. J. Dis. Children*, 1933, 46, 743–750.

classed as "problems" in relation to food were found in other members of the family.[21] Such studies as these well illustrate the established fact of the influence of social contacts on the satisfaction of biogenic needs. And here we see one instance of how more or less lasting attitudes are built up.

Effects of Motivation as Revealed by the Experimental Approach

Until very recently the experimental study of the effects of motives was carried on almost exclusively on animals. From these studies we have learned a great deal concerning the effects of motives on learning, discrimination, problem-solving processes, motivational reinforcement, etc. Fundamentally, these problems have much in common for animals of various species. Such studies have shown us the directive role of motivation on behavior and helped to accentuate the conception of the organismic (molar) character and purposive nature of the behavior of organisms as *naturalistic* phenomena.[22] (Formerly, total and purposive manifestations of behavior were utilized as evidence of the philosophical doctrines of vitalism, entelechy, etc.). Convenient surveys of experimental animal studies are presented in such works as those by Hilgard and Marquis [23] and Stone.[24] With full awareness of the fact that results obtained on the animals of one species are not always valid for the members of different species—especially for Homo sapiens, because of the almost staggering effects of social phenomena—we shall briefly summarize a few representative animal studies as a general orientation to our own level. We must also keep in mind the fact which has been experimentally demonstrated by investigators in the field of animal psychology, that even in infra-human organisms which have no culture, social situations and complications produce differential effects.

[21] D. McCarthy, Children's feeding problems in relation to the food aversions in the family, *Child Develop.*, 1935, 6, 277–284.

[22] See E. C. Tolman, *Purposive Behavior in Animals and Men*, New York: Appleton-Century, 1932, and Motivation, learning, and adjustment, *Proc. Amer. Philos. Socy.*, 1941, 84, 543–563.

[23] E. R. Hilgard and D. G. Marquis, *Conditioning and Learning*, New York: Appleton-Century, 1940.

[24] C. P. Stone, "Motivation," in F. A. Moss (ed.), *Comparative Psychology*, New York: Prentice-Hall, rev. ed., 1942, pp. 65–97.

In the preceding chapter we noted that one important feature of most experiments on animal learning involves the deprivation of some basic need for a definite period of time before the animal is introduced to the experimental situation. It is an accepted fact in animal psychology that when an animal is thus deprived, acts leading to the attainment of an appropriate goal object or reward are reinforced and are therefore more likely to occur when the animal is again placed in the situation.[25] Thus, when an animal is hungry, the presentation of food "reinforces" the acts which preceded the getting of food, etc.

After reviewing the experiments on animal learning, McGeoch concluded: "Within limits not yet clearly defined, learning is a function of the strength of motives which are operating. . . . "[26] For example, Ligon's study showed that the rats which had been deprived of food for the longest period of time performed best in the maze, whereas those who were fed just before entering the maze gave the poorest performance.[27] Within limits, the amount of conditioned salivation varies with the length of the period of food deprivation.[28] The major importance of the strength of drive as a factor in the learning process is brought out even more strikingly in a study by Tolman, Honzik, and Robinson, which showed that *hungry* rats learn better than *less hungry* rats (i.e., those deprived of food for a shorter period) even when they are not given food as a reward.[29] Varying degrees of deprivation produce similar results upon the resistance of a learned response to extinction when it is no longer rewarded. In Sackett's study, the rats who were deprived for the longest period (30 hours) *continued more frequently* to press a bar for food *after the food reward was removed* than the animals deprived for a shorter period (6 hours).[30]

[25] E. R. Hilgard and D. G. Marquis, *op. cit.*, pp. 81–82.

[26] J. A. McGeoch, *The Psychology of Human Learning*, New York: Longmans, Green, 1942, p. 265.

[27] E. M. Ligon, A comparative study of certain incentives in the learning of the white rat, *Comp. Psychol. Monogr.*, 1929, 6, No. 2.

[28] G. Finch, Hunger as a determinant of conditional and unconditional salivary response magnitude, *Amer. J. Physiol.*, 1938, 123, 379–382.

[29] E. C. Tolman, C. H. Honzik, and E. W. Robinson, The effect of degrees of hunger upon the order of elimination of long and short blinds, *Univ. Calif. Publ. Psychol.*, 1930, 4, 189–202.

[30] R. S. Sackett, The effect of strength of drive at the time of extinction upon resistance to extinction in rats, *J. Comp. Psychol*, 1939, 27, 411–431.

Tolman keenly observed that differences in the demand for various objects "are dependent not upon the character of the goal-object per se but rather upon their character with reference to conditions of physiological drive." [31] The interrelated effect of the need for food and the consummatory act upon learning in animals is aptly illustrated in a study by Blodgett. In this experiment, the rats, even though hungry, made comparatively little progress in learning when they did not receive food in the maze. When these same rats were rewarded with food, their performance improved markedly. [32] Similarly, if a food reward has been given to hungry rats but is removed during the course of learning, the performance degenerates. [33]

The learning process in animals has been shown to be affected by the appropriateness of the reward (or goal object) to the organic need motivating the animal. *Very thirsty* animals show a marked improvement in maze performance when *water* is given instead of only slightly moistened *food*. Conversely, learning in *hungry* rats decreases when *water* is given instead of *food*. [34] As Grindley demonstrated, the *amount* of food given to *hungry* chickens affects the speed of learning. When the food was only *shown*, they evidenced slight learning. [35] Animal studies also indicate that certain preferred rewards (e.g., bran mash) function as more effective incentives to a deprived (hungry) animal than certain less preferred rewards (e.g. sunflower seed). [36]

The studies of Warden and his associates reveal the relative persistence of goal seeking in different degrees of various kinds of deprivation. The number of times a rat will withstand electric shock to reach food, water, or a sex object was found to vary with the amount of deprivation. For example, the thirst drive was relatively most persistent in rats after a day of deprivation.

[31] E. C. Tolman, *Purposive Behavior in Animals and Men*, p. 68.

[32] H. C. Blodgett, The effect of introduction of reward upon maze learning of rats, *Univ. Calif. Publ. Psychol.*, 1929, 4, 113–134.

[33] E. C. Tolman and C. H. Honzik, Introduction and removal of reward and maze performance in rats, *Univ. Calif. Publ. Psychol.*, 1930, 4, 257–275.

[34] M. H. Elliott, The effect of appropriateness of reward and of complex incentives on maze performance, *Univ. Calif. Publ. Psychol.*, 1929, 4, 91–98.

[35] G. C. Grindley, Experiments on the influence of the amount of reward on learning in young chickens, *Brit. J. Psychol.*, 1929, 20, 173–180.

[36] R. Simmons, The relative effectiveness of certain incentives in animal learning, *Comp. Psychol. Monogr.*, 1924, 2, No. 7; M. H. Elliott, *op. cit.*

From that time on, the animals' willingness to withstand the shock for a small amount of water decreased slowly until death.[37]

The following observation by Richter, an outstanding investigator of motivation, embodies the main features of the effects of deprivation on the behavior of an animal:

In experiments on one animal [the rat] a liberal supply of building material,—sticks, rope, stones, and cloth,—was placed in the large central cage. This animal had habitually deposited its feces in the water-cup. Usually the water was changed every day, but on one occasion, by some neglect, it was not changed for several days, so that the resulting odor became very unpleasant. At this point the animal started to cover the hole over the water-cup. It first removed part of the upper layer of the cardboard bottom of the large central cage, and dragged it into the water-box. It placed the cardboard over the cup and smoothed it down on all sides until the hole was perfectly covered. Then from the bottom of the central cage it lifted stones larger than its head by three inches into the drinking cage and placed them over the cardboard cover. Besides the large stones numerous pebbles and sticks were used until the water-box was completely blocked. The animal had cut off its only water supply by this performance. Since we wished to see what it would do when it became very thirsty, the material was left undisturbed and no other water was given. After three days, the animal pushed all of the sticks and stones from the drinking cage into the large central cage, tore up the cardboard seal, and drank its fill of the polluted water.[38]

One of the important aims of animal motivation studies is to "measure the relative strength" of various needs in relation to each other in a conflict situation; i.e., an animal motivated by two different drives is placed in a situation in which it has to orient itself to one or the other of two incentives (e.g., food, sex object).[39] It will be factually dangerous to *carry over to the human level the findings concerning the relative strength of different motives in animals without first taking seriously into account the intricate complications of human culture.* In this connection, the

[37] C. J. Warden, *Animal Motivation: Experimental Studies on the Albino Rat*, New York: Columbia University Press, 1931.

[38] P. Richter, Animal behavior and internal drives, *Quart. Rev. Biol.*, 1927, 2, 341–342.

[39] See, for example, C. Tsai, The relative strength of sex and hunger motives in the albino rat, *J. Comp. Psychol.*, 1925, 5, 407–415; C. P. Stone, *op. cit.*; C. J. Warden, *op. cit.*

conclusion drawn by P. T. Young after a survey of the relevant experimental literature is pertinent:

> . . . There is no doubt that hunger behavior dominates thirst if the animal has been long deprived of food and only recently of water, and that thirst dominates hunger under a reversal of conditions. Also the preferential order for foods varies with the constituents of the animal's diet. Similarly, exploratory behavior inhibits sexual aggression, eating, and drinking, if rats are placed in a novel environment. Many such examples can be found to show that *the relative dominance of behavior patterns is largely dependent upon circumstances.* We are forced to conclude that *there is no immutable hierarchy of drives.*[40]

As the above intimates, it may be much to the point here to keep in mind the periodic or cyclic appearance of the various drives. Different drives recur in full strength at shorter or longer time intervals and are also subject to some variation from individual to individual. For example, in the human adult, hunger and thirst are aroused in more or less regular cycles which are of shorter duration than the sleep cycle; and probably the need for sleep ordinarily recurs in shorter cycles than the sex drive. (See Chapter 2, pages 40–43.)

Aside from the necessity for testing the applicability of facts concerning motivation at the animal level to the human level where the *emergence* of culture is a factor to be duly considered, we must be cautious about generalizing on the subhuman level without taking social or environmental factors into account. In studies of motivation even on animals, the introduction of social factors has been found to alter the results. Thus, Jenkins, studying sex behavior,[41] and Nissen, studying maternal behavior,[42] found that the usual goal objects and responses of the white rat were modified when certain social influences were introduced. For example, mother rats will ordinarily withstand relatively frequent electric shock in order to reach their young; but if separated from the litter for a few hours, they show a considerably decreased tendency to reach their young.

[40] P. T. Young, *Motivation of Behavior*, New York: Wiley, 1936, p. 152 (first italics mine).

[41] M. Jenkins, "The Effect of Segregation on the Sex Behavior of the White Rat as Measured by the Obstruction Method," in C. J. Warden, *op. cit.*, pp. 179–261.

[42] H. W. Nissen, "A Study of Maternal Behavior in the White Rat by Means of the Obstruction Method," in C. J. Warden, *op. cit.*, pp. 334–350.

Before we consider experiments on the motivation of human beings in the next chapter, Stone's caution in relation to the sex drive will be an appropriate conclusion for these brief illustrations of the findings of studies on animal motivation.

In closing, it seems appropriate to voice a word of caution against inordinate avidity for utilization of behavioral data on sex phenomena collected from the lower animals for the elucidation of human sexual problems, *in the absence of appropriate factual data on the feasibility of such applications.* The utmost reserve is justified, for even among the lower animals only rigidly controlled experiments suffice to bring out similarities and differences between the species. Vast intellectual and cultural differences between men and the lower animals must certainly restrict rather than enlarge the range of applicability of behavioral data.[43]

[43] C. P. Stone, "Sex Drive," in Edgar Allen (ed.), *Sex and Internal Secretions*, Baltimore: Williams and Wilkins, 1939, p. 1258.

4.

The Effects of Deprivation
at the Human Level (Individual and Social)

IN RECENT YEARS, THE EXPERIMENTAL APPROACH HAS BEEN put to fortunate use in studying the effects of biogenic motives at the human level. In reviewing the representative studies by Sanford, Murphy and his students, and Bruner on the psychological consequences of biogenic need deprivation on human subjects, we shall find clear-cut evidence of the functionally unified organization and operation of motivational and cognitive (perceptual and symbolic) factors. When human beings undergo deprivation of the biogenic needs, even for the relatively short periods possible in the usual experiment, their psychological functions are rendered highly selective in the direction of the appropriate goal objects or situations.

In the next section of this chapter we shall report some results of an experiment on human beings in prolonged semi-starvation. This experiment gives a startling and clear-cut substantiation of observations hitherto obtained only from everyday life situations. Then, bearing in mind the leads afforded by these experiments, we shall cite a few examples of deprivation in actual social life.

The *selectivity* of perception, remembering, and other "higher" processes as determined by external stimuli and internal factors has been demonstrated by many experiments and observations from life. Of the studies showing the effects of attitudes acquired during the individual's development, that of Bartlett [1] is outstanding. Studying first the way individuals *perceive* their surroundings, Bartlett pointed out the effects of socially acquired attitudes upon perceiving, re-

---

[1] F. C. Bartlett, *Remembering: A Study in Experimental and Social Psychology,* Cambridge: University Press, 1932.

membering, and imagining. The studies to be reviewed here demonstrate such *selectivity* as determined largely by the biogenic needs.

On the basis of the observation that abstinence from food leads to selective preoccupation and to thoughts and dreams of food, Sanford set out to test the hypothesis that the amount of imagining about food varies with the length of deprivation. As the first step, he tested a group of school children shortly before and after their regular meals. At both times, the children were presented with words to which they were to respond with the first word that came to them, and pictures of incomplete situations, such as a pointing finger or a baby reaching out with its hands, which they were asked to complete. He found that the children gave about twice as many food responses to the words and pictures *before* meals as they did *after* meals.[2]

In a further study using college students as subjects, Sanford made interesting findings relevant to the *cyclical nature of hunger* as modified by social factors, and to certain social factors that affected the reaction of his subjects to deprivation.[3] He set out to compare the variation in preoccupation with food (1) after a 24-hour fast and (2) during the normal eating cycle. All the subjects were told that they were being tested for speed of response. After a few conventional speed tests, they were asked for word associations, interpretation of incomplete pictures, chain associations, completion of drawings, and completion of words of which two letters were given. In the author's words, the findings were as follows:

"1. Food responses increase with the time during the normal eating cycle and over a 24-hour period.

"2. Over a 24-hour period, the increase in food responses is not in direct ratio to the increase in time, the fasters' average being only slightly greater than that of subjects examined near the close of the normal eating cycle" (p. 155).

The latter point is particularly enlightening in view of the facts stated in Chapter 2 concerning the periodicity of hunger *as modified by prevailing social schedules* (i.e., a "food habit"),

[2] R. N. Sanford, The effects of abstinence from food upon imaginal processes: a preliminary experiment, *J. Psychol.*, 1936, 2, 129–136.

[3] R. N. Sanford, The effects of abstinence from food upon imaginal processes: a further experiment, *J. Psychol.*, 1937, 3, 145–159.

which is important in regulating the selectivity of humans in relation to the goal object (food). Whereas the "physical need for food" was surely greater, on the whole, for subjects deprived of food for 24 hours, the total food responses for this group were only slightly greater than for subjects before one of their regular meals. This modified hunger cycle or "food habit" also accounts for the finding that subjects tested *before* breakfast (a meal which is often light or at times omitted, especially by college students), when they had not eaten for from 8 to 20 hours, made significantly *fewer* food responses than those tested near the latter half of their normal eating cycle ($2\frac{1}{2}$ to 5 hours after eating).

The effects of social factors upon perceptual selectivity after deprivation are revealed in the finding that physical education students, whose program included vigorous exercise, made twice as many food responses as liberal arts students who were tested after an equivalent period of abstinence from food. Here the *line of study* that involved greater energy output increased the *psychological effects* of deprivation as well as the greater actual need for food.

Before we leave Sanford's study, it is worth noting that the reactions he observed in subjects who fasted for 24 hours revealed certain psychological dynamisms which at least some psychoanalysts tend to present dramatically only in the case of sexual deprivation. As Sanford's illustrations show, "frustration mechanisms" tend to accompany the deprivation of any biogenic need. The following conversation between the experimenter and a subject shows one of the devices used to avoid preoccupation with food.

E. Well, how did it go?
S. It was kind of tough—thanks to my roommate.
E. What do you mean?
S. Well, it seemed that just about the time *I got thoughts of food put out of my mind* my roommate would say, "How would you like to have a nice, big, juicy steak?" (P. 158; italics mine.)

Another example of reaction to deprivation is seen in the subject who *forgot* that he was supposed to be abstaining from food: "I missed my supper, as I was supposed to do, and was driving

home from a date when I thought, 'Gosh, I'm hungry.' I parked
the car and went into a drugstore to get a sandwich, and then
the thought struck me, 'Oh golly, I'm supposed to be fasting'"
(p. 158). Psychoanalytic literature is full of cases of forgetting
and other slips associated with prolonged sexual deprivation.

An excellent illustration of research in which cognitive and
motivational factors are conceived of as functionally interrelated psychological processes is Levine, Chein, and Murphy's

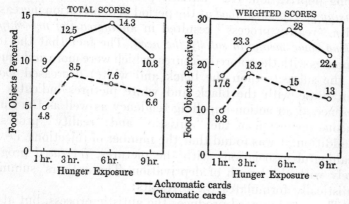

Achromatic cards
Chromatic cards

FIG. 7. The effect of food deprivation on perception.
These are the average scores of all experimental subjects. The total scores
give the average of all food responses made. Weighted scores were computed
by assigning different values to items referring to meat, fruits or vegetables,
and eating utensils. (From R. Levine, I. Chein, and G. Murphy, in *J.
Psychol.*, 1942, 13, p. 291.)

experiment, "The relation of intensity of a need to the amount of
perceptual distortion." [4] These experimenters took perception
as the prototype of "higher processes" with which to study the
"tendency of cognitive processes to move in the direction of
drive-satisfaction" (*autism*) (p. 283). College students were
asked to interpret pictures, some of which were black and white
and some of which were colored. Both groups of pictures included meaningless drawings, ambiguous drawings of food
articles, and drawings of various household articles. Each sub-

[4] R. Levine, I. Chein, and G. Murphy, The relation of the intensity of a need to the
amount of perceptual distortion, *J. Psychol.*, 1942, 13, 283–293.

ject was tested once a week at various periods of time after eating (1, 3, 6, 9 hours). Fig. 7 shows the results. As this figure shows, the number of food responses tended to increase with the length of deprivation up to a certain point, after which there was a slight decrease in number. It should be noted that this decrease occurred *earlier* (at 3 hours) with the colored than with the black and white pictures. The authors interpret these findings as indicating that two processes operated simultaneously during deprivation. An "autistic process" resulted in an *increasing perception of food* as the period of deprivation increased, and a "reality process" resulted in an *increasing necessity of finding some means to satisfy the need*. The fact that the food responses with the colored pictures (which were more ambiguous for the subjects than the black and white) decreased *sooner* than those with the black and white pictures indicates the presence of an action-impelling tendency as well as the simultaneous operation of the "autistic" and "reality" processes. In addition, it was found that the number of rejections, i.e., no meaningful associations with the pictures, *increased* progressively with the length of deprivation. The authors' summary realistically formulates these results:

"The growing need produces the autistic process, but at the same time makes it more imperative to find some means to satisfy the need, i.e., it stimulates the reality process. Even the less ambiguous figures (those which are more easily and consistently seen as food) do not *satisfy* the need. ... We should expect that as he becomes hungrier, he may ultimately stop looking at pictures altogether, particularly where all he has to do is to leave the experiment" (p. 292).

In a further study, Schafer and Murphy [5] investigated "the role of autism in the determination of the figure-ground relationship." For this purpose, reversible contour lines were designed which could be seen as one or the other of two profiles (Fig. 8). For the training series of the experiment, these profiles were separated so that there were four profiles, each bounded by a semicircle (Fig. 9). These profiles were presented in random order. The subjects were given a nonsense syllable for each pro-

[5] R. Schafer and G. Murphy, The role of autism in a visual figure-ground relationship, *J. Exper. Psychol.*, 1943, 32, 335–343.

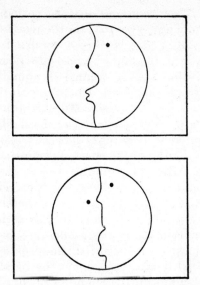

FIG. 8. The two stimuli presented in the post-training series. (From R. Schafer and G. Murphy, in *J. Psychol.*, 1943, 32, p. 337.)

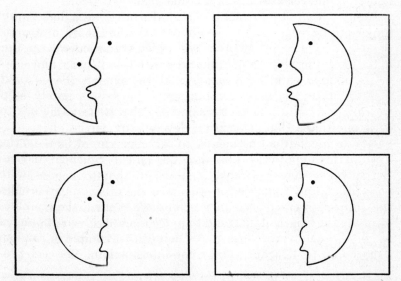

FIG. 9. The four stimuli presented in the training series. (From *ibid.*, p. 336.)

file which they were required to learn to associate with the appropriate face. They were told that when they saw either of two of the four faces they would be rewarded, but when they saw the other two they would be punished. The two faces for which the reward was given were determined by the experimenters and always included *one* profile from each of the drawings in Fig. 8. Since in such a study it would be extremely difficult to reward some biogenic need directly, the experimenters chose money as a reward because it "has been ingrained by conditioning as a means of fulfilling a wide variety of needs" (p. 335). After this training period, the subjects were shown the contour lines when placed together as in Fig. 8. No rewards were given, the subjects being asked merely to write down the names of the profile they saw. In this series the subjects tended to perceive in the contour lines the profile for which they had previously been rewarded; the profile for which they had been punished tended to become the background for the other profile. A "significantly high number" of perceptions after training occurred in connection with the profiles which carried a reward. Hence, "autism can function in the determination of the figure-ground relationship in a visual field" (p. 343).

Another study by Proshansky and Murphy [6] has a direct and important bearing on the role of motivation in the learning and organization of cognitive processes, which we considered briefly in the preceding chapter in connection with the effects of biogenic needs upon a child's psychology. At the outset, the experimenters state: "It is the hypothesis of the present paper that we *learn to perceive* in much the same way that we *learn to act*. . . . It is our thesis that perception develops by virtue of its capacity to mediate adjustments, to serve needs . . ." (p. 295). To test this hypothesis, they designed an experiment in which the subjects were rewarded (again with money) for certain perceptions and punished for others. In the pretraining period, the subjects were placed in a semi-dark room and asked to estimate the length of lines and to judge the heaviness of various weights. Some of the lines were "long" (5 to 7 inches), some "short" (2 to 4 inches), and some intermediate. The weights

---

[6] H. Proshansky and G. Murphy, The effects of reward and punishment on perception, *J. Psychol.*, 1942, 13, 295–305.

varied similarly. During the training period, the subjects again made their judgments, being rewarded with fifteen cents for each long line and each heavy weight. For the short lines and light weights, they had to forfeit fifteen cents. Rewards and punishments were given for the intermediate lines and weights on a "planned haphazard" schedule. In the final testing period, the subjects judged the intermediate lines and weights (without reward or punishment). These judgments were then compared to the initial judgments of the intermediate lines in the pretraining period. Whereas the judgments of control subjects, who were not rewarded and punished, showed no change, the judgments of the subjects who were rewarded *increased significantly in the direction of greater length and weight*. Thus, the reward resulted in selectiveness of perception *in the direction of the reward*.

A neat substantiation of this study was given by Haggard and Rose,[7] who showed the effects of reward upon perception, using the autokinetic phenomenon (see pages 162–163). The subjects were instructed to judge the direction and distance in which a light moved (actually it did not move at all). They were told that only part of the trials would count. In half of the trials in which a subject responded that the light moved to the left, he was rewarded with five cents. Even with the relatively few rewards, a majority of the subjects saw movement more often to the left than to the right. The average distance which the light seemed to move to the left was longer than the average distance to the right. And all the subjects were more confident of their judgments of movement to the left than to the right.

Another particularly clear-cut experiment showing how motivational factors enter into the organization and functioning of perceptual processes was recently carried out by Bruner and Goodman.[8] These authors also urge the necessity of conceiving of perception and other cognitive processes as functions in which both external and internal (e.g., motives) factors enter in a functionally interrelated way. Criticizing those who would put perception in a separate cognitive department of psychol-

[7] E. A. Haggard and G. J. Rose, Some effects of mental set and active participation in the conditioning of the autokinetic phenomenon, *J. Exper. Psychol.*, 1944, 34, 45–59.

[8] J. S. Bruner and C. C. Goodman, Value and need as organizing factors in perception, *J. Abn. & Soc. Psychol.*, 1947, 42, 33–44.

ogy, they emphasize the necessity for studying "the variations perception itself undergoes when one is hungry, in love, in pain, or solving a problem" (p. 33). For this purpose, they designed

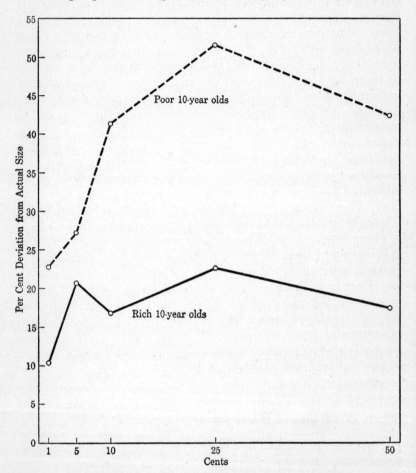

FIG. 10. Size estimation of coins made by well-to-do and poor ten-year-olds. (From J. S. Bruner and C. C. Goodman, in *J. Abn. & Soc. Psychol.*, 1947, 42, p. 40.)

an experiment to test "the tendency for sought-after perceptual objects to become more vivid" (p. 37). The subjects were 10-year-old school children. One group came from a school attended by the children of prosperous business and professional people, and another came from a settlement house in the Boston slums. There was also a control group. The children were asked to estimate the sizes of coins from a penny up to a half dollar by turning a knob that regulated the size of a patch of light on a screen. The control subjects estimated the size of gray cardboard disks which were the same size as the coins. The findings show that the coins (which, as has been suggested, have come to stand for the satisfaction of many needs) were consistently judged by these subjects as larger than were gray disks of the same size. Of particular interest here is the comparison of the judgments of the rich and poor children. In the authors' words, "poor children have a greater subjective need for money than rich ones" (p. 39). These results, which are shown in Fig. 10, clearly indicate that poor children, with the greater need, over-estimated the size of coins considerably more than rich children. This overestimation by the poor children tended to be relatively greater as the value of the coins increased.

These few experiments on the effects of a relatively brief deprivation of biogenic needs at the human level are valuable as leads in handling the observation of deprivation in everyday life. They have the advantage of the control of variables that is possible in the experimental situation, but at the same time they are restricted because of the impracticability of prolonged experimental deprivation in most instances. In the next section we shall consider human behavior under prolonged deprivation, in the light of tested findings from animal and human experiments.

Effects of Prolonged Deprivation

The consequences of prolonged deprivation due to famine, economic depression, foreign occupation, or chaotic socioeconomic situations are well known. The psychology of prolonged deprivation will be the concern of Chapter 16.

But no systematic step-by-step treatment of such deprivation is available as yet. For this reason, the one experimental study of prolonged semi-starvation carried out at the University of Minnesota by Keys, Brozek, Henschel, Mickelsen, and Taylor on conscientious objectors during World War II constitutes a milestone in the scientifically controlled investigation of prolonged deprivation.[9] This admirably controlled study of prolonged deprivation will certainly for decades constitute a mine of facts, with an abundance of direct implications for any formulation of motivation, value-drive relationship, and personality in social psychology, as well as for physiology and practical dietary schedules.

The subjects, all of whom were volunteers from Civilian Public Service, came from different states in the Union. Originally there were 36 subjects, but for several reasons two were dropped before the final stage of the study, and two others were eliminated from the statistical analysis. They were thoroughly informed about the aim, procedures, rigors, and dangers involved in the prolonged experiment. Their ages ranged from 20 to 33 years, and their initial weights from 135 to 187.7 pounds. They were all normal men in good physical health. In intelligence they were "considerably above average" (p. 11).

After a three-month period of standardization (in physical and psychological respects), they were *systematically subjected to semi-starvation for six months*. Then they were rehabilitated. (Unfortunately we cannot devote any space here to the equally interesting results of the period of rehabilitation). At the end of the six months of semi-starvation, they had lost about 25 per cent of their normal weight. (See Fig. 11). Before we give the major findings relevant to our purposes, it is necessary to call attention to two facts which are useful in interpreting the results. This will help us to be a little cautious in applying the conclusions drawn from this experiment to cases of deprivation under actual chaos, insecurity, danger, oppression, and starvation. As Guetzkow and Bowman, who collaborated in the experiment, point out in their more psychological account of the investigation,[10] the subjects "had complete security, in that they were under constant medical supervision and knew they would be taken out of the experiment if anything serious went

[9] A. Keys, J. Brozek, A. Henschel, O. Mickelsen, and H. L. Taylor, *Experimental Starvation in Man*, Laboratory of Physiological Hygiene, University of Minnesota, October 15, 1945.

[10] H. S. Guetzkow and P. H. Bowman, *Men and Hunger, a Psychological Manual for Relief Workers*, Elgin, Ill.: Brethren Publishing House, 1946.

wrong." They were not exposed to persecution or enemy attack.
"They had the safety and security of the average American
civilian in the continental United States" (p. 15). The subjects
were motivated rather highly by the belief that they were serving humanity by the conclusions that might be drawn from the
experiment, which was conducted while the war against fascism

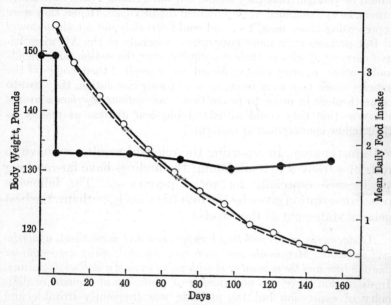

FIG. 11. Average Loss of Weight During 6 Months of Semi-Starvation.

Average Weights, 34 men. Predicted (broken line) and actual (solid line)
body weights are shown as bi-weekly means for the entire group of 34 men.
The actual food intakes, as calories, are also shown. Food intake in thousands
of calories. (From *Experimental Starvation in Man*, by Keys, Brozek,
Henschel, Mickelsen, and Taylor. Used by courtesy of Dr. A. Keys, Director
of the Laboratory of Physiological Hygiene, University of Minnesota.)

was being waged by their country. This motive is revealed by
the fact that some of them showed concern over whether they
would be able to undergo the rigors of deprivation and that
fairly strong feelings of remorse were shown by those who broke
down under the voluntary starvation. In the words of one of the
experimenters:

The 36 conscientious objectors finally selected for the starvation experiment felt themselves privileged, for they alone of the approximately 170 original applicants had survived the screening given by the Laboratory.

They felt a sense of responsibility to the men who were deprived of this opportunity. If they did not come through with flying colors, it would be thought that they should not have come. There were many others, as well qualified as they, denied the privilege. Hence, they were representing these men, too, and could certainly not let them down.

But perhaps even more important, especially as the AP wires began carrying stories of their experiment over the nation, and friends and brothers in army camps abroad began sending them copies of the articles which now were receiving world-wide circulation, they had to come through in order to prove that *conscientious objectors were not slackers*—that they could withstand physical distress as readily as their fellow countrymen in uniform.[11]

Unfortunately, in reporting the relevant results, we have to restrict ourselves to a minimum; the findings have far-reaching significance especially for social psychology. The following broad description given by the investigators is, perhaps, the best general statement of the effects:

As starvation progressed they became more and more silent, apathetic and immobile. Movements were slow and restricted; stairs were mounted one at a time and the men sat or stood leaning against a wall while waiting. In discussion there was no evidence of confusion of thought or difficulty of expression but the attitude was frequently irritable and morose. Trivial incidents were productive of exaggerated annoyance and complaint. *Favorite topics of conversation were food, farming and rural life, a fact which was bitterly resented by some of the men.*

All of the men continually complained of feeling cold, and even in the warm weather of July most of them wore heavy clothes. The conclusion was clear that any lack of heat in the building would have produced bitter suffering. *Another frequent complaint was the sensation of being "old."*

A number of men were bothered by vivid dreams, particularly dreams of breaking the diet, with attendant great remorse.[12]

The deprivation did not affect all the subjects identically, of course. There were individual differences in the effects pro-

---

[11] Personal communication from Harold Guetzkow of the University of Michigan.
[12] Keys, Brozek, *et al.*, *op. cit.*, pp. 25, 26 (all italics mine).

duced. *These differences, which are important in the formulation of the psychology of personality, should be utilized with full weight given to the more general fact that the broad trend of the effects took the same direction.* "The normal range of differences between individuals was greatly widened during semi-starvation. Without exception, however, each man experienced some of the behavior patterns and reactions which are described."[13] One of the most revealing facts regarding the differential thresholds of the learned value system of the individual under conditions of stress was shown by the following:

A few of the men were unable to remain voluntarily on the restricted diet throughout its entirety. Some of the violations were of a minor nature and did not jeopardize the experimental conclusions; in those few cases where major deviations occurred the subject was excluded from the experiment, or the data obtained were discarded. This deterioration of their ethical control was all the more remarkable because these men had shown themselves to be sincere and upright throughout the two or more years of work they had performed in civilian public service units before coming to the laboratory. . . . The semi-starvation pressure of hunger was, however, too much—their very beings revolted against the restriction. One of the individuals not only bought food, but also stole some from "locked" storerooms. Another individual sublimated his food cravings by stealing china cups from coffee shops. Although fasting is said at times to quicken one spiritually, none of the men reported significant progress in their religious lives. Most of them felt that the semi-starvation had coarsened rather than refined them, and they marveled at how thin their moral and social veneers seemed to be (pp. 31–32).

Under ordinary conditions of civilized life, biogenic motives become dominant (over most motives) with the recurrence of the need cycle as regulated by the social milieu, within certain limits of variation. Now the individual attends to hunger, now to thirst, and now to sleep or sex. These needs having been satisfied, at least to a minimum degree, he strives for other higher and more refined ends—status, better position, science, art, etc. "In starvation this pleasant balancing process is upset, and the hunger drive gradually dominates more and more of the person's activities and thoughts. Concomitant with this is a

[13] H. S. Guetzkow and P. H. Bowman, *op. cit.*, p. 22.

lessening of other drives, such as diminution of sexual urges" (p. 23). Developing this point, Guetzkow and Bowman state:

Contrariwise, their sexual urge gradually decreased, and it was the rare individual who continued courtship at the end of the starvation. Budding romances collapsed, and some men wondered how they could have been so interested in *that* girl. One fellow's girl friend visited him from a distant city during the low days of starvation, and she found his ostensible affection disappointingly shallow. His reservoir of affectional responses was drying up. . . . Dancing was not fun—he would rather go to a movie. The men seldom fatigued in a healthy way; they felt old, stuporous (p. 24).

Fig. 12. A starving man's thoughts and fantasies center on food. (From H. S. Guetzkow and P. H. Bowman, *Men and Hunger*, Brethren Publishing House, 1946.)

Even though intellectual capacities were not impaired, it seems, the psychological world of these subjects became more and more focused on food. Again in the interesting words of the authors of *Men and Hunger:*

The intensive preoccupation with food made it difficult for the men to concentrate upon the tasks they had intellectually decided they would work on. If a man tried to study, he soon found himself day-dreaming about food. He would think about foods he had eaten in the past; he would muse about opportunities he had missed to eat a certain food when he was at this or that place. Often he would daydream

by the hour about the next meal, which was not very far away:
"Today we'll have menu No. 1. Gee, that's the smallest menu, it
seems. How shall I fix the potatoes? If I use my spoon to eat them
I'll be able to add more water. Should I make different varieties of
beverages tonight? Haven't had my toast yet today. Maybe I should
save some for a midnight snack with my buddy. What kind of a
sandwich could I make? Maybe I'd better write these ideas down, so
I don't forget them. If I eat a little faster the food would stay warm
longer—and I like it warm. But then it's gone so quickly . . .
(pp. 32, 41).

Food and topics connected with food acquired almost a sacred
halo. Some of these grown-up men did not mind licking their
plates in the presence of others to avoid waste, to the disgust of
certain others who deliberately tried to drop the everlasting
discussion of food topics.

As to emotional effects: "The most important emotional
change coincides with this motivational apathy; namely, that
there was a dulling of the emotional response of the individual
with concomitant depression. Humor was gone. The men did
not sing or whistle of their own accord. Music did not bring its
former warmth. The dejection was exhibited in the lack of conversation at mealtimes. The men had not talked themselves out,
but lacked the spark that fires curiosity" (p. 26). Yet they
tended to be more irritable on ordinarily insignificant provocation. "Petty defects became very important and were the source
of much irritation. Standing in line at the diet kitchen before
being served was the source of explosive conduct. Indecisiveness
on the part of the servers would give rise to ire, and to suspicion
that perhaps the cooks did not know what their ration should
really be. The men 'blew up' at each other on occasion. Manner-
isms which formerly went unnoticed now became sources of
friction" (p. 27).

And for the topic most central for social psychology:

One of the more profound changes which took place was the decreased *sociability* of the men. There were important exceptions to
this, but even the men who managed to continue their social contacts
often felt animosity toward strangers, merely because they were
strangers. *The men built up a tremendous in-group feeling that tended
to exclude both their non-starving friends and the administrative and*

technical staff. They were apart from others—those who had been well fed. They were especially alienated by the individual who supposed he knew what it was like to be hungry because he had gone without food for a couple of days. It was hard to sit near one's comrade who had extra food. They became provoked at the laboratory staff for giving "too much" food to some, and thought it criminal to restrict the rations of others, even though they clearly understood the experimental plan demanded such adjustments in rations (p. 30; italics mine). . . . Often they realized they were not gentlemen in the gallant way they formerly had been, and they did not care. What difference did it make if they were unshaven and sloppily dressed? They would prefer to go to the movies alone, while formerly a "show" was not real entertainment unless a companion could share the fun. Humor often eases the tensions which arise in normal social situations, but these starving men lacked humor—they could not pull quips; they could not make light of things (p. 31).

Some of the items which the men jotted down in their diaries at different stages of semi-starvation further reflect the foregoing results. We quote only a few:

The time between meals has now become a burden. This time is no longer thought of as an opportunity to get those things done which I have to do or want to do. Instead, it's time to be borne, killed until the next meal, which never comes fast enough (p. 19).

It wasn't what the boys did with their food that I didn't like but it was their method. They would coddle it like a baby or handle it and look over it as they would some gold. They played with it like kids making mud pies (p. 20).

This week of starvation found me completely tired practically every day. If they want to get any more work out of me, they're going to have to feed me (p. 20).

Stayed up until 5:00 A.M. last night studying cookbooks. So absorbing I can't stay away from them (p. 21).

Evidence from Siriono Culture. The foregoing experimental results concerning the effects of prolonged semi-starvation, with all their psychological and cultural consequences, are amply observed in actual life situations of hunger, as we shall see in the next section. Ethnological field work in societies in which securing food is a constant concern for all members will demonstrate in a striking way the crucial determination of major individual and social values and practices by hunger frustration. Recently Holmberg undertook a comprehensive field study with this consideration in mind.[14] Many investigators have recognized the effects of biogenic needs in determining the characteristics and values of social groupings and the personality of their individual members. But no one had, as yet, dealt in a comprehensive way "with a society in which the drive of hunger is so constantly frustrated as to have become the dominant motivating force in shaping habit and custom. Siriono society seems clearly to be such a society" (p. 274).

The food supply of the Siriono, though sufficient for survival, is persistently inadequate. The tropical climate is highly unfavorable for food preservation or storage. The Siriono must make arduous hunts for food almost daily, about a fourth of which are unsuccessful. They have only the most primitive weapons and few agricultural tools or skills. Domestication of animals is unknown. In short, the Siriono's waking hours are necessarily occupied with the exhausting and dangerous job of hunting and collecting enough food to subsist.

The psychological effects of this deprivation are far reaching. Here we can hardly do more than list some outstanding examples. Food and food-getting are the topics of the Siriono's major anxieties. When food is obtained, it is eaten without ritual, often furtively or at night so that it need not be shared. Quarrels over food constitute the greatest single source of conflict in the group. Almost no food preferences are shown, a hawk being devoured as voraciously as a partridge. *Food and successful hunting almost dominate the dreams and fantasy of the Siriono;* "sex dreams and fantasies are rarely encountered" (p. 288). The only stealing observed was the taking of food on those infrequent occasions when some was left unguarded. Food is used as a lure for obtaining a partner in sexual activities; when it is scarce, there is little sexual activity. Sexual orgies follow a successful hunt.

The adult Siriono is characterized generally as aggressive, individualistic, and uncooperative. There is no evidence which indicates that such characteristics develop on the basis of

[14] A. R. Holmberg, The Siriono. A study of the effect of hunger frustration on the culture of a semi-nomadic Bolivian Indian society. Doctorate dissertation on file in the library, Yale University, July, 1946.

experiences in infancy or early childhood. The Siriono child is considerably indulged and frustrated little. He has an ample food supply until he is weaned at about three years. Only as he grows older and younger children come into the picture does he share adult hardships. "By the time a youth reaches the age of twelve he is already manifesting most of the signs of adult behavior toward food. In general, he is aggressive in all matters that pertain to food" (p. 283).

The scarcity of food and the almost constant pangs of hunger are reflected in the social values and practices of Siriono culture. *Status* and *prestige* are based chiefly on hunting prowess and food-getting ability. The chief is always a good hunter. The best hunter or food collector is the most desirable mate. The sick and the *aged*, not being able to obtain food, are liabilities and are treated as such. "Consequently, people who are extremely ill or decrepit and whose period of usefulness is over, are abandoned to die" (p. 286).

Since a man can seldom collect more food than is necessary for his family, the family is the functioning economic and social unit, the usefulness of the Siriono band being limited chiefly to serving as a source of sex and marital partners. Since the Siriono often move in their search for hunting grounds, individual ownership of a garden plot, tree, etc., is recognized only when such articles are used. Finally, the almost constant preoccupation with food and the rigors of obtaining it has resulted in a sparse development of art forms, folk tales, or mythology. The magic extant relates chiefly to food. The Siriono's concern merely to survive leaves no time for intellectual activity or for speculations on deities or an afterworld.

The Effects of Deprivation in Social Life

Facts from everyday life concerning the effects of prolonged deprivation of biogenic needs as observed by reporters and persons experiencing these effects high-light in a crucial way the tendencies indicated in experimental situations. For, after all, the generality of any finding, the validity of any theory in social psychology must finally be tested on the basis of its adequacy for handling events of everyday life, when human beings carry on the business of living. We shall consider first relatively simple instances of the effects of deprivation, and then go on to see how, when deprivation is sufficiently prolonged and intense, it may result in almost completely transforming an individual's usual ways of experiencing and behaving.

Ernie Pyle, who shared the lot of American G. I.'s in combat in the North African campaign, reported an incident in which, because of the lack of variety in the battle rations, the appearance of a hog took on all the halo which these G. I.'s might have associated with the sight of a beautiful girl in their ordinary conditions of life. In Pyle's words:

One day I was at a command post in a farmyard in a prosperous irrigated valley. The grounds were full of officers and soldiers who had just arrived. All of a sudden across the barnlot there came plodding a huge white hog.

It was touching and funny to see the wave of desire that swept over the soldiers. Everybody looked longingly at that hog. Everybody had some crack to make. . . .

A year before none of us would have looked twice at a hog. *But then the mere grunting passage of a swine across a barnlot brought a flood of covetous comment.*[15]

G. I.'s who were fascist prisoners for any length of time knew even better the pangs of hunger. One ex-soldier, reporting his experiences as a German prisoner, emphasized with the following anecdote the intensity with which preoccupation with food dominated the lives of the prisoners:

When we were prisoners in Stalag Luft III in East Prussia, the food situation got bad during the winter of 1944. Red Cross packages were keeping us alive, but they weren't getting through regularly, and the Nazis were content to let us starve on a daily bowl of watery soup and a bit of bread.

Food became our principal topic of conversation; we planned menus, compared favorite dishes and reminisced on the last square meal we'd had, months, even years, before. Finally our senior officers and chaplains decided that this constant thinking about food was undermining morale, and a directive went around the compound that edibles were not to be talked about any more.

[15] Ernie Pyle, *Here Is Your War*, New York: The World Publishing Company, 1945; Henry Holt, 1943; pp. 113–114 (italics mine).

One day when several of us were sitting around shooting the breeze, a sergeant muttered, "Boy, I wish I had a nice thick steak."

A major, who was passing, turned around and warned him, "Hold it, sergeant! No more talk about food, you know."

The sergeant looked glumly at the ground, and somebody quickly changed the subject, "Well . . . I wonder what the new-model cars are going to be like?"

So we talked about cars, about new designs, probable speed, mileage, cost, and how soon we could get delivery after the war.

After a long time the sergeant looked up at us. "I wish I had one of those new cars right now," he said, "smothered in mashed potatoes and gravy." [16]

Similar preoccupation with and actual dreams about food were reported [17] by the men in Peary's expedition to the North Pole who were forced to live on the simplest diet, and by a group of fliers wrecked in the antarctic in the recent expedition to the south polar regions.[18]

As a result of the accumulation of a body of psychoanalytic literature, instances of intense preoccupation with goal objects and situations in the case of sexual deprivation are well known. As we have already observed, these preoccupations, distortions, and various frustration mechanisms come into play, in various degrees, whenever an individual is deprived of the satisfaction of any basic need (drive, instinct) for a significant period of time. In recent years, the clinical and experimental use of the Rorschach (ink-blot) test has resulted in many examples of the perceptual distortions that occur when individuals suffer such deprivation. The results of this test may be taken as exemplifying the effects of various internal factors (e.g., motives, attitudes) upon the perception of an unstructured or ambiguous stimulus situation (ink blots in this case). For example, in his report on Rorschach results with representative clinical cases, Beck includes the case of a 37-year-old man who, among other things, "showed no interest in girls." In eight of the ten ink-blot pictures in the test, this man reported seeing the pelvis

---

[16] E. R. Ivy, The Sergeant Changed the Subject, *Saturday Evening Post*, February 15, 1947, p. 62.

[17] Reported in P. T. Young, *Motivation of Behavior*, New York: Wiley, 1936.

[18] O. McCarty, "Dead" Men's Diary, *Saturday Evening Post*, May 17, 1947, pp. 15 ff.

region. Of another figure, "After overt panicky behavior, in which he speaks only with greatest difficulty, he expresses apprehensions more and more and finally . . . [he says that it] 'arouses sexual fears because it is like the feet of a woman.'" Here is an example of perceptions dominated by the effects of sexual deprivation. "The focus of these strong feelings is obviously the sex hunger." [19]

In many European countries today, the picture is so grim that those involved cannot make light of even the results of their deprivation. A recent poll of German working girls revealed that they were haunted by dreams and nightmares of hunger.[20] When asked, "Do you really want to be loved by someone?" these girls replied with such answers as "I have no time," "I'm too busy with my job and my hunger," "Today is no time for love." Under the grim pangs of hunger, the relative importance of other motives, such as sex, tends to fade.

In the stringently rationed prisoner-of-war camps of World War II, the men experienced and observed many instances of the *selectivity* of various functions (perception, discrimination, memory, etc.), as well as the breakdown of the acquired attitudes which, in large part, represent the sociogenic motives. In describing his years of captivity under the Japanese, General Jonathan Wainwright recorded facts which give us, among other things, further insight into the psychology of motivation.[21] In the prison camps at Tarlac and Karenko, a group of high Allied officers underwent prolonged starvation. The men began to be "haunted by hunger" and food "became a mania" with them. They "woke up each morning with hunger paramount in [their] minds" and "went to sleep to dream of food" (p. 200). Under such intense and prolonged deprivation, the range of stimuli which served as goal objects widened far beyond the usual range as modified by cultural influences. After a long period in which they had no animal protein, the officers greedily ate animal stomachs, intestines, and lungs. They searched the ground for "large tough" snails which, although dreadful to

---

[19] S. J. Beck, *Rorschach's Test. Vol. II, A Variety of Personality Pictures*, New York, Grune and Stratton, 1946, pp. 239, 241.

[20] Reported in *Newsweek*, January 20, 1947, p. 37.

[21] General J. M. Wainwright, *General Wainwright's Story*, R. Considine (ed.), New York: Garden City Publishing Co., 1946; Doubleday, 1945.

the taste, were "wolfed" down by those lucky enough to find them. And, looking for "the tiniest nutrition," they ate worms and black weevils along with their meager rice portions (p. 201).

In these desperate circumstances, "We took to counting the two or three beans which sometimes appeared in the bottom of our soup pail, and *if a man received a bean in his soup, and another did not, it made for hard feeling.* This must be hard to imagine, but it is true" (p. 187; italics mine). So the officers asked one man to divide the food as impartially as possible; but he quit the job shortly because they all insisted on standing over him to watch. "*Major General Moore . . . accepted, but with the reservation that he could attend to the splitting of the rice and the soup behind a closed door. . .* " (p. 188). Here we see the intense factor of hunger coming into conflict with the structural properties of the group (see Chapters 5 and 6).

With such a diet, the officers' elimination systems became upset. Frequently in the night they plodded to the latrine, even though they knew that this was the guard's favorite spot for beating them (p. 200).

When the Japanese kept Red Cross parcels from these men, "the frustration was more numbing than any beating we had ever taken" (p. 206). On one occasion the guards gave them a starved cow which broke away as it was being unloaded. Frantically the prisoners chased after it as it ran out of the prison camp, and brought it back; "and in their gnawing hunger some of the men did not even know they had been out of bounds" (p. 163). Here, hunger loomed to obliterate even the much-longed-for freedom.

The fortitude with which these men stood on their dignity as Allied officers in captivity, in accordance with the Geneva Convention, and refused to work for the Japanese soon broke down when they were promised a small extra portion of "work rice" (p. 190).

In areas of starvation and misery in the world today, many cases of actual psychological preoccupation and ultimate disintegration have been observed. It is authentically reported that during the fascist occupation of Greece 14- or 15-year-old Greek girls yielded themselves to the hated enemy soldiers merely to secure a little bread for themselves and their families.

In Italy and elsewhere, mothers and sisters went to the extent of sending little boys or girls to solicit the sexually deprived men who had food, as one means of just obtaining some food.

In a recent account of conditions in post-war Vienna, a physician in charge of children's clinics has produced equally grim evidence concerning the breakdown or disintegration of the socially acquired values and norms under prolonged hunger:

The hunger . . . is worse than the cold. You can do something about the cold. You can find something else to put over the shoulders or wrap around the feet. Or, you can go to bed and stay there. You can wait the cold out, for there is a beginning and an end to cold, but there is no end to hunger.

And being hungry *you do things you thought you never would do.* You send your children out to trade on the black market. It would go hard on you if you got caught, but with the children, if they get "picked up," the authorities will be more lenient.

You learn, too, not to ask your children too many questions when they bring food home. You don't ask anybody questions about where food comes from. You eat it, and while you are doing so *you hope no one will come in with whom it ought to be shared.* Adversity does not bring out the best in people, not when it is a question of who shall live and who shall starve (p. 1). . . . When you're hungry you'll eat anything—and people do. *They eat what is there to be eaten, though ordinarily it would turn their stomachs.* And they drink what's to be drunk; they do not have pasteurized milk and they do not have refrigerators nor do they always have the means to boil water.

Death takes whole families—sometimes there is no one left to notify. Death also leaves many orphans. The younger ones are cared for in institutions. The older ones look after themselves, and "juvenile delinquency" in their case is a way of saying boys and girls are hungry. They take as they can; they oppose with violence the peasant or anyone else who tries to stop them. The girls have their own ways of getting along. *Young as they are they come to terms early, as hungry people everywhere come to terms.* Even their own mothers must sometimes come to terms.

Of course, one is ashamed when the authorities come because one's children are running the streets at night, and one cannot tell the authorities about the soldier who comes to call while the children are out. But the soldier brings food and what is better? That one's children go hungry? The neighbors know; the authorities know; and someday one's own husband, now a prisoner of war, will have to know. Who is to say who is a good mother and who is not, in times like these? (p. 2) [22]

As a foreign observer in the hunger-ridden Volga region in 1921, Anna Louise Strong saw hundreds of cases of such breakdowns under the grip of starvation.[23] Once, as she was riding in a train that was taking food to the stricken population, she heard a baby crying. "Its mother had laid it on our car-steps at one of our halts, crying: 'Take it. Otherwise I must leave it in the market-place. I have no food; without the baby I may fight my way to regions of bread'" (p. 105).

And as she herself lay in a hospital convalescing from an illness, "I saw in the next room a young woman doctor, who was convalescing from typhus, go crazy at the news her mother brought. They had sold household treasures and bought one hundred pounds of flour and ten of sugar; but robbers had broken into the house and stolen the flour. The doctor went into hysteria; she rose and rushed out to seek the flour, though she had as yet no strength for walking. This was the meaning of bread even to doctors on government rations" (p. 121).

We shall reserve for a later chapter (Chapter 16) any consideration of the effects of prolonged deprivation on a mass basis and its profound consequences on the whole structure of social organization. Unfortunately, these grim facts have not succeeded as yet in making their way to the rank of major problems for social psychologists, even though politicians seem to have learned their implications more realistically. Herein lies a fertile field for social psychologists, as their recent serious concern indicates. Aside from its realistic consequences, the facts concerning prolonged mass deprivation can give us a more adequate social psychology of motivation.

[22] A. Wawerka, What It Is Like to Starve. A Doctor Tells the Story, *Our Nation's Children*, May, 1947, Federal Security Agency, Social Security Administration, U. S. Children's Bureau, Washington, D. C. (italics mine).
[23] A. L. Strong, *I Change Worlds*, Garden City Publishing Co., New York, 1937.

PART TWO

Groups and Norms (Values)

Introduction

A FEW PARAGRAPHS WILL SERVE AS A GENERAL ORIENTATION
to the psychology of groups and norms which will be the concern of Part II of this book. Nowhere in the world today do we
see man securing a means of livelihood by himself. Pursuit of
the satisfaction of even basic needs is carried on in groups,
small or large. Nowhere do single individuals secure the necessities of life to the point of any degree of self-sufficiency. Even
in the most primitive social organizations, the individual is
dependent on others to some degree, and others are dependent
on him to a lesser degree. If a state of nature ever existed in
time immemorial, in which every person was self-sufficient in
an appreciable degree and was a law unto himself, we are not
in a position now to ascertain it. Like the great majority of
other animals, man is dependent on a member of the opposite
sex for mating. To a far greater extent than any other animal,
even subhuman primates, he is utterly helpless at birth, and
his helplessness is far more prolonged. The mother has to take
care of him longer than does the mother of any other animal.
Equipped with the potentiality of grasping reciprocal relationships and of retaining these relationships longer, because of the
relatively much greater size of his frontal lobes, he cannot help
building up more or less lasting psychological effects (attachments) in the course of tending to or being tended, and the
mutual sharing of sex and other activities.

In carrying on the activities necessary for making a living,
which take place on the basis of give-and-take and, hence, interacting relationships, tools of production and symbols of communication are standardized and accumulated; and some
routine of work and rest is established peculiar to the locality and
social unit. In the process of group interaction in pursuing the

necessities that satisfy vital needs, there emerge more or less lasting relative roles for the individual members, standards of action, rules regulating reciprocal relationships, values, or norms in matters which become of growing concern for the group. In short, in interacting to secure value objects and situations (like food and shelter), new values emerge. These new values, when standardized, come to regulate the very needs whose promptings were originally responsible for the actions which resulted in the emergence of these rules, values, or norms. With new developments and differentiations in the organization of the interacting group, new values arise which may not have anything to do directly with the satisfaction of vital needs. The accumulating and standardizing routines of action, tools, and techniques, the symbols of communication, and these new values, in turn, come to regulate the individual's behavior and to set standards of work and attainment, and also new aspirations and goals to follow.

In short, during the course of the efforts of men and women who are interacting in group units (small or large) in the most urgent pursuit of perpetuating their life, a whole *superstructure* of routine, of hierarchical and horizontal roles and statuses, of values or norms, arises and becomes more or less standardized. Hence, there exists a host of folkways, mores, rules and regulations, and social values. Once such a superstructure of standards, rules, and values (we shall refer to it collectively as *norms*) is established, it comes (through social pressure or through attitudes of conforming behavior) to regulate activities directed toward the satisfaction of vital needs. But this is not all. The superstructure comes to shape the individual's tastes to an important degree, his major tastes—concerning objects and situations with which he is in contact in his daily life, *ego-involved aspirations* to be attained in the way of *belongingness, status,* and a higher status; it provides him with values which result in the formation of more or less lasting *attitudes* concerning his own group (*identifications,* loyalties, responsibilities) as well as positive and negative attitudes in relation to other groups (*prejudice*). The *values of the superstructure, which appear first on the stimulus side in relation to a newborn infant, constitute the sources of his sociogenic motives* which he picks up during his development. His "picking up" of such values, which results in his more or less lasting attitudes, constitutes the central trend of his *socialization*. Of course the "picking up" of such values is not a mechanical, haphazard process; it is carried on through contact, by selective perceiving and learning ("fixation," "canalization," etc.). Its psychology is the central theme of the process of socialization. And precisely this, with its subsequent effects on individual behavior and experience, is the main concern of the chapters that follow.

To be sure, perhaps no one individual, no matter how important, how intelligent, how broad his interests may be, represents all the values and conformities characteristic of his general culture, especially in the highly differentiated and developed societies of the present time. An individual's range of socialization is limited by the range of his receptivity (his perceptual range) as determined by his actual contact with persons, objects, and situations. As we shall see later, starting with the family group or nursery group, his major values or attitudes are derived chiefly from his actual *membership groups* (play group, adolescent clique or gang, school, church, factory, union, club, etc.) or his *reference groups* (groups to which psychologically he refers himself or aspires to refer himself—e.g., school, college, social class, club to which he relates or aspires to relate himself).

Psychologically, *membership groups* or *reference groups* express more realistically the social settings which can be concretely handled as actual stimulus situations. Therefore we can dispense with such vague terms as "subculture" that are used by some ethnologists who are concerned with the process of socialization and with the personality of the individual members of a culture and who psychologize on that basis.

Consequently, with the differentiation of interdependent social units on the basis of organization and function in society, there will be differentiated sets of values in each unit. For example, capitalist values and aspirations (hence mentality and morality) differ from working-class values and aspirations. So with differentiated values, expectations, and impositions standardized according to sex, and to age (child, youth, adult); the resulting attitudes and sociogenic motives in each case will differ to fit the prevailing social image. No matter what the specific superstructure of norms may be and no matter how much it may vary from culture to culture, the same social psychological principles should be valid—if these principles have any claims to scientific generality.

Until recently, social psychologies were written and experiments were carried out in the image of the prevailing norms of the culture or of the prevailing academic trend of the times which lacked perspective and principles that could be applied to other cultures. Under the impact of the comparative data of sociology (ethnology included), the swing during the past two decades has been in the opposite direction. As a consequence, it has been almost assumed that, because of the unique properties of certain cultures, the psychology of each culture can be accounted for in terms of principles unique to itself. Of course such a view is utterly untenable and is disappearing.

Further difficulty in studying the social psychology of groups and norms arises from the fact that there are not even relatively static cultures in the world today. Almost all cultures are undergoing transition at a greater or lesser tempo as the result of technological developments, World War II, and the impact of the new social order of the Soviet Union on one-sixth of the world. It is no coincidence that problems of culture change, "acculturation," have come to the foreground in the social sciences. Scientifically valid social psychological principles should be valid in the case of individuals in rapidly changing societies as well as in the relatively static ones on which ethnologists have spent a disproportionately long time collecting data.

All kinds of social stimuli—including the mother and other grown-ups, the superstructure of norms of the individual's society, etc.—are first on the stimulus side in relation to this or that particular child. In the course of his contacts, he faces, and *makes his own*, certain already established social routines, the norms regulating interpersonal and intergroup relationships, and other values of his groups. He and his generation do not ordinarily create them anew. The origin of such standardized social products (language, religious and other values, family, etc.) is still a controversial problem. But on all grounds it is safe to assume that they have not dropped out of a clear sky, but are products of group interactions. Therefore, the formulation of the psychology of group interaction, the emergence of new qualities peculiar to the group in group situations in general, the rise and standardization of group norms in particular, and the subsequent effects of these norms on the experience and behavior of the individual members will give us in a nutshell the basic principles involved. In the chapters to follow we shall present them in brief outline, with some crucial illustrative material. Relatively small experimental groups and actual groups with various degrees of structure usually embody in themselves the essential earmarks of any group in any culture. A carefully planned experimental group, a clique or gang, more or less structured group formations in combat situations, relatively isolated groups in prisoner-of-war camps and concentration camps, a college community, a prison community, yield themselves as prototypes for the formulation of the essential principles involved in any group situation. Accordingly, our first task will be a brief account of group situations. The main points reached in the study of groups will prepare us to handle more adequately the problems of *attitude*, personal and group identifications (*ego-involvements*), adolescent cliques, and prejudice. We say more adequately, because if the interrelatedness of these problems to group situations is not pointed out and they are treated as rather discrete items, some of their most significant functional properties will remain obscured.

5.

Properties of Group Situations in General

THAT GROUP SITUATIONS PRODUCE DIFFERENTIAL EFFECTS ON the behavior of participating individuals has appeared in the general and experimental treatment of the subject for years. In the relatively early accounts, rather extreme group situations, i.e., crowd behavior, were a major concern. Dramatic descriptions mixed with theorizing were advanced by authors like Le Bon [1] and Ross.[2] On the other hand, in the early period of the experimental study of groups, the investigators were primarily concerned with the rather discrete effects of group situations on various functions—association, attention, affective degree, work output, etc. The pioneering works of Moede and Allport, among others, are examples. A brief summary of a few of the results obtained in some of Allport's experiments will give a concrete idea of the disconnected social "increments" and "decrements" appearing in group situations, i.e., the gain or loss in output of work resulting from the presence of others.[3] One of the experiments in the series involved an association test, i.e., putting down words "as rapidly as they came to mind." The majority of the subjects in this experiment showed "an increase in speed and quantity of work under group influence."

In another experiment the subjects judged, both alone and in groups, the degree of pleasantness or unpleasantness of odors ranging from the putrid to perfumes. In the group situations the extreme judgments of pleasantness or unpleasantness were

---

[1] G. Le Bon, *The Crowd, a Study of the Popular Mind*, London: T. Fisher Unwin, 1914 ed.

[2] E. A. Ross, *Social Psychology*, New York: Macmillan, 1908.

[3] F. H. Allport, *Social Psychology*, Boston: Houghton Mifflin, 1924, pp. 260–285.

avoided in general: "The unpleasant odors therefore were estimated as *less unpleasant* in the group than when judging alone;
and the pleasant were estimated as *less pleasant* in the group
than in the solitary judgments." This shows a leveling effect
in the group situation. A similar leveling effect was obtained in
the judgment of weights in the group situation. Allport describes this effect as a "basic human tendency to temper one's
opinions and conduct by deference to the opinion and conduct
of others."

In the 'thirties, under the impact of sociological findings on
groups and, especially, the experimental work in psychology
that definitely demonstrated the functional interrelatedness of
parts in the whole, investigators took a more comprehensive
approach. With this new approach, the problems were formulated so that it was possible to point out the implications which
were closer to the experience and behavior of the individual in
actual group situations and in his culture. Stress was now
placed on the emerging qualities and products in group situations. The sociologists' great objection to experimental work was
that it consisted mainly of discrete laboratory artifacts which
lacked the concrete and living character of the qualities emerging in actual social interaction. The study of structural properties peculiar to the group, as opposed to the picking up of
unrelated effects, became the central theme of group studies.

In all group situations new psychological effects peculiar to
the group situation are produced in the participating individuals. They arise in all group situations, whether they be momentary groups, such as a group discussing some controversial
current problem, even though the participants might have been
strangers up to the time of the meeting, or whether they be
more or less lasting groups, such as a clique, a gang, a club, a
church, a college community, a union, a military unit, or jail
community, or manufacturer's organization, etc.

Relatively small groups, especially those that are spontaneously formed, such as cliques and gangs, are excellent prototypes for the formulation of the principles of group psychology.
They embody the essential features of the rise of new qualities,
group norms, which subsequently manifest themselves in the
attitudes and behavior of the individual members. In the socio-

logical literature—in the works of Thrasher, Zorbaugh, Clifford
Shaw, and Whyte, for example—we find neat cases of such
group formations.[4] We shall give some concrete cases later
(see pages 122–134).

Having in mind especially such groups, we find that certain
characteristic features stand out. It will more than pay us if we
look for the following features in studying any group:

1. In bringing and holding group members together, there is
a *motivational factor*. This motivational factor may be either
biogenic or sociogenic. It may be the securing of a means of
livelihood (e.g., food, shelter, etc.) or other economic means.
The gangs formed by economically deprived youngsters, business organizations, professional groups, labor unions, etc., are
examples. In some cases the motivational basis may be primarily sex, as in adolescent cliques or gangs, nudist colonies, or
the various Bohemias of especially large cities. In other cases,
particularly among people who are far above the subsistence
level, the motivation may primarily be the gaining of distinction. The types of sociogenic motives involved in the formation
and functioning of groups vary, of course, from culture to culture and from class to class. Therefore, an enumeration of them
will be futile; they multiply with the development and differentiation of social organization. They may include such various
and specific tastes as represented by Rotary clubs, vegetarian
groups, Longfellow societies, or a society for the prevention of
cruelty to cats. The motivational factor naturally will have a
great deal to do in determining the kind and direction of the
group's activities, the type of values or norms that will come
forth, and consequently the kind of attitudes the individual
members will develop.

One further point should be stressed here. No matter what
biogenic or sociogenic motive may be primarily effective in first
bringing the group members together, a group, once formed,
becomes instrumental in satisfying an important aspect of

[4] See F. M. Thrasher, *The Gang*, Chicago: University of Chicago Press, 1927; H. W.
Zorbaugh, *The Gold Coast and the Slum*, Chicago: University of Chicago Press, 1929;
C. R. Shaw, *The Jack-Roller*, Chicago: University of Chicago Press, 1930; C. R. Shaw,
The Natural History of a Delinquent Career, Chicago: University of Chicago Press,
1931; C. R. Shaw (ed.), *Brothers in Crime*, Chicago: University of Chicago Press, 1938;
W. F. Whyte, *Street Corner Society*, Chicago: University of Chicago Press, 1943.

human motivation. Whether or not it is formed initially to serve these ends, it gives a *feeling of belongingness*, a status and a hierarchy of statuses (positions) which in turn come to regulate aspirations of distinction in the group. We shall say a few words more about this presently (see point 3).

2. In the process of interaction in group activities, whether momentary or lasting, all the psychological functions (perception, discrimination, judgment, thinking, emotion, personality features, etc.) are affected to a lesser or greater degree, depending on the properties of the group "atmosphere." These differential effects represent not merely something added or subtracted, but are qualitative. Differential effects leading to qualitative changes are not unique qualities of group situations; they are embedded in the basic psychology of the individual in any situation. But it is an undeniable fact that groups, especially intense crowds and mass meetings, are particularly conducive to profound behavioral modifications. In experimental studies and observations of group behavior, this fact comes out almost invariably. Later in this chapter we shall briefly present the representative findings of Lewin and his associates in this connection.

3. If the group interaction is lasting to some degree, there is a tendency to the *formation of a structure*. The appearance of relative, interdependent roles for individual members in a hierarchical order at relative distances from a leader is one of the evidences of the formation of a structure. Such structuration seems to be general whether or not it is achieved through formal previously adopted rules. It follows that the leader role is determined not by absolute traits and capacities, but by the demands of the situation at hand. In one situation it may be physical power or bravery; in another it may be intelligence or some other special talent; in still another it may be the family background or an already established prestige. As Thrasher pointed out in his comprehensive study of gangs, the qualities or talents necessary for gaining leadership and keeping it depend on the kind and direction of the work that the group engages in. After a comprehensive survey of the studies on leadership up to 1947, Jenkins concluded as follows: "Leadership is specific to the particular situation under investigation. Who becomes the

leader of a given group engaging in a particular activity and what leadership characteristics are in a given case are a function of the specific situation including the measuring instruments. Related to this conclusion is the general finding of wide variations in the characteristics of individuals who become leaders in similar situations, and even greater divergence in leadership behavior in different situations." [5]

As Whyte pointed out, certain *expectations* are reciprocally built up on the basis of relative positions. The higher up a member is in the hierarchy, the greater is the strength of the demand on him to live up to the expectations of other members. Otherwise he is likely to be dropped down in the hierarchy of positions. [6]

The group structure generates differentiated *"in-group"* ("we" experience) and *"out-group"* ("they" experience) attitudes in the members. The usual group experience may be characterized as an experience of belongingness, solidarity, and loyalty to the interests and norms of the group in spite of various degrees of intra-group rivalries and friction. As Whyte pointed out, the structure of the in-group and out-group delineation need not be recognized by the group members, including the leader, themselves. This is inferred from the differential reactions of the members to each other and to outsiders. If the individual members carry rivalry, friction, and deviation beyond a certain degree (that degree may be different in different groups depending on the demands of loyalty and discipline of the particular group), they will face various kinds of correctives, including demotion, punishment, and ostracism.

Some of the most convincing illustrations of the fact that new in-group attitudes of solidarity, common in-group lingo, jokes, and feelings arise in newly formed groups are reported by those in close contact with the daily life of army units. Just as in-group attitudes are formed by the child in connection with his family, just as the closely knit sorority or fraternity group marks off its own group from others, so the army unit becomes the center

⁵ W. O. Jenkins, A review of leadership studies with particular reference to military problems, *Psychol. Bull.*, 1947, 44, 75.

⁶ W. F. Whyte, *op. cit.*

and focus of the men's experience and activities. Through sharing common experiences, hardships, and risks, the members of the various army units develop, in time, feelings of in-group solidarity and unit pride. Ernie Pyle reflected this fact in the following words:

"The hundred men in that camp were just like a clan. They had all been together a long time and they had almost a family pride in what they were doing and the machinery they were doing it with. . . . Private Wolfson, Sergeant Harrington, and Major Robb had one thing in common with every soldier in the army—they thought their division was the best extant. Since I was a man without a division, I just agreed with them all." [7]

Bill Mauldin also observed the in-group pattern, and vividly drew its products and their subsequent effects:

While men in combat outfits kid each other around, they have a sort of family complex about it. *No outsiders may join.* Anybody who does a dangerous job in this war has his own particular kind of kidding among his own friends, and sometimes it doesn't even sound like kidding. Bomber crews and paratroopers and infantry squads are about the same in that respect. If a stranger comes up to a group of them when they are bulling, they ignore him. If he takes it upon himself to laugh at something funny they have said, they freeze their expressions, turn slowly around, stare at him until his stature has shrunk to about four inches and he slinks away, and then they go back to their kidding again.

It's like a group of prosperous businessmen telling a risqué joke and then glaring at the waiter who joins in the guffaws. Combat people are *an exclusive set,* and if they want to be that way, it is their privilege. They certainly earn it. New men in outfits have to work their way in slowly, but they are eventually accepted. Sometimes they have to change some of their ways of living. An introvert or a recluse is not going to last long in combat without friends, so he learns *to come out of his shell.* Once he has "arrived" he is pretty proud of his clique, and he in turn is chilly toward outsiders.

That's why, during some of the worst periods in Italy, many guys who had a chance to hang around a town for a few days after being discharged from a hospital where they had recovered from wounds, with nobody the wiser, didn't take advantage of it. They weren't eager to get back up and get in the war, by any means, and many of

[7] Ernie Pyle, *Here Is Your War,* New York: The World Publishing Company, 1945; Henry Holt, 1943, pp. 122, 233.

them did hang around a few days. But those who did hang around *didn't feel exactly right* about it, and those who went right back did it for a very simple reason—not because they felt that their presence was going to make a lot of difference in the big scheme of the war, and not to uphold the traditions of the umpteenth regiment. They went back because they knew their companies were very shorthanded, and they were sure that if somebody else in their own squad or section were in their own shoes, and the situation were reversed, those friends would come back to make the load lighter on *them*.[8]

In proportion to the degree of the hierarchical importance of the groups he belongs to in various capacities (for in highly differentiated modern societies he may belong to several), the individual's striving to keep his position and to raise it will vary. All more or less lasting groups have their peculiar structures, with relative positions from the leadership at the top down to the lowest member of the rank and file. Usually in social life, new members find the structure ready made as they enter the group, and they may strive to attain a higher and higher place in the hierarchy. But if a group of individuals gets together through some unusual circumstance, especially if there are dangers to be shared or vital ends to be secured, soon such hierarchical structures develop *spontaneously*, as we have seen in the above examples and shall see later.

Whether the individual finds his place in an established group (such as a family, church, social class) or participates in the formation of a group, he comes to experience a feeling of belongingness. Subject to individual variations, he strives to maintain this feeling, and to hold his place or a better one in the group. This, in brief, constitutes psychologically his *status* and *vertical mobility*—status and vertical mobility being sociological designations. When his belongingness or position is threatened, his very identity becomes disturbed or shaky. These strivings, as we noted earlier, are an important part of the individual's *sociogenic motives*. Since the problem of accounting for these strivings and for the insecurity which arises when group belongingness or status is threatened cannot be considered adequately without more fully discussing established

[8] From *Up Front* by Bill Mauldin. Copyright, 1945, by Henry Holt and Company, Inc. (all but last italics mine).

facts concerning the psychology of groups (Chapters 5–7) and the genetic development and functioning of the ego, we shall treat them in later chapters (Chapters 11 and 12). Only then will our account of group psychology be rounded out. In anticipation, we can state that the individual in any human grouping develops an ego which more or less reflects his social setting and which defines in a major way the very anchorages of his identity in relation to other persons, groups, institutions, etc. As we shall see later, disruption of these anchorages, or their loss, implies psychologically the breakdown of his identity. Such a disruption or loss of the individual's moorings is accompanied by anxiety or insecurity. Consequently, struggles to establish some sort of new moorings occur, for anchoring one's ego securely in some setting is a psychological necessity (Chapter 11, pages 270–276).

4. In a good many cases the individual forms his attitudes on the basis of the values and norms of the groups he joins. He becomes a good member to the extent to which he assimilates these norms, conforms to them, and serves the aims demanded by them. This is the main source of his sociogenic motives. In groups in which no previously standardized norms exist, norms will arise in the course of the interaction of the members (see Chapter 7), and, once established, will determine or alter the individual's experience and behavior in situations, group or individual, which call on them to function.

The place and functional meaning of the individual's social attitudes, belongingness (identification), and status aspirations and strivings become more real if they are related to groups from which they are derived. In other words, the individual's standards, attitudes, and status aspirations stem from and are related to certain groups. We shall refer to these groups as the individual's *reference groups*. In many cases his reference groups are groups of which he is an actual member—*membership groups*. But this is not always so. He may be actually a member of one group, but through his contact with the attitudes and aspirations of another he may do his best to relate himself, his standards, his aspirations to that group. For example, individuals of the middle class may try to regulate their standards and aspirations in relation to leisure-class values. Or through some circumstance, an individual may be living with a group of people who are not his group and to whom he does not relate himself. With such cases in mind, it is psychologically useful to have two different concepts—*membership groups* and *reference groups*. Of course, usually one's reference groups and membership groups are the same. The discrepancies between the two, i.e., the cases in which individuals actually live in one group but aspire to belong to or are made to relate themselves to another, cause a number of conflicts and frictions which will be touched upon later. The marginality and out-of-context strivings of tactless social climbers are illustrations of the point.

Crowd Situations, Their Negative and Positive Effects and the Rise of New Norms

Before presenting some of the crucial findings concerning the validity of the foregoing generalizations, we shall briefly characterize the general properties of extreme cases of group interaction and the rise of new norms on these occasions. Especially important for us are the characteristics of interacting groups and crowds. A slogan or a short-cut formula may come forth at a group meeting and, even when the individual is no longer surrounded by the members of the group, may serve as a guide whenever it is invoked. Here appears an approach to the problem of the formation of norms. It is, therefore, worth our while to glance at some of the important properties of crowds. It is emphasized by sociologically inclined authors that the individual in a crowd situation is no longer his individual self; his individual experience is in the powerful grip of the occasion; his actions are his no more; he is simply a tool responding to the whims of the leader or the violence of the group. To revive the properties of the crowd situation in our minds, we may give one instance which, in his own words, "had an important share" in the education of George Bernard Shaw. He saw a crowd of people; it was a genuinely "popular movement" and it started with a "runaway cow."

The individual in an intense group situation acts as a member of the group; the group situation demands conformity. Whether the individual would *like* to conform or not (if he were to weigh the different aspects of the situation and his own interests from many angles), being a part of the situation imposes conformity on him. He is no longer "the kind of man who would take this or that into consideration before acting." If a participant does manage to oppose the group he usually succeeds in doing so by exerting a proportional effort.

Some writers on the subject have emphasized the intellectual inferiority of the crowd to the individual when alone. They have also given pathetic pictures of the demoralizing effects of crowds, and have even recommended "prophylactics against the mob mind." Such admonitions are appropriate if we pick out only the unfortunate cases and blind ourselves altogether to the elevating effects of crowds. It is true that there are instances in which the individual commits inhuman acts under the grip of a general outburst of mob fury. On the other hand, the group may produce the highest deeds of morality and self-sacrifice. A man whom we know to be stingy may surprise us by generous contributions in a group situation; heroism and stoical self-control are common experiences on the battlefield and in the great crises and revolutions of every era. In World War II, neighbors of mild-mannered, easygoing boys were surprised by their heroic deeds on the battlefields. Ordinarily they might have expected such heroic deeds only from those who exhibited bravery in civilian life.

To give a concrete instance that can be easily verified, we may refer to the Halifax disaster following an explosion in 1917 —an intensive crisis that brought people into close psychological contact. At Halifax many individuals, as well as whole families, refused assistance that others might be relieved. Individual acts of the finest type were written ineffaceably upon the social memory of the inhabitants. There was the child who used her teeth to release the clothes which held her mother beneath a pile of debris; a wounded girl saved a large family of children, getting them all out of a falling and burning house; a telegraph operator at the cost of his life stuck to his key, sent a warning message over the line, and stopped an incoming train. "The illustrations of mutual aid at Halifax would fill a volume. Not only was it evidenced in the instances of families and friends, but also in the realm of business. Cafes served lunches without charge. Drug stores gave out freely of their supplies. Firms released their clerks to swell the army of relief." [9] Similar acts of self-sacrifice and heroism were reported among the residents of Texas City when explosions devastated a good part of the city in 1947.

Thus the effect of the crowd situation on the individual is not always to reduce him to the state of a beast, setting him free to destroy. There are crowd orgies in which he may regress to the point of allowing the irresponsible domination of instinct. On the other hand, there are many cases in which important popular movements in history have achieved definite aims under the stress of disaster, or in opposition to the cruelty of the conditions of life imposed upon the people or the rigidity of the social norms governing their lives.

A glance at Freud's *Group Psychology* is pertinent in this connection. It will help to make clear the formation of social products as the result of the contact of individuals—products which are not found ready-made in the instinctive or unconscious repertory of the human organism.

The crux of the position taken by Freud may be summarized in a few sentences. [10] According to him, the main and, in fact, the only important effect the group situation brings about in the individual is to strip from him the superstructure of social norms, or conscience if the moral aspect is in question, and to give free rein to the satisfaction of the libido; and the only important thing that finds expression is what is stored in the unconscious. This idea is expressed in unequivocal terms: "From our point of view we need not attribute so much importance to the appearance of new characteristics. For us it would be enough to say that in a group the individual is brought under conditions which allow him to throw off the repressions of his unconscious instincts. The apparently new characteristics which he then displays are in fact the manifestations of his unconscious, in which all that is evil in the human mind is contained as a predisposition. We can find no difficulty in under-

[9] S. H. Price, "Catastrophe and social change—based upon a sociological study of the Halifax disaster," in *Columbia University Studies in History, Economics and Public Law*, 1920, 94, 36–57.

[10] S. Freud, *Group Psychology and the Analysis of the Ego*, London: International Psychological Press, 1922.

standing the disappearance of conscience or of a sense of responsibility in these circumstances" (pp. 9–10). According to Freud, the basic undercurrent of all social action and organization is the sex impulse; he finds, "First, that a group is clearly held together by a power of some kind; and to what power could this fact be better ascribed than to Eros, who holds everything in the world?" (p. 40). This means that, according to Freud, the direction of action in a group situation, as well as the emotional quality attained, is stored in the unconscious and ready in advance.

It is true that there are group situations conducive merely to strong sex manifestations, but the crowds that have a lasting effect are those that achieve a social end. In these cases not only is behavior not directed to the satisfaction of the libido, but the individual in the grip of a powerful movement at times cannot help sacrificing himself.

In some crowd situations, formulas or slogans arise or become standardized—achieving the status of common property dear and sacred to every participant—which on later occasions may move the individual to action or may even become the focal point in his life. Consider the "Liberty, Equality, Fraternity" of the French Revolution; the American Revolution's "Life, Liberty, and the Pursuit of Happiness"; the World War I phrase, "To Make the World Safe for Democracy"; and the "Four Freedoms" of World War II. Once such a slogan reaches this status, it can be used and abused to move individuals to action; in its name a great many things can be done. Symbols, slogans, and values, when once standardized for groups, are no longer mere trifles but may have great vitality as rigid stereotypes.

Once a group or crowd takes a definite direction and gains considerable momentum, the leader who started it or who distinguished himself by some outstanding deed may not escape ridicule and even punishment. Slogans have their own history, short or long, depending on the situation and their appropriateness in changing situations. The boos that MacDonald received from his old comrades in the British elections in the 'thirties afford a fitting instance. The tragic fate of Pétain, the patriot idolized in World War I, is another striking illustration of the point.

The denial of the special characteristics of the group situation and the psychological value of its special properties amounts to ignoring some well-established and basic facts of psychology. Even the mere presence of lines or dots near a line at which we are looking influences our perception of it, sometimes considerably. A psychological group situation likewise alters the individual's perception, and the group products that thus come to be standardized are important realities. To be sure, the basic reality beneath all social and cultural realities is the individual organism; but, once the superstructure rises, new factors emerge on their own level.

Thus Freud's *Group Psychology*, which starts by breaking down the artificial dualism between individual and social psychology, turns out to be an individualistic psychology based on the Eros and the storehouse of the unconscious. This one-sided thesis ignores facts established in the psychology of perception, namely, the *interdependence of individual parts*. Freud proceeds as if the *isolated* individual could serve as a clue to the group.

What happens in a group or crowd situation is not restricted to the breaking down of the individual's moral and social norms, but involves the rise and the incorporation of new norms or slogans. Thus, studying crowds or mobs only at the hour of turmoil and outburst, without going back to the causes that produce them and the effects that follow, again shows a lack of the perspective necessary in the study of the problems of social psychology.

The immediate circumstances that give rise to a crowd situation may be important and vital. Such are the prolonged hunger and cold which may result in strikes and violence in great masses of people. Or the precipitating circumstances may be unimportant and trivial in themselves—such as a quarrel over a strip of bathing beach in the Chicago riots of 1919. Nevertheless, the basic psychological processes must ultimately be explainable by common psychological laws. Perhaps comparatively simple crowd situations will enable us to approach nearer the basic principles, because the causes and the manifestations, as well as the effects, may be traced more easily.

A keen observation made by Charlie Chaplin in Vienna

analyzes the instantaneous organization of a crowd of short
duration: "There is a psychology in the gathering of crowds. I
can be walking along a thoroughfare with an occasional recognition. People just look and nudge one another; then go on
their way. But occasionally an excitable wench will exclaim, 'Oh,
look, there's Charlie Chaplin!' and the crowd immediately takes
on her excitement and gathers round until I have to make for a
taxi." [11]

This simple and clear-cut case, although it does not involve
all the aspects of a typical mob gathering and ending in action,
is important for us because it illustrates the following points:
The sudden discovery of a celebrity (Charlie Chaplin is a personality with prestige—a true celebrity to millions of people
all over the world wherever there is cinema) is an event that
stands out from the ordinary run of familiar happenings on the
street—the movement of traffic and the passing of unknown
pedestrians. The unexpected discovery of a person of note
arouses some sort of emotion in most people. Yet what we may
do or not do on the street is prescribed by certain norms—we
are not supposed to look intently at a person; we are not supposed to give overt expression on the street to every surprise or
sudden emotion, attracting to ourselves the attention of everyone around us. Self-respecting people do not do so. Consequently, most "people just look and nudge one another." (We
are allowed to nudge a companion to call his or her attention to
something that has to be noticed.) But there are those, less
firmly bound by social norms, who easily give expression to
excitement when they face a situation that is out of the ordinary. The sudden appearance of Charlie Chaplin is one of
these situations, and an excitable woman may easily break
through the norms regulating behavior on the streets. Her ex-
clamation, "Oh, look, there's Charlie Chaplin!" attracts attention. People stop to look, and those who would otherwise go
on their way after nudging one another make a little crowd
around the person with prestige. The feeling of his importance
is the *common* element in their experience that gathers them into
a momentary crowd, even though they do not know one another

[11] C. Chaplin, A Comedian Sees the World, *Woman's Home Companion*, October,
1933, p. 102.

and will perhaps never even see one another again. This situation does not involve a lasting common tie important enough to hold them together or to result in collective action or the expression of slogans. Yet the incident is sufficient to illustrate how a common background, a common frame of reference, may make possible the sudden precipitation of a crowd situation—when one individual breaks through the norm of decorum and restraint.

Experimental Demonstration of Group Effects by Lewin and His Associates

The fruitful results which may be obtained by the experimental study of group formation, group structure and products, and the subsequent effects on individual behavior are shown by a series of experiments on "social atmosphere" (e.g., "properties of the social group") by Lewin and his associates. In harmony with Lewin's formulations of Gestalt psychology (i.e., "field-theoretical" approach), a group is conceived of as a "dynamic whole" functioning with the "interdependence of the members (or better, of subparts of the group)." [12] This "field-theoretical" approach made possible the study of "the individual psychology of the group member and the collective behavior of the group regarded as a dynamic unity." [13] The techniques used in the experiments were determined accordingly. For example, total behavior observations were made, rather than discrete "atomistic" records of each member's behavior without reference to the total picture in which it took place.

In the first experiment, Lippitt organized two clubs of 10-year-old children who engaged in theatrical mask-making for a three-month period.[14] The leader conducted one group in an "authoritarian" manner and the other in accordance with "democratic" procedure. Four observers made detailed observations of the ongoing activity at each meeting. As the

[12] K. Lewin, Field theory and experiment in social psychology: concepts and methods, *Amer. J. Sociol.*, 1939, 44, 868–896.

[13] R. Lippitt, Field theory and experiment in social psychology: autocratic and democratic group atmospheres, *Amer. J. Sociol.*, 1939, 45, 28.

[14] *Ibid.*, pp. 26–49.

"authoritarian" leader, Lippitt was more "ascendant," initiated more action for the group, was less "objective" in his
dealings with the group members, than as "democratic" leader.
As a result of this differing leader behavior, the structure emerging in the "democratic" group tended to include the adult
leader as a member of the group (i.e., he "was treated more
nearly an equal by child members"), whereas the structure of
the "authoritarian" group tended to center around the adult
leader to whom the children maintained a relationship of "sub-

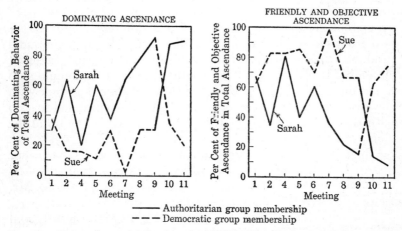

FIG. 13. Comparison of behavior classified as dominating ascendance and
as friendly, objective ascendance for members transferred from one group
to another. (From R. Lippitt, in *Amer. J. Sociol.*, 1939, 45, p. 39.)

mission" (pp. 34–35). The differential effects of these two group
structures on individual behavior are strikingly shown by a
comparison of certain types or categories of behavior of two
members who were transferred from one group to the other.
Fig. 13 shows how the amount of "dominating ascendance"
and "friendly and objective ascendance" exhibited by Sue and
Sarah changed when they shifted groups at the tenth meeting.
    Before Sue, who was first in the "democratic" group, left
her group, she had acquired a feeling of *belongingness* to it as a
result of interaction with its members and identification with its
activities and products. "Two meetings passed before the mem-

ber shifted from the D- to the A-club referred to her new group as 'we.' Until then she had continually made such remarks as, 'Ours is better than yours,' 'You're different in this group, aren't you?' and 'I don't like yours'" (p. 38).

The "democratic" group engaged more frequently than the "autocratic" group in unified activity and talked more in terms of "*we, us,* and *ours*" than of "*I, me,* and *mine*" (pp. 32–33). Whereas the authoritarian leader imposed his own goal on the group and "frustrated spontaneous goals," the democratic leader suggested several goals and let the final goal emerge from group decision. As a result, members of the "democratic" group took group goals as their own. The differences between the two groups in solidarity and identification with group goals and products are shown clearly in the results of two votes taken at the end of twelve weeks: "(*a*) whether the meetings should stop or continue for a longer period, and (*b*) what should be done with the group property, the masks. All of the A-group voted to stop with that meeting; four of the D-group voted to continue the club meetings. All of the A-group members claimed some mask for their own, to take home (e.g., 'Give me mine,' 'Give us our masks'); all of the D-group members suggested a group disposal of one or more of the masks (e.g., 'Give the pirate to Mr. Lippitt,' 'Give the black one to the teacher')" (p. 37).

This experiment lead to another by Lewin, Lippitt, and White in which four comparable clubs of 10-year-old boys each passed through periods in which they had adult leaders who followed "democratic," "autocratic," and "*laissez-faire*" procedures (i.e., the leader kept out of group activities as much as possible).[15] The behavior and position of the various kinds of leader are summarized in Table 1.

Here too the autocratic leaders tended to be outside the group as far as the boys were concerned. In the boys' own words: "*He didn't let us do what we wanted to do,*" "*He made us make masks, and the boys didn't like that,*" "*We didn't have any fun with him,— we didn't have any fights.*" But the "democratic" leaders tended more to be accepted in the group: "*He was a good sport, worked*

<hr>

[15] K. Lewin, R. Lippitt, and R. K. White, Patterns of aggressive behavior in experimentally created "social climates," *J. Soc. Psychol.*, 1939, 10, 271–300. Table 1 is on p. 273.

TABLE 1

Authoritarian	Democratic	Laissez-faire
1. All determination of policy by the leader.	1. All policies a matter of group discussion and decision, encouraged and assisted by the leader.	1. Complete freedom for group or individual decision, without any leader participation.
2. Techniques and activity steps dictated by the authority, one at a time, so that future steps were always uncertain to a large degree.	2. Activity perspective gained during first discussion period. General steps to group goal sketched, and where technical advice was needed the leader suggested two or three alternative procedures from which choice could be made.	2. Various materials supplied by the leader, who made it clear that he would supply information when asked. He took no other part in work discussions.
3. The leader usually dictated the particular work task and work companions of each member.	3. The members were free to work with whomever they chose, and the division of tasks was left up to the group.	3. Complete non-participation by leader.
4. The dominator was "personal" in his praise and criticism of the work of each member, but remained aloof from active group participation except when demonstrating. He was friendly or impersonal rather than openly hostile.	4. The leader was "objective" or "fact-minded" in his praise and criticism, and tried to be a regular group member in spirit without doing too much of the work.	4. Very infrequent comments on member activities unless questioned, and no attempt to participate or interfere with the course of events.

along with us and thinks of things just like we do" (p. 284). Although the *laissez-faire* leader was preferred by most boys to the "autocrat," he too was an outsider: "*We could do what we pleased with him*" (p. 285). As a result of these leader-member relationships, the frequency of "group-minded remarks to the leader" of the democratic group was much greater than to the other leaders.

This experiment yielded ample evidence concerning the formation of group structures and the rise of group products with which members identified themselves in varying degrees. Unfortunately we can consider here only a fraction of the evidence and colorful illustrations of group effects. Perhaps one of the clearest examples of the different effects of group structures on the members concerns differing amounts of certain behavior displayed by the same members in different "atmospheres"— behavior which was never overtly prohibited or encouraged by any of the leaders. For example, in autocratic groups which were characterized as "submissive" in their reaction to the autocratic structure, "normal free-and-easy sociability between the boys" was surprisingly low. This may have been at least in part because the dominating leader prevented the spontaneous formation of group structures and products among the boys—as indicated, for example, by the fact that these "submissive" autocratic members were lowest of all groups in "group-minded remarks" either to the leader or to other members and tended least of all to talk in terms of "*we*." [16]

Figs. 14 and 15 show graphically the differing amounts of aggression expressed by the same groups under different types of leadership. The authors, warning against a "one-factor" theory of aggression to account for these differences, conceive them as a result of the "specific constellation of the field as a whole" (p. 297). Of particular interest is the very slight change in the amount of aggression shown by Group III (Fig. 15) in different atmospheres. Here it seems that one important factor in the total field was the fact that the boys first were almost without adult supervision (*laissez-faire*) and that certain ways of behaving (i.e., "running wild") spontaneously became standardized for them. These standardized behavior norms were then more potent in determining their behavior than other

---

[16] R. Lippitt, and R. K. White, "The 'Social Climate' of Children's Groups," in R. G. Barker, J. S. Kounin and H. F. Wright (eds.), *Child Behavior and Development*, New York: McGraw-Hill, 1943, pp. 485–506.

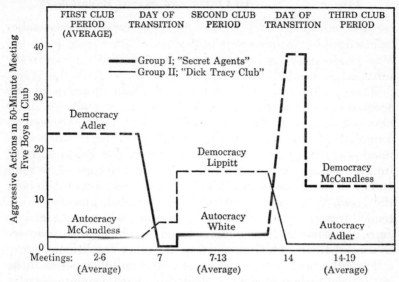

Fig. 14. Aggressive behavior in Groups I and II under different methods of leadership. (From K. Lewin, R. Lippitt, and R. K. White, in *J. Soc. Psychol.*, 1939, 10, p. 280.)

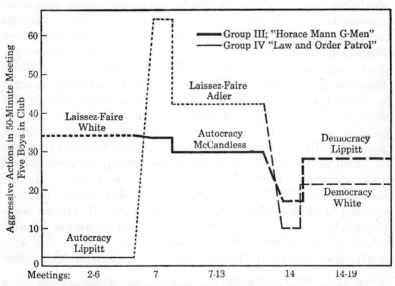

Fig. 15. Aggressive behavior in Groups III and IV under different methods of leadership. (From *ibid.*, p. 282.)

factors which (in other groups) operated toward different behavior in different atmospheres.

In the *laissez-faire* groups, the boys were, for the most part,
interacting spontaneously and were relatively free from adult
influence. The emerging structures tended toward a united
group in which the members experienced feelings of belongingness and solidarity. There was a "high frequency of proposals
for united action" and a "surprisingly high proportion of group-
minded conversation" (p. 138). However, the group activity
(mask-making) was too difficult for these 10-year-olds to plan
and execute without adult help. The members struggled to hold
the group to a united course but often failed, and the group
tended toward disorganization. As a result, when in the *laissez-
faire* atmosphere these boys engaged much more in play activities of their own than when under other conditions.

The autocratic leaders tried to set their (adult) goals as those
of the group while frustrating goals which arose spontaneously,
and therefore the members of the autocracies did not identify
themselves with the goals. They tended to do simply "what *he*
wants me to do." When the leader was away, work on mask-
making flagged. But in the democratic group, the members
themselves selected goals among those suggested by the leader.
These goals became *their* goals. The leader's presence in the club
then made comparatively little difference in the group activity.
This group was allowed to form and function more or less
spontaneously by the leader, who tried to participate in the
group and to help in problems too tough for the boys. In this
group "spontaneous cohesion" ("working toward common
goals, thinking in terms of 'we' rather than 'I,' showing friend-
liness rather than hostility toward other group members, etc.")
was "decidedly higher" (p. 134). A later study by Lewin
showed how identification with group goals makes possible
changes in individual tastes, in this case for food. The subjects
who participated in making a group decision for action felt and
acted as though the decision was *theirs*.[17]

This does not mean that unified group action, identification

---

[17] K. Lewin, "The Relative Effectiveness of a Lecture Method and a Method of
Group Decision for Changing Food Habits," State University Iowa Child Welfare
Research Station, 1942.

of members with the course of action of the group, did not occur in the other groups. For example, in the "aggressive autocracy," in which a generally rowdy atmosphere among members prevailed, the group showed its solidarity in rebelling against the dominating adult leader. "About the middle of the series of six meetings the club members went to their teacher with a letter of resignation signed by four of them. They asked their teacher to give this to the leader when he came to get them after school. The teacher refused to act as a go-between, suggesting that the boys go to the leader directly, but when he appeared after school, courage seemed to wane and they all went to the meeting as usual." [18]

During the process of interaction in the group and identification with its activities and products, the individual comes to think of it as *his* group (in-group) as opposed to *other* groups

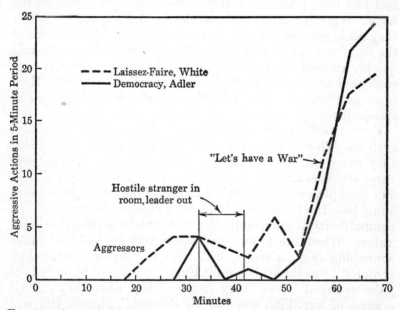

FIG. 16.   Aggressive behavior due to in-group and out-group delineations; the amount of such behavior between members of democratic and of *laissez-faire* groups is shown. (From *ibid.*, p. 285.)

[18] K. Lewin, R. Lippitt, and R. K. White, *op. cit.*, p. 288.

(out-group). He can then oppose other groups and can protect his own group from the attack of others. In the experimental situations such "out-group aggression" appeared. In view of the relative solidarity of the various groups, it is interesting that the skirmishes occurred in both cases between a *laissez-faire* and a "democratic" group. As shown in Fig. 16, the first "war" began with one or two *laissez-faire* members calling names and bickering with the "democratic" group. As the curve shows, the "democratic" group responded in kind. When the *laissez-faire* group decided to "have a war," the "democratic" group responded with even greater aggressive action. (This consisted chiefly of throwing water, pieces of clay, and paint.) A second fight occurring between the same groups was "legalized" as it started, with the words, "It's a war all right." In the authors' words: "On the later occasion the pattern of inter-group conflict had been established; it was, by that time, a part of the boys' 'cognitive structure'—a clearly defined region which they could enter or not as they chose; and since they had found the first 'war' to be very pleasantly exciting, they readily and quickly entered the same region again when the general psychological situation was conducive to conflict" (p. 287). Here is an excellent example, in experimentally created groups, of standardized aggression toward an out-group.

Even experimentally created groups do not function as closed systems. When the subjects enter the experimental situation, they carry with them attitudes formed in other groups; and these attitudes affect their reactions in the new group situation. For example, excerpts from the record of the *laissez-faire* group show how the behavior of two boys changed in terms of the compatibility of group activities with certain of their dominant values. When the group was attempting to build or make something (e.g., a map), Bill, who is "highly adult-value-centered" was the leader, while Finn, "who is not at all 'adult-value-centered'" was "very restless." But when they started a game of war, Finn was "in his element," whereas Bill was "miserable" (pp. 129–130).

Another example of the influence of outside groups was the fact that the only boy who preferred the autocratic leader to the democratic leader was the son of an army officer. As a result of belongingness in his own family group, he "consciously put a high value on strict discipline" (p. 284).

One major finding of these studies is that genuine cooperation and participation on the part of the individual appear when he identifies himself with the task or situation at hand (i.e., when he becomes ego-involved). As the foregoing experiments indicate, democratic participation in the group is usually conducive to such identification. But, as with the army officer's son, if personal identification is otherwise established (autocratically in this case), this established identification prevails over democratic situations. Reports from present-day Germany showing that many people are at a loss as to what to do with democracy give the point a grim reality. The important practical implication of this fact is that, to get the individual identified with democratic practices, it is not sufficient to put him in a democratic atmosphere; it is also necessary to destroy the effects of the background inimical to it. This point will come out again when we consider the effects of membership and reference groups on a change in attitudes (in the Bennington study, see pp. 139–155).

6.

Effects of Membership and Other Reference Groups

IN THE PRECEDING CHAPTER WE DISCUSSED BRIEFLY THE RISE, in group situations, of new products, goals, and structures, the parts of which are functionally interdependent. We gave a brief summary of representative experiments definitely demonstrating such group effects. In this chapter, we shall first present some additional evidence from life situations which sociologists have been accumulating for nearly three decades—most notably represented in the works of Thrasher, Zorbaugh, Clifford Shaw, Whyte, etc. After all, the final test of psychological formulations, no matter how brilliant they may appear to be in themselves, lies in their validity in actual life situations.

During the past decade, the fact that group effects arise, understandable only in terms of the interdependence of parts (the roles of individual members), and that standards or norms peculiar to the group also arise, has become established in psychology. This basic orientation, perhaps more than any other single development, helped to save social psychology from being a compendium of discrete facts, and brought it in line with the reality of the phenomena of concrete social relationships at the level of the social sciences.

But from here we have to go further. For *groups*, especially today, are *not closed systems.* The integrated or contradictory nature (as to direction, interests, values, status relationships, etc.) of different groups which are functionally related (in positive or antagonistic ways) has also to be faced as one of our major problems at the psychological level. The currently vital issues of socio-economic class groupings and antagonisms, issues of prejudice based on these groupings and on other less significant in-group and out-group formations, the agonizing issue of "marginality," and "dilemmas and contradictions of status" so prevalent today in "casually patterned" western societies forcibly impose this major problem on us. We can no longer be complacently satisfied by announcing, as a major finding, that the individual experiences and behaves differently in group situations as determined by the structural properties of the group. Many a person today necessarily moves in different groups which may and *do* exert different and contradictory demands on him. They tend to pull him in different directions, to give rise in him to different (and not infrequently contradictory) values, norms, loyalties, and conformities. They certainly contribute their share to conflict situations with unfortunate consequences for him.[1]

This state of affairs is mainly responsible for the appearance of a *discrepancy* for the individual in regulating his attitudes, loyalties, and conformities. This discrepancy, the consequences of which are far reaching, may be summarized as follows. Ordinarily the attitudes, identifications, loyalties of an individual are largely derived from the values, norms, status regulations of the group or groups of which he is an actual member. These groups to which a person actually belongs, *informally* (as the son of a family, a member of a clique or gang or economic class, in the choice of which he had no part, etc.) or *formally* (as a student of a college, member of a club, union, etc.), may be designated as his *membership groups*. Ordinarily his attitudes and identifications, and subsequently his diverse specific reactions, are regulated and determined by such membership groups. But not always. He may actually be a member of a particular group, but psychologically *refer* himself to a different group and regulate his attitudes and aspirations accordingly (i.e., in reference to that other group). The case of a member of the working class or the middle class who, consciously or unconsciously, relates himself to a higher class and tries to adjust his living and his experiences accordingly is a concrete illustration of the point. Particularly since Veblen's *The Theory of the*

[1] Psychoanalytic literature is replete with material showing the consequences of this state of affairs. See, for example, K. Horney, *New Ways in Psychoanalysis*, New York: Norton, 1939; E. Fromm, *Escape from Freedom*, New York: Rinehart, 1941; H. S. Sullivan, *Conceptions of Modern Psychiatry*, Washington: William Alanson White Psychiatric Foundation, 1947.

Leisure Class, the problems that arise from this discrepancy have been dealt with in various sociological and psychological works. *In short, evidence indicates that the individual's standards and aspirations are regulated in relation to the reference group to which he relates himself.* Usually the reference group to which the individual relates himself is his actual membership group. But, especially in highly competitive societies (such as the capitalist societies of America and Europe), the hierarchical arrangement of which is based on sharp and yet not impregnable vertical class lines, this is frequently not the case. There may be, at times at least, a discrepancy between the individual's actual *membership group* and the *reference group* which he uses to regulate his standards and aspirations. In the next section of this chapter, we shall present an extensive study illustrating the effect of membership groups and of outside reference groups in changing attitudes.

The Effects of Membership vs. Outside Groups and Situations

Groups formed spontaneously as a consequence of informal contacts of individual members may be taken as excellent prototypes for studying various aspects of group interaction and group products.

Adolescent cliques, especially gangs, and groupings formed among people isolated from the main stream of social life are examples *par excellence* of such spontaneously formed groups. They embody in themselves the motivational factors that bring individuals together; they illustrate the way a more or less stable group structure is formed, with roles emerging for the individual members, including the leader; they indicate that in the process of formation, norms (codes) and identifications, solidarity and loyalty, with their appropriate expectations peculiar to the group in question, arise and regulate the behavior of the members in various matters of concern to them all. Consequently the conduct of the individual members is evaluated accordingly.[2]

---

[2] In the extensive studies of Thrasher, Zorbaugh, Clifford Shaw, and Whyte, we find a mine of excellent data concretely illustrating these various aspects of group psychology. The longitudinal case studies of Clifford Shaw (the cases of Stanley,

Practically all such spontaneously formed informal groupings (cliques and gangs) serve two functions. (1) They *organize* activities which *actually or vicariously satisfy the deprivations* (e.g., food, clothing, sex) that made the individuals gravitate toward each other initially. (2) They give the individual members *a sense of belongingness* and *status*. This is especially true in cliques or gangs the members of which lacked a sense of belongingness to any social group, including family. These informally organized membership groups become the main sources of some sense of security for such individuals. In groups (clubs) whose members were above the subsistence level initially and did not suffer a gnawing sense of lack of belongingness, the activities may be directed toward achieving *distinction* and providing mutual aid in securing certain motivational ends.

Whyte's Study of the Street Corner Boys

In the recent work of Whyte we find a concise treatment of the formation and functioning of informal group structures against the background of a slum area, with its peculiar problems arising from its relative segregation from society at large.[3] Particularly, the Street Corner Boys group that he studied shows the main features of group structures: the rise of relative roles, including leadership, the emergence of group norms and group conduct. One of the merits of this study is that Whyte went beyond the in-group picture of the grouping. He deliberately made a special point of studying the impact of the outside groups and situations on the group in general and on individual members in particular.

The Street Corner Boys group arose from the conditions existing in a slum area of a large eastern city in America. As Thrasher and Clifford Shaw pointed out, such areas—still in the process of "settling down" in the general pattern of American life—are particularly conducive to the spontaneous forma-

---

Sidney, and the Martin brothers, for example) are among the most valuable for the students of individual-group relationships. See C. Shaw, *The Jack-Roller*, Chicago: University of Chicago Press, 1930; C. Shaw, *The Natural History of a Delinquent Career*, Chicago: University of Chicago Press, 1931; C. Shaw (ed.), *Brothers in Crime*, Chicago: University of Chicago Press, 1938.

[3] W. F. Whyte, *Street Corner Society*, Chicago: University of Chicago Press, 1943.

tion of informal group structures. The social stability in these slum areas is precarious. One of the best indexes of the peculiar state of slum areas (which have a relatively large number of non-citizens) is that they are looked down upon and segregated in various ways by the main group of established respectability. Cornerville (this particular slum area) has a high percentage of foreign- and American-born Italian inhabitants. The district "has become popularly known as a disordered and lawless community. He is an Italian, and the Italians are looked upon by upper-class people as among the least desirable of the immigrant peoples. . . . The Italians have had to build up their own business hierarchies, and when the prosperity of the twenties came to an end, it became increasingly difficult for the newcomer to advance in this way" (p. 273).

For the people who live in Cornerville, social life does not present a picture of confusion and lawlessness. It is fairly well organized, with hierarchies of socio-economic groups. "According to Cornerville people, society is made up of big people and little people—with intermediaries serving to bridge the gaps between them. The masses of Cornerville people are little people. They cannot approach the big people directly but must have an intermediary to intercede for them. They gain this intercession by establishing connections with the intermediary, by performing services for him, and thus making him obligated to them. The intermediary performs the same functions for the big man. The interactions of big shots, intermediaries, and little guys build up a hierarchy of personal relations based upon a system of reciprocal obligations" (pp. 271–272).

The Street Corner Boys, also known as the Nortons, stem from the representative mass of people of Cornerville—the little guys. Several of these boys frequently do not have any money to spend. At the time the study was carried out, in the late 'thirties, several of the Nortons including the leader, Doc, did not have any steady jobs even though they were well over 20 years old. All the Norton boys grew to adolescence and adulthood under the uncomfortable feeling of being little guys even in their own community. From occasional encounters with the more respectable and high-brow groups or clubs in their own community, they knew that they were treated as rough little guys, and the tendency was to put them in their "place." These circumstances certainly helped to make them gravitate toward each other, to have a standing in the world and to secure mutual help from their fellow men. Thus motivated, the Street Corner Boys group makes a clear, well-structured picture, worthy of study by the social psychologist as being representative of other such groups. The group is not a creation peculiar to Norton Street alone. In almost any city with a similar street, on which boys grow up with various kinds of deprivations and lack social belongingness in relation to society in general, there is a similar sort of in-group.

Still on the fringe of the main vertical current of social organization in relation to economic standing and status, still left to themselves, these boys (like boys in hundreds of cities in similar conditions) gravitate toward each other in their search to relieve their deprivations and to achieve some sense of the belongingness that is one of the essential conditions of psychological security. In the course of their reciprocal contacts, a group structure is patterned with its own peculiar hierarchical arrangement of positions. As Thrasher pointed out in the 'twenties, even the emergence of the leader is a function of the group. Usually the group shapes the leader, of course on the basis of some special capacity demanded by the particular group. In one case it may be physical strength; in another it may be shrewdness; in a third it may be something utterly different. In the case of the Corner Boys the capacity that determined the person of the leader was toughness. On the basis of this characteristic the leader emerged. Doc was first a lieutenant of the leader of the gang, but when he repeatedly licked the leader (Nutsy), the group centered around Doc.

Once a group is crystallized in the course of contacts and events of significance to the members, some sort of in-group formation, a group structure, emerges. Henceforth, the relationship between members and the attitudes toward "outsiders" are largely determined by the group. The higher the place of the member in the group, the more stringent are the expectations placed upon him. In Whyte's words:

Each member of the corner gang has his own position in the gang structure. Although the positions may remain unchanged over long periods of time, they should not be conceived in static terms. To have a position means that the individual has a customary way of interacting with other members of the group. When the pattern of interactions changes, the positions change. The positions of the members are interdependent, and one position cannot change without causing some adjustments in the other positions. Since the group is organized around the men with the top positions, some of the men with low standing may change positions or drop out without upsetting the balance of the group. For example, when Lou Danaro and Fred Mackey [members with low positions in the group] stopped participating in the activities of the Nortons, those activities continued to be organized in much the same manner as before, but when Doc and Danny [members with high positions in the group] dropped out, the Nortons disintegrated, and the patterns of interaction had to be reorganized along different lines (pp. 262–263).

These hierarchical positions of membership are represented by Whyte in the simple diagram shown in Fig. 17.

Once such a group structure is patterned, group action is determined along certain lines. "Group activities are originated by the men with the highest standing in the group, and it is natural for a man to encourage an activity in which he excels and discourage one in which he does not excel" (p. 24). A more or less lasting set of expectations from each and to each member is largely determined by the relative positions in the group. (This established level of a set of expectations is perhaps one of the most telling indexes of the reality of the group structure.)

This can be concretely illustrated by incidents observed in one of the major lines of activities of the Norton group. At one time, the Nortons were seriously interested in bowling. *The performance in bowling became, more or less, the sign of distinction in the group.* As a consequence of this, the high performance of the top-ranking members was accepted as natural and was encouraged. But not so with the high performance of members with low relative standing. That their performance might surpass that of high-ranking members was something that simply did not fit into the picture of established expectations. Hence, they were put "in their place." Take the case of Frank, a member with a rather low standing. Frank was a good player in his own right, yet "he made a miserable showing" *while playing in his own group.* In Frank's words: "I can't seem to play ball

THE NORTONS
Spring and Summer 1937

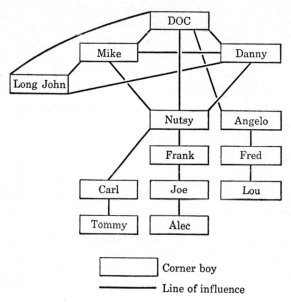

FIG. 17. Hierarchical arrangement of members' positions and lines of influence in the Nortons. (From W. F. Whyte, *Street Corner Society*, University of Chicago Press, 1943.)

when I am playing with fellows I know, like that bunch. I do much better when I am playing for the Stanley A.C. against some team in Dexter, Westland, or out of town." Whyte concludes: "Accustomed to filling an inferior position, Frank was unable to star even in his favorite sport when he was competing against members of his own group" (p. 19).

Once a group is formed, the activities run in relation to the focal position of the leader. The disputes and frictions, as well as the positive actions, ultimately get settled or find expression through him. If some group members are dissatisfied with the direction of activities or think certain individuals in their group are not living up to the group code, they sooner or later

complain to the leader. They try to get him to act in the desired
direction or to bring decisive pressure on the non-conformists.
The individual prestige of the member is an important factor in
determining individual behavior and performance in relation to
others. For example, when Doc moved to the top as a consequence of excellence in fighting, a serious challenge came from
Tony Fontana. Here Doc's established prestige saved the situation for him. As he put it:

> Tony was in my gang when we were kids together. He was a good
> fighter. When he entered the ring as an amateur, he started off winning
> three fights by knockouts. When he turned pro, he was still knocking
> them out. . . . At that time I was the leader of the gang. I was the
> tough guy. But he began to get fresh with me. One night he began
> pushing me around and talking big. I listened to him. I thought, "He
> must be tough. All those knockouts have got to mean something."
> So after a while I said, "I'm going up to bed." I got undressed and
> went to bed, but I couldn't sleep. I put on my clothes and came down
> again. I said, "Say that to me again!" He did and I let him have it—
> pow! . . . But he wouldn't fight me. Why? Prestige, I suppose. Later
> we had it out with gloves on the playground. He was too good for me,
> Bill. I stayed with him, but he was too tough. . . . Could he hit!
> (pp. 4–5).

On the other hand, the authority and prestige that the leader
enjoys have their counterparts in the expectations and the degree of responsibility demanded of him. If he does not live up
to this level he suffers loss of prestige and even position to a
corresponding degree. "When he gives his word to one of his
boys, he keeps it" (p. 259). Likewise, "The leader need not be
the best baseball player, bowler, or fighter, but he must have
some skill in whatever pursuits are of particular interest to the
group" (p. 259).

The members with low status do not lose face if they do not
live up to the group code and expectations, but the leader does.
For example, whereas the lesser members of the group did not
have strict scruples about their money dealings, Doc made
strict rules for himself in the use and securing of money. He had
to be more generous in spending while his boys were around,
but he was almost always broke and unemployed. Lack of
money also troubled him in relation to group activities. If an

activity required the spending of money and he was broke as
usual, he would discourage the line of action; and if he failed to
do so, he would simply find an excuse to get out of it.

   In the binding in-group formation, the real identifications
of individual members are anchored to the group. A sense of
loyalty and solidarity is generated in them as a natural process
which manifests itself in actual behavior. To this effect, Whyte
observed: "Out of such interaction there arises a system of
mutual obligations which is fundamental to group cohesion. If
the men are to carry on their activities as a unit, there are many
occasions when they must do favors for one another. The code
of the corner boy requires him to help his friends when he can
and to refrain from doing anything to harm them" (p. 256).
(In Clifford Shaw's longitudinal case studies we find striking
incidents which verge toward self-sacrifice on the part of group
members not to let down the fellows in their gang.)

   Among many other incidents indicating group solidarity,
Whyte reported the following. Helen, whom the Nortons
thought was Doc's girl friend, was sick in bed. The boys knew
that he had no money to spend on her by way of showing his
consideration. A few fellows got together, raised five dollars,
and sent flowers to Helen as though they were sent by Doc.
Danny, one of the Nortons, who told this incident, added,
"But what things we couldn't do with that $5" (p. 33).

   Solidarity is not a one-way affair, i.e., only from the boys to
the leader. The leader exhibits it to an even greater extent,
proportional to his high position. Doc's refusal to accept a girl's
invitation in order to stick with his gang, who were socially
slighted, illustrates this fact. Shortly after the above incident
took place, the following incident occurred:

   When the fellows were in Jennings', one of the girls was kidding
Doc about his reputation as the great lover and claiming that he was
afraid to go out with her. As he told the story: ... "All right, I said I
would go out with her. But she said, 'First you must come to my
party.' I asked her, 'Who's going to be there?'

   " 'Tony Cardio, Chick Morelli, and Angelo Cucci,' she says.

   " 'Who else?'

   " 'Nobody else.'

   "That steamed me up. Danny, Long John, and Frank were at the same table with me, and she didn't invite them. . . . I told her, 'No, I'm going some place that night.'

"She says, 'That's not true, you just don't want to come.'

"'All right,' I said, 'I don't want to come.'

"And she steamed up. When she went back to her table, I turned to the boys. They were very depressed. I told them, 'Pay no attention to it, she's stupid. She's tactless'" (pp. 33–34).

As will be further elaborated in the next chapter, in the interaction of members in forming an in-group a set of standards or norms invariably arises to regulate the activities of the group as a whole and of the individual members, and to set goals and aspirations for them. For example, the following observation reported by Whyte shows how sexual behavior is regulated by the prevalent norms of the group.[4]

The incest taboo operates in Cornerville, as elsewhere, to prohibit access to females of certain specified familial ties. While marriages may be contracted beyond these incest limits, the corner-boy code also prohibits nonmarital access to relatives who are not blood relations (for example, the brother-in-law's cousin) and to relatives of friends. A corner boy described such a case to me. He was careful to explain that his friend, the girl's cousin, knew that she was a "lay" and would have been glad to have him enjoy himself. Furthermore, the girl was chasing after him so that she was practically forcing the sex relationship upon him. When he was about to have intercourse, he thought of his friend, and, as he says, "I couldn't do a thing." It is only with an outsider, with someone who is not related to him or to a friend, that the corner boy feels free to have sexual relations (p. 28).

The standards are being continually defined in action and in group discussion. The corner boys are continually talking over the girls that they know and others that they have observed in terms of all these categories. Consequently, a high degree of consensus tends to arise in placing the individual girl in her position in each category. The men then know how they are supposed to act in each case; and the observer, equipped with this conceptual scheme, is able to predict how, as a general rule, the men will attempt to act (p. 29).

Disintegration of the Group

Groups, especially spontaneously formed ones, are not fixed, immutable entities. Almost constantly factors from within the

[4] W. F. Whyte, A slum sex code, *Amer. J. Sociol.*, 1943, 49, 24–31.

group (such as friction between members over status, the lack of fulfillment of expectations especially on the part of those who are in higher positions, dominance of individual motives over group norms, etc.) and from without (e.g., the impact of other groups and of society at large) tend to break down the grouping.

The "getting settled down" of group members (particularly the high-ranking ones) in other groupings and positions not compatible with the preoccupations of the group is the major factor in the disintegration of the gang. The "settling down" may be a result of getting married, or of obtaining a steady job with its own opposite demands, or of holding a position in the hierarchy of society at large. The decisive effect of settling down in some such way has been amply elaborated in the writings of Thrasher, Clifford Shaw, Whyte, and others. This again indicates in a negative way the function that the spontaneously formed group serves in the life of individual members. The group gave its members a feeling of belongingness and security, among other benefits. When these are achieved elsewhere, the identification with the informal gang drops away. But as long as settling down is not achieved elsewhere, no amount of preaching and punishment can change group affiliation or activities. A great bulk of evidence could be cited to support this.

In the case of the Nortons, disintegration came when the leader suddenly let the boys down. Doc, the leader, was running for an office with the knowledge and the enthusiastic support of all the Nortons. Without the knowledge of his boys, who were doing their level best for his election, Doc announced abruptly one day his withdrawal from the contest. This was a clear case of letting down the boys who were looking up to him.

"The news of Doc's withdrawal hit the Nortons with devastating effect" (p. 40). Their faith in him was shaken. "When a corner-boy leader mobilizes his friends and arouses their enthusiasm in the support of a candidate and then the candidate suddenly withdraws, the group suffers a serious let-down. The leader has committed his group to the wrong man, and his prestige suffers. The candidate is suspected of having sold out his friends, of having made a bargain with another politician whereby he capitalizes upon their support in order to gain some material advantage." [5] In short, the shocking effect is proportional to the level of expectation—the higher the expectation, the greater is the reaction when the expected course of action is violated. Doc was no longer the leader of the Nortons; he was not even in a position to discuss politics. He lost his magic and became a nobody, though he continued to hang around as an unattached individual.

The Nortons thereupon disintegrated as a group unit. Some of the boys formed a new gang, this time crystallized around a new leader, Angelo. One night, Doc happened to be in the hangout of Angelo and his boys—the new group. Doc suggested to some of them, among them his former lieutenants, that they go some place together. His word carried no weight. The boys answered separately that they preferred to hang around with Angelo. (But the fate of the new gang is not our concern here.)

Doc was prompted to reach his precipitate decision by the demands of the situations outside of his group to which he exposed himself by his candidacy in the main current of sociopolitical life. As Whyte pointed out, one cannot be a good member of the informal groups in Cornerville and of the respectable groups outside them at the same time. The two come into conflict, with subsequent reverberations on the individual. For the two worlds (even two functionally related in the whole socio-economic setup) are not harmoniously integrated. It is tough, especially on a sensitive man like Doc. We shall briefly touch on the effects of such outside influences.

The Impact of Functionally Related Out-Groups and Situations

No matter how well structured a group is, no matter how strongly it influences the identifications and loyalties of the individual members, *the psychology of groups is doomed to remain academic if the factors almost constantly impinging from the general social setting are not included in the study of it.* Only by considering the impact of the general social setup in which these group formations operate (or any group formation, for that matter) can we hope to do justice to the total situation. Other-

[5] W. F. Whyte, *Street Corner Society,* p. 41.

wise insistence on the inclusion of major features of the total
situation will not promote this excellent methodological stand
except by paying it lip service.

As pointed out by many sociologists, the rise of various types
of gangs in the cities is due (in Clifford Shaw's words) to "processes more or less common to American cities." Further evidence from the Cornerville group shows that the main activities
it was engaged in (e.g., bowling, baseball, taking girls out in
automobiles, political campaigns, etc.) are characteristically
American activities. This is so in spite of the fact that this
particular group happened to belong to an Italian ethnic group
in an Italian slum district and was regarded with considerable
aloofness and discrimination by the established and respectable
people in the old New England city.

In the Cornerville slum itself (even though considered by
other districts an area of chaos and confusion), the social life is
hierarchically organized with a minority of "big shots" and a
great majority of little fellows. And our Street Corner Boys
(Nortons) stem from the bottom stratum of working people.
During the depression when the group membership was at
its height most of the members were either totally unemployed
or only partially employed. There are innumerable other boys'
gangs of their class and of higher classes, up to college boys and
their clubs. The Settlement House on the Nortons' street is
above their social level. As Long John (one of the Nortons from
the lowest level of society) remarked during a short period
when they frequented the Settlement House, even it represents
an exclusive set: "I think that everybody that goes in there
thinks they're a little better than the next fellow" (p. 27).

The encounter of the Corner Boys with a group of girls (The
Aphrodite Club) who ranked socially a little higher illustrates
neatly how sex motives directed to females higher in the social
scale act as factors disruptive of group unity. Education, good
manners, and appearance had great value in the eyes of these
girls. They were anxious to make friends with the regular boys
of the Settlement House, whose position was a little higher than
their own. Finally, after considerable discussion, the Norton
boys created a situation which enabled them to meet the girls
in a group. For a short period the association with the girls was

the chief preoccupation of the boys. Then the top members began to worry that living up to the girls, preoccupation with them, and the jealousy they might cause between the boys would disrupt their unity. The top members went to work to get their group separated from the girls' group. After much friction and effort, they succeeded. The group regained its solidarity but not without a loss. A few of the boys remained loyal to the girls, and their place in the Corner group became "rather tenuous."

As we have seen, it was the impact of the larger social setting which brought about the ultimate disintegration of this group. The picture is concisely drawn by Whyte:

No politician in Cornerville can be successful without the support of corner boys, and many corner-boy leaders enter politics. The corner-boy leader performs some of the politician's functions for his followers. He looks after their interests and speaks for them in contacts with outsiders. Yet there are a number of things he cannot do. He cannot get them political jobs or favors unless he subordinates himself and his group to some politician. *It frequently occurs to him and his followers to ask themselves why the leader should have to subordinate himself.* He feels that the politicians have neglected the people's interests. His friends try to persuade him to enter the contest. If he has any capacity for public speaking, their urgings will be hard to resist. He will begin to extend his contacts so that he moves in wider and more influential social circles.

In his first campaign he simply tries to prove that he has enough support to be taken seriously. When he has shown his strength, he is in a position to stage a more vigorous campaign or to make terms with his rivals. If he becomes an important figure, he will be offered money or perhaps even a political job if he will drop out of the contest and support another politician. *If he accepts, his followers feel that he has "sold out," and it is difficult for him to continue as a political figure of any prominence.* He may be able to retain some personal following if he is able to do favors for the boys, but he will no longer have a chance to win an election.

If he refuses to compromise himself and continues to run for office, *the politician must find a way of financing his campaigns. Furthermore, he is required by the nature of his position to spend a great deal of money that he need not spend as a private citizen.* Whenever a local organization gives any sort of entertainment, he is expected to contribute an advertisement for the program book or to buy a number of tickets.

People know that the politician cannot afford to turn them down, and they put him at the top of the "sucker list." He is expected to be a free spender in entertaining his friends and acquaintances. *His corner boys can contribute little to help finance such political activity.* If the politician has built up his own political club, he may obtain a campaign contribution from its treasury, but it is a rare club which has much to spare even for this purpose in the first few years of its existence. *Since a man becomes obligated to those who contribute money to his campaign, the high cost of political activity tends to draw Cornerville politicians away from their original group ties.*[6]

Doc was encouraged by his own boys to run for an office and he was loyally supported by them. But his campaign required money; and he was penniless. He could not bring himself to sell out to outside politicians. His way out of the conflict between the two worlds was to drop out of the contest, saying that there were too many candidates and he had no chance. But his real reason, the conflict between the world of the Corner Boy and the world of the politician, comes out in his own simple description:

The more there were in the fight, the better it was for me. . . . It was the social demands that were too much for me. When I'm down at Jennings' with the boys, somebody comes up to me and wants me to buy a ticket for something. I'm batted out, so I have to refuse. That happens all the time, Bill. . . . As a politician, I'm supposed to go to dances and meetings, and I can't go because I haven't got the money. Fellows come up to me and ask for cards with my name on them and stickers and signs. I can't give them any. . . . You can't be that way in politics. They hold it against you. If you don't buy their ticket, they call you a cheap bastard. They cut you up behind your back. . . . I worried about it. Many nights I walked the floor until three or four in the morning. That was too much, Bill. . . . It was tough getting out. The *paesani* in Welport were all steamed up. So many people had pledged their support to me. And I never asked anybody for his support. Not once! They all came to me. Now that it's all over, I think I could have won. I really think so. . . . Next time I won't get in the fight unless I have $200 in my pocket. But this was really the time for me. In two years—who knows what will happen? . . . Well, it was fun while I was in there (pp. 39–40).

[6] W. F. Whyte, *Street Corner Society*, Chicago: University of Chicago Press, 1943, pp. 209–210 (italics mine).

We shall have more to say about the disintegration or collapse of groups later when we deal with the psychology of social change.

The Effects of Reference Groups on Attitudes and Attitude Change

It has become clear by this time that groups play a major role in shaping attitudes in man. In fact, it may be safe to assert that the formation and effectiveness of attitudes cannot be properly accounted for without relating them to their group matrix. The converging line of evidence coming from sociologists on one hand (Thrasher, Zorbaugh, Clifford Shaw, Whyte, etc.) and from psychologists on the other (Piaget, Healy, etc.) established this fact. The picture presented by the new generation of the Soviet Union—a structurally new, integrated social order, showing a complete reversal of attitudes in millions of individuals—should make this fact incontestable to anyone.

Especially important in this connection is the implication of Hyman's work on the psychology of status. Hyman found that standards people set for themselves are determined largely by reference groups to which they relate themselves and that "within each status dimension an individual's judgment of his status shifts when reference groups are changed." [7]

Many studies have been conducted on changing attitudes by exposing people to material designed to effect a change in some direction. They have at times obtained some results, but by far the most successful in obtaining radical change is T. M. Newcomb's extensive longitudinal study. The subjects were students in a college with a well-integrated liberal trend. The many different phases of college life pulled in the same direction—a direction, in some cases, at variance with the background groups (e.g., family, clique) of the students. As we shall see in a moment, the net result of the study showed that the greater the degree of identification with the college community (i.e., the actual membership group) the greater was the change in attitude. On the other hand, the more the individual was

[7] H. H. Hyman, The psychology of status, *Arch. Psychol.*, 1942, no. 269, p. 49.

under the influence of his previous groups serving as his reference group, the less the attitude change. (Of course, there still
remains one problem: Why did some come to accept the actual
membership group as their reference group, whereas others
stuck to their previous groups? We shall touch upon this problem in Chapter 17.) But it is a fact of utmost importance that
the change or maintenance of attitudes is, to a large extent, a
function of the reference group to which the individual relates
himself.

Before presenting Newcomb's impressive study in his own
words, we should clarify once more the characterization of
reference groups. The individual relates himself, in any society,
to a group or groups; these are his reference groups. Usually,
especially in undifferentiated societies and in rural areas, one's
reference group is his actual group. But diverse groupings in
modern differentiated societies make necessary a delineation
between reference group and membership group. An individual
in a big city actually may belong to diverse groups—his various
membership groups. Or circumstances may be such that he
may live as a part of an actual group (membership group) but
psychologically may relate himself to a different group and
regulate his experience and set his aspirations accordingly. In
such cases, his reference group may be different from his membership group (at least at the time).

Attitude Development as a Function of Reference Groups: The Bennington Study [8]

In a membership group in which certain attitudes are approved (i.e., held by majorities, and conspicuously so by leaders), individuals acquire the approved attitudes to the extent
that the membership group (particularly as symbolized by
leaders and dominant subgroups) serves as a positive point of
reference. The findings of the Bennington study [9] seem to be
better understood in terms of this thesis than any other. The
distinction between membership group and reference group is

---

[8] T. M. Newcomb of the University of Michigan has kindly written up the study
for this book.

[9] T. M. Newcomb, *Personality and Social Change*, New York: Dryden Press, 1943.

a crucial one, in fact, although the original report did not make explicit use of it.

The above statement does not imply that no reference groups other than the membership group are involved in attitude formation; as we shall see, this is distinctly not the case. Neither does it imply that the use of the membership group as reference group necessarily results in adoption of the approved attitudes. It may also result in their rejection; hence the word "positive" in the initial statement. It is precisely these variations in degree and manner of relationship between reference group and membership group which must be known in order to explain individual variations in attitude formation, as reported in this study.

The essential facts about the Bennington membership group are as follows: (1) It was small enough (about 250 women students) so that data could be obtained from every member. (2) It was in most respects self-sufficient; college facilities provided not only the necessities of living and studying, but also a cooperative store, post office and Western Union office, beauty parlor, gasoline station, and a wide range of recreational opportunities. The average student visited the four-mile-distant village once a week, and spent one week-end a month away from the college. (3) It was self-conscious and enthusiastic, in large part because it was new (the study was begun during the first year in which there was a senior class) and because of the novelty and attractiveness of the college's educational plan. (4) It was unusually active and concerned about public issues, largely because the faculty felt that its educational duties included the familiarizing of an oversheltered student body with the implications of a depression-torn America and a war-threatened world. (5) It was relatively homogeneous in respect to home background; tuition was very high, and the large majority of students came from urban, economically privileged families whose social attitudes were conservative.

Most individuals in this total membership group went through rather marked changes in attitudes toward public issues, as noted below. In most cases the total membership group served as the reference group for the changing attitudes. But some individuals changed little or not at all in attitudes

during the four years of the study; attitude persistence was in
some of these cases a function of the membership group as reference group and in some cases it was not. Among those who did
change, moreover, the total membership group sometimes
served as reference group but sometimes it did not. An over
simple theory of "assimilation into the community" thus leaves
out of account some of those whose attitudes did and some of
those whose attitudes did not change; they remain unexplained
exceptions. A theory which traces the impact of other reference
groups as well as the effect of the membership group seems to
account for all cases without exception.

The general trend of attitude change for the total group is
from freshman conservatism to senior non-conservatism (as the
term was commonly applied to the issues toward which attitudes were measured). During the 1936 presidential election,
for example, 62 per cent of the freshmen and only 14 per cent
of the juniors and seniors "voted" for the Republican candidate, 29 per cent of freshmen and 54 per cent of juniors and
seniors for Roosevelt, and 9 per cent of freshmen as compared
with 30 per cent of juniors and seniors for the Socialist or Communist candidates. Attitudes toward nine specific issues were
measured during the four years of the study, and seniors were
less conservative in all of them than freshmen; six of the nine
differences are statistically reliable. These differences are best
shown by a Likert-type scale labeled Political and Economic
Progressivism (PEP) which dealt with such issues as unemployment, public relief, and the rights of organized labor, which
were made prominent by the New Deal. Its odd-even reliability
was about .9, and it was given once or more during each of the
four years of the study to virtually all students. The critical
ratios of the differences between freshmen and juniors-seniors
in four successive years ranged between 3.9 and 6.5; the difference between the average freshman and senior scores of 44
individuals (the entire class that graduated in 1939) gives a
critical ratio of 4.3.

As might be anticipated in such a community, *individual
prestige was associated with non-conservatism.* Frequency of
choice as one of five students "most worthy to represent the
College" at an intercollegiate gathering was used as a measure

of prestige. Nominations were submitted in sealed envelopes by 99 per cent of all students in two successive years, with almost identical results. The non-conservatism of those with high prestige is not merely the result of the fact that juniors and seniors are characterized by both high prestige and non-conservatism; in each class those who have most prestige are least conservative. For example, 10 freshmen receiving 2 to 4 choices had an average PEP score of 64.6 as compared with 72.8 for freshmen not chosen at all (high scores are conservative); eight sophomores chosen 12 or more times had an average score of 63.6 as compared with 71.3 for those not chosen; the mean PEP score of five juniors and seniors chosen 40 or more times was 50.4 and of the 15 chosen 12 to 39 times 57.6, as compared with 69.0 for those not chosen. In each class, those intermediate in prestige are also intermediate in average PEP score.

Such were the attitudinal characteristics of the total membership group, expressed in terms of average scores. Some individuals, however, showed these characteristics in heightened form and others failed to show them at all. An examination of the various reference groups in relation to which attitude change did or did not occur, and of the ways in which they were brought to bear, will account for a large part of such attitude variance.

Information concerning reference groups was obtained both directly, from the subjects themselves, and indirectly, from other students and from teachers. Chief among the indirect procedures was the obtaining of indexes of "community citizenship" by a guess-who technique. Each of 24 students, carefully selected to represent every cross-section and grouping of importance within the community, named three individuals from each of three classes who were reputedly most extreme in each of 28 characteristics related to community citizenship. The relationship between reputation for community identification and non-conservatism is a close one, in spite of the fact that no reference was made to the latter characteristic when the judges made their ratings. A reputation index was computed, based upon the frequency with which individuals were named in five items dealing with identification with the community, minus the number of times they were named in five other items dealing with negative community attitude. Examples of the former items are: "absorbed in college community affairs," and "influenced by community expectations regarding codes, standards, etc."; examples of the latter are: "indifferent to activities of student committees," and "resistant to community expectations regarding codes, standards, etc." The mean senior PEP score of 15 individuals whose index was + 15 or more was 54.4; of 63 whose index was + 4 to − 4, 65.3; and of ten whose index was − 15 or less, 68.2.

To have the reputation of identifying oneself with the community is not the same thing, however, as to identify the community as a reference group for a specific purpose—e.g., in this case, as a point of reference for attitudes toward public issues. In short, the reputation index is informative as to degree and direction of tendency to use the total membership group as a *general* reference group, but not necessarily as a group to which social attitudes are referred. For this purpose information was obtained directly from students.

Informal investigation had shown that whereas most students were aware of the marked freshman-to-senior trend away from conservatism, a few (particularly among the conservatives) had little or no awareness of it. Obviously, those not aware of the dominant community trend could not be using the community as a reference group for an attitude. (It does not follow, of course, that all those who are aware of it are necessarily using the community as reference group.) A simple measure of awareness was therefore devised. Subjects were asked to respond in two ways to a number of attitude statements taken from the PEP scale: first, to indicate agreement or disagreement (for example, with the statement: "The budget should be balanced before the government spends any money on social security"); and second, to estimate what percentage of freshmen, juniors and seniors, and faculty would agree with the statement. From these responses was computed an index of divergence (of own attitude) from the estimated majority of juniors and seniors. Thus a positive index on the part of a senior indicates the degree to which her own responses are more conservative than those of her classmates, and a negative index the degree to which they are less conservative. Those seniors whose divergence index more or less faithfully reflects the true difference between own and class attitude may (or may not) be using the class as an attitude reference group; those whose divergence indexes represent an exaggerated or minimized version of the true relationship between own and class attitude are clearly not using the class as an attitude reference group, or if so, only in a fictitious sense. (For present purposes the junior-senior group may be taken as representative of the entire student body, since it is the group which "sets the tone" of the total membership group.)

These data were supplemented by direct information obtained in interviews with seniors in three consecutive classes, just prior to graduation. Questions were asked about resemblance between own attitudes and those of class majorities and leaders, about parents' attitudes and own resemblance to them, about any alleged "social pressure to become liberal," about probable reaction if the dominant college influence had been conservative instead of liberal, etc. Abundant information was also available from the college Personnel Office and from the college psychiatrist. It was not possible to combine all of these sources of information into intensive studies of each individual, but complete data were assembled for (roughly) the most conservative and least conservative sixths of three consecutive graduating classes. The 24 non-conservative and 19 conservative seniors thus selected for intensive study were classified according to their indexes of conservative divergence and of community reputation. Thus eight sets of seniors were identified, all individuals within each set having in common similar attitude scores, similar reputations for community identification, and similar degrees of awareness (based upon divergence index) of own attitude position relative to classmates. The following descriptions of these eight sets of seniors will show that there was a characteristic pattern of relationship between membership group and reference group within each of the sets.

1. *Conservatives, reputedly negativistic, aware of their own relative conservatism.* Four of the five are considered stubborn or resistant by teachers (all five, by student judges). Three have prestige scores of 0, scores of the other two being about average for their class. Four of the five are considered by teachers or psychiatrist, or by both, to be overdependent upon one or both

parents. All of the four who were interviewed described *their major hopes*, on entering college, *in terms of social rather than academic prestige;* all four felt that they had been defeated in this aim. The following verbatim quotations are illustrative:

E2: "Probably the feeling that (my instructors) didn't accept me led me to reject their opinions." (She estimates classmates as being only moderately less conservative than herself, but faculty as much less so.)

G32: "I wouldn't care to be intimate with those so-called liberal student leaders." (*She claims to be satisfied with a small group of friends.* She is chosen as friend, in a sociometric questionnaire responded to by all students, only twice, and reciprocates both choices; both are conservative students.)

F22: "I wanted to disagree with all the noisy liberals, but I was afraid and I couldn't. *So I built up a wall inside me against what they said. I found I couldn't compete, so I decided to stick to my father's ideas. For at least two years I've been insulated against all college influences.*" (She is chosen but once as a friend, and does not reciprocate that choice.)

Q10: (who rather early concluded that she had no chance of social success in college) "It hurt me at first, but now I don't give a damn. *The things I really care about are mostly outside the college.* I think radicalism symbolizes the college for me more than anything else." (Needless to say, she has no use for radicals.)

For these four individuals (and probably for the fifth also) the community serves as reference group in a *negative* sense, and the home-and-family group in a positive sense. Thus their conservatism is dually reinforced.

2. *Conservatives, reputedly negativistic, unaware of their own relative conservatism.* All five are described by teachers, as well as by Guess-Who judges, to be stubborn or resistant. Four have prestige scores of 0, and the fifth a less than average score. Each reciprocated just one friendship choice. Four are considered insecure in social relationships, and all five are regarded as extremely dependent upon parents. In interviews four describe with considerable intensity, and the fifth with more moderation, pre-college experiences of rebuff, ostracism, or isolation, and all describe their hopes, on entering college, in terms of making friends or avoiding rebuff rather than in terms of seeking pres-

tige. All five felt that their (rather modest) aims had met with good success. Each of the five denies building up any resistance to the acceptance of liberal opinions (but two add that they would have resented any such pressure, if felt). Three believe that only small, special groups in the college have such opinions, while the other two describe themselves as just going their own way, *paying no attention to anything but their own little circles and their college work*. Typical quotations follow:

Q47: " I'm a perfect middle-of-the-roader, neither enthusiast nor critic. I'd accept anything if they just let me alone . . . I've made all the friends I want." (Only one of her friendship choices is reciprocated.)

Q19: " *In high school I was always thought of as my parents' daughter.* I never felt really accepted for myself . . . I wanted to make my own way here, socially, but independence from my family has never asserted itself in other ways." (According to Guess-Who ratings, she is highly resistant to faculty authority.)

L12: " What I most wanted was to get over being a scared bunny . . . I always resent doing the respectable thing just because it's the thing to do, but I didn't realize I was so different, politically, from my classmates. At least I agree with the few people I ever talk to about such matters." (Sociometric responses place her in a small, conservative group.)

Q81: " I hated practically all my school life before coming here. I had the perfect inferiority complex, and I pulled out of school social life—out of fear. I didn't intend to repeat that mistake here. . . . I've just begun to be successful in winning friendships, and I've been blissfully happy here." (She is described by teachers as " pathologically belligerent "; she receives more than the average number of friendship choices, but reciprocates only one of them.)

For these five individuals, who are negativistic in the sense of being near-isolates rather than rebels, the community does not serve as reference group for public attitudes. To some extent, their small friendship groups serve in this capacity, but in the main they still refer such areas of their lives to the home-and-family group. They are too absorbed in their own pursuits to use the total membership group as a reference group for most other purposes, too.

3. *Conservatives, not reputedly negativistic, aware of their own*

relative conservatism. Three of the five are described by teachers as "cooperative" and "eager," and none as stubborn or resistant. Four are above average in prestige. Four are considered by teachers or by Guess-Who raters, or both, to retain very close parental ties. All four who were interviewed had more or less definite ambitions for leadership on coming to college, and all felt that they had been relatively successful—though, in the words of one of them, none ever attained the "really top-notch positions." All four are aware of conflict between parents and college community in respect to public attitudes, and all quite consciously decided to "string along" with parents, feeling self-confident of holding their own in college in spite of being atypical in this respect. Sample quotations follow:

Q73: "*I'm all my mother has in the world. It's considered intellectually superior here to be liberal or radical. This puts me on the defensive,* as I refuse to consider my mother beneath me intellectually, as so many other students do. Apart from this, I have loved every aspect of college life." (A popular girl, many of whose friends are among the non-conservative college leaders.)

Q78: "*I've come to realize how much my mother's happiness depends on me, and the best way I can help her is to do things with her at home as often as I can.* This has resulted in my not getting the feel of the college in certain ways, and I know my general conservatism is one of those ways. But it has not been important enough to me to make me feel particularly left out. If you're genuine and inoffensive about your opinions, no one really minds here if you remain conservative." (Another popular girl, whose friends were found among many groups.)

F32: "*Family against faculty has been my struggle here.* As soon as I felt really secure here I decided not to let the college atmosphere affect me too much. Every time I've tried to rebel against my family I've found out how terribly wrong I am, and so I've naturally kept to my parents' attitudes." (While not particularly popular, she shows no bitterness and considerable satisfaction over her college experience.)

Q35: "I've been aware of a protective shell against radical ideas. When I found several of my best friends getting that way, I either had to go along or just shut out that area entirely. I couldn't respect myself if I had changed my opinions just for that reason, and so I almost deliberately lost interest—really, *it was out of fear of losing my friends.*" (A very popular girl, with no trace of bitterness, who is not considered too dependent upon parents.)

For these five the total membership group does not serve as reference group in respect to public attitudes, but does so serve for most other purposes. At some stage in their college careers the conflict between college community and home and family as reference group for public attitudes was resolved in favor of the latter.

4. *Conservatives, not reputedly negativistic, not aware of their own relative conservatism.* All four are consistently described by teachers as conscientious and cooperative; three are considered overdocile and uncritical of authority. All are characterized by feelings of inferiority. All are low in prestige, two receiving scores of 0; all are low in friendship choices, but reciprocate most of these few choices. Two are described as in conflict about parental authority, and two as dependent and contented. All four recall considerable anxiety as to whether they would fit into the college community; all feel that they have succeeded better than they had expected. Sample statements from interviews follow:

D22: "I'd like to think like the college leaders, but I'm not bold enough and I don't know enough. So the college trend means little to me; I didn't even realize how much more conservative I am than the others. *I guess my family influence has been strong enough to counterbalance the college influence.*" (This girl was given to severe emotional upsets, and according to personnel records, felt " alone and helpless except when with her parents.")

M12: " It isn't that I've been resisting any pressure to become liberal. The influences here didn't matter enough to resist, I guess. *All that's really important that has happened to me occurred outside of college,* and so I never became very susceptible to college influences." (*Following her engagement to be married, in her second year, she had " practically retired " from community life.*)

Q68: "If I'd had more time here I'd probably have caught on to the liberal drift here. But I've been horribly busy making money and trying to keep my college work up. *Politics and that sort of thing I've always associated with home instead of with the college.*" (A " town girl " of working-class parentage.)

Q70: " Most juniors and seniors, if they really *get excited about their work, forget about such community enthusiasms as sending tele-*

grams to Congressmen. It was so important to me to be accepted, I mean intellectually, *that I naturally came to identify myself in every way with the group which gave me this sort of intellectual satisfaction.*" (One of a small group of science majors, nearly all conservative, who professed no interests other than science and who were highly self-sufficient socially.)

For none of the four was the total membership group a reference group for public attitudes. Unlike the non-negativistic conservatives who are aware of their relative conservatism, they refer to the total membership group for few if any other purposes. Like the negativistic conservatives who are unaware of their relative conservatism, their reference groups for public attitudes are almost exclusively those related to home and family.

5. *Non-conservatives, reputedly community-identified, aware of their relative non-conservatism.* Each of the seven is considered highly independent by teachers, particularly in intellectual activities; all but one are referred to as meticulous, perfectionist, or overconscientious. Four are very high in prestige, two high, and one average; all are "good group members," and all but one a "leader." None is considered overdependent upon parents. All have come to an understanding with parents concerning their "liberal" views; five have "agreed to differ," and the other two describe one or both parents as "very liberal." All take their public attitudes seriously, in most cases expressing the feeling that they have bled and died to achieve them. Interview excerpts follow:

B72: "*I bend in the direction of community expectation*—almost more than I want to. I constantly have to check myself to be sure it's real self-conviction and not just social respect." (An outstanding and deeply respected leader.)

M42: "My family has always been liberal, but the influences here made me go further, and for a while I was pretty far left. Now I'm pretty much in agreement with my family again, but it's my own and it means a lot. It wouldn't be easy for me to have friends who are very conservative." (Her friendship choices are exclusively given to non-conservatives.)

E72: "I had been allowed so much independence by my parents that I needed desperately to identify myself with an institution with which I could conform conscientiously. Bennington was perfect. I drank up everything the college had to offer, including social attitudes, though not uncritically. I've become active in radical groups and constructively critical of them." (Both during and after college she worked with CIO unions.)

H32: " I accepted liberal attitudes here because *I had always secretly felt that my family was narrow and intolerant, and because such attitudes had prestige value.* It was all part of my generally expanding personality—*I had never really been part of anything before.* I don't accept things without examining things, however, and I was sure I meant it before I changed." (One of those who has " agreed to differ " with parents.)

Q43: " It didn't take me long to see that liberal attitudes had prestige value. But all the time I felt inwardly superior to persons who want public acclaim. Once I had arrived at a feeling of personal security, I could see that it wasn't important—it wasn't enough. *So many people have no security at all. I became liberal at first because of its prestige value.* I remain so because the problems around which my liberalism centers are important. What I want now is to be effective in solving the problems." (Another conspicuous leader, active in and out of college in liberal movements.)

The total membership clearly serves as reference group for these individuals' changing attitudes, but by no means as the only one. For those whose parents are conservative, parents represent a negative reference group, from whom emancipation was gained via liberal attitudes. And for several of them the college community served as a bridge to outside liberal groups as points of reference.

6. *Non-conservatives, reputedly community-identified, not aware of their own relative non-conservatism.* The word "enthusiastic" appears constantly in the records of each of these six. All are considered eager, ambitious, hard-working, and anxious to please. Four are very high in prestige, the other two about average. None is considered overdependent upon parents, and only two are known to have suffered any particular conflict in achieving emancipation. Each one came to college with ambitions for leadership, and each professes extreme satisfaction with her college experience. Sample quotations follow:

Qx: " Every influence I felt tended to push me in the liberal direction: my under-dog complex, *my need to be independent of my parents, and my anxiousness to be a leader here.*"

Q61: " I met a whole body of new information here; I took a deep breath and plunged. When I talked about it at home my family began to treat me as if I had an adult mind. *Then too, my new opinions gave me the reputation here of being open-minded and capable of change.* I think I could have got really radical but I found it wasn't the way to get prestige here." (She judges most of her classmates to be as non-conservative as herself.)

Q72: " I take everything hard, and so of course I reacted hard to all the attitudes I found here. I'm 100% enthusiastic about Bennington, and that includes liberalism (but not radicalism, though I used to think so). Now I know that you can't be an *extremist if you're really devoted to an institution,* whether it's a labor union or a college." (A conspicuous leader who, like most of the others in this set of six, *judges classmates to be only slightly more conservative than herself.*)

Q63: " *I came to college to get away from my family,* who never had any respect for my mind. Becoming radical meant thinking for myself and, figuratively, thumbing my nose at my family. *It also meant intellectual identification with the faculty and students that I most wanted to be like.*" (She has always felt oppressed by parental respectability and sibling achievements.)

Q57: " It's very simple. *I was so anxious to be accepted that I accepted the political complexion of the community here.* I just couldn't stand out against the crowd unless I had many friends and strong support." (Not a leader, but many close friends among leaders and non-conservatives.)

For these six, like the preceding seven, the membership group serves as reference group for public affairs. They differ from the preceding seven chiefly in that they are less sure of themselves and are careful "not to go too far." Hence they tend to repudiate "radicalism," and to judge classmates as only slightly less conservative than themselves.

7. *Non-conservatives, not reputedly community-identified, aware of own relative non-conservatism.* Each of the six is described as highly independent and critical-minded. Four are consistently reported as intellectually outstanding, and the other two occasionally so. All describe their ambitions on coming to college in intellectual rather than in social terms. Four of the five who were interviewed stated that in a conservative college they would be "even more radical than here." Two are slightly above average in prestige, two below average, and two have zero

scores. Three have gone through rather severe battles in the process of casting off what they regard as parental shackles; none is considered overdependent upon parents. Sample interview excerpts follow:

Q7: "*All my life I've resented the protection of governesses and parents.* What I most wanted here was the intellectual approval of teachers and the more advanced students. Then I found you can't be reactionary and be intellectually respectable." (Her traits of independence became more marked as she achieved academic distinction.)

Q21: "I simply got filled with new ideas here, and the only possible formulation of all of them was to adopt a radical approach. *I can't see my own position in the world in any other terms. The easy superficiality with which so many prestige-hounds here get 'liberal' only forced me to think it out more intensely.*" (A highly gifted girl, considered rather aloof.)

C32: "*I started rebelling against my pretty stuffy family before I came to college.* I felt apart from freshmen here, because I was older. Then I caught on to faculty attempts to undermine prejudice. I took sides with the faculty immediately, against the immature freshmen. I crusaded about it. *It provided just what I needed by way of family rebellion*, and bolstered up my self-confidence, too." (A very bright girl, regarded as sharp tongued and a bit haughty.)

J24: "*I'm easily influenced by people whom I respect*, and the people who rescued me when I was down and out, intellectually, gave me a radical intellectual approach; they included both teachers and advanced students. *I'm not rebelling against anything.* I'm just doing what I had to do to stand on my own feet intellectually." (Her academic work was poor as a freshman, but gradually became outstanding.)

For these six students it is not the total membership group, but dominant subgroups (faculty, advanced students) which at first served as positive reference groups, and for many of them the home group served as a negative point of reference. Later, they developed extra-college reference groups (left-wing writers, etc.). In a secondary sense, however, the total membership group served as a negative point of reference—i.e., they regarded their non-conservatism as a mark of personal superiority.

8. *Non-conservatives not reputedly community-identified, not*

aware of own relative non-conservatism. Each of the five is considered hard-working, eager and enthusiastic but (especially during the first year or two) unsure of herself and too dependent upon instructors. They are "good citizens," but in a distinctly retiring way. Two are above average in prestige, and the other three much below average. None of the five is considered over-dependent upon parents; two are known to have experienced a good deal of conflict in emancipating themselves. All regard themselves as "pretty average persons," with strong desire to conform; they describe their ambitions in terms of social acceptance instead of social or intellectual prestige. Sample excerpts follow:

E22: "*Social security is the focus of it all with me.* I became steadily less conservative as long as I was *needing to gain in personal security, both with students and with faculty.* I developed some resentment against a few extreme radicals who don't really represent the college viewpoint, and that's why I changed my attitudes so far and no further." (A girl with a small personal following, otherwise not especially popular.)

D52: "*Of course there's social pressure here to give up your conservatism.* I'm glad of it, because for me this became the *vehicle for achieving independence from my family.* So changing my attitudes has gone hand in hand with two *very important things: establishing my own independence and at the same time becoming a part of the college organism.*" (She attributes the fact that her social attitudes changed, while those of her younger sister, also at the college, did not, to the fact that she had greater need both of family independence and of group support.)

Q6: "I was ripe for developing liberal or even radical opinions because so many of my friends at home were doing the same thing. So it was really wonderful that I could agree with all the people I respected here and the same time move in the direction that my home friends were going." (A girl characterized by considerable personal instability at first, but showing marked improvement.)

Qy: "I think my change of opinions has given me *intellectual and social self-respect at the same time.* I used to be too timid for words, and I never had an idea of my own. As I gradually became more successful in my work and made more friends, I came to feel that it didn't matter so much whether I agreed with my parents. It's all part of the feeling that I really belong here." (Much other evidence confirms this; she was lonely and pathetic at first, but really belonged later.)

These five provide the example *par excellence* of individuals who came to identify themselves with "the community" and whose attitudes changed *pari passu* with the growing sense of identity. Home-and-family groups served as supplementary points of reference, either positive or negative. To varying degrees, subgroups within the community served as focal points of reference. But, because of *their need to be accepted, it was primarily the membership group as such which served as reference group for these five.*

Summary

In this community, as presumably in most others, all individuals belong to the total membership group, but such membership is not necessarily a point of reference for every form of social adaptation, e.g., for acquiring attitudes toward public issues. *Such attitudes, however, are not acquired in a social vacuum. Their acquisition is a function of relating oneself to some group or groups, positively or negatively.* In many cases (perhaps in all) the referring of social attitudes to one group negatively leads to referring them to another group positively, or vice versa, so that the attitudes are dually reinforced.

An individual is, of course, "typical" in respect to attitudes if the total membership group serves as a positive point of reference for that purpose, but "typicality" may also result from the use of other reference groups. It does not follow from the fact that an individual is "atypical" that the membership group does not serve for reference purposes; it may serve as negative reference group. Even if the membership group does not serve as reference group at all (as in the case of conservatives in this community who are unaware of the general freshman-to-senior trend), it cannot be concluded that attitude development is not a function of belonging to the total membership group. The unawareness of such individuals is itself a resultant adaptation of particular individuals to a particular membership group. The fact that such individuals continue to refer attitudes toward public issues primarily to home-and-family groups is,

in part at least, a result of the kind of community in which they
have membership.

In short, the Bennington findings seem to support the thesis
that, in a community characterized by certain approved attitudes, the individual's attitude development is a function of the
way in which he relates himself both to the total membership
group and to reference group or groups.

7.

The Formation of Group
Standards or Norms

EVERY SOCIAL GROUP, SMALL OR LARGE, WITH SOME DEGREE of in-group and out-group delineation, has an organization defining the roles (statuses and functions) of individual members, has attitudes toward persons in the in-group and toward those in out-groups, and requires certain conformities in action and aspiration from the individuals who belong. All this is determined or regulated by a set of standards or norms of the group. In short, wherever we see a group which is organized to some degree, we see a set of norms shaping and regulating the attitudes and behavior of the members and of the group itself. We shall deal with the effects of group norms on experience and behavior in the next chapters.

In social groups which are already organized (such as family, church, school, union), the new member becomes a good member by assimilating the already existing standards or norms of the group. (This, of course, does not preclude the possibility that he may later effectively participate in changing them.)

But when individuals unite *to act together* in a situation brought about by common motives, interests, or deprivations, or by some turn of events, the interaction tends to produce some sort of new group formation which may be temporary or lasting, depending on the situation. In the process of group formation certain norms are standardized as the common property of the group, henceforth prescribing relative roles for the individual members at least in matters which have been of concern in group interaction. Children's play groups, adolescent cliques, gangs in large cities, and formations of a group of individuals in social isolation, are concrete illustrations of the point. In the preceding two chapters we have given some examples of such spontaneous group formations, and in the last part of this chapter we shall present a few more illustrations.

In short, there is an invariable tendency for group inter-action to give rise to a set of standards or norms in matters that involve the group. Once such a set of standards or norms arises, it becomes the common property of the group. Hence-forth it sets the tempo, the characteristic features of the group in action, loyalty, and other aspects of conformity.

Many sociologists have recognized this fact and theorized about it. It was argued in some sociological accounts that the behavior of groups (with their new qualities, their supra-individual organizational features, and new products) was different from the behavior of the individuals and, hence, that group action and group quality were governed by altogether different, supra-psychological principles.

Major research developments during the last decade or so did much to break down this conception of a dichotomy in the principles governing individual behavior and group behavior. We have seen representative samples of the converging lines of research in the last two chapters.

It is becoming a recognized fact that the emergence of dif-ferent or new qualities—structural transformations—occurs not only on the level of human group interaction, but also on all levels of physical, biological, and historical events. In particular the work of Gestalt psychologists on perception and in other fields has helped to establish the fact of structural properties of wholes, interdependence of parts, qualitative transformations with the coming of new factors into the situation. For example, it has been shown that the qualitatively distinct character of perception of form, melody, rhythm, meaning, is not derived from the distinct properties of the parts in isolation, but that (on the contrary) the parts derive their quality from their functional membership in the whole. The delineation and deter-mination of figure-ground properties,[1] transposition effects in melody, etc., all go to establish this conclusion.[2] In short, the emergent qualities and products that unmistakably appear in

---

[1] For an example, see pp. 214 f.

[2] For authoritative treatments of the subject see, for example, W. Köhler, *Gestalt Psychology*, New York: Liveright, 1929; and M. Wertheimer, in W. D. Ellis (ed.), *A Sourcebook of Gestalt Psychology*, New York: Harcourt, Brace, 1938.

group situations are embedded in the basic psychology of the individual.

Another important general fact embedded in the basic psychology of the individual in any situation (individual or group, laboratory or everyday life) is that reactions take place within reference frames in which certain reference points stand out. The concept of reference frame is not an abstract notion. It simply designates the well-known fact that reaction to stimulus is not a discrete affair, peculiar to this or that factor, but that it is the outcome of the functional interdependence of all factors (internal and external) operative at a given moment. The special mention of reference points in such a functional interdependent whole is made because they are outstanding features determining or modifying the general character of the frame.

For example, when we judge distances, magnitudes, weights, etc., we do so within certain reference frames or scales. A distance is far or near, a magnitude is big or small, a weight is heavy or light, with all gradations between the limiting points, according to the frames or scales we are using or are *forced to use* (usually by the compellingness of the objective situation) at the given moment. These are some simple examples of reference frames (scales). Certain salient, compelling features, end points, standards, etc., in the situation determine or modify the frame or scale. The experiences of far, near, late, early, for example, have hardly any meaning without reference to some consciously or unconsciously operating end points. These are some samples of reference points (or anchoring points). It has been shown time and again in the laboratory that with the shifts of reference points, experiences in question are correspondingly altered.

A few concrete illustrations from everyday life may make the point more real. A ten-story building around Rockefeller Center in New York seems to be a dwarf; a similar building in a small town may give a towering impression. To a peasant in Asia, $300 income a year is a sizable fortune, whereas to a vacationing banker in a large concern, it is nothing. It has been found by actual observation that what is consistently heavy to a professor, who is not used to lifting weights, is not so heavy to a person who lifts them in his daily work. These examples can be multiplied almost indefinitely.[3]

The "organization" of experience in the direction of definite structures seems to be a primary psychological principle (Köhler). Whether or not there already are definite structures and definite standards—outstanding features as reference (anchoring) points in the external situation—individuals form their reference frames and points in their reaction to new situations.

In cases in which the objective stimulus situation is well structured, the psychological reference frames and points are compellingly determined by it in some way. The reaction (perceptual, judgmental, etc.) of the individual is regulated by some reference frame or points. But in unstructured ("indeterminate," vague, ill-defined) situations, internal and internalized factors (motives, values, norms, group pressure, prestige, etc.) act as major factors to determine or alter the reaction. If, for example, a formal standard for judging a graduated series of stimuli (e.g., magnitudes, weights, etc.) is lacking, end points may be (in fact are, as the evidence shows) chosen as major reference (anchoring) points in relation to which other stimuli in the series are judged. A vague and ill-defined situation becomes a plastic canvas on which our preoccupations, motives, and stereotyped attitudes block in the picture. In the findings of investigators using such vague stimulus material (e.g., ink blots), we find innumerable demonstrations of this fundamental psychological tendency. The work of Luchins [4] and others shows that the greater the vagueness of the stimulus field, the greater the influence of internal (e.g., motives) and internalized factors (social attitudes, identifications, ego-involvements, etc.) as well as the effects of suggestion, prestige, social pressure, propaganda. This conclusion is not a discovery of academic psychologists. Fishing in muddy waters has almost

[3] For a fuller treatment and presentation of evidence on reference frames and points, see M. Sherif, *The Psychology of Social Norms*, New York: Harper, 1936, chap. 3; M. Sherif and H. Cantril, The psychology of attitudes, *Psychol. Rev.*, 1945, 52, 306–314.

[4] A. S. Luchins, On agreement with another's judgment, *J. Abn. & Soc. Psychol.*, 1944, 39, 97–111; A. S. Luchins, Social influences on perceptions of complex drawings, *J. Soc. Psychol.*, 1945, 21, 257–273.

always been a flourishing trade for politician and demagogue. Also, the unstable, fluid, and critical situations which usually occur as a consequence of depression, mass deprivation, and misery have been fertile ground for the revolutionary. A treatment of this problem will be our main concern in Chapter 16.

On the basis of this sketchy summary of some basic psychological facts, we can proceed to the specific problem of the chapter. It is in unstable conditions, in situations of group interaction which lack an established organization and established norms, that new group structures and new standards or norms arise. A clear-cut demonstration of this tendency will help to show the basic psychological process involved in the rise of group norms, and their effect on the individual participating member once they are adopted by him. In this demonstration our concern is with the main process—not with its manifestation in any concrete issue.

Before showing how the process is built up in the individual —alone and in group situations—clarification of one point is necessary. A situation may be unstructured or vague in general, or in some aspect. If the particular aspect is one of the major concerns of the group in question, it constitutes a plastic component which may be shaped, crystallized, and standardized in this or that way. A good illustration of this is reported by Ernie Pyle in *Here Is Your War*. When the first convoys left England at the time the North African offensive was launched against Hitler, the men on board were kept in the dark as to the *destination* of their journey. They knew they were going into battle service, because other men sailing with them and objects on the boats were clear-cut indications. But the *destination* of their convoy was a matter of conjecture for them. Consequently rumors sprang up which the men came to regard as true until they were contradicted by facts and other rumors. Many men shared these rumors, at least for a short time. One officer in the convoy even experimented with a rumor as to the destination, and it came back to him as he planted it after it went around to other men on board. Ernie Pyle says:

Of all the spots on earth where rumors run wild, I think a convoy trooper must lead, hands down. Scores of rumors a day floated about the ship. We got so we believed them all, or didn't believe any.

It was rumored we would rendezvous with a big convoy from America; that an aircraft carrier had joined us; that we'd hit Gibraltar in six hours, twenty-four hours, two days; that the ship behind us was the *West Point*, the *Mount Vernon*, the *Monterey;* that we were eighty miles off Portugal, and two hundred miles off Bermuda. None of these turned out to be true.

The rumormongering got so rife that one officer made up a rumor to the effect that we were going to Casablanca, and timed it to see just how long it would take to encircle the ship. It came back to him, as cold fact right from the bridge, in just half an hour.[5]

Hypothesis to Be Tested

We have seen that if a reference point is lacking in the external field of stimulation, it is established internally, as the temporal sequence of presentation of stimuli goes on.

Accordingly we raise the problem: What will an individual do when he is placed in an objectively unstable situation in which all basis of comparison, as far as the external field of stimulation is concerned, is absent? In other words, what will he do when the external frame of reference is eliminated, so far as the aspect in which we are interested is concerned? Will he give a hodgepodge of erratic judgments? Or will he establish a point of reference of his own? *Consistent* results in this situation may be taken as the index of a subjectively evolved frame of reference.

We must first study the tendency of the individual, in order to do away with the dualism between "individual psychology" and "social psychology." In this way we can determine the differences between individual responses in the individual situation and in the group situation.

Coming to the social level we can push our problem further. What will a group of people do in the same unstable situation? Will the different individuals in the group give a hodgepodge of judgments? Or will they establish a collective frame of reference? If so, of what sort? If every person establishes a norm, will it be his own and different from the norms of others in the group? Or will there be established a common norm

[5] Ernie Pyle, *Here Is Your War*, New York: The World Publishing Company, 1945; Henry Holt 1943, pp. 7–8 (italics mine).

peculiar to the particular group situation and dependent upon the presence of these individuals and their influence upon one another? If they in time come to perceive the uncertain and unstable situation which they face in common in such a way as to give it some sort of order, if they establish a reference frame and point among themselves, and if this frame of reference is peculiar to the group, *then we may say that this is at least the prototype of the psychological process involved in the formation of a norm in a group.*

The Autokinetic Effect, Its Possibilities for Our Problem

With these considerations clearly in mind, our first task will be to find objectively unstable situations that will permit themselves to be structured in several ways, depending on the character of the subjectively established reference points. From among other possible experimental situations that could be used to test our hypothesis, we chose to use autokinesis in this particular series of experiments.

The conditions that produce the autokinetic effect afford an excellent experimental situation. We can easily get the auto-kinetic effect. In complete darkness, as in a closed unlighted room, or on a cloudy night in the open when there are no lights visible, a single small light seems to move, and it may appear to move erratically in all directions. If you present the point of light repeatedly to a person, he may see the light appearing at different places in the room each time, especially if he does not know the distance between himself and the light. The experimental production of the autokinetic effect is very easy and works without any exceptions, *provided, of course, that the person or the experimenter does not use special devices to destroy the effect.* For in a completely dark room a single point of light *cannot* be localized definitely, because there is nothing in reference to which you can locate it. The effect takes place even when the person looking at the light knows perfectly well that the light is not moving. These are facts which are not subject to controversy; anyone can easily test them for himself. In this situation not only does the stimulating light appear erratic and irregular to the subject, *but at times the person himself feels insecure about his spatial bearing.* This comes out in an especially striking way if he is seated in a chair without a back and is unfamiliar with the position of the experimental room in the building. Under these conditions some subjects report that they are not only confused about the location of the point of light; *they are even confused about the stability of their own position.*

The autokinetic effect is not a new artificial phenomenon invented by the psychologists. It is older than experimental psychology. Since it sometimes appears in the observation of the heavenly bodies, the astronomers had already noticed it and offered theories to explain it.[6]

We studied the influence of such social factors as *suggestion* and the *group situation* on the extent and direction of the perceived movement. The study of the extent of the experienced movement permits a quantitative study for the approach to the formation of norms. We shall therefore report on the extent of movement.

Procedure. We studied the extent of the movement experienced in two situations: first, when *alone*, except for the experimenter—in order to get the reaction of the individual unaffected by other experimentally introduced social factors, and thus to gain a basic notion about the perceptual process under the circumstances; second, when the individual is in a *group situation*—in order to discover modifications brought about by membership in the group.

The subject was introduced into the group situation in one of two ways: He was brought into a group *after* being experimented upon when *alone*. This was done to find out the influence of the group situation after he had an opportunity to react to the situation first in accordance with his own tendencies and had ordered it subjectively in his own way. Or he was *first* introduced to the situation *in the group*, having no previous familiarity with the situation, and was *afterwards* experimented

---

[6] For a concise history of the autokinetic effect as a scientific problem, see H. F. Adams, Autokinetic sensations, *Psychol. Monog.*, 1912, no. 59, 32–44.

Several theories have also been advanced by psychologists to explain the nature of the autokinetic effect. These are immaterial for our present problem. The important fact for us to remember is that the autokinetic effect is produced whenever a visual stimulus object lacks a spatial frame of reference.

upon individually. This was done to find out whether the perceptual order or frame (scale) that might be established in the group situation would continue to determine his reaction to the same situation when faced alone. This last point is crucial for our problem. The others lead up to it and clarify its implications.

The subjects, apparatus, and procedures used will be only briefly outlined here. They are reported in full elsewhere.[7]

The experiments were carried on in dark rooms in the Columbia psychological laboratory. (See Fig. 18.) The subjects were graduate and undergraduate male students at Columbia University and New York University. They were not majoring in psychology and did not know anything about the physical stimulus setup or the purpose of the experiment. There were 19 subjects in the individual experiments; 40 took part in the group experiments.

Individual Experiments. The stimulus light was a tiny point of light seen through a small hole in a metal box. The light was exposed to the subject by the opening of a suitable shutter controlled by the experimenter. The distance between the subject and the light was 5 meters. The observer was seated at a table on which was a telegraph key. The following instructions were given in written form: "When the room is completely dark, I shall give you the signal READY, and then show you a point of light. After a short time the light will start to move. As soon as you see it move, press the key. A few seconds later the light will disappear. Then tell me the distance it moved. Try to make your estimates as accurate as possible." (See Figs. 18 and 19 for the experimental setup.)

These instructions summarize the general procedure of the experiment. A short time after the light was exposed following the READY signal, the subject pressed the key; this produced a faint but audible ticking in the timing apparatus indicating that he had perceived the (autokinetic) movement. The exposure time, after the subject pressed the key to indicate that he had begun to experience the movement, was two seconds in all cases.

[7] M. Sherif, A study of some social factors in perception, *Arch. Psychol.*, 1935, no. 187.

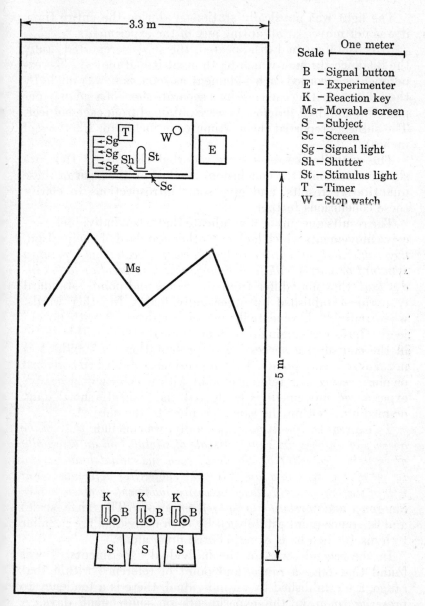

FIG. 18. Plan of the experimental room used in group experiments.

The light was physically stationary during the entire time; it was not moved at all during any of the experiments.

After the light had disappeared, the subject reported orally the distance through which he thought it had moved. The experimenter recorded each judgment as soon as it was made by the subject, writing each one on a separate sheet of a small paper pad. One hundred judgments were obtained from each subject. The subjects reported their estimates in inches (or fractions of inches).

The quantitative results are reported elsewhere.[8] Here we shall present only the conclusions reached on the basis of these quantitative results, and give some introspections to clarify these conclusions further.

The results unequivocally indicate that when individuals perceive movements which lack any other standard of comparison, *they subjectively establish a range of extent (a scale) and a point (a standard or norm) within that range which is peculiar to the individual* (they may differ from the range and point—standard or norm—established by other individuals). In other words, when individuals repeatedly perceive movement with no objective basis for gauging its extent, there develops within them, in the course of a succession of presentations, a standard (a norm or reference point). This subjectively established standard or norm serves as a reference point with which each successive experienced movement is compared and judged—short, long, or medium—within the range peculiar to the subject.

To express the point more generally, we conclude that *in the absence of an objective range or scale of stimuli and an externally given reference point or standard, each individual builds up a range of his own and an internal (subjective) reference point within that range, and each successive judgment is given within that range and in relation to that reference point.* The range (scale) and reference point established by each individual are peculiar to himself when he is experimented upon alone.

In the second series of the individual experiments, it was found that once a *range*, and point of reference within that range, are established by an individual, there is a tendency to preserve them in the experiments on subsequent days. A

8 *Ibid.*, pp. 24, 34–41.

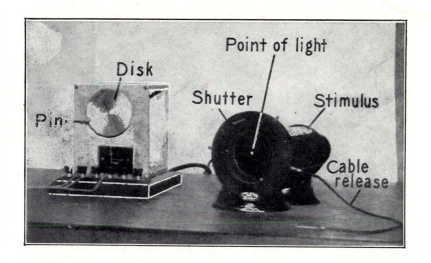

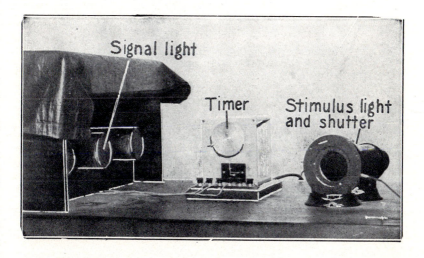

Fig. 19. (Above) Apparatus for individual trials with screen removed. (Below) Apparatus for group experiments with screen removed.

second and third series of 100 judgments each show a median score for a given subject very similar to that found in the first series, but with a reduced variability.

The written reports obtained from every observer at the end of the experiment further corroborate these conclusions. Summaries of the following sort, which are typical, show that the subjects at first found it hard to estimate distance because of the lack of externally given reference points or standards:

"Darkness left no guide for distance."

"It was difficult to estimate the distance the light moved, because of the lack of visible neighboring objects."

"There was no fixed point from which to judge distance."

Other observations indicate that the subjects developed standards of their own in the absence of objective ones:

"Compared with previous distance."

"Used first estimate as standard."

This reveals once more the general psychological tendency to experience things in relation to some frame of reference, as we shall see in our review of related findings in various major fields of psychology. (See pp. 217 ff.)

In the group experiments, this finding of experimental psychology was carried into social psychology, and its operation noted when the individual was in a group situation.

Group Experiments. On the basis of the results, the problem which we must study in the group situation becomes self-evident. To recapitulate, the individual experiences the external field of stimulation in relation to a frame of reference; when such a frame is given in the objective situation, this will usually determine in an important way the structural relationships of the experience—all other parts will be organized as determined or modified by it. But when an objective frame of reference is lacking—when the field of stimulation is unstable, vague, and not well structured—the individual perceives the situation as shaped by his own internally evolved frame of reference. The questions that arise for the experiment in the group situation, then, are the following:

How will the individual members in the group situation perceive the stimulus field? Will there again evolve in each one a range and a standard (norm) within that range which will be peculiar to him, as happened when individuals were experimented on alone?

Or will group influences prevent him from establishing any well-defined range and reference point within that range, and thus spoil his capacity to perceive the uncertain situation in any sort of order?

Or will the individuals in the group act together to establish a range, and a reference point within that range, which are peculiar to the group?

If such a range and reference point are established, what will be the influence of such a group product on the individual member when he subsequently faces the same stimulus situation alone?

These questions represent more or less pure cases. There are, of course, possibilities that lie between.

These questions lead us directly to the psychological basis of social norms. We must admit that we have reduced the process to a very simple form, but the first fundamental psychological problem is the way an individual perceives a stimulus situation. His behavior follows upon this perception rather than upon the bald physical presence of the stimulus. There is no direct and simple correlation between the stimulus and the subsequent behavior, especially on the level of behavior with which we are dealing. A simple perceptual situation is the first requirement for experimental analysis of the problem.

We purposely chose a stimulus situation in which the external factors are unstable enough, within limits, to allow the internal factors to dominate in establishing the main characteristics of organization. This enables us to say that any consistent result in the experience of the individual members of the group, differing from their experience as isolated individuals, is a function of their interaction in the group.

We have already emphasized the fact that we do not face stimulus situations involving other people or even the world of nature around us in an indifferent way; we are charged with certain modes of readiness, certain established norms, which enter to modify our reactions. This important consideration shaped the planning of the group experiments. We studied the differences between the reactions (a) when the individuals first faced the stimulus situation in the group, and (b) when they joined the group after first establishing their individual ranges and norms alone with the experimenter. Accordingly, 20 of the subjects began alone and were then put into groups in subsequent experimental sessions; the other 20 started with group sessions and ended with individual sessions.

This rotation technique enabled us to draw conclusions regarding the following important questions:

How much of his independently established way of reacting to a situation does the individual carry over when facing the same stimulus in a group? How much will he be influenced by his membership in the group after his range and norm have once been established when alone?

How will he experience the situation when alone, after a common range and norm have been established peculiar to the group of which he is a member? Will the common product developed in the group serve as a determining factor when he subsequently faces the same situation *alone?*

The experimental setting was in general the same as in previous experiments. Of course, additional techniques were necessary to handle two or more members of a group at the same time. One major addition was the use of signal lights. The experimenter could not tell from the voice alone who was giving a judgment; so as each subject gave his judgment aloud, he pressed a push button connected with a dim signal light of a particular color by which the experimenter might know who the speaker was. (See Figs. 18 and 19.)

There were eight groups of two subjects each and eight groups of three subjects each. Four groups in each of the two categories started with the individual situation (one whole session for each individual), and then functioned as groups. Four groups in each category started in group situations for the first three sessions on three different days (all members of the group being present) and were then broken up and studied in the individual situation.

In order to make the relation of individual members to one another as natural as possible, within the limits of the experimental setting, the subjects were left free as to the order in which they would give their judgments. In fact, they were told

at the start to give their judgments in random order as they
pleased. Whether the person who speaks first has more influence than the others becomes a study in leadership—which
is a further interesting problem. (Perhaps such studies will give
us an insight into the effect of polarization on the production
of norms in a group situation.) But from the examination of
our results, we can say that the reporting of the judgments has
a gradual cumulative effect; aside from whatever influence the
first judgment may have on the second or third, the judgments
of the third individual at a given presentation affect the subsequent judgments of the first subject in the round of presentations following. Thus the production of an established group influence is largely a temporal affair and not the outcome of this or
that single presentation. We shall refer to this point again later.

Besides the quantitative judgments obtained during the experiments, the subjects were asked at the end of each session
to write down their observations. Questions were asked which
aimed at finding out whether they became conscious of the
range and norm they were establishing subjectively. These
questions were: "Between what maximum and minimum did
the distances vary?" "What was the most frequent distance
that the light moved?"

Certain facts stand out clearly from our results, and may be
summarized in a few paragraphs.

When an individual faces a stimulus situation which is unstable and not structured in itself, *he establishes a range and
norm (a reference point) within that range.* The range and norm
that are developed in each individual are peculiar to that individual, and may vary from the ranges and norms developed
in other individuals in different degrees, revealing consistent
and stable individual differences. The causes of these individual
differences are difficult to determine; their understanding
may prove to be basic to a satisfactory understanding of our
problem. But for the time being it may be worth while to work
on our main theme.

When the individual who develops a range and a norm within
that range independently is put into a group situation together
with other individuals who also enter the situation with their
own ranges and norms established in their own individual ses-

sions, the ranges and norms tend to converge. But the convergence is not so close as when they first work in the group situation and have less opportunity to set up stable individual norms. (See left-hand graphs, Figs. 20 and 21.)

When individuals face the same unstable, unstructured situation as members of a group for the first time, a range and a norm (standard) within that range are established which are peculiar to the group. If, for the group, there is a rise or fall in the norms established in successive sessions, it is a group effect; the norms of the individual members rise and fall toward a common norm in each session. To this the objection may be raised that one subject may lead, and be uninfluenced by other members of the group; the group norm is simply the leader's norm. To this the only possible empirical reply is that in our experiments the leaders were constantly observed to be influenced by their followers—if not at the moment, then later in the series and in subsequent series. Although the objection has occasional force, the statement regarding group norms is in general true. Even if the group norm gravitates toward a dominating person, the leader represents a polarization in the situation, having a definite relationship toward others which he cannot change at will. If the leader changes his norm after the group norm is *settled* he may *thereupon cease to be followed*, as occurred several times in our experiments. In general, however, such cases of complete polarization are exceptional. (See right-hand graphs, Figs. 20 and 21.)

The fact that the norm thus established is peculiar to the group suggests that there is a factual psychological basis in the contentions of social psychologists and sociologists who maintain that new and supra-individual qualities arise in group situations. This is in harmony with the facts developed in the psychology of perception. (See Chapter 9.)

When a member of a group subsequently faces the same situation *alone*, after the range and norm of his group have been established, he perceives the situation in terms of the range and norm that he brings from the group. This psychological fact is important in that it gives a psychological approach to the understanding of the "social products" that weighed so heavily in the discussion of groups.

MEDIANS IN GROUPS OF TWO SUBJECTS

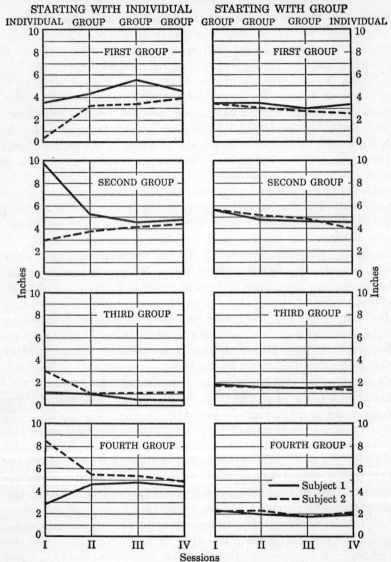

STARTING WITH INDIVIDUAL   STARTING WITH GROUP
INDIVIDUAL GROUP   GROUP GROUP   GROUP GROUP   GROUP INDIVIDUAL

FIRST GROUP

FIRST GROUP

SECOND GROUP

SECOND GROUP

THIRD GROUP

THIRD GROUP

FOURTH GROUP

FOURTH GROUP

——— Subject 1
- - - Subject 2

Inches

Inches

I   II   III   IV   I   II   III   IV
Sessions

FIGS. 20 and 21. Where individual sessions came first (I), divergent norms were established, giving rise to "funnel-shaped" figures as a result of the convergence of the subjects' norms in the subsequent group sessions (II,

MEDIANS IN GROUPS OF THREE SUBJECTS

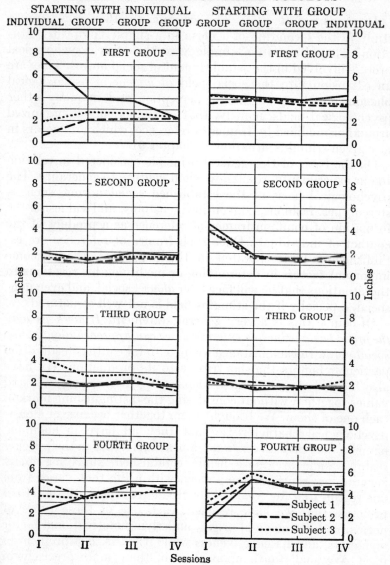

STARTING WITH INDIVIDUAL   STARTING WITH GROUP

INDIVIDUAL GROUP   GROUP GROUP GROUP GROUP   GROUP INDIVIDUAL

Subject 1
Subject 2
Subject 3

Sessions

III, IV). (See left-hand graphs in both figures.) Where the group sessions
preceded the individual ones, the convergence of norms was apparent from
the first session, and remained throughout, including the (final) individual
sessions. (See right-hand graphs in both figures.)

Discussion of Results. The experiments, then, constitute a study of the formation of a norm in a simple laboratory situation. They show in a simple way the basic psychological process involved in the establishment of social norms. They are an extension into the social field of a general psychological phenomenon that we find in perception and in many other psychological fields, namely, that our experience is organized around or modified by frames of reference, which are factors in any given stimulus situation. (Chapter 9)

On the basis of this general principle considered in relation to our experimental results, we shall venture to generalize. The psychological basis of the established social norms, such as stereotypes, fashions, conventions, customs, and values, is the formation of common frames of reference as a product of the contact of individuals. Once such frames of reference are established and incorporated in the individual, they become important factors in determining or modifying his reactions to the situations that he will face later *alone*—social, and even non-social, especially if the stimulus field is not well structured.

Of course this is a very general statement. *It gives us only the broad basic principle with which we can approach any specific social norm.* In each instance we have to take into consideration particular factors that contribute to its production. We have also lumped stereotypes, fashions, conventions, customs, and values together, without considering the distinguishing mark of each one of them. We brought them together because of a basic psychological characteristic that they all have in common, namely, that they all serve as frames of reference in their proper realms. Some are more firmly established, surviving many generations; some are temporary, with a life that varies from one season to a few years. Though all are related to the broad principle that we have reached, each one of these types of norms, with its mode of origin, underlying motivational factor or factors, and its effectiveness while it exists, is a problem in itself. We shall touch upon some of these more precisely in subsequent chapters.

Our experiments merely show the formation of a specific frame of reference in a group situation. The experimental situation does not represent a pressing social situation such as is found in everyday life with its intense hunger, sex, and ego (status) factors. It is simply one unstable, unstructured situation that is new for the subjects. They have no set norms of reaction to it, and therefore it is plastic enough to be structured by the effect of experimentally introduced social factors such as suggestion, prestige, and other group influences.

In this situation, *within certain limits*, there is no "right" or "wrong" judgment. One subject demonstrated this spontaneously during the experiment by suggesting, in spite of the fact that he was not supposed to talk: "If you tell me once how much I am mistaken, all my judgments will be better." Not being sure about the correctness of his judgments, the subject feels uneasy, as we know from the introspective reports. In *the individual situation*, the individual structures the unstructured situation by furnishing his own peculiar range and reference point. In *the group situation* the members of the group tend to structure the situation by converging toward a common norm in their judgments. If in the beginning of the experimental session they start with widely different judgments, in the course of the experiment they come together, the divergent one feeling uncertain and insecure in the solitude given by his judgments. This convergence is not brought about instantly by the direct influence of one or two judgments of the other members of the group; it exhibits a temporal pattern. The following analysis by a member of one of the groups, written in answer to the question, "Were you influenced by the judgments of the other persons during the experiments?" illustrates our point. This subject wrote, "Yes, but not on the same observation. My judgment in each case was already made, and I did not change to whatever the other person said. But on subsequent observations my judgments were adjusted to their judgments. After a number of observations, the previous agreement or lack of it influenced me in adjusting my own perspective."

Despite the above case, *every individual is not necessarily aware of the fact that he is being influenced in the group situation*, or that he and the other members are converging toward a common norm. In fact, the majority of the subjects reported not only that their judgments were made before the others spoke, *but that they were not influenced by the others in the group.*

This fact is in harmony with many observations in the psychology of perception; we know that the general setting of a stimulus influences its properties, and that unless we take a critical and analytic attitude toward the situation we need not be aware that its properties are largely determined by its surroundings.

It must be said that in our experimental setting the subjects were not moved by a common interest or drive such as is found in a group that faces a common danger, such as starvation or the cruel authority of a tyrant. In these vital situations there is a certain gap that has to be filled, some urgent deprivation to be satisfied. Until the need is satisfied, to some degree at least, the instability of the situation continues. If the norms and slogans that arise under the stress of a tense and uncertain situation do not meet the situation adequately, the instability is not removed, and new norms and new slogans are likely to arise until the tension is relieved. For example, in a mass of hungry people searching for food, a leader or a small party may standardize certain norms or slogans as guides to outlook and action. But if these norms do not lead to the satisfaction of hunger, other leaders or interested parties may and do spring up and standardize other norms or slogans. This dynamic process moves on and on until norms or slogans are reached appropriate to the situation.

Before closing this discussion a word should be said about the positive and negative, or lowering and uplifting, effects of the group situations. This is necessary because of confusing discussions on group products. We have already seen in Chapter 5 (pp. 107 ff.) that it is futile and one-sided to take an absolutistic stand on the problem of whether group interaction results in ennobling or degrading effects. Taking sides either way is factually erroneous. Depending on the motivational factors, the background, and the general social setup in which the group interacts, emerging group products and group direction will vary. For example, delinquent gangs have harmful effects, yet they are perhaps among the most democratically formed groups. No norm, not even a leader is imposed on them from without. The norms (the code), the leader himself emerge in the very process of interaction. The mass meetings of the Hitler Jugend in which the conquest of the world usually became a fixed, standardized delusion illustrate the degrading effects of group interaction. A lynching mob is another good example. On the other hand, as we saw in the case of the Halifax disaster (p. 107) and in the tremendous sacrifices that revolutionary group leaders are willing to make, some of the loftiest deeds of human selflessness may emerge in intense group interactions. Therefore, we have to be careful about drawing one-sided moralistic conclusions from the formal characteristics of group interaction and group products. The safest thing for the social psychologist to do is to cling to his major finding which, of course, has important ideological implications. But these have to be worked out against the whole background of the socio-economic setup and the motives of men involved in the interaction.

The social psychologist's important finding is:

that in the course of interaction relative roles emerge for the members;

that group products peculiar to the group arise;

that these group norms enter to shape the reactions of the individual member even when he is no longer actually in his group;

and that group standards *rise* or *fall* as a function of group interaction and not individually (see the graphs of the second and fourth groups of three subjects, Fig. 21).

The Rise of Standards or Norms in Actual Social Groups (Groups in Social Isolation)

The final test of the validity of a generalization in psychology is, of course, its validity in actual situations. The work of the psychologist is not an exclusive preoccupation of academic people. We must, therefore, find counterparts of our findings in actual social situations. It has been shown that in vague, ill-defined, and confusing situations, group norms appear and eventually regulate the reactions of the individual. We shall deal with intense cases of group interaction in situations of confusion and instability in Chapter 16. Here we shall present only some milder illustrations at random.

The cases of isolated groups of individuals in situations

where their old established standards no longer operate effectively afford us fine testing grounds for our hypothesis. Everyone is familiar with the rise of codes in adolescent cliques, gangs, and close friendship circles. We had occasion to refer to concrete illustrations of these in preceding chapters. We shall consider adolescent cliques later (Chapter 13).

In the following paragraphs we shall present some cases of the rise of group norms (standards) in social isolation brought about by various circumstances. They can be multiplied almost indefinitely.

The most clear-cut cases for our present purpose are those in which individuals are isolated from the general run of things, and face common deprivations, dangers, etc., which necessarily lead them to interact as demanded by the urgency of the situation. The reports of men under the stress of battle or imprisonment in World War II are full of such instances. They reveal how norms which are prevalent in society become ineffective and tend to break down under the stringent conditions of the front line, and how new norms are generated through the interaction of the men in this new situation. We have already seen how a psychological in-group formation arose in the Italian front and how peculiar jokes and interests were standardized for the group (pp. 103 f.). Little things which were scarce, such as a can opener, comb, or nail clippers, meant a great deal to the men. And they felt no scruples about taking them. As Pyle said: "Stealing ceased to be just stealing when something a man needed badly was taken." [9] A doctor who had lived for a year in an isolated logging camp related similarly that the norms defining stealing in the camp were quite different from those in the outside world. For example, taking bottles of liquor from another man's ample supply was not considered stealing; but taking a man's cheap flashlight (which was irreplaceable) was a heinous offense.

When life is, at the very least, uncomfortable and little luxuries are scarce (as they were on the battlefront), certain behavior may be standardized and practiced even though the behavior does not relieve an actual lack or discomfort. As Ernie Pyle related: "Everything was so scarce we always took any-

[9] Ernie Pyle, *op. cit.*, p. 149.

thing that was offered us whether we needed it or not. I took a
proffered cigarette while already smoking one. I drank wine,
which I detest, just because somebody was sharing his bottle.
I had no shame about accepting candy, cigarettes, clothing or
anything else anybody offered. We all learned to live on the
policy which Colonel Raff put in these words: '*I never refuse
anything*'" (p. 149, italics mine).

During General Jonathan Wainwright's long imprisonment
under the Japanese, he himself was a member of a group of
high-ranking Allied officers who together struggled to keep
their courage up and to keep alive in the grim isolation of the
prison camp.[10] We have already seen in Chapter 4 how standardized means of dividing food became necessary under the
almost unbearable duress of hunger (pp. 87–88). Food, in
fact, became so central in the thoughts of the group members
that anyone who could steal or smuggle food or tobacco into
the camp was very "clever" indeed and became almost a
hero (pp. 247 ff.). The tantalizing sight of the cartloads of food
which the Japanese hauled in for their own use and which they
paraded past the hungry prisoners became a subject of much
concern. A name expressing the common reaction of the hungry
members to this sight became standardized. The carts were
called "hope carts" (p. 204). In the horrifying conditions of
group life, many of the established army statuses (ranks) broke
down, even though the Japanese separated officers from en-
listed men. For example, on one occasion Captain Turner vol-
unteered to serve as orderly for a high British officer who was
ill, even though this meant less comfort for himself. Wainwright
was willed a razor hone by a sergeant. Because of this precious
possession, he became the razor sharpener for the group and
"was kept busy at it through most of each day" (p. 255).
The interaction of these men struggling to keep alive and keep
hope alive resulted in all sorts of group products. Late at night,
slips of paper with pledges and slogans were circulated secretly
from bed to bed, usually pledging their intention to live through
their prison horror (p. 236). One favorite slogan was "Home
Alive in '45." Passwords (e.g., "Butch") were standardized to

[10] J. M. Wainwright, *General Wainwright's Story*, R. Considine (ed.), New
York: Garden City Publishing Co., 1946; Doubleday, 1945.

serve as warnings against the approach of guards (p. 249). And one group of officers even composed songs and lyrics to keep up the morale of the group.

As societies become more highly differentiated, it has happened that groups of people voluntarily isolate themselves from the community at large to develop their own values and way of life. The history of the Protestant religions is full of such self-imposed formations. For example, the Shakers and Mormons "voluntarily isolated themselves from the larger community because their contacts with the community were unpleasant." [11] The Shakers originally had no doctrine or creed, in fact protested against the rigidity of formal doctrine. However, as they became a group apart and carried on their activities, a *doctrine* arose. "The natural transformation of custom into doctrine is a slow process; but opposition hastens the formulation of creed. For the creed becomes the defense, the justification and the rationalization of the custom" (p. 66). The Mormons did not establish and standardize polygamy as a mode of conduct for the group until they had journeyed to and lived in the wilderness of Utah. "Through the independent social control made possible by isolation distinctive group characteristics were formed and impressed upon succeeding generations. Mormons are Mormons not through anything inherently Mormon in a portion of human nature, but because they have developed group characteristics independently of the community mores" (pp. 118–119). The complicated codes or norms resulting in the two groups mentioned, including a certain desired "type of personality," "ideals," ways of disciplining obstreperous members (e.g., "disfellowship," or putting into "avoidance"), are standardized and are available for the inculcation of succeeding generations.

The prisons of established society represent another situation in which men come together in a group more or less isolated from the rest of society. Clemmer made an extensive study of life in a large penitentiary.[12] When men enter the prison, they are, for the most part, "confused and uncertain about the

[11] R. Shonle, *The Isolated Religious Sect*, M.A. Thesis, Sociology, University of Chicago, August, 1923, p. 1.

[12] D. Clemmer, *The Prison Community*, Boston: The Christopher Publishing House, 1940.

social world they have left" (p. 99). And as each becomes an inmate—one number among thousands—he feels "swallowed up" and experiences a "loss of identity" (p. 102). But this state of extreme confusion does not last long. In the first place, thousands of men, experiencing this lost feeling and striving to get along, have already interacted in such a way as to produce a certain *code* of behavior. There are accepted ways of communication, treatment of officials and fellow prisoners, methods of satisfying the intense sexual deprivation, etc. All of these norms have arisen in prisons and are, for the most part, specifically relevant to the prison situation (although some are brought in from the gangs of the "underworld"). There is a prison *argot*—words and phrases standardized in the prison to express the situations of prison life. In the second place, within the larger prison community, hundreds of spontaneous smaller groups develop. And in these small groups too, norms regulating the behavior of members arise. Clemmer found that the degree to which the prisoners are successful in taking as their own the norms (*code*) of the prison community and of the groups within it had a very real bearing on the reaction to the prison situation. If the world outside seems confused to a man and if he cannot accept the prison code which might serve as a reference frame in interpreting the "atomistic" prison life, he may be "swallowed up" and become quite a different person.

By observing such origins of norms and values in isolated group situations, we see in bold relief the operation of certain psychological principles which are equally applicable in the case of the individual facing an unstructured situation or to the rise of group norms on a mass basis.

Even in more or less haphazard associations of a short duration, we see unmistakable manifestations of a spontaneous group structure and the rise of norms. For example, a group may form among individuals temporarily out of their customary social surroundings on a train or a bus when some circumstance or event brings them together. The following illustration, though it comes from a novel and not from observed evidence, must have happened to some of us in a similar situation. In Steinbeck's novel, *The Wayward Bus*, the passengers maintained the usual reserve prescribed for their situation until Mr. Pritchard, a dignified businessman, accidentally fell sprawling onto the lap of a pretty girl. "Everyone laughed. And suddenly the bus was not full of strangers. Some chemical association was formed." [13] When a train is delayed or wrecked, the passengers may group together and even produce norms, in the way of catch words, rumors about the outcome of the situation, jokes, etc.

Social psychology may be able to formulate general principles about group formation and the rise of norms (values), applicable to any group organization with its system of codes, if we learn to extract the basic structural common properties that prevail in all of them. Otherwise, the almost innumerable social organizations and the diverse systems of norms peculiar to each of them will remain discrete items, as is the case today. We cannot hope to achieve a science of social life as long as we remain dumfounded by the unique qualities of every social pattern.

The basic principles underlying any group formation—the rise of a group structure and products (norms) in more or less casual groupings of short duration, as well as well-structured, lasting groups—must be the same. The artificiality and, in fact, the fallacy of making sharp demarcations in relation to the basic properties of groups was noted by Sapir, who used a group at an automobile accident and a Senate body as examples:

There is in reality no definite line of division anywhere along the gamut of group forms which connect these extremes. If the automobile accident is serious and one of the members of the crowd is a doctor, the informal group may with comparatively little difficulty resolve itself into something like a medical squad with an implicitly elected leader. On the other hand, if the government is passing through a great political crisis, if there is little confidence in the representative character or honesty of the senators or if an enemy is besieging the capital and likely at any moment to substitute entirely new forms of corporate authority for those legally recognized by the citizens of the country, the Senate may easily become an unimportant aggregation of individuals who suddenly and with unexpected poignancy feel their helplessness as mere individuals.[14]

[13] J. Steinbeck, *The Wayward Bus*, New York: The Viking Press, 1947, p. 151.
[14] E. Sapir, Group, in *Encyclopædia of the Social Sciences*, New York: Macmillan, 1932, 7, 178–182.

8.

The Formation
and Effects of Concepts

THE EFFECTS OF GROUP INTERACTION ON INDIVIDUALS ARE NOT
confined simply to the duration of the interaction. As we have
seen, group products—tools, concepts, norms (values) etc.—
come into existence, are standardized and accumulated. The
individual uses them and responds to them in his daily life—in
company of others or alone. He is almost constantly dealing
with the products of group interaction. This means that he is
ever carrying on his life activities on the level of the accumulated group products of his time and social setting. In this
chapter we shall deal briefly with the effects and genetic development of the concepts expressed in language—perhaps the
most important single item in the whole process of human
socialization. In the chapters to follow, we shall deal with the
effects of other social products.

Some Effects of Concepts

As social psychologists, we must study the effects of language
on the behavior of human individuals. Surely no function of the
adult human escapes the influence of his language symbolisms
(including the use of tools). Although an adequate treatment
of the psychology of language is beyond the scope of an outline
of social psychology, we can, by orienting the problems involved, clarify the discussions of the psychological concepts
dealt with in the chapters to follow. After gaining some perspective on the general nature of concepts and their psychological effects, we shall consider briefly their genetic formation
as basic to the process of socialization.

Historical and anthropological material makes evident the

fact that the concepts of a group are not dropped from the blue or the result of the inventive genius of one individual (for his creation must be in harmony with the temper of his times).[1] Concepts arise during group interaction. The crucial way in which they act to determine the experience, thinking, and behavior of the group is not, perhaps, quite so evident.

A glance at even sketchy accounts of the rise and effects of some important concepts is relevant. Concepts of number, weight and measure, and time may be taken as examples.[2] There was a time in the early history of every society when no one could count. Some tribes without accurate concepts of number exist today. A shepherd, for example, kept track of his sheep by calling each by name. During the long and complicated development of concepts of number, different systems arose in the history of different groups. Thus, the Old Babylonians developed a "sexagesimal system" in which 60 was a higher unit, as 100 is for us today. What is known of the fascinating history of the "zero," so important in the development of mathematics and consequently of science in general, clearly shows that it "came into use so gradually and its value was established by the cooperation of so many people that it can hardly be said to have had an inventor" (a, p. 16).

The history of measures is chiefly one of standardization of units for ever-enlarging groups of people. For example, in ancient times, measures of length were based on parts of the body and consequently varied from person to person. The ways which were worked out for standardizing such measures for a community seem very colorful today. In one German community, the following method was agreed upon: "Stand at the door of a church on a Sunday, and bid 16 men to stop, tall ones and small ones, as they happen to pass out when the service is finished; then make them put their left feet one behind the

[1] Even scientific concepts have been found to reflect the run of events in human history. See, for example, Conant's evidence and comments on this fact in his lectures: J. B. Conant, *On Understanding Science*, New Haven: Yale University Press, 1947.

[2] The material in the following paragraphs is taken from a series of pamphlets prepared and distributed by the American Council on Education, 744 Jackson Place, N.W., Washington 6, D. C. They are: (a) "The Story of Numbers," Achievements of Civilization, no. 2, 1932; (b) "The Story of Weights and Measures," no. 3, 1932; (c) "Telling Time Throughout the Centuries," no. 5, 1933; (d) "The Story of Our Calendar," no. 4, 1933.

other and the length thus obtained shall be a right and lawful rood [rod] to measure and survey land with, and the sixteenth part of it shall be a right and lawful foot" (b, p. 11). During the Middle Ages, with its feudal organization, almost every town had its own measuring units. Of course, a great deal of confusion (psychological and otherwise) could result when individuals from different towns attempted to trade. Measures of surface developed chiefly as a result of the need for units of land measure. The Romans and other European groups used as a unit the amount of land a certain amount of grain would plant. In medieval England, land was measured in terms of the number of yoke of oxen or plows needed to cultivate the land. Probably the measurement of weight did not assume much importance until trade in precious materials began.

The importance of time concepts in modern life is almost taken for granted. Yet not only were time concepts relatively less important in earlier periods of history, they were for the most part exceedingly inaccurate and varied tremendously from group to group. Even as recently as 1850, people in America laughed at the idea of a factory producing seven watches a day—for who would want them? (c, p. 1). In modern life, time may become so important that some people are considerably upset if they "lose track of the time" or are a few minutes early or late. This seems perfectly natural to us—as "natural" as a 24-hour day or a 7-day week. Yet "the moment man began dividing the time from sunrise to sunset into equal periods, he left natural time-telling behind him. As has been pointed out, our hours, minutes, and seconds are not marked in any way by nature. There is, moreover, nothing natural in numbering our hours from one to twelve and then beginning over again with one. . . . It is not natural to have the calendar day begin at midnight . . . the calendar day itself is an artificial unit although it began as a natural one—it is now the *average* solar day" (c, pp. 63–64).

Our concept of months and years may seem to many people simply a part of nature, but "for many, many centuries such an expression as 'two moons ago' or 'three harvests ago' was an accurate enough way of dating any event. When men did try to fit days, months, and years together into a single scheme for reckoning time, they found the task of making a good calendar very difficult" (d, p. 8). Early calendars often varied in terms of the activities of the group. For example, Babylonian months were determined by the seasonal activities carried on, such as plowing, brick-making, herding, etc. Whereas some calendars were based on cycles of the moon, the Egyptians based theirs on the sun—with three seasons based on the condition of the Nile and their consequent agricultural activities. And just as values standardized by the group may continue after the conditions which gave rise to them disappear, so concepts of time may remain in use though no longer appropriate. In Babylonian history, the month units, because they were based on in-accurate units of the solar cycle, slipped from their proper places in the seasons. In time, the plowing month fell in the wrong season for plowing and so forth.

Now such variations in the concepts of a language produce almost overwhelming differences in the consequent experience and reactions of the group. The fact that Eskimos use three different words for snow, depending on its state, and the Hopis use two words for water surely has a consequential effect upon the users of the terms. The anthropologists, Kluck-hohn and Kelly, have emphasized this point on a more com-prehensive scale by illustrating the different results of the structure of a language on the experience of the users:

Especially the morphology of a language preserves the unformu-lated philosophy of the group. For example, Dorothy Lee has shown that among the Trobriand Islanders " the sequence of events does not automatically fall into the mold of causal or telic relationship." Be-cause of the mold which grammar imposes upon our " thinking " these people find certain types of communication with Europeans difficult since Europeans almost inevitably talk in causal terms.

The very morphology of any language inevitably begs far-reaching questions of metaphysics and of values. A language is not merely an instrument for communication and for rousing the emotions. *Every language is also a device for categorizing experience.* The continuum of experience can be sliced very differently. We tend all too easily to assume that the distinctions which Indo-European languages (or our own particular language) force us to make are given by the world of nature. As a matter of fact, comparative linguistics shows very plainly that any speech demands unconscious conceptual selection on the part of its speaker. No human organism can respond to all the kaleidoscopic stimuli which impinge upon it from the external world. *What we notice, what we talk about, what we feel as important is in some part a function of our linguistic patterns.* Because these linguistic habits tend to remain as unquestioned "background phenomena," each people tends to take its fundamental categories, its unstated basic premises for granted. It is assumed that others will "think the same way," for "it's only human nature." When others face the same body of data but come to different conclusions, it is seldom thought that they might be proceeding from different premises. Rather, it is inferred that they are "stupid" or "illogical" or "obstinate." [3]

Some psychologists have gone so far as to equate language and thinking. Although it is not our problem here, the relationship of language and thought and its effects on various functions is surely an important area of study, especially for social psychology. For, as we shall see presently, the whole process of socialization is linked with language development, perhaps more than with any other single aspect of development. But let us start with some relatively simple examples of the effects of concepts upon experience and behavior.

As Gemelli has reported, a very frequent form of response to a perceptual situation is simply to name the perceived form or object.[4] A few examples of the effects of naming from the research of Bartlett will illustrate how concepts enter to affect the structure of perception and memory.[5] Bartlett found that even very simple line designs were spontaneously named by his subjects. Naming of these *simple, structured* drawings had little effect on their subsequent reproduction. But the naming of slightly more detailed designs had definite effects. Here, according to Bartlett,

Naming occupied a position of greater importance. It not only satisfied the observer, but helped to shape his representation. For example, [one figure] was once called a "pick-axe" and was represented with pointed prongs. Once it was termed a "turf-cutter" and made with a rounded blade. It was called in part a key (the handle),

[3] C. Kluckhohn and W. H. Kelly, "The Concept of Culture," in R. Linton (ed.), *The Science of Man in the World Crisis*, New York: Columbia University Press, 1945, pp. 100–101 (italics mine).

[4] A. Gemelli, *Arch. Ges. Psychol.*, 1928, 65, 207.

[5] F. C. Bartlett, *Remembering: A Study in Experimental and Social Psychology*, Cambridge: University Press, 1932.

and in part a shovel (the blade), and changed accordingly in representation. Six observers called it an " anchor," and exaggerated the size of the ring at the top. Once only was the point in the blade correctly reproduced—by a subject who said that the design represented a "prehistoric battle-axe." . . . All this neatly illustrates how great a variety of names may be given to simple observational material and also—a point more to our purpose—how *the name, as soon as it is assigned, immediately shapes both what is seen and what is recalled* (p. 20, italics mine).

If a figure appeared odd, disconnected and unfamiliar, it was in almost all cases attacked at once by analogy. So naming came in again, in a different way. For the analogy had practically always to do with the shape of the figure, or with the disposition of its lines and curves. When [a certain figure] was shown to a mathematical student, he at once remarked: "That arrangement of lines reminds me of a 'determinant.'" His immediate reproduction was accurate and several weeks later he still recalled and correctly reproduced this figure (p. 21).

We see that the particular concept used served as an anchorage for the individual, determining his reactions in relation to the stimulus. McGranahan, after surveying the literature on such effects of language, came to the conclusion: "The effect of language on perception appears to be to make those features of the objective world that are represented by linguistic forms stand out in greater articulation, to give greater individuality to the object or event so represented, to cause similarities to be seen in things similarly represented, and in general to influence perception in the direction of the speech-forms." [6]

In the learning process, too, concepts may serve as anchorages for the individual, thus having marked effects upon the course of learning. Warden found that a maze was learned with considerably greater efficiency when verbal cues were employed.[7] An adequate learning theory will necessarily be one that can handle such facts.

The American standard intelligence tests (Stanford-Binet, especially Form L) simply are not applicable for children in other cultures—in the rural sections of Turkey, for instance. Aside from the verbal tests, even the pictures of many "com-

[6] D. V. McGranahan, The psychology of language, *Psychol. Bull.*, 1936, 33, p. 202.
[7] C. G. Warden, The relative economy of various modes of attack in the mastery of a stylus maze, *J. Exper. Psychol.*, 1924, 7, 243-275.

mon" objects are not understood, because the objects do not
have the same symbolic value in America and in rural Turkey.
Because concepts function as anchoring points and frames
in relation to which experience is structured, the acquisition of
concepts leads to a more or less characteristic organization of
response. It has been reported that the behavior of children
who are deaf and blind from an early age is disorganized and
diffused until they learn some definite concepts.[8]

Luria has emphasized that language, by providing organized
and guiding cues, gives to behavior its organized and *voluntary*
character.[9] The findings related to the decrease in the speed of
conditioning in older children owing to emergence of "voluntary" factors would seem to give support to this contention.
Genetic study of the central control of conditioning reveals
that there is no evidence for such control *"in the first year of
human life, this control making its first appearance at the age of
3–5, probably coeval with the child's instrumental mastery of his
verbal and conscious processes."*[10] It has been observed that in
many cases of insanity the language of the patient runs a retro-
gressive course concomitant with a deterioration of organized
behavior patterns.[11]

Concepts inherent in the language have, then, important demonstrable effects on the psychology of individuals. Many of the
individual's attitudes are formed in relation to concepts during
the course of his development. The capacity for functioning on
a conceptual level makes possible the development of the
individual's conception of himself and of his relationship to
other persons and objects around him. And it is of utmost importance that this conceptual level of psychological functioning
emerge in the scale of the animal kingdom only on the human
level.

In a simpler form, we see the capacity for the formation of
concepts in the lower animals. Here the process is referred to
as "generalization." For example, a rat which has been con-

[8] D. McGranahan, *op. cit.*, p. 205.
[9] A. R. Luria, *The Nature of Human Conflicts*, New York: Liveright, 1932.
[10] G. H. S. Razran, Conditioned responses: an experimental study and a theoretical analysis, *Arch. Psychol.*, 1935, no. 191, p. 118.
[11] A. A. Low, Studies in infant speech and thought, *Ill. Med. Dent. Monogr.*, 1936,
1, no. 2.

ditioned to jump when presented with a tone of 1,000 cycles will respond also to a 2,000-cycle tone. Somewhat nearer the formation of concepts is the observation by several experimenters of an animal's response to form *as such*, independent of position. Thus it has been found that rats, raccoons, cats, and monkeys can be trained to respond equivalently to triangles, even when they are inverted.[12] But a 2-year-old child is apparently better able than a chimpanzee to make this discrimination.[13]

Chimpanzees can learn to use tokens to obtain food from a vending machine. The tokens then acquire symbolic value and become "adequate incentives" for the animal in learning situations. However, as Cowles found, they are not as effective as a food reward itself. Furthermore, when food is not given for the tokens—the response is not "reinforced"—their effectiveness as incentives disappears in time. "There is considerable evidence that the food-token was an adequate incentive for learning and retention only by virtue of its exchange for food."[14] Man's reactions to symbols acquire immeasurably greater significance. Not only will he save money when its exchange for food is not possible; he will even continue to accumulate money far past the point necessary to feed, clothe, and otherwise satisfy the basic needs of himself, his family, and even future generations. As Hayakawa has noted: " . . . a chimpanzee can be taught to drive a car, but there is one thing wrong with its driving: its reactions are such that if a red light shows when it is halfway across a street, it will stop in the middle of the crossing, while if a green light shows while another car is stalled in its path, it will go ahead regardless of consequences. In other words, so far as a chimpanzee is concerned, the red light can hardly be said to *stand* for stop; it *is* stop."[15]

It may be useful to distinguish between reactions which are

[12] For reviews of this research, see N. L. Munn, *Psychological Development*, Boston: Houghton Mifflin, 1938, p. 148; and C. T. Morgan, *Physiological Psychology*, New York: McGraw-Hill, 1943, pp. 109 ff.

[13] L. W. Gellerman, Form discrimination in chimpanzees and two-year-old children. I. Discrimination of form per se, *J. Genet. Psychol.*, 1933, 42, 1–50.

[14] J. T. Cowles, Food-tokens as incentives for learning by chimpanzees, *Comp. Psychol. Monogr.*, 1937, 14, no. 5, p. 94.

[15] S. I. Hayakawa, *Language in Action*, New York: Harcourt, Brace, 1941, p. 26.

perceptually and those which are *conceptually* symbolic. For although animals are able to react to stimuli with different characteristics as *equivalent*, they are not able to divorce this equivalence from specific perceptual situations. As we shall see, this is also characteristic of many of the symbolic reactions of young children. In man, the range of this equivalence is vastly extended by his ability to function conceptually, apart from a specific perceptual context. This capacity of functioning on a conceptually symbolic level makes possible the formation and accumulation of concepts encompassing a tremendous range of stimuli. Hayakawa has illustrated this capacity and almost infinite scope of generalization in "The Abstraction Ladder." (See Fig. 22.)

It is true, of course, that there is no *necessary* correspondence between every concept and the objects, situation, or class of stimuli it represents. But we must point out that concepts must to some degree accurately epitomize the objective world so that man's life activities will continue. Sometimes concepts are used after the situation that gave rise to them is over or after the concept has been proved erroneous, but sooner or later a new concept will be formed to express the actual state of things. This carry-over of concepts, the resistance to change, and the rise of new concepts have been observed in science, as well as in other activities of man.[16]

New concepts are constantly arising as conditions change. "Quisling," "jitterbug," "juke box," "fifth column," "denazification," "atom bomb," "normalcy" are examples. The study of the origin of such new concepts will be profitable for social psychologists as well as for social scientists. The "New Words Section" of a standard dictionary, such as Merriam-Webster, is a good source for such study, since the compilation of a modern dictionary consists mainly in checking the appearance and use of a word as it is spoken and written in daily life.[17]

A large proportion of the most recent edition of a standard dictionary's New Words Section is composed of military words. And about half of them concern airplanes and bombing raids.

[16] See J. B. Conant, *op. cit.*

[17] C. D. Rice, "Do You Speak English?" *This Week Magazine*, December 1, 1946, pp. 8–9 and 25.

Here is a rather neat demonstration of the fact that a new situation, particularly one of such overwhelming importance as World War II, gives rise to new concepts expressing the new conditions and objects. The rising pressure of labor-owner problems is attested to by a large number of new words, such as "sit-down strike" and "fink." The appearance of a new style of music is marked by a whole collection of new words— "jive," "hepcat," "alligator," "boogie-woogie," etc. Sometimes, of course, a new word may be intentionally coined by one person. If it "catches on," it is because certain conditions or objects exist which need crystallization for those who come into contact with them.

However, the truth or falsity of a concept in terms of the objective world is not in itself a psychological problem. Its appropriateness to the world of objects and events can be ascertained by scientists in the specific fields, e.g., physics, biology, etc. For example, the frequently used and abused concept, "race," can be brought into line with objective facts by the science of biology.

What is the explanation for the emergence of the conceptually symbolic level of functioning in man? It is surely not his organs of speech, for many animals have these same organs. As Sapir observed: "Physiologically speech is an overlaid function, or, to be more precise, a group of overlaid functions. It gets what service it can out of organs and functions, nervous and muscular, that have come into being and are maintained for very different ends than its own." [18] Biological scientists agree that the answer lies in the fact that man has more extensive cortical development, especially of the frontal areas, than any of the subhuman animals. It is this development on the human level which makes possible the rise and especially the *accumulation* of concepts and norms. In summarizing these points, the anthropologist White notes that even man's use and accumulation of tools—so vital in the whole rise of civilization —are made possible by this conceptual level. For although the higher apes can indeed use and make tools, they are limited by their perceptual range. "Tool-using among apes is thus a dis-

[18] E. Sapir, *Language, an Introduction to the Study of Speech*, New York: Harcourt Brace, 1921, p. 8.

THE ABSTRACTION LADDER
Start Reading from Bottom *UP*

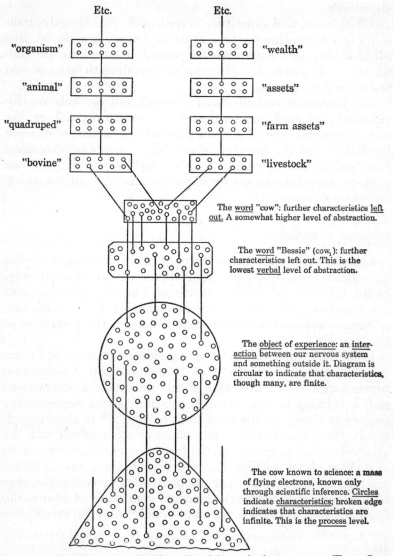

The *word* "cow": further characteristics left out. A somewhat higher level of abstraction.

The *word* "Bessie" (cow₁): further characteristics left out. This is the lowest *verbal* level of abstraction.

The *object* of *experience*: an *interaction* between our nervous system and something outside it. Diagram is circular to indicate that characteristics, though many, are finite.

The cow known to science: a mass of flying electrons, known only through scientific inference. Circles indicate *characteristics*; broken edge indicates that characteristics are infinite. This is the *process* level.

FIG. 22. The Abstraction Ladder. Read from the bottom up. (From *Language in Action* by S. I. Hayakawa (Harcourt, Brace). Adapted from the "Structural Differential" in *Science and Sanity* copyrighted by A. Korzybski.)

continuous psychological process subjectively as well as objectively.

"With man, tool experience is quite different. Overtly, tool-using is a discontinuous process as, of course, it must be. But subjectively, tool experience in man is continuous and enduring." [19] For man, tools become also symbols to be passed on to future generations.

The formation and effects of concepts and symbols are, for the most part, problems on the level of human psychology. We cannot pretend here to give an adequate treatment of concept formation. But the problem is so basic to man's psychological functioning, and especially to his socialization, that we can achieve some orientation by inquiring how the individual acquires these concepts.

Concept Formation

Language concepts are products of the interaction of human individuals in groups. Their acquisition is of utmost importance in the socialization of the individual. Once formed, concepts enter to structure his experience and behavior. Individuals may, in turn, participate as members of groups in the formation of new concepts.

From the results of a series of experiments on concept formation, Heidbreder concluded that "the attainment of concepts is psychologically a modification of the perception of objects, and that it is likely to conform to the pattern of the perception of objects as closely as the conditions permit." [20] In these experiments, the concepts of concrete objects were attained with the greatest ease, concepts of spatial forms less easily, and concepts of numbers least readily. This order would seem also to follow the relative distance of the concepts from a perceptual level to higher levels of abstraction. Concepts were attained more easily from pictured than from verbal material.[21] And the attainment

[19] L. A. White, On the use of tools by primates, *J. Comp. Psychol.*, 1942, 34, 369–374.

[20] E. Heidbreder, Toward a dynamic psychology of cognition, *Psychol. Rev.*, 1945, 52, 1–22.

[21] E. Heidbreder, A study of the evolution of concepts (abstract), *Psychol. Bull.*, 1934, 31, 673.

of a concept was found to vary not with the relative ease or difficulty of memorizing its name (nonsense syllables) but rather "by the relation between its reference and the perceptual situation in which it is presented." [22]

Hull found that calling the individual's attention to the elements common to several stimuli while they were before him "consistently increases the efficiency of the process." [23] On the other hand, when the common elements are directly given to the individual out of the perceptual situation, the efficiency of concept formation was no greater than when no hints were given at all.

Linking concept formation with *perception* in this crucial way gives us a general orientation. But we must not forget that a concept also involves abstraction and *generalization*. As Smoke found, "The process of concept formation appears to involve grouping. The learner tends to envisage certain stimulus patterns as constituting a *group to which any given stimulus pattern does or does not belong*." [24]

There may be considerable substance in Sapir's conclusion that "the speech element 'house' is the symbol, first and foremost, not of a single perception, nor even of the notion of a particular object, but of a 'concept,' in other words, of a convenient capsule of thought that embraces thousands of distinct experiences and is ready to take in thousands more. If the single significant elements of speech are the symbols of concepts, the actual flow of speech may be interpreted as a record of the setting of these concepts into mutual relations." [25]

But if the problem were left here, one might conclude, as some investigators have, that concepts are "logical constructs." Such a view ignores the findings of genetic psychology, which indicate that motivational factors enter into the attainment of concepts; and that concepts are not static entities but change and develop as the individual develops. As a result of intensive investigation, Vigotsky concluded that "from the psychological

[22] E. Heidbreder, Language and concepts, *Psychol. Bull.*, 1936, 33, 794.
[23] C. L. Hull, Quantitative aspects of the evolution of concepts: an experimental study, *Psychol. Monogr.*, 1920, 28, no. 123.
[24] K. L. Smoke, An objective study of concept formation, *Psychol. Monogr.*, 1932, 42, no. 191, p. 35 (italics mine).
[25] E. Sapir, *op. cit.*, p. 12.

point of view the meaning of a word is nothing but a generalization or concept. . . . The main result of our investigation . . .
is the thesis that the meaning of words develop." [26] With this
orientation, there seems little point in separating psychologically concepts of value and concepts of reality. Psychologically,
both would seem to be attained by the same process, with
greater or lesser degrees of motivational and affective components.

With the above considerations in mind, let us turn now
specifically to evidence from genetic psychology concerning
the development of children's concepts.

In discussing the role of biogenic needs in the behavior of the
infant, we mentioned the results of research on children's perceptions (see pp. 53–55). Very young children tend to perceive
the world around them in terms of undifferentiated, meaningful wholes. And those objects or persons which are meaningful are those with biological value in terms of satisfying basic
needs. It is true, of course, that the child is not always under
the grip of a biological need, and that reactions to social objects
and situations begin very early. And as soon as socially derived, learned (sociogenic) motives begin to come into the
picture, they too exert a directive effect on the perceptual
process.

Even in experimental situations, it is found that young
children tend to notice large, moving stimuli rather than fine
details, unless they are specifically motivated otherwise (see
p. 55). After reviewing the research on children's reactions to
perceptual situations, Vernon concluded that "children are not
interested in the discrimination of sensory qualities, but only
in the broad perceptual outlines of meaningful wholes." [27]
Their reactions tend to be to the outstanding features of a
situation. If such aspects are not determined by the need or
wish dominant at the moment, they are usually those which are
most prominent in the situation itself. For example, a baby will
generally notice a large red toy rather than a small pink one by
its side.

With age comes an increasing tendency to distinguish detail

[26] L. S. Vigotsky, Thought and speech, *Psychiatry*, 1939, 2, 29–54.
[27] M. D. Vernon, *Visual Perception*, Cambridge: University Press, 1937, p. 182.

and the qualities of things (e.g., color).[28] Thus on the standard Binet intelligence tests, discrimination of size comes at the 4-year-old level and discrimination of color and weight at the 5-year level. There seems to be little doubt that the increasing discriminativeness of perception is related to the acquisition of concepts. It would seem that concept formation is first limited and regulated by the child's perception (see below), which in turn is reacted upon by the acquisition of concepts.

In view of the experimental results indicating the close relationship between perception and concept formation, it is not accidental that the development of children's early concepts also seems to follow a course similar to that of their perceptions. The early words of children are almost always nouns referring to objects or persons related to the satisfaction of their desires, feelings, and especially of their basic needs.[29] Even for children 2 to 5 years old, the most commonly used concepts are those related to mother, home, father, and brothers and sisters—in other words, the sources of satisfaction for their biogenic needs and other desires which are beginning to appear at these ages.[30] These early concepts have been compared to one-word sentences. They are largely undifferentiated and are used at first in direct relation to specific situations.

The fact that children's early concepts are closely tied to perceptual situations has been observed by many investigators. By noting the relative order in which the various parts of speech enter the child's repertoire of language responses, we may have some indication of the relationship between perception and concept formation. McCarthy has mentioned the "naming stage in which, after making the important discovery that everything has a name, he asks many 'what questions' in order to learn the names of the various objects in his environ-

[28] See for example the research of W. Line, The growth of visual perception in children. *Brit. J. Psychol. Monogr. Suppl.* 1931, 5, no. 15; V. Hazlitt, Children's thinking, *Brit. J. Psychol.*, 1930, 20, 354–361; R. Staples, The response of infants to color, *J. Exper. Psychol.*, 1932, 15, 119–141.

[29] For relevant literature on this point, see D. McCarthy, Language development in children, chap. 10, pp. 476–581, in L. Carmichael (ed.), *Manual of Child Psychology*, New York: Wiley, 1946; and E. Dewey, *Infant Behavior*, New York: Columbia University Press, 1935, p. 251.

[30] M. M. Shirley, Common content in the speech of preschool children, *Child Develop.*, 1938, 9, 333–346.

ment."³¹ But names for classes of stimuli not directly per-
ceivable appear comparatively late. For example, the concept
"metal" appears fairly late and is accurately used only when
a mental age of about 11 has been reached.³² It is significant,
too, that verbs, which are usually acquired after nouns, at
first refer only to the immediate situation in which the child
finds himself.³³ And even when past and future tenses are used,
the time which is so conceptualized refers at first to the very
near past or future.³⁴ This point is well illustrated by Bean's
observations of his child at 2½ years of age;³⁵ the child used
"yesterday" to refer to all past time and "this afternoon" to
refer to all future time. Concepts of time, then, seem to be
detached from the immediate very slowly indeed.

Adjectives, which are the next parts of speech to be used,
increase with age—with definite adjectives becoming relatively
fewer and indefinite adjectives increasing.³⁶ This would be expected from the genetic studies of children's perceptions. As
Bean concluded, "Despite adult obtrusion of qualities into the
experience of children . . . they are so busy acquainting themselves with objects and *their uses* that the qualities of objects
play a less important part in their mental life, and therefore in
their language, until there is a large enough fund of nouns, and
until the nouns are familiar enough to lend definiteness of meaning to their modifiers."³⁷

Relational words appear after adjectives, and pronouns are
just coming into use around the end of the second year (at
least for the American children studied).³⁸ As we shall see in a
later chapter, the attainment of that level of functioning in
which "I," "me," "mine," "you," "yours," and finally "we"

³¹ D. McCarthy, *op. cit.*, p. 508.
³² A. F. Watts, *The Language and Mental Development of Children*, London:
George G. Harrap and Co., Ltd., 1944, p. 22.
³³ M. M. Lewis, The beginning of reference to past and future in a child's speech.
Brit. J. Educ. Psychol., 1937, 7, 39–56.
³⁴ S. Adams, Analysis of verb forms in the speech of young children and their relation to the language learning process, *J. Exper. Educat.*, 1938, 7, 141–144.
³⁵ C. H. Bean, An unusual opportunity to investigate the psychology of language,
J. Genet. Psychol., 1932, 40, 181–202.
³⁶ J. B. Carroll, Determining and numerating adjectives in children's speech,
Child Develop., 1939, 10, 214–229.
³⁷ C. H. Bean, *op. cit.*, p. 193 (italics mine).
³⁸ E. Dewey, *op. cit.*, p. 251.

are clearly conceptualized has profound effects upon the child's awareness of himself and his relationships with others (pp. 252-262). We shall pause here only to note McCarthy's conclusion concerning the effects of language on social development: "During the early preschool period when the child's language is not yet very useful as a means of communication, he is still definitely an individualist, and it is probably significant that a marked degree of socialization of behavior occurs during the later preschool period when language itself is becoming a more efficient means of intercommunication." [39] The development of language responses as a means of *intercommunication* makes possible the child's eventual grasp of reciprocal relationships with other people.

The relationship between perceptual development and concept formation is at first so close that different opportunities for contact with the environment produce definite variations in the concepts formed. Thus, Bean reports that nearly 90 per cent of the concepts used by his child, who was nearly blind from birth, were derived "from tactual, auditory, gustatory and motor senses and the few visual ones that related only its light and color, which was all that he could sense before the operations." [40] After the operations in which sight was restored, words that referred "to visual objects were rapidly added." Varieties of experience and travel have also been found to be followed by a rapid increase in *conceptual* development. [41] And it is not unlikely that the differences in conceptual development found between children of different socio-economic classes may be in no small part affected by the differences in perceptual and practical situations presented by their respective environments.

Initially, then, the child's concepts follow the course of his perceptions, being at first largely undifferentiated and more or less dominated by his basic drives and wishes or desires. Many children, in their contacts with the external world, form concepts distinctly their own. For example, Watts reports that a 16-months-old boy he observed had found "that certain things

[39] D. McCarthy, *op. cit.*, p. 550.
[40] C. H. Bean, *op. cit.*, p. 191.
[41] D. McCarthy, *op. cit.*, pp. 559 ff.

in his environment were sufficiently alike for his purposes to be conveniently referred to as *yo-yos* and that among the *yo-yos* there existed a sub-class of *go-gos*." [42] The "yo-yos" were any portable objects with handles, while the "go-gos" had not only handles, but lids. Thus a fairly wide range of generalization, regulated by the child's play interests, was possible. Children may continue to form and use their own distinctive concepts, particularly if their parents encourage them. Other parents, more anxious for their child to attain linguistic maturity, discourage such individual activities early. At any rate, the child must eventually use the concepts as standardized in his society (for example, with their dictionary meanings), if he is to become an active participant in his group—for reciprocal communication can be carried on only on this basis.

The possible range of stimuli to which a young child may give an equivalent response is extremely large. For example, it has been experimentally demonstrated that children under 2 years of age can generalize "chair" even to a folded chair, "ball" to a collapsed ball, rectangularity to a picture frame and to L-shaped figures.[43] Whereas this is possible for clearly perceptible objects, it is more difficult for the young child in the case of "class" or abstract concepts, even when the child is specifically trained in this direction.[44]

Only as the child develops, extends his experience, and uses concepts do they become increasingly specific, more rich in detail, and detached from immediate perceptual situations. In Munn's words: "It is quite evident . . . that words spoken by others elicit increasingly fine differential reactions as the child grows older. Similarly, the use of words becomes increasingly discriminative. Both of these trends indicate that, as the child grows older, words are, to him, taking on *a closer approximation to their fullest conventional representative significance as this has developed during the social history of the group*." [45]

In his research on children's concepts, Vigotsky found that

[42] A. F. Watts, *op. cit.*, p. 35.
[43] L. Welch, The span of generalization below the two year age level, *J. Genet. Psychol.*, 1939, 55, 269–297.
[44] L. Welch and L. Long, The higher structural phases of concept formation of children, *J. Psychol.*, 1940, 9, 59–95.
[45] N. L. Munn, *op. cit.*, p. 387.

the qualities of objects were irrevocably connected with the objects themselves for preschool children. If a preschool child was persuaded to change the name of, say, "dog" to "cow," he proceeded to talk of the object (the dog) as though it were a cow—having horns, giving milk, etc.[46] But this "complete fusion" of the perceptual and conceptual begins to break up as the child grows older, and the separation increases with age. As he develops, the child becomes able to function psychologically on a conceptually symbolic level. More and more, his concepts take on the standardized meanings of the group in which he lives. These meanings are simply generalizations which have been standardized by the group in their past interactions, and which serve to classify or categorize experience, both cognitive and affective. Henceforth, the individual's psychological functions are regulated in general by these standardized concepts. And in particular, his reactions to social stimuli—his likes and dislikes, his aspirations and loyalties—are regulated by norms or values, which are special cases of the concepts of his group.

[46] L. S. Vigotsky, *op. cit.*, p. 36.

9.

Attitudes

Man's Socialization Revealed Mainly Through Attitudes and Conforming Behavior

AS WE SHALL ELABORATE LATER, ATTITUDES ARE FORMED IN relation to situations, persons, or groups with which the individual comes into contact in the course of his development. Once formed, they demand that the individual react in a *characteristic* way to these or related situations, persons, or groups. This characteristic feature, which is inferred from behavior (verbal or non-verbal), denotes a *functional state of readiness* in relation to stimulus situations which elicit it. For example, when we see a person or group of persons react to a flag with respect, we infer that they have an attitude toward the flag. When we see millions of people observe a certain day, say the Fourth of July, with certain words and deeds, we infer that they have an attitude toward that particular day. Likewise, people's preoccupation with and struggles toward obtaining certain objects (e.g., money), emulating certain persons (a superior, leader, actress, etc.), joining certain groups (union, college, ethnic group, nation, etc.), seeking certain social positions, may be cited as indexes of major attitudes. These are not mere generalities—every one of them can be demonstrated in single members of the groups in question. For example, if an individual belonging to group *A* reacts unmistakably negatively to an individual in group *B* without first forming an opinion about that person, we may say that he has an attitude of prejudice toward group *B*. If he is a "good member" of group *A*, very probably his attitude is shared by other "good members" who constitute the majority of people in that group.

The above examples apply to *social* attitudes, but not all of an individual's attitudes are social. We develop attitudes in relation to any stimulus object or situation (social or non-social) with which we come into contact repeatedly. Since this invariably occurs after, say, a few encounters, we are seldom impartial in our reactions to situations or persons. We may develop a special liking for a particular bird, a special view, a special food. We may and do develop special likes and dislikes for friends, personal enemies, or rivals, for special events peculiar to ourselves and determined by our motives and individualities.

Of course, our special concern in this book is with the *social attitudes*. The feature that makes certain attitudes *social* is that they are formed in relation to social stimulus situations; we have already mentioned this (Chapter 1). We saw there that social stimulus situations are persons, groups, and the products of human interaction—material and non-material, i.e., the man-made environment of things, technological devices, and values or norms. Attitudes formed in relation to these constitute the main body of what is socialized in man. The major feature that makes a man a good member of his particular reference group (be it a clique, a gang, a school, a church, a union, a nation) is the attitudes he forms in relation to them. The concrete signs that give an individual the characteristic imprint of his groups and his culture (whatever this culture may be) are, in terms of psychological units, the attitudes he reveals in concrete situations. For they are the psychological products *par excellence* of his socialization, i.e., his becoming a Frenchman, an Eskimo, a Hopi, an American, a Chinese, etc. Of course, the range of his attitudes as a good Frenchman, Eskimo, etc., is limited to the range of his receptivity. No one is subjected to all the social and cultural products of his group, especially in a society with some degree of differentiation. In short, man's socialization is revealed mainly in his attitudes formed in relation to the values or norms of his reference group or groups. Many of these attitudes represent his sociogenic motives. His conception of the scope of his world, his standards of living, his aspirations toward wealth, women, and status are regulated, his goals are set, by the prevailing hierarchy of social organization and norms of his group. Hence his sociogenic motives and the regulation of his biogenic motives are reflected in his social attitudes. The main constituents of his ego are these attitudes. Although a fuller discussion of this will be given in Chapters 11 and 12, the foregoing is sufficient to indicate why attitudes have been a central theme for social psychologists, and why literally hundreds of papers (experimental and otherwise) have been devoted to the subject.

Some behavioristically inclined social psychologists refer to attitudes as conforming behavior. They represent a social attitude by a curve, the J-curve,[1] which graphically represents the distribution of the attitude in a representative sample of the

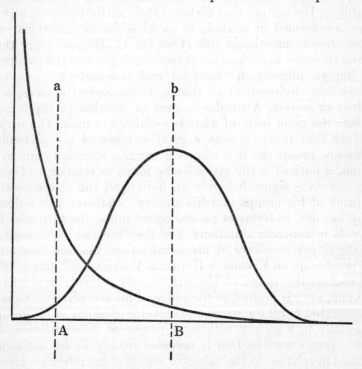

Fig. 23. "Two theoretical behavior distributions and their medians. Distribution A is J-shaped, distribution B is normal. The dotted lines *a* and *b* represent the medians of the two distributions." (By permission from *Psychology at Work*, edited by P. S. Achilles, Copyrighted, 1932, by the McGraw-Hill Book Company, Inc.)

[1] See F. H. Allport, The J-curve hypothesis of conforming behavior, *J. Soc. Psychol.*, 1934, 5, 141–183.

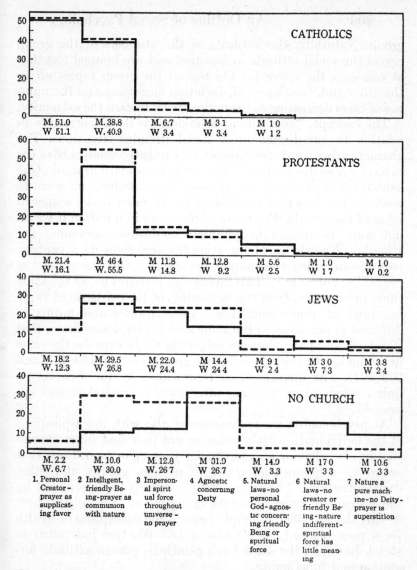

FIG. 24. "Distribution of percentages of 1,219 students of the College of Liberal Arts of Syracuse University upon the question of the existence and nature of the deity."

On 7 opinions about the nature of the deity (specified on the abscissa), distribution of Catholics approaches most closely the J-curve of conformity. Most divergent distribution is "No Church" subjects. Men's opinions, solid line; women's, broken line. (From D. Katz and F. H. Allport, *Student's Attitudes*, Syracuse: The Craftsman Press.)

group. Naturally, the *majority* of the members of the group reveal the social attitude in question and are lumped together at one end; the curve for the rest of the group tapers off to the other end, the degree of deviation increasing and the number of cases decreasing as the curve moves toward the extremity.

The concept, "conforming behavior," is itself suggestive in relation to our discussion of social stimulus situations. The characterizing word, "conforming," explicitly denotes that the behavior is so designated in relation to a standard or norm. One cannot speak of conformity if there is no standard, no norm to conform to. As social psychologists, we must make a special issue of the standard or norm *of the group* in question if we do not want to remain in complete confusion concerning the stimulus. Knowledge of the stimulus *first* gives us a vantage point from which to examine the group in question and the prevailing norms in it. This knowledge prepares us, at the same time, to be aware, from the beginning, of the existence of varying (and at times conflicting) value frames and norms in different groups even in the same society. Evidence shows that standards and judgments are subject to shifts, even for the same individual, with shifts in reference groups (see pp. 139–155, and 300–301). The quantification represented by the J-curve acquires much more meaning after such a methodological approach.

As psychologists we are concerned also with the aspirations of the individual—with whether or not they find overt expression in his behavior at a particular time. The aspirations that are at all consequential relate to persons, groups, and other social situations. The range of their variety is determined by the prevailing range of values or norms of the social milieu. A sum like $100,000. is simply beyond the conception of wealth for a poor peasant. (See Chapter 15.) Whether individual or social, however, the same basic principles govern attitude formation and functioning.

Some Principles at the Basis of Attitudes

As we have seen, an attitude is inferred from the *characteristic, selective* nature of reaction to situations. In other words, reaction revealing the existence of an attitude in the individual is not evoked alone by the properties of the external stimulus. The characteristic or selective nature of reaction is a function of the factors within the individual himself; there is implied a functional *state of readiness* in relation to the stimuli in question. Hence, the psychology of attitudes consists of accounting for this established state of readiness. It is embedded in the general selectivity of the whole organism. For example, perception, judgment, learning, remembering, etc., are highly selective affairs, being jointly determined by the state of the organism at the time and the properties of the stimulus field. Organisms are hardly ever impartial to their environment. To take the state of the organism first—the motivated or emotional condition, prior stimulation, fatigue, drowsiness, personal involvement, etc.—all these factors influence perception, judgment, learning, remembering, thinking, and make him selective to various degrees depending on the intensity of the factors producing the state. Established attitudes also have differential effects on all these processes. As for the stimulus, the degree of compellingness of the stimulus field (such as a loud noise, a perfect form) decreases the effects of selectivity as determined by internal factors. We shall return to this point later (pp. 224–227).

It is, then, evident that attitudes alone do not account for the states of readiness determining a characteristic or selective type of response. There are different kinds of states of readiness. Attitudes denote those which are learned (formed) in relation to definite stimuli (objects, persons, situations, values, or norms) and which are more or less lasting. (This differentiates an attitude from a momentary motivational or emotional state.) Therefore, attitudes always imply a *subject-object relationship*. The object of an attitude is of *value* to the individual. This affective property of an attitude is due either to the intrinsic, direct, or "instrumental" motivational appeal of the stimulus (such as food, a sex object, mother, milk bottle, a period of romance) or to the socially invested stamp of *value* on the stimulus. For example, in itself a flag is a piece of cloth of some color. The value of the flag in the eyes of the individual is derived from the socially standardized value attributed to it. A great many attitudes are formed in relation to social values or norms. Attitudes concerning the nation, family, or constitution are examples. These are usually incorporated in the individual through short-cut value judgments supplemented with all sorts of correctives in cases of deviations from the norm. The value judgments encompass a great many stimuli in their range ("extension"). Consequently, an attitude based on such a value judgment will be tapped by any stimulus related to it. For example, an attitude of prejudice toward "foreigners" in America will embrace diverse kinds of individuals who are related to the attitude in various degrees. It has become an established fact that the meanings of concepts (including value concepts) are immediate and do not require the recurrence of specific past associations.

Now, having differentiated attitudes from other kinds of states of readiness, we may return to an account of the principles underlying them. For, unlike judgment or perception, an attitude does not denote a distinct psychological phenomenon; it is a composite formation based on various factors.

Since attitudes are psychological formations learned in the course of the individual's development, a genetic start will be most helpful in understanding the underlying principles. As we elaborated at some length earlier (Chapter 3, pp. 51–60), the first *values* of the infant are stimuli which directly satisfy or are instrumental in satisfying his biogenic needs. As the child grows, he builds up attitudes (positive and negative) in relation to other objects, persons, or groups which may or may not have a bearing on his biogenic needs. As formulated by Tolman, "Instrumental values, however, are attached not only to the final environmental consummatory and evoking situations *but also to ordinarily neutral environmental objects (or situations)* in so far as these latter come to serve as consistent *means* or *hindrances* towards consummatory situations or away from the evoking situations." [2]

The infant is first so dominated by his momentary organic needs (food, sleep, etc.) that he is, in Gesell's words, "socially deaf and blind" to the provocations of social stimuli around him, including people and even the mother who feeds him. He

[2] E. C. Tolman, Motivation, learning and adjustment, *Proc. Amer. Philos. Soc.*, 1941, 84, p. 551 (first italics mine)

does not respond in a discriminatory or perceptive way to objects or persons around him except as they satisfy or prevent satisfaction of the dominant need of the moment. As Lewin says, "For the infant of a few weeks or months the valences [the values] depend essentially on his *own* needs and their momentary condition. If he does not want a food he cannot be moved by psychological means to eat it. He simply spits it out." [3]

As he grows older, he is made to observe routine practices and good manners (for his age) through power, prestige, momentary inclination to do things that others are doing, or through physiological habits. He has as yet to develop attitudes which he will consider his—attitudes which he will feel an urge to observe without any external pressure or coercion. In order to be able to achieve this, he has first to reach the level of psychological functioning at which he is able to delineate what is subjective (i.e., what is his whim, desire, or wish) and what is objective reality (physical phenomena, the point of view of others, natural laws, social standards, norms, etc.) For, as made evident in the extensive studies of Piaget, the infant up to a certain age of development cannot distinguish what is mere desire and whim and what is reality outside of him (physical and social). His own psychological world consists so dominatingly of his needs and desires that objects, persons, and the rest of his surroundings, are (to him) merely means for satisfying his ever-changing whims. Hence the lack of delineation between fantasy, wish, and reality. It is not a coincidence that the definitions of simple, already learned words expected of a three-year-old on standard intelligence tests (e.g., Stanford-Binet) are based on *use*, i.e., the way these objects are instrumental to him. He is unable to grasp and retain socially standardized rules or norms. To achieve this he has to be able to stick, with at least some consistency, to some point of view required by a rule or standard which may be at odds with his own mercurial needs. Similarly, for the same reason, he cannot carry on, for any appreciable time, give-and-take

[3] K. Lewin, "Environmental Forces in Child Behavior and Development," in C. Murchison (ed.), *A Handbook of Child Psychology*, Worcester: Clark University Press, 1931, p. 101.

relationships with other individuals, including other children because this requires seeing himself and the other person from the points of view of both.

Consequently, the child cannot as yet have consistent social attitudes outside of his attachments and aversions to things and persons based on the fulfillment or hindrance of his needs. Social attitudes, which are derived from established standards or rules, require conformity whether or not they are in line with the ups and downs of one's desires at the moment. To achieve conformity to a rule or standard requires a level of psychological development which distinguishes whim from reality (social and physical). This level is reached by the development of the ego, with resistances met socially and physically, and participation in group activities, particularly with age-mates. We shall elaborate on this in later chapters. Fuller implications of these developmental stages will emerge forcibly in the discussion of group prejudice (Chapter 14), but we may mention in passing that it is only after some degree of ego development, a stage at which the main social anchorings of the individual are established, that "race" prejudice becomes for him what it is for his group.

The foregoing paragraphs give only the main points of the general developmental picture in which attitudes are formed. We have yet to treat specifically the selective role of perception and judgment in which the selectivity of the attitude is embedded.

The selectivity of perceiving, judging (discriminating), and other major processes comes out strikingly, if we again start with the reactions of the infant. As we have seen before (Chapter 3, pp. 53 ff.), a child's earliest perceptions and discriminations are centered in the objects and persons that have something to do, directly or indirectly, with the satisfaction of his needs. He can be led to make finer discriminations if we succeed in arousing his biogenic motives to do so. The same is true of language development. His vocabulary and its growth are linked with his motives. In short, children's early cognitive functions (perceptions, discrimination, learning, etc.), as well as other functions, are at first dominated almost completely by his needs (motives), which render them highly, well-nigh

Attitudes

exclusively, selective. The selectivity of cognitive functions as well as other functions is not peculiar to children. Perceiving, judging, remembering, function selectively on the adult level too, as determined by biogenic needs and sociogenic motives.[4] The above discussion, together with the main line of evidence that stood out in our discussion of motives (Chapters 2–4), helps us to clarify our understanding of the *selectivity* revealed in perception, judgment, and other functions. It became quite evident that perceiving, discriminating, learning, etc., are not unrelated functions in the psychology of the individual. They are determined not only by the properties of the external field alone, but also by the internal factors (needs, attitudes, previous stimulation, etc.). Under the grip of intense motivation and attitudinal sets, internal factors may enter as limiting factors, especially if the external situation is vague or unstructured. The widespread use of projective techniques (Rorschach and others) and their at times remarkable predictive value provide major evidence for the point.

There is no way, psychologically, of detecting factors of motivation other than by their unmistakable differential effects on perception, learning, and other functions. The motivational factors (e.g., stomach contractions, depletion of water, accumulation of sex hormones) or the physiological humoral state produces (directly or indirectly) a "central motive state." The "central motive state," in turn, plays a dominant role in determining the perceptions, discriminations, learning that are taking place at the time. Therefore, when one talks about the *selectivity* of perception, learning, etc., one is really talking most of the time about the effects of motivational factors (sex, food, attitude, etc.). Unless we are working on the physiological

[4] The works of Bartlett, Murphy and Levine, Marks, Seeleman, Clark, Sanford, and Guetzkow and Bowman may be cited to this effect from an ever accumulating bulk of evidence. See F. C. Bartlett, *Remembering; A Study in Experimental and Social Psychology*, Cambridge: University Press, 1932; J. M. Levine and G. Murphy, The learning and forgetting of controversial material, *J. Abn. & Soc. Psychol.*, 1943, 38, 507–517; E. Marks, Skin color judgments of Negro college students, *J. Abn. & Soc. Psychol.*, 1943, 38, 370–376; V. Seeleman, The influence of attitude upon the remembering of pictorial material, *Arch. Psychol.*, 1940, 258; K. B. Clark, Some factors influencing the remembering of prose material, *Arch. Psychol.*, 1940, 253; R. N. Sanford, The effects of abstinence from food upon imaginal processes, *J. Psychol.*, 1936, 2, 129–136, and 1937, 3, 145–159; H. S. Guetzkow, and P. H. Bowman, *Men and Hunger*, Elgin, Ill.: Brethren Publishing House, 1946.

level (i.e., dealing directly with hormone factors, various depletions, etc.), there is no way of dealing with motives other than to take differential findings of various psychological phenomena as their indexes. This is, in fact, what "depth" psychologists (e.g., psychoanalysts) are constantly doing. In spite of their scorn of surface data, they are constantly using tiny bits of surface phenomena (various kinds of slips, selective forgetting, preoccupation with certain symbols, etc.) as indexes of the dramatic depth-phenomena complexes, "libido," infantile sexuality, etc.

On the basis of these considerations, we have in mind primarily the motivational factors when we talk about the *selectivity* of perception, judgment, etc. We have already discussed briefly the role of these factors in the selectivity of perception, judgment, memory, etc. To repeat, as the *selectivity* of attitudes is embedded in the selectivity of perceptual and judgmental processes in general, we do not have to make a special issue of the motivational components involved in an attitude. As concisely expressed by Tolman, " . . . purposiveness and cognitiveness seem to go together." [5]

Some Relevant Facts at the Basis of Attitudes

We just said that the selectivity of attitudes is embedded in the selectivity of perception and judgment. Now, since attitudes are formed in relation to stimuli, and since the first encounter of the individual with any stimulus is a perceptual one, some relevant facts from the psychology of perception are in order. And as attitudes are discriminatory affairs, certain findings in the psychology of judgment are necessary for a clarification of these composite formations, i.e., attitudes.

Of course, as vigorously emphasized by Doob recently, attitudes are learned.[6] Without learning, there would be momentary sets only, and no attitude formation. At present, we shall accept these formations in an empirical way as results of learning processes. The problems of just what the learning mecha-

---

[5] E. C. Tolman, *Purposive Behavior in Animals and Men*, New York: Appleton-Century, 1932, p.13.

[6] L. W. Doob, The behavior of attitudes, *Psychol. Rev.*, 1947, 54, 135–156.

nisms are, how many repetitions or "reinforcements" are necessary for such a complicated product as an attitude, how much disuse will cause an attitude to fade out, and other learning problems, are at present beyond our scope. The psychology of learning seems to be still in a highly controversial state especially in relation to complex topics. It will not help social psychologists (as yet) to take sides with a learning theory no matter how vigorous it may appear at first. In dealing with *social* attitudes we are dealing with highly complicated phenomena peculiar to the human level. Besides the structural properties of simple judgments and perceptions, functions at the abstract symbolic (conceptual) level are involved. In the meantime, we must eagerly follow the developments in learning theory, anticipating the filling in of the important bracket of learning mechanisms. The improvisations of learning theory by social psychology have not been happy ones.[7] An adequate psychology of learning that can be extended to social psychology will be one which takes into full account the structural properties of perception and judgment on the symbolic level.

That stimuli do not have absolute stimulating value has

[7] The following report of conditioning on human subjects gives a concrete idea of the implications of uncritically carrying the findings on subhuman animals to the human level, especially in social psychology where we are dealing with relationships of a symbolic and abstract nature: "It has been found that the conditioned salivary response in human subjects is erratic and not predictable from the particular properties of the stimuli and the amount of training. Razran (1935) found that although nearly all of his subjects showed some signs of conditioning, it was often sporadic and variable (cf. L. F. Jones, 1939). Thus one subject might give consistently large secretions, another almost none, and a third actually give a decrease in the flow of saliva in response to the conditioned stimulus. The same subject might react differently when in the presence of a group than when alone, and results might be quite different on successive days. On the assumption that the nature of the conditioned response which a subject yielded was to be attributed to his attitude, Razran attempted to control the attitude experimentally by specific instructions. When subjects were directed to form associations between the conditioned and unconditioned stimuli the responses were greater and more stable than when instructions not to form certain associations were given. On the other hand, when the establishment of such determining attitudes was prevented by forcing the subjects to concentrate on the task of learning a manual maze while the conditioning stimuli were presented, the resulting conditioned response showed a regular progressive acquisition and stable reliable magnitude (Razran, 1936a). In later studies, *by misleading the subjects with respect to the purpose of the experiment,* Razran (1939l) has been able to secure relatively involuntary salivary conditioning which much more nearly follows the rules to be expected from Pavlov." E. R. Hilgard and D. G. Marquis, *Conditioning and Learning,* New York: Appleton-Century, 1940, pp. 261-262 (italics mine).

become almost a truism. This holds in the case of relatively simple perceptual phenomena even without the inclusion of motivational factors in the picture.

Take a cardboard of uniform orange color about 2 feet long and 1 foot wide. Cover half of it with a black paper and look at the uncovered orange part steadily for some minutes—then remove the black cover. For some time the covered part will appear a different shade of orange from the other part. In the same way, a shade of gray may look darker or brighter according to the white or black surroundings, or the general pattern in which, or beside which, it is found. The same tone may seem different when alone and when preceded or followed by other tones in a melody. Within limits, a sound is judged high or low, a weight heavy or light, not only in accordance with its absolute physical value, but also in accordance with the background of sounds or weights that precede.

In these examples, we get different reactions to the same stimuli without preparing ourselves consciously to get them. On the contrary, we often have to force ourselves to destroy these variable reactions, and we do not always succeed.

But there are cases in which our anticipations and attitudes play an important part in determining our perceptions, especially if the external field of stimulation is not well structured. For example, different people may see different forms in indefinite ink blots or as they look at patches of clouds. On a dark night we may see all sorts of animate or inanimate forms as we walk past an old cemetery.

Psychologists usually use ambiguous figures to demonstrate the point. To give some well-known examples: In the same picture there may be hidden the outlines which permit seeing either a vase or two profiles (Fig. 25). In another picture there may be seen either a withered old woman or a smartly dressed young woman. Now in the first picture you will see either the vase or the two profiles first, depending largely upon whether you are prepared to see the one or the other. Also, as we reported from a concrete study, motivational factors may effect such reversals (Chapter 4, pp. 70–72). The same thing is true of the picture showing the old or the young woman. Ordinarily you see one or the other; they do not mix. The one

Fig. 25. When we see a vase, the shape stands out clearly, the rest forming the background. When we see two profiles, the contours of the faces are conspicuous in the foreground, and aspects that are not relevant to the profiles recede into the background. (From E. Rubin.)

you see, vase or profiles, old woman or young woman, as the case may be, stands out with clear contour, and the rest of the picture remains in the background. These and other cases of perception suggest that, whether external conditions are well and definitely structured or not, we ordinarily experience not confusion, but forms and shapes and other definite total structures. These are not arbitrary affairs; they are dependent on the lawful interplay of internal and external factors.

From these considerations we may generalize that even in the case of relatively simple stimulus objects there is no point-to-point correlation between the stimulus and what it arouses in us. Each time it stimulates it may not arouse the same effect. The effects are determined not only by the discrete physical stimulus, but by its place among other stimuli and internal conditions in us at the moment.

Now we may go one step further. Different persons may notice different characteristics of the same stimulus field. Lines and colors may be dominant for one man and ignored by another. It is not enough to have bright stars above you in order to notice and enjoy the constellations. Some do not notice the constellations that others do; and the groupings that are made vary somewhat from man to man and from culture to culture. Each culture emphasizes different aspects of the field, so that the field may take on altogether different modes of organization.

A well-known line of research may furnish us with a simple experimental demonstration of this principle. We refer to the experiments in Külpe's laboratory on the influence of *Aufgabe* (task or instruction) on perception of the stimuli presented.[8] In these experiments, begun in 1900, he briefly presented his subjects with different stimuli, such as printed syllables, about which different aspects or "dimensions" could be reported, e.g., the *number* of letters involved, the *location* of the colors, or the *total pattern* composed by them. Külpe found that more items were noted and more correct judgments made by the subject about that aspect of the stimuli which had been emphasized by the *Aufgabe*. The subjects noticed more fully and in more detail the aspects of the stimulus field that they had set themselves to see. Subsequently Yokoyama and Chapman verified Külpe's results.[9] All these experiments indicate that "the efficiency of report for all tasks is lower under an indefinite *Aufgabe* than under a definite instruction."

Even without such sets produced by deliberate instructions, our reactions to stimuli are not discrete, disjointed affairs. They derive their special significance in relation to reference

---

[8] O. Külpe, Versuche über Abstraktion, *Bericht über den I. Kongress für experimentelle Psychologie*, 1904, 56–68.

[9] Yokoyama, reported by E. G. Boring, Attribute and sensation, *Amer. J. Psychol.*, 1924, 35, 301–304; and D. W. Chapman, Relative eßects of determinate and indeterminate Aufgaben, *Amer. J. Psychol.*, 1932, 44, 163–174.

frames (scales) and points to which they are functionally related.

Perceptions, Judgments, and Other Major Phenomena Take Place Within Reference Frames

Experience appears to depend always upon *relations*. Immediately the question presents itself: What sort of relations? Perception, conceived as illustrative of experience in general, is the result of the organization of external and internal stimulating factors that come into functional relationship at a given time.[10] Factors that come into such functional relationships are interdependent; they affect each other, and the properties of any factor are determined partly by the properties of other factors. In this sense we can say that the external and internal factors that come into relationship form a functional whole. The reality of such functional wholes is amply demonstrated by experiment. For example, the brilliance of a patch of gray or the apparent temperature of an object depends, within limits, upon the brilliancies or temperatures to which the organism has been reacting.

The relational whole in our perceptions, judgments, and other experiences involves definite frames of reference. These frames of reference prove to be, not arbitrary abstractions from the experience, but fundamental characteristics of every situation consisting of external and internal factors which form a functional whole. When we say "up," we mean "up" in relation to something that is below. When we say "far," we mean far in reference to something near.

The frame of reference seems to be a concept of great importance in psychology, for facts implied in it reveal themselves persistently in almost every field of experimentation: in perception, judgment, memory, affectivity, etc. Here we have to restrict presentation of evidence to a few basic fields, viz., the sensory field, judgment, and perception.

In the Sensory Field. We find evidence like the following in any textbook on general psychology. Fill three vessels with

[10] See W. Köhler, *Gestalt Psychology*, New York: Liveright, 1929, especially chaps. 5 and 9.

water, one hot, one lukewarm, and one cold. Immerse one hand in hot water, the other in cold water for a couple of minutes, and then immerse both hands in the water of medium temperature. This same medium temperature will feel cool to the hand coming from the hot water, and warm to the one coming from the cold water. In relation to cold a medium temperature is experienced as warm; in relation to hot the same temperature is experienced as cool. Stimulation by cold or hot causes shifts, within limits, in the physiological zero or indifference point. This fact, one of the striking demonstrations of the phenomenon of "adaptation," is due to a physiological process (studied by Adrian and others). The sense organs first react to stimulation with all the energy at their disposal at the moment. If the stimulation continues, the strength of the reaction decreases. From moment to moment, the organ thus excited reacts differently to the same objective stimulation. In this process we find a physiological basis for the differences in reactions to the same stimulus field. This rough description will suffice to illustrate that the underlying processes in all our cases (and in all experience) are physiological. With this principle in mind, we may hope the physiologists will some day determine the neurological basis that underlies all our experience. But until then we have plenty of work to do on our own level of description. The physiologists' findings will not change the established relationships on our own level of work, but will teach us the neurological dynamics of our facts.

The principle implied in the different experiences excited by the same temperature can be illustrated by visual adaptation. When we come from the light into a dark room, the blackness will be intense; and when we have been in the dark for some time, our study light will appear very bright. A medium gray will appear darker after looking at bright objects, and, conversely, the same gray will seem brighter after looking at dark objects. These are well-known cases of "successive contrast." Likewise, in cases of simultaneous contrast, a gray patch is lighter *against* a black background, and vice versa.

The French psychologist Henri studied localization on the skin over a period of years (1892–1897). He first carried on his experiments at the Sorbonne in 1892–1894 (under the direction of Binet) and continued them at Leipzig in 1894. The results caused him to conclude that there are certain parts of the body, such as joints, that form a *frame of reference* for localization. Spots are localized in terms of distance from these parts of the body. The errors of localization cannot be interpreted without recognizing the role of the reference points involved. In his own words, "Almost always the error of localization is committed in the direction of the points of reference (*points de repère*) which the subject uses in the localization of the spot touched." [11] He further reported that when the subject used one reference point (*point de repère* or *Anhaltspunkt*) within a cutaneous area, there appeared a *constancy* in the direction of errors. With the shift of reference there appears a corresponding shift in the direction of the errors of localization.[12]

In Judgment. An especially striking illustration of the role of the frame of reference appears in a basic and much elaborated field of psychology —psychophysics, the study of the psychology of discrimination and judgment in response to stimuli which are parts of a quantitative continuum. The accumulating work on the "absolute judgment," or estimate of a single stimulus, shows that *in psychophysical judgments the use of a standard stimulus for each comparison is not needed to permit the observer to give a judgment about each stimulus in the series. After a few rounds of presentation, the observers establish a scale; the position of a stimulus is judged against the background of that scale.* A case reported by Wever and Zener is pertinent. Using the method of "absolute judgment" or single stimuli, they gave an observer a "light" series of weights (84, 88, 92, 96 and 100 grams); after this series had become an "established" scale for the observer, they suddenly introduced a "heavy" series (92, 96, 100, 104 and 108 grams). "The effect of the first series on the judgments of the second was quite evident for 20 or 25 presentations, i.e., for four or five rounds judgments of the 'heavy' *predominated* for all stimuli; from this point on, however, *the judgments showed a redistribution* conforming to the second

[11] V. Henri, Recherches sur la localisation des sensations tactiles, *Année Psychol.*, 1895, 2, 168–177.

[12] V. Henri, *Über die Lokalisation des Tastempfindungen*, Berlin: Reuther, 1897, pp. 37–38.

stimulus series." [13] In other words, *when for a stimulus (e.g., 96 grams) the "light series" (84–100 grams) is the frame of reference, the stimulus is experienced as heavy, but when the same stimulus is related to a heavy series, it is experienced as light.*

Wells found the same general principle to be operative in an experiment in which he asked his subjects to arrange a series of aesthetic stimuli in order of their preferences. He comments that "if A and B arranged 10 pieces of music in order of preference, the orders would center about each individual's own standard but if A, B, C, D, etc., arranged ten graduated weights, the orders would theoretically all center about a common standard, the objective order of heaviness." [14]

Hollingworth found comparable effects depending upon the establishment of a median value in the comparison of sizes. "In the experiment on sensible discrimination we become adapted to the median value of the series, tend to expect it, to assimilate all other values toward it, and to a greater or less degree to substitute it for them." [15]

During the last decade, extensive investigations were conducted showing one way or another the referential nature of judgments. For example, Long studied the effect of preceding stimuli upon the judgments of succeeding stimuli. He found that the values of succeeding stimuli were appreciably altered by earlier stimuli.[16]

Particularly interesting for us is the work of Rogers. Using a scale of weights in one experiment, Rogers showed the unmistakable effect of experimentally introduced reference points on the whole scale and on the individual stimuli in the scale. As the reference point is carried away from the scale upward, it expands the scale to a certain point, and as the reference point is moved down into the scale it causes the scale to shrink.[17]

[13] E. G. Wever and K. E. Zener, Method of absolute judgment in psychophysics, *Psychol. Rev.*, 1928, 35, no. 6, 475 ff.

[14] F. L. Wells, On the Variability of Individual Judgment, *Essays Philosophical and Psychological in Honor of William James, by his Colleagues at Columbia University*, New York: Longmans, Green, 1908, p. 152.

[15] H. L. Hollingworth, *Journal of Philosophy, Psychology and Scientific Methods*, 1910, 7, 468.

[16] L. Long, A study of the effect of preceding stimuli upon the judgments of auditory intensities, *Arch. Psychol.* 1937, no. 209.

[17] S. Rogers, The anchoring of absolute judgments, *Arch. Psychol.*, 1941, no. 261.

McGarvey substantiated this finding using verbal material.[18]

It would be one-sided to emphasize only the effect of reference points on the frame to which they are related. The range of the frame and the degree of strength of the frame in the individual will certainly have an effect on the reference point introduced. One new development in this field will be the study of the *reciprocal* effects of reference frames and points.

In this connection, Tresselt's work on the influence of practice in forming a scale of judgment is particularly interesting.[19] It directly connects the work on reference frames with learning. Tresselt had her subjects practice first with a given scale of weights. After various degrees of practice (learning) with this scale, she introduced a new scale. She found (a) that the practiced scale had a significant effect *at first* in the judgments of the values of the new scale until the subject adjusted himself to it, and (b) that, "there is a definite effect of different amounts of practice" upon the new series. "The greater the amount of practice, the more slowly does the scale of judgment shift to its new position" (p. 260). This finding demonstrates the experience of individuals during the period of adjustment to new surroundings, and the difficulty that the people with rigidly established routines undergo in making such adjustments.

In Perception. Gestalt psychologists furnish an infinite number of instances of "anchoring" (*Verankerung*). They insist on the member-character of a part within an organized structure. Thus Wertheimer demonstrated that a line is experienced as horizontal or vertical in reference to the position of other things in the field of stimulation.[20] If the observer's visual field was objectively slanted by means of a mirror, a similarly slanted objective line tended to appear vertical, indicating that the position of an object is perceived in its relation to the whole organized field. Koffka has made a special issue of the notion of "member-character" and *Verankerungspunkte*

[18] H. R. McGarvey, Anchoring effects in the absolute judgment of verbal materials, *Arch. Psychol.*, 1943, no. 281.

[19] M. E. Tresselt, The influence of amount of practice upon the formation of a scale of judgment, *J. Exper. Psychol.*, 1947, 3, 251–260.

[20] M. Wertheimer, *Drei Abhandlungen zur Gestalt-theorie*, Philosophische Akademie, Erlangen, 1925, pp. 93–99.

(anchorage points), and the importance of the ground for the figure. He summarizes the facts and the argument on this point by saying: ". . . All this means that a definite single position exists only within a fixed spatial level. If the conditions for the formation of such a level are absent, localization is no longer possible; for just as the level grows unstable, so does the single point within it." [21]

In discussing the *ground* (in relation to *figure*) he writes: ". . . The ground has a very important function of its own; it serves as a general level (niveau) upon which the figure appears. Now figure and ground form a structure, consequently the former cannot be independent of the latter. On the contrary, the quality of the figure must be largely determined by the general level upon which it appears. This is a universal fact, observed in such products of culture as fashion and style. The same dress which is not only smart, but nice to look at, almost a thing of beauty, may become intolerable after the mode has passed" (p. 566).

This fact suggests directly the relationship involved in figure and ground, first studied extensively by E. Rubin and much emphasized by Gestalt psychologists. In the stimulus field, a part is organized into the figure and stands out with definite shape or form, segregated with clear-cut boundaries or contours; the rest forms the background upon which the figure appears. The picture on page 215 is a good illustration of the point. When one sees in it a vase, the shape of the vase stands out with its own definite contours; when, on the other hand, two profiles facing each other are seen, the contours of the vase slip to the background and the faces pop into the foreground, displaying the distinct contours of the profiles.

The resolution of the stimulus field into figure and ground has been shown experimentally by the present writer to hold on a simple social level as well as with figures such as presented in our example. In this experiment the subjects were seated in a room in which material spoken in a different room could be heard through a loud-speaker. Two short stories of approximately equal length and dealing with similar topics were read

[21] K. Koffka, Perception: an introduction to Gestalt-theorie, *Psychol. Bull.*, 1922, 19, 570.

simultaneously. One of the stories came through the loud-speaker; the other one was read by a person in the same room with the subjects. After the reading the subjects were asked to write down whatever they could remember of the two stories. The result was not the confusion of the two stories coming to their ears simultaneously; but, in a great majority of cases, one story was picked up and heard in a meaningful way as the whole story to the end. These results indicate that when two meaningful materials are presented to the ears simultaneously, one meaningful unity is picked up and followed in such a way that it forms a continuous whole; the other material forms the background, perhaps a more or less disturbing one in our particular case. For our present purposes it does not matter which of the stories was picked up more often—that of the reader or that from the loud-speaker. The results reported above were substantiated later by the experiments of G. Houghton.[22]

Nevertheless, figure and ground are not independent; each influences the properties of the other. In a public place you may be absorbed in conversation with a friend and may be directly noticing only his face and his words. But the general structure of the background, the gaiety or solemnity of the group, the quietness or noise around you, will have an effect on you and your friend despite your absorption in each other. In Koffka's words, "The ground serves as a general level (niveau) upon which the figure appears."

The ground is especially important in social psychology. Group studies would gain much more significance, as we have indicated in Chapter 6, if the subtle relationship between the figure and the background were taken into consideration. For example, when two people are talking in a public place, their conversation and behavior are tinged by the properties of the whole "atmosphere."

The evidence on the referential nature of our reactions can be piled up indefinitely from other fields also—memory,[23]

[22] These experiments are reported in H. Cantril and G. W. Allport's *The Psychology of Radio*, New York: Harper, 1935, p. 150.

[23] For example, see T. Ribot, *Diseases of Memory*, London: Appleton, 1893; M. Halbwachs, *Les cardres sociaux de la mémoire*, Librarie Félix Alcan, 1925; F. C. Bartlett, *Remembering: A Study in Experimental and Social Psychology*, Cambridge: University Press, 1932.

affectivity,[24] personality, etc. In the next chapters, we shall present evidence (from the investigations of Chapman and Volkmann, Sears, Himmelweit, and others) showing that our aspirations and goals are also referential affairs.

Differential Effects of Structured and Unstructured Stimulus Situations

We have already had occasion to refer to the differing effects of the degree to which the external field is structured. Before giving a concise experimental demonstration of the formation of an attitude, we must remind ourselves of the implications of these differential effects. They are basic to the understanding of the major types of attitude formation.

There are cases in which the external field of social stimulation is *well structured*. We see definite shapes in buildings, tables, and books. We hear definite melody and rhythm in the music coming from radio, choir, and orchestra. The field of stimulation is organized into definite structures, the rest forming the background on which these structures stand out with figure-character. In the organization of response to stimulation the essential principle is the *grouping* of different parts of the stimulus field.

Some sort of grouping takes place, whether or not the stimulus field itself imposes the essential conditions for grouping. In cases in which the field of stimulation is well structured, the special characteristics of a grouping are determined by the factors in the external situation. The shape of a square with clear-cut lines will be perceived by everybody as a square. In this case the sharp contours of the four lines unmistakably connected with each other at their extremities are determining factors. The factors determining the structuring of the stimulus field have been studied and found to include among others the following: closeness (proximity), likeness, "common fate," and objective set. If there are dots at irregular intervals before you, the dots which are close together will be grouped together. But if such a spatial factor is lacking and certain of the dots

24 J. Beebe-Centre, *Pleasantness and Unpleasantness*, New York: D. Van Nostrand and Company, 1932; N. E. Cohen, The relativity of absolute judgments, *Amer. J. Psychol.*, 1937, 49, 93–100.

are alike—say, in color or shape—the similar ones are likely to be grouped together.[25]

In actual social life man (in any culture) is surrounded by tools, furniture, buildings, means of transportation, timetables, and other definite schedules regulating the run of vital activities. All these *compellingly* force themselves on the individual (even without direct mediation of other individuals) with their definite magnitudes, proportions, limiting time spans, definite scopes of distance, etc. These compelling features of the "man-made" world produce in the individual definite scales, frames, and standards. These scales (frames), and standards, once they are formed in him, constitute the major source of the formation of his tastes and expectations in relation to things, his conception of the scope of his world, his degree of mobility, his major sense of the proportion of things, his conception of the scale of speed, riches, etc. We have already referred to this field of stimulation as material culture or technology. Together with its psychological effects, namely, the mentality and technology relationship, it is a sorely neglected topic of social psychology. This all-important topic will be our concern in Chapter 15.

Where such objective factors are wanting, i.e., where the stimulus field is *unstructured* in various degrees, the result is usually not a perception of chaos; organization still takes place. But in such cases the internal or internalized factors play the dominant role in organization or grouping. These internal or internalized factors may be attitude, set, drive, emotional state, etc. Consider ambiguous figures and puzzle pictures. These pictures can be seen in different ways, but if you tell an observer one of the possibilities first, he will probably see that one and not the others.

The Rorschach tests are good examples of an indefinite, non-structured field of stimulation. These tests consist of ambiguous ink blots. The subjects are asked to report whatever they see in them. Since the ink blots are irregular and complex, they are open to all sorts of interpretations which reveal certain internal factors in the subject himself. One of the early

[25] See especially M. Wertheimer, *Untersuchungen zur Lehre von der Gestalt, Psychol. Forschung*, 1923, 301–350.

studies, that of Bleuler and Bleuler in 1935, shows concretely how habitual ways of looking at things as a result of cultural peculiarities may cause people to interpret the Rorschach blots in such a way as to reveal the characteristics of their well-established culture products. These investigators gave Rorschach tests to a group of Moroccan subjects. The important result for our problem is that the Moroccans gave "such a wealth of small-detail responses" as is not usually found in European subjects.[26] This very probably may be a reflection of the "love for beautiful detail" in the Moroccan art.

Some good examples of the tendency to form groups and the dominance of internal factors over external are found in the experimental work on rhythm. The essential condition in the perception of rhythm is grouping of stimuli. Usually accent is decisive in determining rhythmic patterns. But even when sounds follow one another fairly rapidly at a uniform rate without intensity or time-interval differences, we cannot help grouping them, and we experience rhythm although rhythm is objectively lacking. The rhythmic grouping of the puffs of the locomotive or the grinding of the train wheels is well known. These are examples of subjective rhythm.

This was experimentally demonstrated by Sherif. The stimulus was a succession of ticks coming from behind a screen at a uniform rate. The groups of subjects were instructed to move their hands in time with the ticks, and to count aloud in a particular grouping given to them by the experimenter: 1–2 or 1–2–3 or 1–2–3–4, as the case might be. While this was in progress, another subject was brought into the experimental room. This new subject was completely ignorant of the fact that the rhythm was prescribed; he was told merely to listen to the rhythm. For a few minutes the other subjects continued in his presence, after which all but the naïve subject were sent out of the room. He was then instructed to beat time to the rhythm of the ticks. Most of these subjects conformed to the grouping that had been suggested by the hand movements and oral counting-off by the other subjects. The usual introspective reports obtained from the naïve subjects revealed a tendency

[26] M. Bleuler and R. Bleuler, Rorschach's ink-blot test and racial psychology: mental peculiarities of Moroccans, *Character and Personality*, 1935, 4, 97–114.

to experience intensity (accent) and time-interval differences. (It would be interesting to compare the reactions of musically naïve subjects with the reactions of musically sophisticated subjects.)

All these illustrations show that whether the external field of stimulation is well structured or not, it is organized into definite frames. If the external field is well structured, the objective factors in the situation chiefly determine what sort of grouping will take place. If the external field is not well structured, grouping still takes place; but here internal or internalized factors such as attitude play the dominating role in determining or completing the grouping. This grouping is a primary experiential fact. Even if this or that pattern depends largely on past associations, it is scarcely likely that the *tendency to organize* a stimulus field is itself merely a product of association.

Of course there are an almost infinite number of gradations of structure of the stimulus field—from, say, the imposing compellingness of Rockefeller Center in New York to the confusion and chaos of a devastated town in which the schedules of public services are disrupted because of war.

In the recent work of Luchins we find a clear demonstration of the graded effects of the degrees of structuration. Luchins studied the effects of social factors (e.g., suggestion) in relation to stimulus objects with various degrees of structuration. The studies show that the greater the degree of vagueness or indefiniteness of the stimulus object, the greater the effect of social factors.[27] On the basis of such findings, we may state that *the effect of social factors coming from without (suggestion, group pressure, etc.) and of internal factors (motivation, attitudes, etc.) increases with the vagueness, "indeterminateness," and decreases with the clarity and structuredness of the stimulus situation.*

Bruner recently expressed the same principle: ". . . The greater the equivocality the greater the chance for behavioral factors in perception to operate, all other things being equal." [28]

[27] A. S. Luchins, On agreement with another's judgment, *J. Abn. & Soc. Psychol.*, 1944, 39, 97–111; A. S. Luchins, Social influences on perception of complex drawings, *J. Soc. Psychol.*, 1945, 21, 257–273.

[28] J. S. Bruner and C. C. Goodman, Value and need as organizing factors in perception, *J. Abn. & Soc. Psychol.*, 1947, 42, 36.

10.

Attitude Formation and Change

IN CHAPTER 7, WE PRESENTED EXPERIMENTS DEMONSTRATING the rise of group norms in relation to an unstructured stimulus situation, and their effect on the individual when he is no longer in the group.

Experimental Production of an Attitude [1]

Proceeding on the basis of these facts and hypotheses, we can undertake the experimental formation of an attitude using the same autokinetic technique. This brings us close to the way many attitudes are formed in actual life. In daily life, many of our major attitudes are formed on the basis of short-cut value dictums coming from other people, *before we make up our minds ourselves through actual contact* with the situations, persons, and things. In other words, the relationships are structured, crystallized for us through these value dictums before we form our own attitudes in relation to them on the basis of sufficient facts. The following experiment was undertaken to demonstrate this fact in a precise laboratory situation.

The experiment to be reported deals with the influence of the pronouncements of another person on the adoption of a prescribed attitude. There were 7 groups in this experiment, each group consisting of 2 members. In every group one subject cooperated with the experimenter, i.e., deliberately distributed his judgments within the range and around the norm assigned to him by the experimenter beforehand. The other subject was unaware of this predetermination. The degree of this "naïve"

---

[1] This study is reprinted with slight changes from M. Sherif, An experimental approach to the study of attitudes, *Sociometry*, 1937, 1, 90–98.

subject's conformity to the norm and range of the cooperating subject may be taken as the index of the social influence. The same subject cooperated with the experimenter in every group in order to keep the influencing member constant in all the groups.

The range and the norm prescribed for every group were different. For the first group, the prescribed range was 1–3 inches, 2 inches being the prescribed norm. For the second group, the prescribed range was 2–4, and 3 inches the norm, and so on to the seventh group for which the range and norm were 7–9 and 8 respectively. It will be observed that the prescribed range was rather narrow; consequently in the course of the experimental period the cooperating subject gave no judgments which deviated from the norm by more than one inch in either direction.

In the first experimental session, both subjects (the cooperating and the naïve) took part. After each exposure of the point of light for two seconds, the subjects spoke their judgments aloud one at a time and the experimenter recorded them. In order not to stress the factor of *primacy*, the cooperating subject was instructed to let the other subject utter his judgment first, at least half of the time. The social influence in our previous experiments with the autokinetic effect was found to be not so much a function of this and that separate judgment as of the temporal sequence of judgments. Fifty judgments were taken from each subject.

In the second session only the naïve subject was present, so that we might see how much of the prescribed range and norm he carried from the group session. Again fifty judgments were taken. As the norm formation in the autokinetic effect is a fragile and, in a sense, artificial formation, such an arbitrary prescription may break down easily after a certain number of judgments. Our whole point is that the autokinetic effect may be utilized to show a general psychological tendency, and not to reveal the concrete properties of attitude formation in actual life situations.

In the presentation of results we give the prescribed range and norm, the number of judgments of the naïve subject falling within the prescribed range, and his norms (as represented by the median of the distribution of his judgments) in the first (group) and second (individual) sessions.

GROUP 1

	Experimentally Obtained (from Naïve S)	
Prescribed	Session I (in Group)	Session II (Alone)
Range 1–3 inches	1–5	1–4
Norm 2	3.36	2.62
No. of the 50 judgments falling within the prescribed range	41	47

At the end of the second (individual) session the subject was asked to answer in writing four questions related to the problem. The answers to two of the questions further verify our earlier results. We shall therefore confine ourselves to the answers given to the other two questions, which are important for our present problem. These questions were: (1) What was the distance that the light most frequently moved? (This was intended to find out whether the subjects became conscious of the norm formed in the course of the experiment); (2) Were you influenced by the judgments of the other person who was present during the first session? (This question was asked in order to find out whether the subjects were conscious of the fact that they were being influenced by the cooperating subject.)

The answers of the subject in Group 1 are important for any theory of suggestion and attitude formation:

1. Most frequent distance was 2 inches. Seemed to be more consistently 2 inches second day than on first day.

2. Yes, they were despite my efforts to be impartial. Probably many of my judgments were inordinately large because of small distances given by other subject. I think this was an attempt at avoiding suggestion and in so doing going to the other extreme. *I do not think I was influenced by first day's judgments on the second day.* I tried to be impartial in my judgments the first day. *I felt resentment toward the other subject the first day because of the successive equal judgments by him.* I tried to be objective toward this feeling: that is to banish the thought. But I feel that this resentment caused my judgments to

differ from his by a greater amount than they would have if the judgments had been kept separate; that is if I had not heard his judgments. *The second day I felt more independence in my judgments and I believe that these judgments were therefore more accurate.*

GROUP 2

	Experimentally Obtained (from Naïve S)	
Prescribed	Session I (in Group)	Session II (Alone)
Range 2–4 inches	1–10	1–5
Norm 3 inches	4.25	3.77
No. of the 50 judgments falling within the prescribed range	30	43

The answers to the two questions were:

1. "Three or four inches were the most frequent estimates."
2. "*No, I was not influenced by the other person.* This I believe was because I stated my estimates first for the most part."

GROUP 3

	Experimentally Obtained (from Naïve S)	
Prescribed	Session I (in Group)	Session II (Alone)
Range 3–5 inches	2–8	3–6
Norm 4 inches	4.61	4.57
No. of the 50 judgments falling within the prescribed range	43	49

The answers follow:

1. "Four inches yesterday. Five inches today."
2. "Yes, my first judgments are much higher than those following. In a way I scaled them down to ranges nearer to his. The majority of times I gave my judgments first. The same distance seemed shorter after a few trials. My judgments were influenced by yesterday's. I measured them by the same scale both days."

GROUP 4

	Experimentally Obtained (from Naïve S)	
Prescribed	Session I (in Group)	Session II (Alone)
Range 4–6	3–6	3–6
Norm 5	5.20	5.21
No. of the 50 judgments falling within the prescribed range	47	46

The reports:
1. "Five inches."
2. "For the first three or four times. After that, no."

GROUP 5

	Experimentally Obtained (from Naïve S)	
Prescribed	Session I (in Group)	Session II (Alone)
Range 5–7	3–7	3–7
Norm 6	5.50	5.42
No. of the 50 judgments falling within the prescribed range	34	35

The reports:
1. "Five inches both days."
2. "No. *I was not influenced by the presence of another person.* But I sincerely believe that my partner was exaggerating the distance when he made his estimate. I say this because it seemed to me that he hesitated several seconds after I gave my estimate. . . ."

GROUP 6

	Experimentally Obtained (from Naïve S)	
Prescribed	Session I (in Group)	Session II (Alone)
Range 6–8	3–8	4–8
Norm 7	5.94	6.18
No. of the 50 judgments falling within the prescribed range	24	27

The reports:

1. "Seven most frequent, 5 next frequent."
2. *"No, I was not influenced."*

GROUP 7

	Experimentally Obtained (from Naïve S)	
Prescribed	Session I (in Group)	Session II (Alone)
Range 7–9	4–12	6–9
Norm 8	7.40	7.83
No. of the 50 judgments falling within the prescribed range	17	40

The reports:

1. "The most frequent distance was about 8 inches. The next most frequent was about 7 inches."
2. "I think it did make a difference when somebody else was with me. When I gave my judgment first, there was no difference, of course, but when he was with me I sometimes, though not all the time, modified my judgment when it was very far from his, and when I thought that I might easily have been mistaken. Of course, this did not occur frequently, but I cannot deny that it happened sometimes."

Conclusion. From these results we may conclude that the subjects may be influenced to perceive an indefinite stimulus field in terms of an experimentally introduced norm. The degree of the influence may be different in different subjects, in line with individual differences. It may be great, as in the case of the subject in Group 4. It may be not so striking, as in the case of the subject in Group 5; or it may be negligible, as with the subject in Group 6. Even in the last case, an influence on the norm (though not on the range) is evident.

The answers reveal that the subjects become conscious of the norm which develops in the course of the experiment. However, they may not all be conscious of the fact that they are being influenced toward that norm by the other member of the group. (See answers given by the subjects in Groups 1, 2, and 4.) And, as determined by personality factors, they may or may

not feel resentment at such influence. But whatever these personality differences, the general fact of the convergence toward
a common attitude is evidenced. In connection with this point,
it is interesting to note that in some cases the *conformity* to
the prescribed range and norm when the *influencing person* is
no longer present (Session II) is closer than the *conformity*
produced by his actual presence. (See the results for Groups 2,
3, 6, 7.)

It seems to us that the psychological process embodied in
these facts may be basic to the daily phenomena of suggestion,
especially to the role of suggestion in the formation of attitudes.
It is not a rare occurrence in everyday life to react negatively or
hesitatingly to a suggestion on some topic made by an ac-
quaintance while in his presence, but to respond positively after
leaving him (perhaps there is a disinclination to accept suggestions readily unless there is a strong prestige or pressing demand; to appear easily yielding is not so pleasant for an ego).

Attitudes, we repeat, imply characteristic modes of readiness
in reacting to definite objects, situations, and persons. This
experiment has demonstrated in a simple way how a *characteristic* kind of readiness may be experimentally obtained in
relation to an indefinite stimulus field.

Extensions to More Concrete Material. The experiment just
reported shows the basic psychological processes involved in
the formation of an attitude. The stimulus object in this experimental situation does not *itself* arouse motivational factors
such as are found in social relationships in daily life, in which
persons are directed toward definite goal objects. However, even
though the stimulus object itself lacks motivational appeal,
questions of competence arise between the subjects because of
the discrepancies of their judgments in relation to the situation.
Discrepancies in judgments in a vague situation in relation to
which the subject feels insecure arouse some ego issues among
the subjects. In spite of such issues, the subjects feel compelled
to converge, because of the insecurity of the situation.

Yet such experimental demonstrations, which emphasize the
process of formation rather than the content of attitudes, may
be mere artifacts of the laboratory. It is necessary to have verifications of the conclusions from studies using more concrete

stimulus material. Of the available material, we shall use only two illustrations.

Experimental verification of these results has been obtained, utilizing stimulus objects having social value. In a series of experiments, Asch, Block, and Hertzman had subjects make judgments of photographs, political figures, professions, and well-known slogans along several dimensions—e.g., intelligence and honesty for the photographs, social usefulness, idealism, etc., for professions, and the like.[2] These situations, for the most part, were "objectively ill-structured and vague" in order "to investigate the dependence of judgments upon subjective factors which function when the objective characteristics of the situation are reduced to a minimum" (p. 219). Particularly in the case of the photographs of strange persons, the subjects had few standards by which to make their judgments. In such a situation, just as in the autokinetic study, the subjects established a frame or scale within which they made judgments concerning each situation. "*The judgments of a single situation are related to each other by a person in accordance with an underlying attitude of acceptance or rejection*" (p. 248). These findings came out most clearly "for situations which are not well-defined objectively." Of course, in the case of stimuli which the subjects (college students) had already faced in daily life, such as professions, this "underlying attitude" was found to correspond rather closely to the "prevailing norms" of "the cultural background of our subjects."

The authors at a later time went on to vary the experimental conditions systematically, introducing "authoritative standards" in order to study their effects on the individual judgments of the stimuli. For example, after the subjects had made their individual judgments, they were given the judgments purportedly made by a group of college students and were then asked to judge the stimuli. The result here was: "*A standard having an authoritative source tends to alter an individual's judgments in its direction*" (p. 249). Such standards were found to be influential "even when they were strongly at variance with those of the subjects" (p. 249). The investi-

[2] S. E. Asch, H. Block, and M. Hertzman, Studies in the principles of judgments and attitudes: I. Two basic principles of judgment, *J. Psychol.*, 1938, 5, 219–251.

gators suggest "that a standard, functioning as a frame of reference, may produce organization at a higher level, when it carries with it the sanction of public approval than when the same or a similar stimulus standard is evolved by the individual himself" (p. 232). Thus, with socially significant material, *conformity to a prescribed standard* was produced in the judgments of the individuals, just as it was in the experiment in which the stimulus had no significance for the subjects.

Of particular interest was the finding that the shifts in the direction of the authoritative standard were *less* for judgments of slogans than for the other materials. In the case of the slogans, although the authoritative standard exerted some influence, the individual's own "scale of reference" tended to be a more decisive factor. The authors interpret this finding in light of the fact that "the subject is being influenced by a background of historical and political knowledge" and that, therefore, the situation is "relatively well-structured" (p. 250). Under these circumstances, his "strongly fixed" attitude functions more effectively than the experimental group standard in determining his judgments. Thus, these results "do not constitute an exception to the findings of the present experiments" (p. 250).

In a further series of similar experiments, Asch found that even when a fictitious standard introduced as that of a group of college students correlated −1.00 (i.e., with an exactly opposite ranking) with the individual's own judgments, the standard effected a shift in individual judgments.[3] Even when the subjects were given their own previous judgments as a standard, they were "*influenced more strongly by the fictitious standard of a congenial group than by their own standards!*" (p. 447).

However, Asch found that a standard imputed to just any group did not have this effect. When the subjects were told that the standard consisted of judgments made by Nazis, there was "a tendency to reject the standards . . . as a basis for judgment" (p. 463). Here we see how previously formed attitudes toward an out-group, and especially an out-group with standards highly

[3] S. E. Asch, Studies in the principles of judgments and attitudes: II. Determination of judgments by group and by ego standards, *J. Soc. Psychol.*, *SPSSI Bull.*, 1940, 12, 433–465.

at variance with one's own group standards, lead to a rejection of the standard, as opposed to the acceptance of the standard of a "congenial" group or *reference group*.

Our second illustration is from a recent work by Stagner and Osgood, showing attitude formation and shifts as found in the actual course of human events.[4] These investigators obtained ratings from college students and adult subjects for various groups (Englishmen, Socialists, Frenchmen, Pacifists, etc.) on an 8-point scale ranging from one extreme value judgment to the other (e.g., kind to cruel, strong to weak, etc.). In addition, certain concepts like "Big Navy," "Neutrality," "Fighting" were similarly judged. Ratings were obtained between April, 1940, just before the Nazi invasion of Norway, and March, 1942, and the changes or shifts of attitude were noted. In this case, the frame to which a judgment was referred was formed from the actual course of events, the opinions of newspapers, radio, and other mass media, as well as from the norms of the individuals' membership groups. For example, in 1940, the subjects tended to be "isolationist-nationalistic, but opposed to intervention." But the "bombs of Pearl Harbor acted upon mental patterns which already had shifted far along the path of war. The sharp impact of that event is shown in the curves for Fighting, Pacificism, and Neutrality" (p. 199).

Particularly relevant to this discussion are the findings about judgments concerning Russians. In the authors' words, "We suspect that most American adults have no more objective data on the cruelty of Russians than Sherif's subjects had on the extent of the autokinetic phenomenon" (p. 213). In such cases, one would expect the judgments made to be particularly liable to social influences. In the beginning of the study, the median judgment of Russians was one of decided disapproval. General approval increased after Hitler's attack on the Russians until by March, 1942, the judgment was slight approval. Particularly striking was the increase in the concept "strong" in relation to the Russians when they "proved their power by unexpectedly holding the Nazis." However, in general the authors

[4] R. Stagner and C. E. Osgood, Impact of war on a nationalistic frame of reference: I. Changes in general approval and qualitative patterning of certain stereotypes, *J. Soc. Psychol.*, 1946, 24, 187–215.

noted that judgments on the "good-bad" dimension are relatively resistant to the impact of events. We shall have more to
say about this point in the next section.

The authors interpret their findings in terms of "the frame
of reference as an interiorization of the culture-pattern. The
individual is trained to accept the judgments of others regarding the allocation of given concepts to certain points on the
approval-disapproval continuum, and even to a considerable
extent on specific gradients, just as Sherif's subjects . . . were
influenced by majority opinion" (p. 213). However, "change
they do," to some extent at least, with the compellingness of
events, such as the decisive defeat of Hitler's army by the Russians (p. 205). Similarly, whereas the general evaluation
concerning Frenchmen remained positive as a result of the prevailing values of American life, the judgments of their strength
decreased increasingly after the fall of Paris and the subsequent
stages of occupation.

Change and Perpetuation of Attitudes

Since attitudes are formed (learned) in relation to objects,
persons, groups, or norms (values), it follows that they are not
unchangeable. So fundamental is the whole problem of change
in the superstructure of "human nature," which consists chiefly
of attitudes of various kinds, that it runs through many sections of this book. It has already been considered briefly in
Chapter 6. The theme will reappear in the chapters on ego-
involvements, in our discussions of adolescence and prejudice,
and will be among our chief concerns in Part III, "Individuals
and Social Change." At present, therefore, only a few general remarks on attitude change are necessary as further verification of
the process of attitude formation outlined earlier in this chapter.

Attempts at changing attitudes or social prejudices experimentally by the dissemination of information or factual argument have been notably unrewarding. Some investigators have
been unable to obtain any change.[5] Others have obtained various
degrees of shift in the desired direction, although there were

[5] See, for example, E. B. Bolton, Effect of knowledge upon attitudes toward the
Negro, *J. Soc. Psychol.*, 1935, 6, 68–90; and D. Young, Some effects of a course in
American race problems on the race prejudice of 450 undergraduates at the University
of Pennsylvania, *J. Abn. & Soc. Psychol.*, 1927, 22, 335–342.

almost always some cases showing negative or no change.[6] And at times the changes produced by such methods were in the opposite direction to that attempted.[7] Although the attempts at changing attitudes through information alone may produce shifts in degree or alteration of items of behavior, these changes are apt to be discrete and rather ephemeral.

It is a common observation of life that individual contact with persons or events the characteristics of which run counter to a well-established attitude seldom has much effect on the individual's attitude. To persons with a strong, unfavorable attitude toward Negroes, individual Negroes who have none of the supposed stereotyped characteristics either are perceived as possessing them anyway or are viewed as exceptional cases. Thus, for a prejudiced person, a Paul Robeson may verify the assumption that "Negroes are musical," or may be considered as an "exception" from the "usual run." Even events of a world-wide scope may leave people unmoved. For example, the Nuremberg trials were a dramatic exposition of the Nazi crimes against humanity. However, according to one member of the American prosecution: "It is certainly true that there remain large bodies of Germans on whom the trials have had no effect whatsoever. . . ." [8] According to another observer, "Not even proof of the bestiality of Belsen guards will show them what the Nazis did." [9] Without doubt, however, at least some Germans were affected by the revelations and events following the Nazi defeat. Still others were perhaps only confused, disillusioned, and embittered. For it is a fact that when established reference frames become shaky or break down, the individual tends to experience uncertainty, ambiguity, or anxiety until he accepts some new reference point or frame. Especially when attitudes

[6] For example, P. W. Schlorff, *An Experiment in the Measurement and Modification of Racial Attitudes in School Children*, Ph.D. thesis, New York University, 1930; M. Smith, A study of change of attitudes toward the Negro, *J. Negro Educ.*, 1939, 8, 64–70; H. H. Remmers, Propaganda in the schools—do the effects last? *Public Opinion Quart.*, 1930, 2, 197–210.

[7] For example, D. D. Droba, Education and Negro attitudes, *Sociol. and Soc. Res.*, 1932, 17, 137–141; A. J. Manske, *The Reflection of Teacher's Attitudes in the Attitudes of Their Pupils*, Ph.D. thesis, Teacher's College, Columbia Univ., 1935.

[8] R. M. W. Kempner, "Impact of Nuremberg on the German Mind," The *New York Times Magazine*, October 6, 1946, p. 66.

[9] I. A. R. Wylie, "Germany Nation of Nazis Still," *Ladies' Home Journal*, 1946, 63, 24 ff.

are related to the individual's very conception of himself, when they involve his anchorage with his surroundings, their break-down may lead to confusion and chaos for him.

If the facts about the matter in question or even concrete experience *alone* are not sufficient to lead to fundamental and lasting attitude changes, what methods are effective? In answering this question, we find that the process of attitude change involves the same factors as those in attitude formation. In the studies of Asch, Block, and Hertzman, and of Asch, we found that the introduction of a standard or reference frame from some "congenial" group (reference group) effected a substantial change in individuals' judgments except for stimuli in relation to which some attitude was already well established. In such cases, the existing frame resulted in the perception of an already structured situation by the individual. The most clear-cut evidence concerning the factors necessary for fundamental change in such well-established attitudes came from Newcomb's Bennington study presented earlier (see pp. 139–155). Here the decisive effect of group membership and identification (ego-involvement) with the group and its products (norms, values) on the process of attitude change came out clearly. Lewin's study showing the superiority of "group decision" to a lecture method for changing food habits is another case in point. Lewin concluded that fundamental attitude change (re-education) was dependent on identification with a group.

Re-education influences conduct only when the new system of values and beliefs dominates the individual's perception. The acceptance of the new system is linked with the acceptance of a specific group, a particular role, a definite source of authority as new points of reference. It is basic for re-education that this linkage between acceptance of new facts or values and acceptance of certain groups or roles is very intimate and that the second frequently is a prerequisite for the first. This explains the great difficulty of changing beliefs and values in a piecemeal fashion. This linkage is a main factor behind resistance to re-education, but can also be made a powerful means for successful re-education.[10]

[10] K. Lewin and P. Grabbe, "Conduct, Knowledge, and Acceptance of New Values," in *Changing Attitudes and Behavior, Publication No. 3*, Research Center for Group Dynamics, Department of Economics and Social Science, Massachusetts Institute of Technology, 1945, p. 12.

This general observation is confirmed by observations of individual members of adolescent gangs, cliques, etc. (pp. 332–336).

Yet, as we saw in the Bennington study, it is inadequate to consider membership in one group alone in relation to attitude change and to reach conclusions on that basis. For in highly differentiated societies, as in the United States today, groups do not exist alone as closed systems. Other groups impinge on the group structure and its individual members and their attitudes, at times, with a compelling impact. So we find some members of an in-group who maintain conflicting attitudes because of outside reference and identification. It would be interesting to have been able to follow those who did change their attitudes in Bennington after they left their college in-group ties. At least some of them must have succumbed to the pressure of established social groups whose norms were contrary to the liberal Bennington trend. Only when the myriad groups of society are *integrated*, with a consequent harmony of norms of behavior, do fundamental and lasting changes in attitudes occur.

Before leaving the problems of attitude change for the time being, we must mention another point which will be expanded in Chapter 15. It is true that discrete events may have no effect whatsoever on an established attitude. However, there are some concrete experiences so overwhelming that attitude changes of a lasting kind do result. This is particularly the case when the experience cannot be handled adequately by relating it to existing attitudes. The impact of technological developments provides clear evidence on this point. Particularly when individuals first come into contact and use the products of modern technology, old attitudes break down and are changed in a sweeping way. For example, within a comparatively short time after going to work in a modern factory, illiterate Chinese peasants may completely revise their attitudes toward family, husband and wife relationships, etc.

In spite of all the forces in society that work toward social change, as a general rule the change in attitudes of individuals and groups tends to lag behind the change in actual conditions. Because of what the sociologists call this "cultural lag," many prevalent attitudes are highly at variance with existing facts, social and otherwise. We cannot go into the complicated problems of the "cultural lag" and its effects here in any detail; its study must necessarily involve data from sociology and economics as well as from psychology. But we shall point out that at least a part of this problem is psychological. Just as our bodies, which we experience as ourselves, are anchored in space, the attitudes which are formed in relation to social objects, persons, and relationships around us serve as anchoring frames in relation to the social world around us. And when the stability of these anchorings is threatened, the individual feels confused, anxious, or insecure. Unless acceptable new anchorings are presented, he will tend to cling tenaciously to the old. The reason for this psychological fact will become evident in the chapters on ego-involvements.

The peculiar picture of individuals and groups who continue to cling to attitudes which do not correspond in point of fact to the world around them would seem a great deal more puzzling, were it not that there are interested groups who exert great effort toward their perpetuation. Before the advent of modern technology, such groups had to exert their influence chiefly through face-to-face contacts. But with the invention of the printing press down to the introduction of television, interested groups have found in these mass media of communication perhaps their most potent weapon.

There is ample evidence to the effect that the mass media in the western capitalist societies today tend to be largely in the hands of a small group of owners who are predominantly conservative. Further evidence for this point will be considered in Chapter 12. As an example, the Commission on Freedom of the Press reported that five advertising accounts made up nearly a fourth of the income of America's major radio networks in 1945.[11] In this connection, Lazarsfeld at the conclusion of his report on his radio study remarks: "Technological innovations have, it is true, a tendency of their own to engender social change. But so far as radio is concerned all signs point to the unlikelihood of its having, in its own right, profound social consequences in the near future. Broadcasting is done in America

[11] Commission on Freedom of the Press, *A Free and Responsible Press, A General Report on Mass Communication*, Chicago: University of Chicago Press, 1947.

today to sell merchandise; and most of the other possible effects of radio become submerged in a strange kind of social mechanism which brings the commercial effect to its strongest expression." [12] As it is easy to verify, almost all the films produced in Hollywood, and consequently those which make up the majority of the world's film fare, can be traced to the efforts of six major companies.

The effect of this leads toward the perpetuation of existing attitudes (stereotypes, prejudices, etc.) even though they may be completely out of line with the trend of science and social life. Detailed evidence concerning various methods used may be found in the work of Doob [13] and other students of propaganda. A few illustrations out of the hundreds coming to light every day will shed further light on the psychology of attitudes.

One technique is to start by preparing an *unstructured* situation. Thus, William Randolph Hearst began discussing the 1936 presidential election as follows: "I do not know what party 1 will support, and I cannot know until the platforms are adopted, and the candidates are nominated."

So he does not seem to know. But one paragraph later, it is evident that he knows as definitely as anyone can know anything. He anchors his certainty to well-established values in the society he is addressing:

"I will say, however, that I think there should be a Jeffersonian Democratic party in the field.

"I think definitely that the historic Democratic party of Jefferson, of Madison, of Monroe, of Jackson, of Cleveland, should nominate candidates who are recognized Democrats, and adopt a platform of sound democratic principles.

"I think, too, that this regular Democratic party should get out an injunction to prevent the Socialist party from using its name." [14]

In a study of attitude (stereotype) perpetuation, the Bureau of Applied Social Research of Columbia concluded that short

[12] P. F. Lazarsfeld, *Radio and the Printed Page*, New York: Duell, Sloan & Pearce, 1940, p. 332.

[13] L. W. Doob, *Propaganda—Its Psychology and Technique*, New York: Holt, 1935.

[14] W. R. Hearst, editorial in the *New York Journal*, August 29, 1935.

stories in 8 representative magazines with national circulation were perpetuating stereotypes of "Anglo-Saxon superiority" with more consistency than other mass media. In their words, "American short story writers have made 'nice people' synonymous with Anglo-Saxons." [15] Similarly, advertising copy circulated through mass media exerts a stereotyping effect. An advertising man quoted in this same study said: " 'You want to sell to the greatest number of people. Therefore in your advertisement you present someone whom they will want to emulate.' This man had actually conducted research of his own to determine what particular Anglo-Saxon names possessed the greatest power to suggest high social and economic status—in other words maximum snob appeal " (p. 11).

Similar surveys are conducted by one of the Gallup organizations for motion picture executives who aim for the highest possible box office receipts. Such surveys tend, of course, further to stereotype the Hollywood cinema. Conducted under the banner of "giving the public what it wants," polls devised to enhance the box office potential of a picture or to create an audience actually have the effect of perpetuating the stereotypes and interests of the public. As one critic of such surveys cogently remarked: "Freedom of choice presupposes a full appreciation of all alternatives involved." [16] A recent more general criticism of the use to which surveys of attitudes are put was leveled by Cartwright, who specifically attacks one of Gallup's fundamental notions concerning the use of public opinion polls: "In the guise of being democratic and of giving the average man a greater voice in social affairs, public opinion research can be used to impede progress through misplacing the function of invention in our society. By asking the public to invent solutions to social problems and by interpreting the absence of new solutions as a desire for the *status quo*, public opinion polls are sometimes employed to bring pressure to bear against innovation and change." [17]

[15] "How Writers Perpetuate Stereotypes," A report by the Writer's War Board, New York, 1945

[16] E. Borneman, "The Public Opinion Myth," *Harper's Magazine*, August, 1947, p. 38.

[17] D. Cartwright, Public opinion polls and democratic leadership, *J. Soc. Issues*, May, 1946, p. 10.

Continuing with this point, Cartwright selects an illustration which is directly pertinent to our present discussion:

Radio programming provides a particularly interesting illustration. People are no more inclined to have suggestions for changing their radio service than they are for changing any other part of their world. Vested interests which wish to maintain present programming in radio can easily collect public opinion data to show how few people have any suggestions for basic changes in their radio service. Experience has shown, however, that new types of programs, once created, may become extremely popular over night. Had a survey been conducted a few years ago asking for suggested changes in radio programs, probably no one would have suggested "a new type of program in which someone asks people questions." But today quiz programs rate high in listener appeal. By the same token it is unjustified to take current polling results that over half of the population have no suggestions for improving radio service as a reason for satisfaction with present standards of radio programming (p. 11).

This is not the place to go into detail regarding the equally important problem of where the individual gets the attitudes and tastes which public opinion surveys tap. From this discussion, we can see, however, that a good share of them are derived at least in part from pronouncements or suggestion of the mass media. Of course, any interpretation of poll results which omits this factor is inaccurate, to say the least.

The stereotyping effects of the Hollywood movies are almost too well known to require mention. Not only in America, but all over the world, one can find individuals whose manners, morals, aspirations, and dreams are patterned after the never-never make-believe of Hollywood. The movie producer aims at a mass audience. He therefore concocts a picture full of the kinds of people, values, manners, etc., that the majority will find attractive. Although only a small segment of the population could live in this manner, the magic of the screen draws more and more to embrace the glamour, wealth, adventure, and romance that are synonymous with Hollywood in the minds of millions of people throughout the world.

This conserving, stereotyping effect of the mass media of communication is not inevitable. Indeed the mass media could be one of the swiftest instruments for effecting social change and reducing the "cultural lag." But for this to happen, the interests of those who control the media must be in harmony with the progress of science and social relationships.

Attitude Studies and the Psychology of Attitudes

We could continue our account of attitudes, building up to a more concrete level with a compilation of summaries of attitude studies, but that is not our present intention. Especially during the last three decades, attitude studies have been piling up. Both psychologists and sociologists have contributed to the accumulation of literature in the field under various titles, such as prejudice (social distance), prestige suggestion, stereotype, etc. Hosts of special cases of attitudes have been studied— from attitudes of "race" prejudice, through attitudes of radicalism-conservatism, attitudes toward peace and war, class and profession, romanticism and various art forms, to special topics such as punctuality. Commercial "public opinion" enterprises, usually motivated by pecuniary interests or by certain interest groups, flourish in the "measurement" of attitudes concerning current industrial, economic, political, military, and social problems.[18]

Even though the bulk is great, such discrete studies have not contributed much to the formulation of a psychology of attitudes. Therefore, compilation of diverse kinds of attitude studies and findings will not help us much, even though some of them give useful data concerning the particular attitudes studied. Usually the attitude is chosen for study for its own sake and not for the principles that may be attained through the specific case. Consequently, the broad principles which are implicit in such studies are often missed. They stand rather as discrete findings, not unified in a conceptual scheme of problems and concepts.

[18] It is not our concern here to take up the question whether or not these public opinion institutes carry on their work with the sole motive of finding facts and reaching scientific conclusions, or whether they sometimes add to the confusion by trying to create a "band wagon" effect by their pronouncements of "majority opinion." For it has been found in several studies that majority opinion influences attitudes. The type of pronouncement of the Gallup poll and Gallup's syndicated articles is too well known to need description here. See also pp. 310–313, Chapter 12.

There is no special physics of trains, automobiles, or refrigerators; they are special applications of certain principles. Likewise, there cannot be an entirely different psychology covering prejudice, conservative-radical attitudes, or the like. There must be some basic principles governing any attitude. And, of course, there are also specific factors in each case. We have already presented some general facts which lie at the basis of any attitude.

In view of the points raised in our general orientation (Chapter 1), it is highly pertinent to proceed to further clarification of our attitude formulation in relation to certain concrete topics. Out of other possible significant ones we chose the topics of *ego-involvements, adolescence,* and *prejudice.*

The psychology of ego formation and ego-involvements will lead us to take up attitudes which define and regulate interpersonal and group relations, which express status and aspirations toward social goals. As such, these ego-attitudes constitute the major, if not the focal, realm of sociogenic motives. This will give us a picture of the formation and functioning of interpersonal attitudes, such as those related to family; masculinity-femininity; relative positions (roles) in the capacities of equal, superior, or inferior; attitudes of belongingness and marginality; attitudes expressing our social aspirations; etc.

The psychology of adolescence affords us an excellent opportunity to point to the relationship and friction between biogenic motives (primarily sex in this case) and the social milieu—and the consequent formation and functioning of new attitudes in the critical situation thus produced. Here we shall see once more the effect of groups in the rise of new norms.

Lastly the psychology of prejudice, which is a special case of an attitude, will be an appropriate topic to clarify our approach to "in-group" and "out-group" relationships—the attitudes produced and perpetuated in the process of group frictions.

Each of these topics (ego-involvements, adolescence, and prejudice) will in various ways help us to pull together motivational, group (collective), and cognitive (perceptual) factors in the formation and functioning of attitudes.

11.

Ego-Involvements

NO MATTER WHAT CULTURAL VARIATIONS IN BEHAVIOR THERE may be, man in all societies is first of all motivated by his biogenic motives. He has to eat, drink, sleep, mate, and satisfy other biogenic needs to achieve at least a minimum subsistence level of living (Chapters 2–4). In early childhood, his whole functioning is dominated by these needs. As he grows, as he becomes a member of the group in so many capacities, he learns to eat certain things, at certain times, in certain settings. Not only the quality of food as such matters, but where he eats it. He may feel *out of place* eating in certain places, staying in certain quarters. This is true of sex and other biogenic motives as well. He desires a sex object, but he also desires the sex mate to satisfy his personal sense of worth—he wants her to have "class," in good standing, to possess qualities which are at a high premium in the eyes of his own group—whatever that group and their valued qualities may be. In short, aside from laws, regulations, and customs imposed from without, the concern over our *personal worth* comes from within to regulate the ways we satisfy even our biogenic motives.

The established norms within a society require conformity from the members or would-be members (children) that live in its atmosphere. The conformity is imposed either through the objective external properties of cultural products, such as the specially standardized proportions and forms of furniture, utensils, clothing, language, houses, etc., that present themselves every day, or through the demands, scolding, example, teaching, cooperation, correction, or punishment of parents, teachers, playmates, equals, superiors, legal institutions, and groups.

Infants are not required at first to conform to rules and regulations of their own accord. As they grow up, customs and traditions are imposed more severely, until the "proper" norms are incorporated in the individual. But to consider the acquisition of social values or norms by the individual solely the consequence of external coercion, or of frustration owing to the mother-father-child relationship, as legalistically-minded writers and orthodox psychoanalysts do, simply does not meet the test of developmental facts. The growing child or youth strives actively to make the standards or norms of his group (play group, clique, school, team, club) *his own*. He does his best to become a good member and to excel in his group. Becoming a good member and excelling necessarily mean enthusiastic incorporation of and willing conformity to the values of his reference group, whatever it may be in a particular culture. Only by this active assimilation and conformity does he become a member in good standing and acquire his relative status in the group. In the adult, the social norms are so well incorporated that he conforms not only in response to pressure from parent or police, but usually of his own accord. There are times when he does not steal, even though he might steal to his advantage, because consciously or unconsciously the norm, "Thou shalt not steal," is effective within him. There are times when he does not commit adultery, because "Thou shalt not commit adultery" has become a part of him. It will hurt *him* to steal; it will injure *his* self-respect to commit adultery. It will be below *his* dignity to do anything that is not *honorable*. Telling a lie will hurt *his* conscience.

Of course, there are times when he yields to "temptation"— temptation as defined in his group, and in situations where it is culturally defined. Of course, too, there are individual differences; different individuals have different thresholds at which they break down under the stress of temptation or other trying crisis or tension. We are not talking about a generalized "prototype" of man.

After yielding to temptation or other strong demands of the moment, an individual may repent, because something in *himself* is hurt. He may feel the necessity of confessing to a priest or to a dear friend, because he feels something restless *in him* which forces him to find some release. Another individual may not confess, but he may still have a sense of guilt in *himself*, because he has done something he should not have done. Many an individual has a *conflict* within *himself* before or after committing an act.

In all cultures, primitive or highly developed, bourgeois or socialist, individuals *belong* to groups. Aside from the fact of group belongingness, social position or *status* has no meaning. We belong or aspire to belong to this or that school, club, class, etc. Everyone is a member of a family, member of this or that church, fraternity, clique, organization, etc. Our very identity as we experience ourselves is derived from such memberships or reference of ourselves to them. After a certain level of development—after the ego develops some degree of stability—lack of belongingness or being left out produces feelings of insecurity or anxiety. The touchingly unfortunate life stories of the "marginal man," [1] isolates, paranoids, misfits are examples of the point. Even anarchists, who are products of bourgeois societies with contradictory forces and values, are no exceptions to the rule. Their highly intense "substitutive activities" and grandiose escape plans reveal what they have to put up with for their professed "doctrine." If this were not so, it seems they would not go to the utmost pains to address themselves (in books, discussions, lectures, and even *organizations*) to certain groups of people. As Whyte has indicated in his *Street Corner Society*, areas of social disorganization are such only for superficial observers. Each of these areas has an internal organization with codes of its own, and demands conformity to them.

Our ego problems arise from our positions in relation to other individuals in our specific groups. These individuals may be persons we are actually in contact with in some capacity, or persons whose attainments in our line we know.

In this connection we have to repeat the truism that individuals do not strive only for belongingness; they strive also in different degrees for position in their groups. First, they may have as their goal just to belong—to a college, organization, "social set," etc. Once this is achieved, they may not feel satisfied unless they reach a certain *standing* in the group.

[1] See, for example, E. V. Stonequist, *The Marginal Man*, New York: Scribner, 1937.

Ordinarily the satisfaction of biogenic needs, the getting of a job, the attainment of wealth or office depends on our being a good member of the group. This is true equally of gangs of the underworld and of "respectable" organizations such as a manufacturer's association. (Of course, the codes differ; activities for the getting of things are regulated by the peculiar norms of each group.) Therefore, being a member in good standing becomes a major concern for us.

The topics touched upon in the above paragraphs constitute the major area of *sociogenic motives*. Such behavior implies, one way or another, involvements of the ego. In the adult, the ego becomes extremely complicated, especially in highly developed bourgeois societies with their great differentiation and contradictory groups and values. If we trace the development of the ego through early childhood (for it does not exist at birth), these formidable-sounding terms "ego" and "ego-involvements" lend themselves to a naturalistic formulation. We shall see that the ego is a genetic formation consisting of attitudes formed in relation to objects, persons, groups, institutions, etc. We shall designate as "ego-attitudes" the attitudes toward things that we consider ours or that are ours (e.g., a house, room, dress, book, etc.); toward persons or groups to which we are personally related in some capacity (as friends, enemies, kin, fellow members, or, in the case of groups, as cooperators or opponents); and toward institutions to which we belong. In short, the ego consists of such attitudes. Related to what we consider *me, I, mine*, these attitudes are not discrete, independent of one another. Their constellation (ego-attitudes) constitutes the ego.

The concept "ego-involvement" is used simply to denote the appearance of ego-attitudes in the psychological functioning at a given moment. Ego-involvements are situationally aroused, as may be seen in everyday life experience. The same joke, say about our ability in some field that matters to us, may be taken in a good-natured way in the circle of our trusted friends; but it may arouse disgust and various sorts of defense reactions in a group consisting of our rivals and proved enemies. Various kinds of ego-involvements have been studied and their differential effects measured with a considerable degree of success, especially during the last decade. As such, the much abused badge of acceptability, "operational," may be legitimately attached to the concept. We shall present some illustrative studies of ego-involvements in the following chapter.[2]

Ego a Genetic Formation

Ego formation belongs to man alone among the many species of the animal kingdom. Not even the highest subhuman animals share it with him. This fact is mainly the result of man's unique capacity for functioning psychologically on a *conceptually symbolic* level. As we have seen (pp. 183–194), it is this same level of psychological functioning that makes possible, as a consequence of *human* interaction, the *rise* and *accumulation* of tools, symbols, concepts of language, and social norms (value judgments) from generation to generation. In the words of the biologist Huxley: "The first and most obviously unique characteristic of man is his capacity for conceptual thought. . . ." [3]

Ego functioning does not come as an innate endowment of man, in the same sense as the capacity for conceptual thought, perception, judgment, and other such psychological functions. The constellation of attitudes in the psychological make-up of the *human* adult which we designate as the ego is a genetic formation. The newborn human child is biologically integrated —but he has no ego. And his ego would not form as he matures were it not mainly for two facts. First, his psychological functioning, and *his alone*, can take place on a conceptually symbolic level enabling him to grasp reciprocal relationships with other humans and to make effective use of the accumulation of tools, concepts, and norms which he will eventually face. Thus animals and human idiots manifest no ego formation. Second, once man is biologically equipped with this possibility (of functioning psychologically on a conceptually symbolic level), he grows into a world of lawful nature and of social relation-

---

[2] For a brief history of the concept of ego-involvements, see R. R. Holt, Effects of ego-involvement upon levels of aspiration, *Psychiatry: J. Biol. & Interpers. Relations*, 1945, 3, 299–317.

[3] J. Huxley, *Man Stands Alone*, New York: Harper, 1927, p. 3.

ships and their products which impose the necessity of adapting himself to them and regulating his behavior accordingly. Without these restrictions, resistances, and rewards of nature and *especially of the established social world around him*—with its diverse material and technological products, its institutions, its accumulated tools, concepts, and norms—the human individual would have no consistent and continuous ego formation. So it is that children reared in isolation from human society have no ego.[4]

Because the group that an individual is born into possesses an accumulation of established tools, symbols, concepts, and norms, the major part of the constellation of attitudes making up his identity is formed in relation to them. Thus it is that the egos of individuals in different social groups and cultures are shaped in their major features in the image of those groups. Just as attitudes are learned in relation to the situations, objects, persons, institutions, etc., around the individual, so the ego is formed. Even the most intimate of relationships— those of kinship—are learned in accordance with norms existing in the particular society at a particular time. The relative closeness, affection, loyalty, and responsibility toward various blood relatives exhibited by an individual will vary in terms of the prescribed norms of his group. The work of ethnologists has convincingly shown that the individual becomes altruistic, individualistic, competitive, cooperative, etc., as determined by the major norms of the group of which he is a member.[5] It is useless, then, to argue over whether "human nature" is basically selfish or altruistic, cooperative or competitive, etc. The attitudes composing the ego are this or that way depending on the content of the values of the society in relation to which they are formed.

The ego is not present at birth in the human child. As we have seen (pp. 51–60), the behavior of a newborn baby in *any* society is dominated by the satisfaction of basic needs. He has yet to become a socialized being. This socialization,

[4] See, for example, A. Gesell, *Wolf Child and Human Child*, New York: Harper, 1940.
[5] See, for example, M. Mead (ed.), *Cooperation and Competition Among Primitive People*, New York: McGraw-Hill, 1943; and M. Mead, *From the South Seas*, New York: Morrow, 1939.

this formation of the ego, is not a mystic process. It is inferred from the behavior of the growing child. And in view of all the controversy centering around man's social nature, it is gratifying to find that the psychology of the early period of ego formation is one of the firmly established, repeatedly verified areas in psychology.[6]

From the mass of observations of child behavior, starting with the works of Tiedemann, Darwin, Preyer, and Shinn,[7] down to the contemporary controlled observations of Gesell,[8] one finds that even the body is not experienced as the individual's own from the outset. Psychologically, the parts of the body *become* his in the course of his genetic development. Through repeated contact, manipulation—even the hitting and banging—of his own body and other objects in his environment the baby learns to differentiate his body from the outside world. One of Preyer's observations of his own child will make the point clearer:

How little is gained for the development of the notion of the "I" by means of the first movements of the hands, which the infant early carries to his mouth, and which must give him, when he sucks them, a different feeling from that given by sucking the finger of another person, or other suitable objects, appears from the fact that, e.g., my child for months tugged at his fingers as if he wanted to pull them off, and struck his own head with his hand by way of experiment. At the close of the first year he had a fancy for striking hard substances against his teeth, and made a regular play of gnashing his teeth. When on the four hundred and ninth day he stood up straight in bed, holding on to the railing of it with his hands, *he bit himself on his bare arm*, and that the upper arm, so that he immediately cried out with

[6] For a partial review of this evidence, see M. Sherif, *The Psychology of Social Norms*, New York: Harper, 1936, pp. 156–164; and for an expansion of this review, M. Sherif and H. Cantril, *The Psychology of Ego-Involvements*, New York: Wiley, 1947, chap. 7.

[7] C. Murchison and S. Langer, Tiedemann's observations on the development of the mental faculties of children, *J. Genet. Psychol.*, 1927, 34, 205–230; C. Darwin, Biographical sketch of an infant, *Mind*, 1877, 2, 285–294; W. Preyer, *The Mind of the Child; Part II, The Development of the Intellect*, New York: Appleton, 1890; M. W. Shinn, *Notes on the Development of a Child*, University of California Publications in Education, Berkeley: The University Press, vol. 1, 1899; vol. 2, 1907.

[8] A. Gesell and H. Thompson, *The Psychology of Early Growth*, New York: Macmillan, 1938; and A. Gesell and F. L. Ilg, *Infant and Child in the Culture of Today*, New York: Harper, 1943.

pain. The marks of the incisors were to be seen long afterward. The child did not a second time bite himself in the arm, but only bit his fingers, and inadvertently his tongue (p. 189).

How little he understands, even after the first year of his life has passed, the difference between the parts of his own body and foreign objects is shown also in some strange experiments that the child conducted quite independently. He sits by me at the table and strikes very often and rapidly with his hands successive blows upon the table, at first gently, then hard; then, with the right hand alone, hard; next, suddenly strikes himself with the same hand on the mouth; then he holds his hand to his mouth for a while, strikes the table again with the right hand, and then all of a sudden strikes his own head (above the ear). The whole performance gave exactly the impression of his having for the first time noticed that it is one thing to strike oneself, one's own hard head, and another thing to strike a foreign hard object (forty-first week) (pp. 190–191).

Thus, at a time when the attention to what is around is already very far developed, one's own person may not be distinguished from the environment. . . . Nay, even in the nineteenth month it is not yet clear how much belongs to one's own body. The child had lost a shoe. I said, "Give the shoe." He stooped, seized it, and gave it to me. Then, when I said to the child, as he was standing upright on the floor, "Give the foot," . . . he grasped at it with both hands, and labored hard to get it and hand it to me (p. 190).[9]

Another concrete example of the fact that the child must learn to differentiate his body from the external world is found in the observations of children's behavior before a mirror. Reports by Darwin, Preyer, and Gesell, for example, all agree that at first the child responds to his image as though it were *another real person*, even engaging in chatter, kissing, etc. In Gesell's words: "It is doubtful whether the infant identifies himself in any way with the image. Even at the age of 5 years a pair of twin girls made misinterpretations of their mirror images. Each considered the image not a self-image, but called it by the name of the co-twin." [10] Of course most children, not having a live "self-image," *learn* that their reflection is an image much earlier.

A more integrated picture of ego formation may be obtained

[9] W. Preyer, *op. cit.*
[10] Gesell and Thompson, *op. cit.*, p. 241.

by reference to the research of Piaget and his collaborators.[11] Piaget's observations indicated that at first the infant psychologically floats "about in an undifferentiated absolute" (p. 128). In this undifferentiated absolute there are no psychological boundaries between one's own body and other objects, between reality and fantasy or wish, between subjective and objective. Thus a distinct ego experience is the "result of a gradual and progressive dissociation, and not of a primitive intuition" (p. 128). The dominant principle that regulates the orientation of behavior at this time, as we have seen earlier, is the satisfaction of the momentary needs or wishes as they arise. Accordingly, one reacts differently to the same objects as one's needs or wishes change. The infant may give a positive reaction toward an object or person now, but may react negatively a little later. From the point of view of the adult, such behavior is "inconsistent." But it is consistent in that it follows the variations in needs or wishes.

On account of the resistances that he meets in the external world, the individual has to make adaptations to reality. This means that he has to make distinctions between what is himself and what is not, what is wish and what is reality. With these distinctions, logical consistency dawns. But at first, the child still acts and talks as though his own wishes and desires were the center of reference of the whole world; hence there is not yet much logical consistency, which is achieved only through sticking step by step to some well-established premise. In this process the undifferentiated absolute breaks down; the realization of reciprocal relations among other people and ourselves evolves. For the realization of reciprocal relations one has to grasp that there are other points of view besides one's own. And in order to grasp this the child must be able to separate himself from the external world.

The main fact that we draw from Piaget is that the child's behavior is at first dominated by autism, which is governed chiefly by the satisfaction of momentary needs or wishes; and that as the child meets external resistances he adapts himself to reality gradually. *In this process the ego develops.*

[11] J. Piaget, *The Child's Conception of Physical Causality*, New York, Harcourt, Brace, 1930; J. Piaget, *Judgment and Reasoning in the Child*, New York, Harcourt, Brace, 1928.

Gesell and Ilg made extensive observations of child behavior at various ages, from which the developing ego formation may be inferred.[12] For example:

By 40 weeks or a year he has made significant advances in self-discovery. Whether sitting up or lying down, his arms and hands now have more freedom of movement, and he uses them to explore his own physical self. . . . In the period from 1 to 2 years there is an increasing amount of social reference. Although the infant-child is capable of long stretches of self-absorbed activity, he is also given to numerous social advances. . . . He extends a toy to a person; he holds out his arm for the sleeve; he says "ta-ta"; he hands the empty cereal dish to his mother; . . . By all these tokens and devices, he builds up a vast body of specific perceptual experience which ultimately enables him to draw the momentous conclusion that there are other persons in the world more or less like himself (p. 336).

Two years is a transitional period when the child both clings to moorings and cuts from them. Johnny is his name, and in his inarticulate psychology, the spoken word Johnny which he hears is nothing more or less than he himself! His name is Johnny as a person. He will soon use the pronouns you, me, and I,—a further indication of a fundamental change in the psychology of his self (p. 337).

Even by the age of 3 years, . . . he knows his own sex with assurance. His interest in human anatomy remains strong; he talks freely and naturally about differences which he has observed (pp. 338–339).

Between 5 and 6 years the child . . . has lost some of the sophomoric traits of 4 year oldness, and has more sense of status and propriety. He has a better appreciation of the folkways of culture. He shows the conservatism of youth in deferring to them, and citing them to his parents for their consideration. He does not want to be different from humanity (p. 340).

Only around the age of 72 months does the child begin "setting up standards for himself."

As Gesell observed, children usually first use their own names in referring to themselves, and only later mine, me, and I, roughly in that order. And the concept we appears considerably later.[13] With language development, a more adequate discrimination between self and not-self is accompanied by the

---

[12] Gesell and Ilg, op. cit.

[13] As reported by M. S. Fisher, Language patterns of preschool children, Bureau of Publications, Teacher's College, Columbia University, 1934.

elaboration of the ego to include attitudes both toward one's self and toward relations to the many objects and persons in one's environment. It makes possible the incorporation of accumulated social norms and values, standards of behaving, aspirations, prescribed loyalties and responsibilities. But at first, the child does not adopt these social norms as his own. They are imposed by grownups and are often followed in an inaccurate way. The following observation illustrates this point: "The little girl has been told she should not let a little boy see her in her underwear. The little boy raps on the door and the little girl who is in her underwear says, 'Wait just a minute.' She takes *off* the unacceptable underwear and now naked, tells the little boy he can come in."[14] Even as the child grows older, he may *know* very well the norms of various groups but may not *act* in terms of them because they are not *his own*.

At this point Piaget's work, *The Moral Judgment of the Child*, is especially illuminating.[15] The findings of a whole series of coordinated investigation are that all rules (of language, logic, morality, and society, including even the rules of games) are first external to the child. Moral rules or norms (as well as others) are at first imposed on him from without (heteronomy). Even though he is made to abide by them because of the authority of grownups, he lapses easily, giving in to his desires whenever he is not under the grip of external authority. For these externally imposed rules or norms have not yet become *his own* rules or norms.

Through participation in age-mate group activities, the child learns to grasp reciprocal human relationships. In Piaget's words: "From the moment that children really begin to submit to rules and to apply them in a spirit of genuine cooperation, they acquire a new conception of these rules" (p. 89). "Henceforward, he will not only discover the boundaries that separate his self from the other person, but will learn to understand the other person and be understood by him" (p. 90). Thus, through cooperative participation he comes to accept the group norms as his own and to develop his identifications, loyalties, and inner responsibilities toward them (autonomy). Otherwise,

---

[14] This observation was communicated to the author by Dr. Mary Cover Jones.
[15] J. Piaget, *The Moral Judgment of the Child*, London: Kegan, Paul, 1932.

he considers norms imposed on him by sheer authority as nuisances to be evaded whenever possible.

On the basis of such concrete results of genetic psychology, Piaget gives an excellent criticism of sociologists like Durkheim who are not greatly concerned with genetic development and who miss the important properties of co-acting social groups in which regulating norms spontaneously arise. By missing this important contribution of child psychology, sociologists of Durkheim's type come to believe that "society [the dichotomy and contrast being between it and the individual] alone stands above individuals; from it emanate all authority and prestige" (pp. 356–357). Such psychology leads to the conception of the child as simply a creature to be filled with the authority and values of society, and to "a defense of the methods of authority " (p. 359).

An effective grasp of the norms of his social groups, of prescribed relations with others around him comes only after the child has assimilated these norms as *his own*. And this effective incorporation is very largely due to the grasping of reciprocal relationships in interactions with other persons, particularly with other children. It has been amply demonstrated that very young children cannot participate in group activities. In fact, one index of ego development is an increasing capacity to take part in play as a member of an age-mate group. The development is revealed as the child grows older by the increasing length of time in which he engages in collective activity, the increasing size of the group (number of members), and the increasing complexity of rules to be observed.[16] Only as he learns his own position relative to other individuals around

[16] See, for example, M. B. Parten, Social participation among pre-school children, *J. Abn. & Soc. Psychol.*, 1932, 27, 243–269; M. B. Parten, Leadership among pre-school children, *J. Abn. & Soc. Psychol.*, 1933, 27, 430–440; M. B. Parten, Social play among pre-school children, *J. Abn. & Soc. Psychol.*, 1933, 28, 136–147; A. S. Salusky, Collective behavior of children at a pre-school age, *J. Soc. Psychol.*, 1930, 1, 367–378; A. P. Beaver, The initiation of social contacts by pre-school children, *Child Develop. Monogr.*, no. 7, Teacher's College, 1932; E. H. Green, Group playing and quarreling among pre-school children, *Child Develop.*, 1933, 4, 302–307; E. V. C. Berne, An experimental investigation of social behavior patterns in young children, *University of Iowa Stud. Child Welfare*, 4, no. 3, 1930; K. M. B. Bridges, *The Social and Emotional Development of the Pre-school Child*, London: Trench, Trubner, 1931; and L. B. Murphy, *Social Behavior and Child Personality*, New York: Columbia University Press, 1937.

him can the child successfully participate in group activities.

A good many studies indicate that some ego formation is necessary before competition, cooperation, sympathy, setting of goals or aspiration levels, or prejudice start to operate as factors, consistently, as they do for adults. (The degree of ego formation necessary for the appearance of various of these factors may differ.) Wolf found that the younger and less mature children in her study gave little indication of a competitive attitude.[17] Berne's results indicate that cooperative behavior and responsibility for self and others increase significantly with age, as Piaget's results also indicate.[18] A significant age trend for the appearance of sympathetic responses to the distress of others was found by L. B. Murphy.[19] The experimental studies of Greenberg[20] and Rosenzweig[21] furnish evidence that the level of aspiration does not seem to appear clearly until the child has formed some conception of his "self," has developed a sense of "pride" which he feels must be maintained. Goodenough made an important link when she noted that "goals are not clearly realized until after the crystallizing effect of verbal formulation has taken place and the distinction between the self and not self has become sufficiently advanced to give form and pattern to the child's social attitudes. . . ."[22]

In her provocative study of racial aspects of self-identification, Ruth Hartley concludes that her data point to a "concept of group consciousness and group identification as an intrinsic aspect of ego development."[23] K. B. and M. K. Clark, who continued this line of research with Negro children, also

---

[17] T. H. Wolf, The effect of praise and competition on the persisting behavior of kindergarten children, *University of Minnesota Institute of Child Welfare Monogr. Series*, 1938, no. 15.

[18] Berne, *op. cit.*

[19] L. B. Murphy, *op. cit.*

[20] P. J. Greenberg, Competition in children, *Amer. J. Psychol.*, 1932, 44, 221–248.

[21] S. Rosenzweig, Preferences in the repetition of successful and unsuccessful activities as a function of age and personality, *J. Genet. Psychol.*, 1933, 42, 423–441.

[22] F. L. Goodenough, *Developmental Psychology*, New York: Appleton-Century, 2nd ed., 1945, p. 423.

[23] For R. Hartley, see R. Horowitz, Racial aspects of self-identification in nursery school children, *J. Soc. Psychol.*, 1939, 7, 99.

found that awareness of membership in a social group is an integral part of ego formation, and that "concepts of self gleaned from concrete physical characteristics of perceived self become modified by social factors taking on a new definition in the light of these social factors."[24]

These results, taken in conjunction with ethnological findings, may be cited as conclusive evidence of the *learned* character of such social components of "human nature" as well as of the genetic character of the ego itself.

But the constellation of attitudes comprising the ego does not consist solely of *social values*. As Wallon has emphasized, and as we shall see in Chapter 15, both the material and the social circumstances surrounding the child determine in a major way the character of his ego.[25] The general technological level of the milieu, the amount and kind of toys and games, the size of the living space, the kind and amount of nourishment, the kinds of material opportunities, and the like, as well as values and norms, enter to shape his psychological identity. Depending on such factors, he may feel strange when only a mile away from his house. If he grew up in a primitive village, he may be overwhelmed by the mere sight of Times Square in New York. Such material circumstances vary vastly from class to class and from society to society.

In stating these broad outlines concerning the trend of ego formation, we have largely ignored the factors leading to variations in the speed of its development, and the tremendous variation in organization and particular components in the individual child. Obviously, every child does not incorporate all of the norms of his general culture or even of his own group. The range of his social contact is restricted by the range of his receptivity. The norms that will be most effective for an individual will be those of his particular membership and reference groups. His ego formation also will vary in its components, its relative rigidity or flexibility, etc., in terms of his case history,

[24] K. B. Clark and M. K. Clark, The development of consciousness of self and the emergence of social identifications in Negro pre-school children, *J. Soc. Psychol.*, 1939, 10, 591–599; K. B. Clark and M. K. Clark, Skin color as a factor in racial identification of Negro pre-school children, *J. Soc. Psychol.*, 1940, 11, 159–169.

[25] H. Wallon, *Les Origines du caractère chez l'enfant*, Paris: Presses Universitaires de France, 1933.

e.g., the kind of treatment received from adults, opportunities for language development, contact with cultural products, treatment by and associations with age-mates, etc. Such variations constitute importa t problems in the study of individual differences.

Regressions and Breakdowns of the Ego Under Given Situations

Since the ego is a genetic formation, since it consists chiefly of attitudes which come to form the individual's identity, it is not fixed or immutable. Various degrees of breakdown or disintegration of the ego-attitudes are facts of everyday experience. Under the overpowering urge of a basic (biogenic) drive, such as hunger or sex, the ego may break down and the organism be directed, without regard for social niceties, toward the biologically significant goal object. In fact, ego-breakdown may be taken as one of the consequences of prolonged deprivations. In Chapter 4, we saw many examples of such breakdowns. Thus, the starving conscientious objectors cared not a whit about appearing to be gentlemen; they even licked their plates clean in the presence of others. Thus General Wainwright and his fellow prisoners dropped their self-respect as Allied officers to do menial tasks for a little more "work rice." Thus, the starving mothers not only engaged in prostitution but sent their children on the streets to get a little more food. And, under the desperate stress of starvation, the mother gave her baby away that she might obtain food. Such examples of breakdowns of ego values could be multiplied almost indefinitely in cases of stress from the various basic drives. For just as norms and values arise from the structure of society through the interaction of individuals and thus comprise the *superstructure* of society, so the interiorized social norms (social inhibitions and aspirations, loyalties and responsibilities, etc.) constitute the *superstructure* of the individual's psychological functioning. This superstructure is subject to breakdown, leaving the organism functioning closer to the biological level. Motives which are part of the ego, *sociogenic motives*, tend to drop out of the picture when the stress of a *biogenic motive* (or motives) becomes unbearable. The necessity for distinguishing the origins of the various motives in man (*biogenic or sociogenic*) becomes even more evident than when the distinction was first made (pp. 12–14).

Less consequential cases of ego-breakdown or regressions may be found merely by looking around us. The top-hatted dignified gentleman who goes to a party with his wife loses all of his pomp after a few drinks of champagne and may begin making obscene remarks and gestures. When tired, the politest of ladies may make rude remarks to all who come her way. Under situations of stress or conflict, a person may act "like a baby," or regress.

Under extreme stress, as during war, catastrophe, or depression, individuals may very well become "different people" or collapse or destroy themselves. Thus, during the depression years after World War I, suicide, the actual destruction of the self, occurred not only among the unemployed, but also among people who had lost their businesses or enough money so that they could not continue life in the manner that they had come to consider *their* way. The psychological effect of prolonged unemployment has been found to include a breakdown of ego-attitudes, a narrowing of the ego boundaries, and even collapse of the ego formation. Thus the unemployed man may come to feel himself as useless, superfluous. He may find that he has to beg, to be humble, unlike his former self. Eisenberg and Lazarsfeld found "that the last stage of unemployment consists of a general narrowing of activities as well as of outlook on life. There is also a narrowing of wants and needs. Yet there is a limit beyond which this narrowing cannot go; otherwise a collapse occurs." [26]

The most vivid illustrations of ego-breakdown perhaps are found in injury or surgical treatment of the frontal lobes. Particularly in prefrontal lobotomy and lobectomy, which have been performed on neurotic and psychotic patients, is demonstrated the dependence of ego formation and functioning on the conceptually symbolic level of functioning—a level made possible by the development of the frontal lobes in man. In lobectomy, a portion of the gray matter is removed. Lobotomy

[26] P. Eisenberg and P. F. Lazarsfeld, The psychological effects of unemployment, *Psychol. Bull.*, 1938, 35, 378.

is a less serious operation involving the severance of fibers between the frontal areas and the thalamus. Here we can mention only those effects of lobotomy which are most relevant to our problem.[27]

We shall see, as reported by Sullivan and others, that anxiety does not develop until the individual's identity is in some degree formed. Conversely, prefrontal lobotomy, while removing the "planning" functions of the brain and hence the individual's ability to act in accordance with the interiorized social norms which constitute such an important part of the ego, results in a *reduction* of anxiety. In reporting the results of prefrontal lobotomies on patients suffering from neurotic symptoms characterized by anxiety, Freeman and Watts say that even in severe cases ". . . prefrontal lobotomy has succeeded in relieving the underlying emotional tension to a degree where the various symptoms are of little importance in the life of the individual. Indeed, this emotional tension underlies so much of the symptomatology that it would seem as if the operation succeeded more or less specifically in removing the basis for the complaint." [28]

Freeman and Watts made the following conclusion concerning the effects of the operation upon behavior: "Inertia and lack of ambition, *loss of what is commonly called self-consciousness, indifference to the opinions of others, satisfaction with performance even though this may be of inferior quality and quantity*—these may be considered among the primary results. Euphoria, evasion, bluffing, talkativeness, moria, aggressive behavior, teasing, *indecent acts*, inattention, poor judgment— these might be classed among the secondary results" (p. 303, italics mine).

The conclusive implication of these findings, indicating that the functioning of ego relationships takes place on a conceptual level, is further substantiated by Landis and Bolles in the following summary of the effects of lobotomy:[29]

[27] For a concise account of these effects, see C. T. Morgan, *Physiological Psychology*, New York: McGraw-Hill, 1943.

[28] W. Freeman and J. W. Watts, *Psychosurgery*, Springfield: C. C. Thomas, 1942, p. 282.

[29] C. Landis and M. Bolles, *Textbook of Abnormal Psychology*, New York: Macmillan, 1946.

The surgical severing of the nerve tracts connecting the frontal lobes and the thalamus has marked psychological effects, *particularly in relation to self-consciousness.* . . . The use of this surgical technique with mental patients produces some astonishing results, particularly *a reduction of self-consciousness and a loss of "psychic pain."* Intellect, as measured by the standard intelligence tests, is usually unchanged after the operation. In many instances *the use which is made of intelligence in social and personal relationships is somewhat diminished.* As a consequence, some patients become indolent and exhibit a marked lack of social tact (p. 431, italics mine).

Patients who have undergone this operation *are different from their prepsychotic selves*, although sometimes the difference is not immediately recognizable. They are apt to be somewhat indolent; they are often outspoken, *saying the first thing that comes into their heads rather than waiting to think what response the remark will produce in others.* They are aware that they are hasty, undiplomatic, and tactless, and often are sorry and apologetic. The emotional reactions are brisk, but shallow and short-lived. They laugh more and are of quicker temper. *There is an absence of brooding melancholia, the hurt feelings, the pouting, and the grim silences which marked them before the operations* (pp. 432–433, italics mine).

A Characterization of the Developing Ego

Ego formation, then, starts with the facing of external reality. In adapting to external reality the child has to distinguish between himself and external things. He meets resistances in his surroundings. Now what do these resistances consist of? They are the resistances of inanimate objects around him, and the opposition and hindrances offered by other people, such as parents and nurses.

But are even the objects around him devoid of social meaning? Most of the objects—chairs, tables, walls, pictures on the walls, etc.—are social products. They are found in certain standardized proportions and forms; and different cultures have different proportions and forms. This is important: these objects represent definite perceptual relationships. They have an effect in shaping his taste for forms and proportions. Consequently, when later the child is surrounded by other proportions representing a different culture, he may find these new objects queer or repugnant.

In addition to protecting the child from dangers and taking care of his basic biological needs, how do the parents and others around him influence him? They develop in him the means of communication (language and gesture); they put limitations on what he can do; they tell him what a good or a bad boy is like, what is proper and what is not proper. All these things are determined by socially prescribed norms. Right from the start the child grows up in an atmosphere heavily charged with socially established values. He is fully immersed in them; they, more than the baptismal water, are what develop him into a good Baptist, for example. He is told that he is Johnny, and Johnny is this or that—that he is a boy, and boys do this and not that.

In short, beginning with his body, what he includes in "I" are the things, meanings, and qualities related to him as "mine" or "me," so that the "I" connections grow numerous and complicated. A complex formation takes place around the "I," and this has relations with many different things, including his own body as a whole, the different parts of his body, his clothes, the people around him—his parents and others who are close—and inanimate objects around him. Thus this formation around the "I" consists of a complex system of relations.

Social values—the socially standardized relations—constitute no small part of the ego. Even in the case of the most obvious and visible content included in "I," namely, one's own body, there are norms attached to it: what part of the body one may expose and what part not, and when; what one has to do with it when meeting certain people or appearing in a certain group; what parts of one's body one can make appear more desirable, and in what ways one may properly do this, as a child, as a woman, as a man. Carrying the burden of our egos, we find ourselves nearly always in situations that impose definitely prescribed demands on us. In the household, in school, in business, in the office, in the meeting, and even in a love situation, we stand in more or less definite socially prescribed relationships to other individuals, and to the whole situation. To a large extent our status, what we are in this situation, and how *we* shall *feel* and *act*, are prescribed by social values. (We have no desire to minimize the role of the unique properties of each specific situation.) Even what a husband and wife may expect from each other, their privileges and duties, vary from one culture to another (and the objective variation in responses is less important than the social adaptation and interpretation). Because of these variations, the ego of a wife in a given culture may be injured by a given act of the husband, whereas in a different culture a wife may not look upon such an act as an ego problem at all, and so does not get hurt. Individual differences enter here, but it is not difficult to find examples in which these standardized ego-involvements stand out strikingly despite the range of individual variation within one culture.

This complex formation revolving around the "I" notion becomes a very important part of the whole psychological make-up of the adult. The *values* form no small part in its constitution; and it determines goals to be attained, and regulates to a large extent our likes and dislikes in the social sphere. It enters as a factor in the regulation and modification of instinctive strivings. Formed in the course of contact with external reality while "floating in an undifferentiated" autism which is moved primarily by the momentary needs and wishes, the ego may be referred to as a "system or complex of systems, a functional part region within [the] psychological totality." [30] Not every experience is a part of the system evolved around the core "I." As the facts reviewed in our short survey of its formation lead us to believe, the ego system segregates itself from the rest of the psychological totality with more or less firm boundaries. The boundaries are not rigid entities; the "boundaries of the ego are variable," and they "will vary from case to case." [31] They shrink and expand with the specific established relationships that are aroused at the moment. Under stress of exhaustion, or drunkenness, or the complete dominance of lust or hunger, the boundaries of the self may be broken through by strong biological impulses, and the result is a regression toward the absolute autism that we saw in children. Of course

[30] K. Lewin, *Dynamic Theory of Personality*, New York: McGraw-Hill, 1935, p. 56.

[31] K. Koffka, *Principles of Gestalt Psychology*, New York: Harcourt, Brace, 1935, pp. 333, 321.

this is not the autism of a helpless child, but the autism of a grownup "making a fool of himself" to others who have not thus regressed; or of a person living as an escape from reality in a self-made world of pure fantasy (a lunatic dreamer); or of a reckless person who gets what he wants because he is powerful.

This brings us close to the important contribution of psychoanalysis, to the basic truth that we cannot help finding in the dramatic conceptualizations of Freud and his followers. Especially impressive is the systematic development presented by Freud in *The Ego and the Id*. In genetic development the child starts with the undifferentiated id, consisting of instinctive strivings that are set for gratification. We have already dealt with the problem of basic drives and the minimum criteria for singling them out. We have seen the fallacy of using any single drive as the magic principle to explain all human behavior and culture (Chapter 2). According to Freud, in this undifferentiated state the child is dominated by the "pleasure principle" unchecked by other internal factors. In consequence of the frustrations that the child meets from the external world, the ego develops. The super-ego is later differentiated from the ego under the influence of the environment. The superego criticizes and checks the domination of the impulses coming from the id. The super-ego is derived from parents and others in authority around the child.[32] It reacts to the instinctive demands with an "inflexible or very nearly inflexible code—religion, ethics, superstition, good manners." [33] *What is this code with its ethics, status regulation, good manners, etc., if not a set of socially established values?*

With respect to structure, the super-ego may be likened to the ego which we characterized as a complex formation around the notion "I," of which social values constitute no small part. We shall continue to use the term ego in this sense. The psychoanalysts themselves are not always sure in certain cases which one of the two, ego or super-ego, to choose.[34]

[32] S. Freud, *The Ego and the Id*, London: L. and V. Woolf at the Hogarth Press, 1927, p. 49.
[33] M. D. Eder, On the economics and the future of the super-ego, *Int. J. Psychoanalysis*, 1929, 10, 251.
[34] See, for example, E. Jones, The origin and structure of the super-ego, *Int. J. Psychoanalysis*, 1926, 7, 307.

Once formed, the ego (this includes the super-ego of the psychoanalysts) clearly displays affective properties. Objects and individuals move us most deeply and arouse in us the strongest reverberations when, besides satisfying the basic needs, they are identified or at least closely linked with our ego. Things and persons are felt with greater warmth, the more intimately they are incorporated into the core of the ego. The main constituents of the ego, social values, are affectively charged fixations.

The affective property of the ego is expressed in Freud's notion of secondary narcissism. One psychoanalyst, James Glover, has expressed this as follows:

When thwarted libido, withdrawn from incestuous love-objects installs in the self the composite image of these objects, so that henceforth a differentiated part of the self is invested with libido formerly attached to supreme love-objects (an image which exercises the prerogatives of observation, criticism, approval, and punishment formerly exploited by its real precursors) then the libido is effectively divided against itself, for the narcissistic recompense for renounced object gratifications so obtained can only be maintained by inhibition, and this inhibition is maintained with the help of affective sanctions as strong or even stronger than these disciplinary self-preservative activities. Just as a threat to survival mobilizes the painful affect of fear, so an infringement of the ego-ideal loosens the secondary narcissism found in the cathexis of the introjected parental image and occasions the painful tension of guilt, etc.[35]

The feeling of guilt caused by violation of the values well incorporated in the ego may be taken as an index of the strong affective properties which the ego displays. The psychoanalysts have furnished us with valuable material indicating the effects of the sense of guilt. The symptoms of the self-corrective behavior that eases the sense of guilt may find expression in various ways. We cite, as an illustration, one pathological case connected with the sense of guilt. "In the case-history of a young patient the manifestations of his acutely conscious sense of guilt played a conspicuous part. When he indulged in the slightest luxury or pleasure he immediately experienced an inner command to be wretched, exhausted and thoroughly ill.

[35] J. Glover, The conception of the ego, *Int. J. Psychoanalysis*, 1926, 7, 418.

He was unable to do any work; his illness had cost him several years that should have been directed to study." In this case it is interesting to note that his "father is a clergyman in a small town. He (the father) belongs to a religious sect that professes a strict moral code, and is narrow and bigoted in his beliefs, although in other respects he is peaceable and easy to get on with." The prohibitions of the mother "concerned not only what related to sex but everything that was at all worldly." [36]

Ego Motives

Before closing our characterization of the ego, we should clarify somewhat the place of ego strivings in the scheme of motivation. An unequivocal clarification of this issue will help to end the futile controversies over "human nature" which are used to justify certain practices of exploitation and prejudice. As became evident in our brief account of its genetic development, the ego is not innate, nor are there any inborn drives or instincts which may be labeled as ego drives.[37] Ego strivings are *learned* and as such vary from culture to culture. Ego strivings have no meaning except in connection with our relationship to other individuals and groups. The standards and aspirations that serve as goals in our personal strivings are determined by our relative positions in relation to other individuals and groups.

Primarily ascendant or submissive, cooperative or competitive, hoarding or collective strivings are not *universal* in all cultures. The main *directions* of ego-striving vary from culture to culture, as is clearly indicated in many sociological works.[38] Even the seemingly most intimate personal attachments, loyalties, and responsibilities represented in kinship relation-

[36] O. Fenichel, The clinical aspect of the need for punishment, *Int. J. Psychoanalysis*, 1928, 9, 49.

[37] For example, the account of the ego in H. Cantril's *The Psychology of Social Movements*, New York: Wiley, 1941, which is presented as based on Sherif's formulation in *The Psychology of Social Norms*, includes a section devoted to ego drives. This was corrected in Sherif's joint work with Cantril, *The Psychology of Ego-involvements*.

[38] For example, in M. Mead (ed.), *Cooperation and Competition Among Primitive People;* B. Malinowski, *The Family Among Australian Aborigines*, London: University Press, 1913, p. 284; W. H. R. Rivers, *The History of Melanesian Society*, Cambridge, England: Cambridge University Press, 1924, vol. 2, p. 147.

ships are, we repeat, regulated by the socially established classifications and standards.[39]

Different virtues may be emphasized in various cultures. The ideal man of the Middle Ages is not among the ideal-man types of today. As we saw before, in one culture the highly competitive successful man may be hailed as hero, but in a different society such a person may be at a disadvantage. For example, in present-day American society, perhaps the great banker or industrialist has the prestige of being the great man. Prize fighters and successful football players and coaches seem to have as much glamour as scientists or artists—or even more. On the other hand, the Trobriander, for example, "wants, if he is a *man*, to achieve social distinction as a *good gardener* and a good worker in general." [40] Consequently, the incentives that move him are different. Individual gain and accumulation of wealth are not his primary values. In the Soviet Union, as actual study has shown, the hierarchy of values attached to professions has been reversed. Thus, laborers stand high in the scale, and bankers and lawyers are rated low.[41]

Since values incorporated in the individual are, in their major outlines, social values, it follows that the order of the hierarchy of values in the personality make-up will correspond in a significant way to that of his class or reference group. This has to be taken into account before we can make a satisfactory attempt to study personality types.

Some concrete illustrations of the social determination of feelings of personal failure and success will be presented in the next chapter. If it were not for our position relative to other individuals or groups, we should be free of ego problems. On the other hand, our strivings for food, sleep, rest, and sex are not dependent from the outset on the presence or absence of other people.

Since ego-strivings are dependent on the development of the

[39] See R. H. Lowie, *Primitive Society*, New York: Boni and Liveright, 1925, p. 80; Rivers, *op. cit.*, vol. 1, p. 50; A. R. Radcliffe-Brown, The study of kinship systems, Presidential Address, *J. Roy. Anthropol. Inst. of Great Britain and Ireland*, 1941, vol. 71, parts i and ii.

[40] B. Malinowski, *Argonauts of the Western Pacific*, London: Routledge, 1922, p. 62.

[41] J. Davis, Testing the social attitudes of children in the government schools in Russia, *Amer. J. Sociol.*, 1927, 32, 947–952.

ego, which is a genetic formation, and since the kind and even the degree of ego-strivings within certain definite ranges are in the image of the social setting in which they take place, ego strivings should be classified with the *sociogenic motives*. But their learned sociogenic character does not make them insignificant, ineffective factors in our lives. Observing the politician's lust for office, or the suffering a person may go through to *belong* to a group, etc., no one can deny the *urgency*, the unmistakable place of ego motives in our lives. To account for the striving nature of the ego, we do not have to posit biogenic ego drives.

The positing of instincts of ascendance, submission, "Drive for Autonomy," "Drive for Social Ties," "Drive for Achievement," "Drive for Recognition," "Drive for Control," has not helped our understanding of ego strivings at all. We must look for our clues elsewhere, in line with the established fact that the ego is *formed in man alone* of all animal species, because only he can function on a conceptual level.

With the above considerations in mind, we cannot help finding a substantial truth in the formulation advanced by Murphy, Murphy, and Newcomb: [42]

The thing known as the self is a selection and organization of experiences involving the visceral tensions, muscular strains, the sound of one's name, one's mirror image, and so on; and the thing which knows this pattern is simply the organism as a whole. If this is correct, it is easy to see that the self, being a primary source of many satisfactions, *must inevitably become a value*. The self is something which we like and from which we expect much. If this simple conception of the self as a value is sound, it becomes possible to eliminate with one stroke the supposed antithesis between Freud's conception of narcissism or self-love as a basis for vanity or craving for status, and the traditional associationist view that we are pleased by prestige, status or flattery because thereby we become more likely to obtain concrete rewards which we desire. Adient responses toward parts of our own body and toward our own voices and mirror images develop parallel with the awareness that the self is the thing which will have to be enhanced, assisted and rewarded if we, as organisms, are to live abundantly and satisfyingly. The special instinct, vanity, as a basis

[42] G. Murphy, L. B. Murphy, and T. M. Newcomb, *Experimental Social Psychology*, New York: Harper, 1937.

for the craving for status, vanishes into thin air, as have so many other specific instincts (p. 210).

The self is not only a value; it is a unique sort of value. It not only represents an immediate object of importance but is also a symbol which stands for many other values which may in time be achieved. When one says that he hopes he is a good enough teacher or bridge-player or diplomat to be successful in new adventures, he relies upon the characteristics of his empirical self, the self as he knows it, to bring other good things within his reach. It is in this sense that the self can properly be called a central or organizing value (p. 211).

The more specific accounting for ego-strivings lies, in our opinion, in the referential nature of experience. As we have found, our perceptions, judgments, memories, etc., take place in relation to more or less definite reference frames. Even in cases of relatively simple events, ambiguity or unstructured-ness delays the judgment time and renders judgmental activity rather tense and difficult. This is not a pleasant experience even on its simplest level. The ego is no exception to the general principle. Once it is formed with all its diverse ties in relation to goal objects, persons, and groups which stand in different degrees of affective relationship to it, the ego has to be anchored safely in many capacities. When these ties are disrupted, we experience insecurity and loss of personal identity. In fact, the feeling of personal security consists mainly of the stability of these ties which originally constitute the formation of the ego. It is not a coincidence that our main concern when we are confused and feel "left out" becomes to *belong*, to belong at any cost. The experiences of *being left out* and marginality in situations we are facing are painful, and may have unfortunate consequences. *Belongingness* in personal and group situations becomes our major effort. One of the telling pieces of evidence in favor of this point is that feelings of *anxiety* appear only after the ego formation has advanced to some degree of consistency. The advent of this significant experience as dependent on the development of the ego is reported by Sullivan and others. Sullivan says:

Along with learning of language, the child is experiencing many restraints on the freedom which it had enjoyed up till now. Restraints have to be used in the teaching of some of the personal habits that the culture requires everyone should show, and from these restraints there comes the evolution of the self system—an extremely important part of the personality—with a brand-new tool, a tool so important that I must give you its technical name, which unhappily coincides with a word of common speech which may mean to you anything. I refer to *anxiety*.

With the appearance of the self system or the self dynamism, the child picks up a new piece of equipment which we technically call anxiety. Of the very unpleasant experiences which the infant can have we may say that there are generically two, pain and fear. Now comes the third.[43]

The social values do not consist only of a set of prohibitions or taboos prescribing what is bad or wrong (the negative values), but include also positive values, putting the stamp of approval or desirability on certain kinds of acts or accomplishments; therefore ego-involvement does not appear as merely a checking or inhibiting factor; it is also a positive indicator of certain lines of action and striving. Attainment along these lines brings satisfaction.

As we have seen, a new generation does not form new fundamental norms. The child is born into society where there are *established* norms. From childhood on, these social fixations or values begin to be interiorized in him, and thus set his goals within bounds. In general, he regulates the activities which center in the satisfaction of his needs along the channels which have the approval of society. If he deviates considerably he is acted against either by various social correctives including the police force, or by his own ego. He also incorporates in himself the values imposing responsibilities and demanding sacrifice. In some few individuals this aspect may become so strong that it overcomes the desires connected with the basic needs.

It is, of course, indisputable that even though a person may have secured some status, he may not be satisfied, but may do all he can to attain a higher position. There are hierarchies of positions, and some people seem to have an insatiable craving

---

[43] H. S. Sullivan, *Conceptions of Modern Psychiatry*, Washington: William Alanson White Psychiatric Foundation, 2nd ed., 1947. Reprinted from *Psychiatry: J. of Biol. and Pathol. of Interpers. Relations*, 1940, 3, no. 1, and 1945, 8, no. 2, p. 9.

for power. In short, there are individual differences in this respect as in other respects.

Once we *belong*, just any position in the group will not do. We cannot help experiencing our position in relation to the existing scale of the group (the scale being hierarchical in the case of social groups). In the next chapter, we shall see in the experimental work of the last decade evidence showing the regulation of behavior in terms of the individual's relative position in the hierarchy of the group.

Now shall we say that at the roots of the ego, which is a genetic formation, there is a "dominance drive" that is of different strength in different individuals? Or shall we accept the instincts of self-assertion and submission? It seems to us that we do not have to postulate instincts or drives of domination or submission to explain observed individual differences. Such drives do not have an assignable locus in the body, such as the needs for food and sex have. Our hypothesis is that the differences in ego-striving may be due to a number of factors. Among them are ability (intelligence) differences, glandular differences that are so important in determining temperament, gratifications or frustrations of the major needs such as sex and food, and the general bodily condition.

We start setting goals on the scale of status as determined by our peculiar personality factors. Failure is painful. After some trials and defeats, one usually gives up grandiose schemes and approximates his goals to his ability (or in special cases he may develop delusions). There are also unfortunate people who keep on fighting—like a Don Quixote. In short, individual differences in dominance are extraordinary, and seem to yield more easily to genetic explanations than to an explanation in terms of a universal and powerful instinct. We shall deal with the variations due to personality factors in Chapter 17. This much we should say here. The results of ascendance and submission studies, as well as studies of other such "personality features," when obtained even on infra-human primates, should not be glibly carried over to the human level to account for differences in ego-strivings. On the human level, different capacities, different "traits" will influence the hierarchical positions in the group, as prescribed by the particular group situation and the special forms that regulate hierarchical arrangements therein.[44]

Ego-Involvement as a Factor in the Regulation of Basic Motives

The members of an adult group do not give in to every stimulus in the satisfaction of their needs or desires; the general orientations of their behavior are not regulated by changes in their momentary needs. When desires and wishes do not harmonize with the demands of the ego, they are usually checked or modified. The term "ego" is historically endowed with a sentimental, fetishistic halo. We must therefore be explicit: *The ego is not a fixed entity.* It is made up of relationships that are formed in the course of one's genetic development, centering in the experience of "I," itself a direct product of contact with reality. There are such different things, such different persons, such different situations linked with "I," "me," "mine," that each special case has to be studied in its concrete relationships and seen in its place in the make-up of the ego. *The ego varies with the varying relationships of members of the main socio-economic classes of humanity.* The ego reflects membership in a professional group, a family; it varies with a man's place as colleague, as teacher, as student, as employer, as employee. In each case what will elate, what will hurt, what will be taken for granted is determined by his own special place in the situation. A few examples will make this clearer.

It is an everyday experience in many social situations that men and women are treated differently. This is especially true in societies where a leisure class serves as a model for the rest of the population. Modes of behavior toward us will be taken as compliment, or as insult, or as something to be taken for granted, depending merely on whether we are male or female.

[44] The following observation by Thrasher is to the point: "The marks of leadership vary from gang to gang. The type of boy who can lead one gang may be a failure or have a distinctly subordinate role in another.... Physical and athletic prowess, which stand the leader in such good stead in most gangs, for example, would not be valued in the following type of group" (p. 344). After naming the special group in question, Thrasher says that "a hunchback was a very successful leader of a gang of healthy boys." F. Thrasher, *The Gang*, Chicago: University of Chicago Press, 1927, p. 350. To this effect, see also Chapter 17.

The attitudes of others toward us, and our attitudes toward ourselves as man or woman, are to a large extent prescribed by social standards and relationships.

In the young child up to approximately 3 years of age there appears "little evidence of any recognition of such [sex] differences." Children use the words "bad boy" indiscriminately to both sexes as a term of opprobrium. But after the age of 3 there is in general "no misapplication of the words boy or girl." [45] With psychological identification of ourselves as boy or girl, and later as man or woman, we incorporate into ourselves the qualities that are considered to go with male or female characteristics in our particular society, and we feel and react in the way "appropriate" to male or female. This is not to deny the feelings connected with male or female physiological peculiarities; these are surely only an elementary core in the complex experience of maleness or femaleness.

If the social custom requires that the woman's place is by the hearth, then the best cook will feel herself to be the best woman. In such a case beauty may be regarded as secondary or even immodest. In good "society" in America the proper procedure is for the gentleman to propose to the lady; the reverse runs counter to a lady's sense of propriety. If she does propose under the stress of strong love, she does it at the cost of her "pride." This practice seems to be just so much "human nature." Perhaps there may be some biological bias in this direction. But among the Eddystone Islanders "the initiative in proposing marriage seems often to come from the women. If a girl takes a fancy to a man, she will carry off his basket and run with it to the bush, a custom evidently closely associated with that of the *tugele*, which is connected with warfare. Carrying off the basket is a definite sign of preference and, if the man is willing, he will begin negotiating with the parents of the girl." [46] Among human groups generally, the courtship pattern may depend largely on the economic relation of the sexes.

The *name* given by the parents to the child and the place it

[45] M. Dillon, Attitudes of children toward their own bodies, *Child Devel. Monogr.*, 1934, especially pp. 165, 172.

[46] W. H. R. Rivers, *Psychology and Ethnology*, London: Kegan Paul, 1926, p. 80.

takes in his ego development is another point of interest. Many things of importance are connected with a person's name. McDougall rightly remarks that one's name "becomes a handle by aid of which he gets hold of himself and acquires facility in thinking and speaking of himself as an agent, a striver, a desirer, a refuser." In many societies individuals must change their names as part of the ceremony when an important stage is reached in their lives. The Andamanese girl gets a new name at the time of first menstruation. This is called the "flower name." [47] Likewise, in one of the Melanesian groups "on marriage both man and woman change their names and assume a common name." [48] The European and American woman's change of surname at marriage marks a new attitude toward the self; the new family officially displaces the name identification of the old. Of special interest is the experience of women who go into professions, and become economically and in some other ways independent; some of them do not use their married names. It would be interesting to discover what type of woman does and what type does not use her married name. The place of the name in the developing ego has interesting research possibilities for social psychology.

Diverse Kinds of Ego-Involvements

As we have indicated earlier in this chapter, the concept of ego-involvement denotes the psychological functioning in which ego-attitudes act as factors, to shape or modify the reaction that results at any moment. Ego-involvement may be a factor in learning, judgment, perception, memory, thinking, and other phenomena, as we shall see in the next chapter.

There are diverse kinds of ego-involvements. We are related to objects, persons, groups, and institutions around us in many different capacities. With our established ego-attitudes, we face diverse kinds of situations, the atmospheres of which are congenial, adverse, demanding, imposing, enhancing, etc. Our ego becomes involved in these as determined by the peculiari-

[47] A. Radcliffe-Brown, *Andaman Islanders*, Cambridge, England: Cambridge University Press, 1922, p. 119.
[48] W. H. R. Rivers, *History of Melanesian Society*, vol. 1, p. 347.

ties of each situation. In one, we may be competing with
rivals in some task, and we come out on top. The result is
ego-gratification. We lag behind; the result is *ego-frustration*.
In a group of friends we may have no *ego-concern*. In a situation in which we feel our personal worth is at stake, we become
highly sensitive. The result is *ego-expansion*. For some reason,
we may find ourselves sleeping or traveling with people that we
consider inferior. We feel out of place (*ego-misplacement*). As
will become evident in dealing with the topic of prejudice, our
relationships to other persons and groups (*ego-links*) may be
expressed, psychologically, as *ego-distances*. Such ego-distances
can be and, in fact, are measured.

We propose, therefore, to use the term *ego-involvement* as a
general concept to encompass all cases of functioning in which
the ego enters as a factor. The specific cases should be expressed by more specific concepts, some examples of which
we mentioned above; their exact terminology should be worked
out. We cannot deal with the whole field in a general outline.
In the section to follow, we shall clarify the fact of ego-involvement by some specific illustrations. (See also Chapter 12.)

Some Illustrations of Ego-Misplacements

Our success or failure in a given task or situation is not attainment as measured objectively, but attainment relative to
the goal set by us at the time; and it is experienced as gratification or frustration of our sense of personal worth. The involvement of the ego-level consequently influences the goals of
performance set by ourselves in concrete situations. If we do not
wish to hurt ourselves by falling below our set goals or aspirations, one way to protect ourselves is to play safe and set them
low.

Here again social norms prescribe for the individual (before
he has time to make his actual contacts with people and situations and thus form his personal standards) *in what situations
the ego has to be involved*, and to how large an extent, whom he
must consider superior and whom inferior to himself. The
socially prescribed norms determining ego-involvements in the
individual are fairly enduring, for they prescribe his established

standing in many respects. As long as we are in our prescribed setting, which raises no problems for us, and carry on the business of our daily routine in conformity with what we *expect* from others and what others expect from us, there are no intense and violent ego issues.

However, the moment strong expectations—personally formed or prescribed by social norms—are violated, the ego becomes involved and may play the dominating role in determining the behavior. The occasions that arouse such ego-expansions include accidents like an insult from a person from whom we expect pleasant treatment, or some loss of status. Intentionally we put the last statement in a general form, because such occasions will differ with the particular status of the person in question. Each case has to be studied in all its aspects. (We do not wish to minimize the importance of the differences in individual sensitiveness; we shall have a word to say about these in Chapter 17.)

The socially established norms of prejudice furnish good illustrations of this point. White people in the southern states take for granted the presence in their homes of Negroes as cooks, as servants, or as nurses in intimate contact with their babies. But the presence of a Negro in the same home, *with equal status*, is something not to be tolerated. The distance between white people and Negroes is not a physical one, or one that is felt through the immediate sense impressions. The distance is an ego-distance or social distance, since social values (positive and negative) are incorporated in the ego. When the socially stamped distance of superior from inferior is violated by the presence of an inferior as equal, the ego-level becomes involved. We may conveniently refer to such cases as instances of *ego-misplacement*.

An individual as a member of a group cannot afford to ignore his place in relation to the social situation. He cannot say that he does not know how he stands in relation to another person or other persons in the situation. As employer or employee, as superior or inferior in office or work, etc., we find certain prescribed requirements determining our status, and we are bound to notice them. If we fail to notice them, the resistance of the other members of the group, strong or weak in proportion to our deviation, will command our attention. Thus certain enduring standards as to when the ego will be involved, and its direction (positive or negative), are seen to be truly "established" for us. In cases of ego-misplacement—e.g., when we are put in a position below our status or dignity—or violations of a set standard, as when we feel that we have committed a deed violating our moral or social values, the degree of frustration, or the intensity of the conflict or sense of guilt, will probably be proportional to the degree of ego-misplacement.

12.

Ego-Involvements in Personal and Group Relationships

SOME OF THE CONCLUSIONS IN THE PRECEDING CHAPTER REACHED on the basis of genetic, psychoanalytic, and sociological (ethnological) work, have been subjected to experimental verification, especially during the past decade. The differential effects of ego-involvements on judgment, perception, memory, and other basic processes have been experimentally obtained and measured with some degree of success. In this chapter we shall present a few studies representative of this rapidly accumulating field of research.

But before considering these experimental findings, we should clarify a point which has been a constant headache in social psychology—the dichotomy between the personal and the social. To be sure, all ego-involvements are involvements of the individual. But the principles governing interpersonal and group relationships are, we repeat, basically the same. In this chapter, we shall distinguish between personal and social involvements so as to follow some order in the presentation of material. Whether revealed in strictly personal relationships (such as marriage, love, friendship) or derived from groups, social norms, or institutions, all sorts of identifications become personal. As Rubinstein aptly indicated, activities in collectives become personal when the individual is ego-involved in them. On the other hand, such involvements and others of social derivation are the social in the individual. Actually, the dichotomy of personal and social is a dualism which has come down with historical intellectual heritages but which has no validity. Also, at least some of the major contradictions that cause conflicts in the individual in "casually patterned societies" are contradictions that exist in the social setting.

It is necessary to note another closely connected fact: the effect of prevailing social norms even on the most intimate personal relationships. As the evidence in the preceding chapters has indicated, there are social norms (differing in different societies, and at different periods in the same society) regulating even the most intimate human relationships. The reciprocal expectations, loyalties, and responsibilities involved in such relationships are regulated in their major aspects by these social norms. A few concrete examples will make the issue real again. Among the peoples whose conception of marriage is formed by the norms of the Mohammedan religion, the practice of a man having more than one wife is not considered outrageous, even by the wives. (Of course, this does not mean that no jealousies are aroused in situations where certain women vie to be favorite wife.) And there are cultures in which polyandry is standardized as a normal practice.

But one does not have to resort to ethnological material. In the United States, for example, the changing conception, rights, status, education of women certainly affected reciprocal expectations, approaches, courtship, responsibilities in marital and love relationships. Consider the American woman of the seventeenth century as depicted in the following description of that period:

> The dutie of the husband is to travel abroad to seeke living: and the wives dutie is to keepe the house. The dutie of the husband is to get money and provision; and of the wives, not vainly to spend it. The dutie of the husband is to deale with many men: and of the wives, to talke with few. The dutie of the husband is, to be entermedling: and of the wife, to be solitarie and withdrawne. The dutie of the man is, to be skilfull in talke: and of the wife, to boast of silence. The dutie of the husband is, to be a giver: and of the wife, to be a saver. . . . Now where the husband and wife performeth the duties in their house we may call it College of Qyietness: the house wherein they are neglected we may term it a hell.[1]

Certainly the reciprocal expectations, duties, and treatment of husband and wife then were not what they are (or the con-

---

[1] Quoted by B. J. Stern in The family and cultural change, *Amer. Sociol. Rev.*, 1939, 4, 203.

flicting trends are) today.[2] The well-known fact that parent-youth relationships are changing, with conflicts resulting from the changing times, should likewise be mentioned in passing.

Some of the strong factors in many cases of binding friendships are determined by group affiliations. Our friends are usually members of our own class, club, fraternity, union, etc. In short, even in the seemingly most intimate personal involvements, collective factors play a major role. Often, when people are introduced to each other, they are not introduced simply as John, James, Mary, or Martha, but as so and so in some organization, club, ethnic group, etc. These labels showing socio-economic standing and other status rankings play a definitive role at the very start. We shall see some specific verifications of such unverbalized and unconsciously achieved effects of group factors later in this chapter. These are taken so for granted that their full significance is glossed over by learned people, who somehow tend to look in psychology for the bizarre and unique rather than the recurrent happenings of our lives. This is true even of the social psychologists, and is one reason why social psychology has been slow in becoming really social.

Ego-Involvements in Personal Relationships

It is a truism to say that we are involved in ourselves, in our kin, in our friends, rivals, enemies, in the achievement of our work. As psychologists, after accepting such involvements as facts, our approach is to handle them in a conceptual scheme and detect and measure them by controlled observation.

Laymen as well as psychologists note in their daily contacts that people react differently to the same remarks, to responses of other persons, depending on the established relationships between them and on the exigencies of the moment. Even when we are not in their presence, the things we do are affected by

[2] A recent popular survey of the differences between women 50 years ago and today in 30 different respects gives a summary view of the psychological changes in women owing, of course, to the transformations brought about by the rapid industrial developments in America. All these changes reflect themselves in the daily reciprocal relationships of men and women in many capacities. See James F. Bender, "How Much Women Change—and How Little," *The New York Times Magazine*, April 27, 1947.

our opinion of what people who matter to us will think of us, how they will appraise us.

Literary works and reports of happenings in actual social life, rather than the analyses of psychologists, are still the best sources of material showing the effects of ego-involvements in their diverse manifestations. Let us look first then to these sources for a few examples.

In a description of the great conductor, Toscanini, by one of the musicians in his orchestra, we see how a person can become so involved, so identified with his work that he is literally deaf and blind to his own behavior. Toscanini has an "unconscious habit" of singing while he conducts. He usually tries to do so, according to this musician, an octave above the instrument playing the "lead," whether it is a piccolo or a bassoon. Although he stops a rehearsal with fury if even one false note is played by some instrument, he simply does not hear his own voice. In one instance, he did hear a voice but was so involved in the music that he had no idea it was his own. As this musician tells the story: "Once, in Salzburg, the Maestro was putting the orchestra through a tense dress rehearsal. His own siren vocalizing soared out above the instruments. Suddenly his face clouded over with a look of impending storm. His baton, descending with a swish against his desk, halted the orchestra.

" 'Silence,' he roared. 'Who is singing here?' He waited for the culprit to identify himself. 'Well, whoever it is will now kindly shut up!'

"With a contemptuous look of warning for all, the guilty one resumed his conducting." [3]

When an individual accomplishes some feat in an activity with which he is ego-involved, the accomplishment may be magnified in his eyes. Just as people's perception of objects which have value for them, like stamps or coins, tends to be distorted or exaggerated, so ego-involvement may lead to perceptual exaggerations. In Simonov's novel of the momentous events in Stalingrad, Konyukov, a middle-aged soldier, captured a German prisoner. Bringing him to his commanding officer, Saburov, Konyukov said:

[3] "I Play for Toscanini," *This Week Magazine, New York Herald Tribune,* March 16, 1947, p. 20.

"I caught him. Look, I caught him and I give him to you. . . ."
Konyukov had the look of a conqueror on his face. Just like Zhuk,
he had tied the prisoner's arms behind his back, but at the same time
he kept clapping him on the shoulder in a friendly way. This German
was his booty. And Konyukov treated him as if he were his property,
as he would treat anything else he owned.

[The capture is so close to Konyukov's heart that he sees it as an
event of first-rate importance]: "What does he say? What does he
say?" Konyukov asked, interrupting the German two or three times.

"He's saying everything he should say," Saburov answered.

"He's hoarse. . . . Listen, he's lost his voice all of a sudden," Konyukov observed with surprise. He was still panting himself from the
fighting. "That's because I strangled him a little. Now he'll be without a voice for a couple of weeks, maybe a whole month," he added,
giving the German an appraising look.

"How far did you get in the old army?" Saburov asked him.

"Sergeant," Konyukov said.

"Well, he's a sergeant, too," Saburov said.

"Well, imagine that," Konyukov muttered in disappointment,
"and I thought he was a colonel." [4]

The love between husband and wife or sweethearts gives us
examples *par excellence* of the effects of ego-involvements upon
many psychological functions. For in addition to the value a
husband, wife, or sweetheart has as a sex object and provider,
he has value as a person with whom one is ego-involved. This
high degree of identification is one of the common elements of
the love stories of all ages. Steinbeck expressed this identification in *The Wayward Bus* when he wrote of Alice, wife of Juan,
the bus driver: "Alice was big in herself and everyone else was
very little, everyone, that is, except Juan. But, then, he was an
extension of herself" (p. 89). "Juan blotted out the universe
to her . . ." and when "she talked to Juan, there were only the
two of them" (p. 35).[5] The importance of ego-involvements in
romantic love comes out with all its color and shading in
Shakespeare's *Romeo and Juliet*. The two young lovers, seeking
to identify themselves with each other, are yet torn by their
conflicting identification with their warring families.

The truly human literature of all times is replete with illus-

---

[4] K. Simonov, *Days and Nights*, New York: Simon and Schuster, 1945, p. 42.
[5] J. Steinbeck, *The Wayward Bus*, New York: The Viking Press, 1947.

trations of ego-involved behavior. But we must turn now to the work of psychologists who have begun, especially in the past decade, to investigate and measure the effects of ego-involvements in many psychological functions.[6] As we have seen, perceptual and symbolic functions of the individual are modified by the stress of a biogenic motive (see pp. 66–75). Similarly, ego-involvements produce different effects. The effects of ego-involvements on perception, learning, memory, erection of aspiration levels, and judgment, for example, have been experimentally demonstrated.[7] The results of these studies may be taken as showing once more the selectivity of psychological processes as well as the organization and functioning of motivational and cognitive factors in a unified way.

The selectivity of memory as a result of ego-involvement is shown in a study by K. B. Clark. The procedure here was essentially that used by Bartlett in his studies of remembering. Boys and girls read twice a paragraph concerning the meeting of a man with a dominating woman. They were then asked to reproduce the paragraph as accurately as possible. Subsequent reproductions were obtained at weekly intervals. Significant differences were found between the recall of the boys and the girls. The boys "tended toward personalization—to identify themselves with the man of the situation and to make their recalls in terms of the 'affective' dynamics of the situation,

[6] Ego-involvement studies have been accumulating over the past decade; they were first surveyed by G. W. Allport in The ego in contemporary psychology, *Psychol. Rev.*, 1943, 50, 451–478.

[7] See, for example, E. Horowitz and R. Horowitz, Development of social attitudes in children, *Sociometry*, 1937, 1, 301–338; J. M. Levine and G. Murphy, The learning and forgetting of controversial material, *J. Abn. & Soc. Psychol.*, 1943, 38, 507–517; T. Alper, Task-orientation vs. ego-orientation in learning and retention, *Amer. J. Psychol.*, 1946, 59, 236–248; K. B. Clark, Some factors influencing the remembering of prose material, *Arch. Psychol.*, 1940, no. 253; R. W. Wallen, Ego-involvement as a determinant of selective forgetting, *J. Abn. & Soc. Psychol.*, 1942, 37, 20–39; A. L. Edwards, Political frames of reference as a factor influencing recognition, *J. Abn. & Soc. Psychol.*, 1941, 36, 34–50; V. Seeleman, The influence of attitude upon the remembering of pictorial material, *Arch. Psychol.*, 1940, no. 258; W. McGehee, Judgment and the level of aspiration, *J. Gen. Psychol.*, 1940, 22, 3–15; R. R. Holt, Effects of ego-involvement upon levels of aspiration, *Psychiatry*, 1945, 3, 299–317; E. Marks, Skin color judgments of Negro college students, *J. Abn. & Soc. Psychol.*, 1940, 22, 3–15; G. S. Klein and N. Schoenfeld, The influence of ego-involvement on confidence, *J. Abn. & Soc. Psychol.*, 1941, 36, 249–258. This representative list includes the studies reviewed in the following pages.

particularly as related to the potential or actual damage to the prestige of the man." [8] In another part of the study, a paragraph concerned with the anxieties of W.P.A. workers was read and recalled by W.P.A. workers and Columbia College students. Whereas none of the college students tended to "personalize" their reproductions, the W.P.A. workers not only did tend to, but a fourth of them actually reproduced the paragraph in the first person singular.

Marks' study on judgments of skin color by Negro subjects shows how judgments in which one is highly involved may be distorted in terms of previously established reference scales. In this case, the judgments were made in terms of a reference scale of skin color in which the subject tended to place himself near the average, independent of his actual skin color (within limits, of course). Thus, the skin color of a given subject would be judged lighter by a person with dark skin than by a person with light skin.[9] The affective components of this scale are, of course, derived in part from the socially established scale in America which places a premium on light skin.

Although psychologists particularly interested in the learning process have not given much attention to the fact, ego-involvements produce differential results in learning. In a study of the learning and retention of pro-Soviet and anti-Soviet material by strongly pro-communist and anti-communist subjects, Levine and Murphy showed that a person's ego-involved frame of reference affects both learning and retention. For example, the anti-communist subjects tended to learn and retain the anti-Soviet selection better than the pro-communist subjects. The authors explain these results in terms of the harmony or threat of the material to the subject's autisms.[10] Alper substantiated the effect of ego-involvements in learning in her study comparing the learning of nonsense syllables and digits by ego-involved and "task-involved" subjects. The experiment was designed in such a way that 3 "laws of learning" formulated on the basis of classical studies were tested. Some of the subjects were told that the experiment was really a test of intel-

[8] Clark, *op. cit.*, p. 61.
[9] Marks, *op. cit.*
[10] Levine and Murphy, *op. cit.*

ligence. Alper found, for example, that while the learning of task-involved subjects was superior to their retention, this was not the case for subjects who were ego-involved. In short, the study shows that ego-involvements are factors which must be considered in an adequate learning theory.[11]

Klein and Schoenfeld decisively showed the differential results of the degree of involvement with the situation in their study of confidence ratings based on a group of pencil and paper tasks. In one situation, subjects were told the tasks were intelligence tests and that the results would be sent to the personnel bureau of the university, whereas in the other situation no such instructions were given. Under the "'stress' or 'ego-involvement' situation," the subjects' confidence ratings showed a generality lacking in the more "neutral conditions" where the confidence ratings in various tasks showed little relationship.[12] McGehee found differential results for his subjects' judgments of their own future performance (erection of aspiration level) and their judgments of another person's performance.[13]

Some light is thrown on these and other studies by C. Sherif's study of individuals' judgments of their own performance and that of another person with whom they maintained a definite personal relationship.[14] Each subject participated with another person in a dart-throwing game, which they were told was a test of eye-hand coordination. Each pair of subjects in the first group consisted of a parent and his or her child. The pairs in the second group were husband and wife. After a few practice trials by one member of the pair, the second member wrote an estimate of the first member's next score, keeping his estimate a secret. The subject who was throwing the darts then estimated aloud the score he expected to make on that trial. This procedure was followed for a series of 25 trials. Then the subjects changed places, the second member of the pair becoming the thrower and estimating his own performance. The identical procedure was followed with the second subject. Each

[11] Alper, *op. cit.*
[12] Klein and Schoenfeld, *op. cit.*
[13] McGehee, *op. cit.*
[14] Presented at the Eastern Psychological Association meeting, Atlantic City, New Jersey, April 26, 1947.

subject thus made a series of 25 judgments of his own future performance and 25 judgments of his partner's future performance.

In this situation, the subjects tended to be as ego-involved with their partner's (parent, child, husband, or wife) performance as with their own. In some cases, more ego-involvement was shown with the partner's performance. As a result, the judgments of their own and the partner's future performance tended, on the average, to resemble each other in many respects, such as accuracy, "rigidity" (or tendency to hold the level of judgments or goals constant), and the tendency toward shifts in judgments as performance improved or deteriorated. The spontaneous remarks and reactions of the partners in this study substantiate the results in a crucial way. Many of the subjects were considerably more loquacious, tenser, and more pleased with the performance of their child, or parent, or mate than with their own. The records of the spontaneous remarks of the subjects during the course of the experiment reveal this both when judging one's partner's performance and when judging his own.

The subjects quite frequently gave spontaneous suggestions to their partners on the best techniques of holding and throwing darts, standing, etc. There was, of course, nothing in the instructions conducive to such reactions. The subject who was throwing was often advised by his partner: "Don't tighten up"; "Take it easy"; "Get a good grip on the dart"; "You're taking it too casually, dear"; etc.

Every subject made encouraging remarks to his partner for example, mother to son: "Get that yellow, S——! Get it for Daddy!" "Come on, honey, really do me proud. You have a better eye than that." Wife to husband: "I want you to make 80, H——. I want to tell the children about it." Mother to son when he estimated his score lower than his previous score: "Oh, no! You'll do more than you bid, not less."

All the subjects showed enthusiasm for their partner's successes, in some cases more than for their own. For a partner's successes, there were whistles and even shouts of enthusiasm: "Yippee! The best yet!" "Come on, Robin Hood, do *that* again!" "You look like you've been on shipboard a lot. You're *good*, Mommie." "You see, I knew my faith in you was justified. . . . You're going to make it again this time."

Some subjects offered excuses for their partner's "failures." For example, one husband explained that his wife hadn't been feeling well that day, but the explanation came only after a long series of low scores on her part. A mother explained her daughter's low score on one trial by saying, "I think that dog running by the window threw you off." One daughter hid her face in her hands and groaned or giggled every time her mother missed the target, a reaction quite similar to her reactions to her own "failures."

In some cases there was considerable awareness of the way the partner looked while throwing, as indicated by such remarks as: "Isn't she cute? Doesn't she look cute doing this?" "Mommie looks so funny throwing those!" "I wish your father could see you do this."

Several subjects remarked spontaneously that it seemed more difficult to estimate for their partner than for themselves— A wife: "It's so much easier to estimate for myself than for A——." A mother writing down her estimate before her daughter made hers: "The funny thing is that I seem to be estimating just what C—— bids every time." (As a matter of fact she was not.) A father: "It's easier to judge myself than E——. His score seems to fluctuate more than mine. (Looks at score sheet) I don't know. He's staying fairly constant, isn't he?"

Data concerning the nature of the relationship and the degree of identification and of motivational attachment between the subjects who were partners in this experiment would have been interesting and would help to clarify the differential results obtained from pair to pair. Several of the husband-and-wife pairs revealed more or less typical American husband-and-wife attitudes. In various degrees, the husbands tended to be protective of their wives, encouraging them and comforting them. One husband consistently kept his estimates lower than his wife's score when her score was low, raising them above her score only when her performance was clearly improving. The wives, in various degrees, tended to maintain an admiring role in relation to their husbands' performance.

As revealed in the spontaneous remarks, the subjects made

judgments of both their own and their partner's performance in terms of expectations and goals established through personal association and through the interiorization of social reference frames relating to the relationship (e.g., toward one's husband or child). Further variation would be expected if the subjects were involved with each other in a negative way, e.g., as bitter personal rivals, competitors, or members of antagonistic groups.

A word should be said now about the psychological significance of ego-involved and non-ego-involved (or "task-involved") situations. Task-involved situations, we should say, take place discretely without being referred to an established reference scale or frame, such as a scale of goals. Consequently, no special effort is called for to approximate certain levels and goals. On the other hand, ego-involved situations put us in a position relative to standards set by ourselves in the past, by others, or in relation to established scales of achievement of individuals or groups who are superior, inferior, or equal in our eyes. It is this reference to a scale, or standard of achievement, with which we are involved that produces results that differ in so many respects. This hypothesis would seem to be substantiated in part by Klein and Schoenfeld's finding of low intercorrelation of confidence ratings under "neutral conditions" and Holt's finding that the setting of goals for one's own performances "is more specific, more peripheral and responsive to outer environmental forces" when there is little ego-involvement in the situation.[15]

If reactions are regulated in terms of an ego-involved reference frame or scale in which one's self and other persons occupy relative positions, it should be possible not only to produce such modified reactions momentarily but also, knowing the frame and the relative positions of two persons in it, to predict the direction in which the reaction would be modified. We have already seen how admirably the autokinetic phenomenon lends itself to the study of the process of norm formation in group situations, and of attitude formation (pp. 162 and 228). In 1936, this same stimulus situation was used to demonstrate how judgments may be regulated momentarily by ego-involvements as determined by the position of another person relative to the

[15] Holt, *op. cit.*, p. 314.

subject.[16] In this case, the cooperating subject had prestige in the eyes of the naïve subject. The following is a verbatim account by the subject cooperating with the experimenter:

Miss X and I [Assistant in Psychology, Columbia University] were subjects for Dr. Sherif. I was well acquainted with the experiment but Miss X knew nothing whatsoever about it. Since she was a close friend of mine, and I carried some prestige with her, Dr. Sherif suggested that it would be interesting to see if we could predetermine her judgments. It was agreed beforehand that I was to give no judgments until she had set her own standard. After a few stimulations it was quite clear that her judgments were going to vary around five inches. At the next appropriate stimulation, I made a judgment of twelve inches. Miss X's next judgment was eight inches. I varied my judgments around twelve inches and she did the same. Then I changed my judgment to three inches, suggesting to Dr. Sherif that he had changed it. She gradually came down to my standard, but not without some apparent resistance. When it was clear that she had accepted this new standard, Dr. Sherif suggested that I make no more judgments lest I might influence hers. He then informed her on a subsequent stimulation that she was underestimating the distance which the point moved. Immediately her judgments were made larger and she established a new standard. However, she was a little uneasy with it all, and before the experiment had progressed much farther whispered to me, "Get me out of here."

When we were again in my office, I told her that the point had not moved at all during the experiment. She seemed quite disturbed about it, and was very much embarrassed to know that we had been deceiving her. Noting her perturbation, I turned the conversation to other matters. However, several times during our conversation she came back to the subject, saying, "I don't like that man" (referring to Dr. Sherif) and similar statements indicating her displeasure with the experience. It was not until some weeks later when she was again in my office that I discovered the full extent of her aversion. I asked her to serve as a subject for me in an experiment and immediately she exclaimed, "Not down in *that room*," pointing to Dr. Sherif's experimental room.

In 1946, Zeaman again demonstrated the regulation of ego-involved reaction as determined by the relationship between the subjects. In this demonstration, two cooperating subjects

[16] M. Sherif, An experimental approach to the study of attitudes, *Sociometry*, 1937, 1, 90–98.

were used, one for whom the naïve subject felt a good deal of affection and one for whom he tended to feel antagonism.[17] In Zeaman's words:

One male graduate student of the Anthropology Department at Columbia was used as subject. He was cooperative, and intelligent, but entirely naïve about the experimental procedure and apparatus, and about the autokinetic effect. The relationship between the observer and the two experimenters was primarily that of very close friendship although after a period of sharing an apartment for one year, different modes of behavior had set in on the part of the subject with respect to the male and female experimenter. It is ... this difference in relationship that forms the independent variable in this experiment. The relationship between the subject and the female experimenter was a non-competitive, pleasantly affectional relationship. ... Between the subject and the male experimenter, on the other hand, there existed a relationship characterized by a mutual striving for ascendancy, aggression ... and a consequent tendency to deprecate the judgments of the other person. Over a period of many months, these relationships had proved relatively invariable.

The naïve subject first gave his judgments individually. Then:

The female experimenter left the room under a pretext, to make a quick average of the judgments in order to fix her own. Upon returning, thirty-five judgments apiece were recorded for the female experimenter and subject together. The subject controlled his key (and hence the duration of the light) and alternated with the experimenter in giving first judgments.

Following a brief rest, thirty-five additional judgments were taken for the subject in an " alone " situation before it was " spontaneously " decided to "fill-out the curve" of the male experimenter. In this second social situation the female experimenter manipulated the experimenter's switch and recorded the judgments of the subject together with the male experimenter. During the rest, the male experimenter had previously left the room to inspect the subject's " alone " judgments. The second social situation was conducted in the same manner as the first, with the subject and experimenter alternating in giving the first judgment for each stimulus. A final " alone " was then given.

[17] Mr. David Zeaman of Columbia University reported the demonstration for this book.

[Before the experiment] The prediction had been made . . . that the observer's positive and negative attitude towards the female and male experimenter respectively would be reflected in his perception of an ambiguous stimulus. Specifically it was predicted that the female experimenter would be able to shift the subject's norm in the direction of her judgments, while the effect of the male experimenter's judgments would be to shift the subject's norm in a direction away from the norm assumed by the male experimenter.

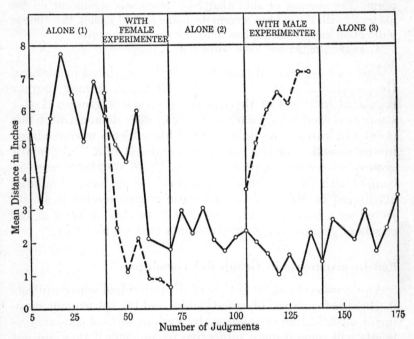

FIG. 26.   The effects of positive and negative personal involvements on judgment.

The means of each 5 successive judgments of distance of autokinetic movement are indicated on the unbroken line.   The two experimenters' "planted" judgments are shown on the broken lines.   The 5 situations are specified at the top of the figure.   (Courtesy of D. Zeaman.)

Figure 26 shows the mean of each 5 successive judgments for the naïve subject (the solid line) and the two cooperating subjects (dotted lines).   Zeaman summarized the findings as follows:

The subject assumed a norm at approximately 5.9 inches in the first " alone " situation, and was shifted down to 3.4 inches by the female's judgments which averaged 1.9 inches. This drop is significant on the .01 level. A further decrease occurred in the next " alone " situation with the subject's norm leveling off at 2.4 inches as an average for thirty-five judgments.

The male experimenter then set his norm at 5.9 inches to discover the amount and direction of shift that would occur in the subject's norm. The amount of shift that took place was significant on the .05 level, with the subject's norm dropping to 1.57 inches, this time in a direction away from that assumed by the experimenter.

Thus the predictions were borne out. . . .

Just as ego-involved reactions may be regulated in terms of the position of another person relative to us, so may they be regulated in terms of the relative position of groups. Asch's study reviewed briefly earlier (pp. 235–237) demonstrates this point admirably. The judgments of his subjects were modified in the direction of the supposed standards of a "congenial" group (reference group) even when those standards were in conflict with the individual's own. On the other hand, standards attributed to Nazis (an antagonistic group) tended to be rejected as a basis for judgment.[18] It is to this problem of the effects of groups on ego-involvements that we now turn.

Ego-Involvements in Group Relationships

Any ego-involvement is that of the individual who manifests it. But the formation of ego-attitudes and the subsequent shaping or modification of reactions by various sorts of ego-involvements will remain mere subjective phenomena if they are not related to the social situations which produce them. It became evident in the preceding chapter that the major ego-attitudes defining our position in relation to others are derived from the status ranking prescribed by social organizations (family, school, profession, club, etc.) and the norms and goals prevailing in them. Formally or informally organized groups of any kind are necessarily hierarchical—with their peculiar *status* and

---

[18] S. E. Asch, Studies in the principles of judgments and attitudes: II. Determination of judgments by group and by ego standards, *J. Soc. Psychol.*, *SPSSI Bull.*, 1940, 12, 433–465.

prestige scales. Family, church, gang, professional organization, union, club, university—all have their own status and prestige scales. Individuals in every society are members of some group or groups. As we trace the differentiation of groups from relatively simple primitive societies to highly variegated bourgeois societies, the groups that the individual belongs to increase in number and complexity. (Here we shall not digress to discuss the effects on the individual of the integration or lack of integration [conflicts] of the groups of which he is a member.) The status and prestige standards of individual members are determined largely by those of the groups of which he becomes a member or to which he refers himself.

Status is a sociological denotation. Status is a standardized position in the group. As the anthropologist Linton states, "In all societies certain things are selected as reference points for the ascription of status." [19] The scale of status positions is a stimulus for the would-be member; hence the status positions of a group are data of sociology. The individual learns them as he comes to belong *psychologically* and to participate in his groups. In its main features his ego consists of a series of belongingnesses. Social psychologists must learn a great deal from the social scientists about these status positions, for they can be studied sociologically on their own level without reference to this or that individual. For example, the relative roles of father and mother, and the range and particular roles of kinship relations can be studied without reference to particular individuals in those particular roles. As clearly pointed out by Piaget, at first the family is a perceptual pattern to the child and a place of satisfaction of his needs. It is only after a certain degree of ego development that he grasps the significance of reciprocal roles in the family as they are standardized in the particular social setting.

Therefore it becomes imperative for the social psychologist to learn something about the sociology of *status*, if he wants a proper perspective toward the stimulus situations. An outline of social psychology is not the place to bring together the scattered sociological literature on status. Consequently we

[19] R. Linton, *The Study of Man: An Introduction*, New York: Appleton-Century, 1936, p. 215.

shall mention in passing only a few relevant points inspired by Benoit-Smullyan's concise discussion of status, status types, and status interrelations.[20] Everywhere, group organizations are hierarchical affairs. These hierarchies may be based on diverse criteria of which economic and political power are major. In lesser organized groups other criteria may determine status. For example, in a schoolroom, a hierarchy is established among the pupils according to the degree of success in school subjects. Status may be defined "as relative position within a hierarchy" (p. 155). Benoit-Smullyan says:

By a hierarchy we mean a number of individuals ordered on an inferiority-superiority scale with respect to the comparative degree to which they possess or embody some socially approved or generally desired attribute or characteristic. A hierarchal position is thus always a position in which one individual is identified with others with regard to the possession or embodiment of some common characteristic, but differentiated from these others in the *degree*, or *measure*, to which the characteristic is possessed or embodied. The three chief hierarchies with which we will be concerned are: the economic hierarchy, the political hierarchy, and the prestige hierarchy. Relative position within these hierarchies constitutes economic status, political status, and prestige status respectively (pp. 151–152).

Economic status, political status, and prestige status are the three primary or basic types of social status. The individual's position may not be on the same level in these three major types of status, i.e., he may be high in prestige status and not so high in economic status. After pointing to certain concrete cases of such discrepancies, Benoit-Smullyan comes, however, to the conclusion that "in fact, *the data suggest that economic status has been the dominating element in our own* [American] *recent history* . . . " (p. 151, italics mine). "Wealth is frequently 'converted' into power by direct or indirect bribery, by purchasing posts of command or weapons of coercion, by hiring the services of guards or soldiers or propagandists"(p. 159).

In a society dominated by private property relationships, all prestige sooner or later has to be regulated by economic status. "It is significant that the dispossessed aristocrat does not in-

---

[20] E. Benoit-Smullyan, Status, status types and status interrelations, *Amer. Sociol. Rev.*, 1944, 9, 151–161.

definitely retain his prestige unless he is sooner or later able to win back his power. Similarly, the *nouveaux riches*, though snubbed persistently, do sooner or later gain in prestige status providing they retain their money. We have to do here with one phase of an interesting social process which we may name 'status conversion' " (p. 159).

Particularly significant for the social psychologist is the concept of *status equilibration* that Smullyan introduces. He characterizes the concept as follows: "As a result of status conversion processes which are normally at work in every [capitalist] society, there exists a real tendency for the different types of status to reach a common level, i.e., for a man's position in the economic hierarchy to match his position in the political hierarchy and for the latter to accord with his position in the hierarchy of prestige, etc." (p. 160).

The concept of *status equilibration* is particularly useful for the social psychologist, for in actual life the status equilibration process brings together strange companions (e.g., professor, businessman, and politician). Let us illustrate the point from a plausible case of a professor and a businessman; this could happen in any distinguished university town having a "good" address. A certain professor has prestige because of his university position, but, not having broken down in himself the hierarchy of economic values of his setting, he gets ideas from his businessmen neighbors, who live with the luxurious standards of rich country squires. One neighbor is a multimillionaire. He wants prestige commensurate with his wealth, but has not attained this level of prestige as yet. People know him chiefly through the advertisements of his products. The result is that the two men "team up" in order that each may attain the level of economic or prestige status that he wants. Of course the professor in question represents the type who keeps intact in himself the contradictory hierarchy of values of his setting, in spite of his polysyllabic utterances to the contrary in print. The illustration may be extended to cover the politician-scholar-businessman triumvirate.

We are deliberately excluding concrete studies dealing with socio-economic status and the ego-involvements determined by them, restricting ourselves here to simpler and less conse-

quential data to formulate the principle. Before we proceed
with such data, a few words giving the implications of the foregoing discussion for the problem of ego-involvements are in
order. The sociological concept, *status*, denotes a relative position in a hierarchy (scale) of positions. The status of an individual is the position he holds in the hierarchy of his group,
whatever it may be. In order to have a relative position in the
group, of course, he has first to relate himself, or belong, to it.
Belongingness in a group produces in him the experience of the
hierarchy or scale of the group. Once a member, his status
aspirations and standards of attainment are determined accordingly. These status aspirations and standards are revealed
psychologically through his ego-attitudes and ego-involvements.

The conclusion indicated in the foregoing discussion is substantiated in its major features by a number of studies made
during the last decade.[21] We shall here summarize briefly a few
representative ones.

In Hyman's study of the psychology of status, already cited,
we find an experimental demonstration of the fact that the
standards people set for themselves are determined by the
standards of the group or groups to which they relate themselves (their reference groups). Hyman first conducted intensive
interviews to discover the individual's dimensions of status, his

[21] See, for example, D. W. Chapman and J. Volkmann, "A social determinant of
the level of aspiration, *J. Abn. & Soc. Psychol.*, 1939, 34, 225–238; H. H. Anderson and
H. F. Brandt, A study of motivation involving self-announced goals of fifth grade
children and the concept of level of aspiration, *J. Soc. Psychol.*, 1939, 10, 209–232;
E. R. Hilgard, E. M. Sait, and G. A. Magaret, Level of aspiration as affected by relative standing in an experimental social group, *J. Exper. Psychol.*, 1940, 27, 411–421;
R. Gould and H. B. Lewis, An experimental investigation of changes in the meaning
of level of aspiration, *J. Exper. Psychol.*, 1940, 27, 422–438; P. S. Sears, Levels of
aspiration in academically successful and unsuccessful school children, *J. Abn. & Soc.
Psychol.*, 1940, 35, 498–536; A. MacIntosh, Differential effect of the status of the
competing group upon the levels of aspiration, *Amer. J. Psychol.*, 1942, 55, 546–554;
F. W. Irwin and M. G. Mentzer, Effect of differences in instruction and motivation
upon measures of level of aspiration, *Amer. J. Psychol.*, 1942, 55, 400–406; H. H.
Hyman, The psychology of status, *Arch. Psychol.*, 1942, no. 269; H. B. Lewis, An
experimental study of the role of the ego in work: I. The role of the ego in cooperative
work, *J. Exper. Psychol.*, 1944, 34, 113–126; H. B. Lewis and M. Franklin, An experimental study of the role of the ego in work: II. The significance of task-orientation in
work, *J. Exper. Psychol.*, 1944, 34, 195–215; H. T. Himmelweit, A comparative study
of the level of aspiration of normal and of neurotic persons, *Brit. J. Psychol.*, 1947,
37, 5–59.

reference groups and individuals, the genesis, criteria, and values of status and his satisfaction with his status. Among the interesting findings here was the "rare occurrence of the total population as a reference group and the great frequency of more intimate reference groups. . . . Individuals operate for the most part in small groups within the total society, and the total population may have little relevance for them. Far more important are their friends, people they work with. Consequently, objective measures of status will very likely differ from subjective measures if total population is the basis for the determination of objective status" (p. 24).[22]

Hyman then went on to construct scales to measure "subjective status" in several respects, e.g., economic, intellectual, cultural, social, etc. He showed how judgments of an individual's own status in these respects shift when related to different reference groups. He also found that: "striving for status is generally directed in the channel of the most valued status," i.e., toward the highest in the hierarchy of statuses. Dissatisfaction with status was found to vary "inversely with the level of status," showing how one's position on the scale may influence one's aspirations and strivings. The findings concerning "lack of concern with status" are revealing. Lack of concern was evident among those individuals (1) whose status was similar to the status of their reference group; (2) who maintained a status high in the hierarchy and took their position for granted; and (3) who rejected the scale of status established in the social order around them in judging their own status. Finally, "the values of an individual are set into operation by certain reference groups, in which case specific statuses contribute to general status in accordance with their value" (p. 91).

The most clear-cut formulation of the problem of the erection of goals of achievement in a task, as regulated by groups whose achievement *in our eyes* are consistently established as superior, inferior, or on the same level with ours, was advanced, in 1939, by Chapman and Volkmann.[23] They start by calling attention

[22] This shows that such terms as "culture" and "subculture" are loose terms to use in accounting for the social influences on the individual, as we indicated earlier (pp. 95-96). On the other hand, the concepts of membership and reference groups put the individual in a concrete social situation in terms of the range of his receptivity.

[23] Chapman and Volkmann, *op. cit.*

to the principle that "the conditions which govern the setting of a level of aspiration (*Anspruchsniveau*), in the sense of an estimate of one's future performance in a given task, may be regarded as a special case of the effect upon a judgment of the frame of reference within which it is executed" (p. 225). For, as we have pointed out, all judgmental activities tend to "take place within such referential frameworks," whether they are ego-involved or not. In cases in which ego-involvement of some sort enters as a factor, the major anchoring points are determined by that factor. Chapman and Volkmann asked their subjects to predict their future performance on a literary test. The subjects (college students) had no objective criteria in relation to which they could make such an appraisal. The experimenters, however, furnished the subjects with such anchorings by giving them the alleged performances of groups who stood in different positions relative to the subjects, such as literary critics (higher) and W.P.A. workers (lower). The group of subjects who compared themselves to the "superior" standard *lowered* their goals. On the other hand, the "inferior" standard (W.P.A. workers) introduced for the other group had the effect of *raising* the goals of that group.

But when the subjects' own standards in a task (a test) were previously established, the introduction of various group standards produced practically no shifts based on these group standards. These findings were later substantiated with different stimulus material and different reference groups.

Another comprehensive formulation of the principle is that offered by P. Sears in her work on the level of aspiration of academically successful and unsuccessful school children.[24] Sears' experimental verification is especially significant in that she utilized a hierarchy of success and failure already established in a school situation. She conclusively showed how relative standing established in a success-failure hierarchy in the school group influences the standard of performance on a subsequent occasion. Sears then went on to create experimental "success" and "failure" for the children's performances. She found that even in such experimentally created situations, the children set their goals in accordance with what they believed

[24] Sears, *op. cit.*

to be their position relative to the social norms of performance they had accepted. In explaining the findings of different characteristics of the aspiration level for successful and unsuccessful children, Sears concludes: "The cultural pressure to excel and to keep the performance improving, plus the cognizance of the position of the self relative to social norms, seems to account for most of the results obtained in the present investigation" (p. 528).

Recently, Lewin, Dembo, Festinger, and Sears gave a concise statement of the principle that appears in all these and similar studies, when they stated, in line with the previous formulations, that such influences as temporary situational factors and standards of one's own and other groups governing setting a level of aspiration "may be conceived of as frames, involving a scale of values, within which the individual makes his decision as to a goal."[25]

More recently, Himmelweit, taking his lead explicitly from the work of Sears, demonstrated how the individuals in a group set apart, who see themselves in a definitely inferior position in relation to "normal" people, regulate their goals as prescribed by the established standing of their group. Himmelweit studied the judgments made by hospitalized neurotic patients of their own past and future performances on a simple motor task. He found that the judgments were affected by the degree of ego-involvement of the subjects in their performance. While recognizing the particular influence of individual differences of neurotic patients, Himmelweit assigned to first place in factors explicitly determining the degree of ego-involvement "the environmental factor or reference scales against which the individual evaluates his performance" (p. 43). He concludes: "In the case of the anxious and depressed patient, no outside group norm is imposed—it is rather an interiorized one, based upon the conception the patient has of his ability in relation to those of the group. Since he considers himself inferior, i.e., below the standard of the group, he behaves as if his performance had been compared with that of a superior group."[26]

[25] K. Lewin, T. Dembo, L. Festinger, P. Sears, "Level of Aspiration," in J. McV. Hunt (ed.), *Personality and the Behavior Disorders*, New York: Ronald Press, 1944, vol. 1, p. 337.

[26] Himmelweit, *op. cit.*, p. 57.

A telling substantiation of the effects of the reference scale of the group to which an individual belongs psychologically upon his aspirations and actual performance is a study by M. Dalton of production in an industrial department.[27] In this department, 100 men worked under a piece-rate system in which they received a bonus for production over 66%. However, through the interactions of the group a "well recognized rule" had been established that no worker must produce over 150% on any job. The striking finding was that a majority of the men consistently made a bonus, but were careful not to exceed 150%. Ten men disregarded the rule and averaged between 150% and 200%, whereas 18 men averaged below 100%. After finding that *skill alone* did not account for this range of performance, Dalton demonstrated that it could be fully accounted for in terms of (1) the social backgrounds and (2) present social activities of the individual members of the group. The findings are summarized by Whyte:

(1) "Most of the bottom production group grew up in large cities where for years they had been active in boys' gangs. Such activity tends to build loyalty to one's own group and opposition to authority—whether from parents or management. The rate busters all grew up on farms or in small towns where they lived under the close supervision of parental authority and had little time or opportunity to develop gang activities and the accompanying loyalty to the gang.

(2) "In terms of present social participation, the restricters [who averaged below 100 per cent] are the men who lead an active social life *in the shop*. Furthermore, they lead a highly active group life outside of work." (Italics mine.) In other words, these are the men who are *good* members of the group. On the other hand, "these findings suggest that he [whose average is over 150%] is either a lone wolf in factory and community or else an individual with a strong drive toward social mobility, who thus cuts himself off from others on the same level and seeks association with those of superior status." This conclusion was further substantiated by other behavioral indexes. For example, the "restricters" were the most generous in giving to the group charities and the "rate busters" the most stingy.

[27] This study is summarized by W. F. Whyte in an unpublished study "Economics and Human Relations in Industry," which was kindly made available by Dr. Whyte.

These findings recall the Bennington study (pp. 139–155) in which conformity or non-conformity to the liberal Bennington values was wholly intelligible in terms of the degree of absorption in the college group and the relative attachment to outside groups whose values conflicted with those of Bennington.

With these considerations in mind, we will clarify our present problem by returning briefly to the implications of group psychology outlined in earlier chapters.

Ego-Involvements and Groups

An ever-accumulating bulk of evidence indicates that one's reference groups are major factors in determining one's personal goals. In our discussion of the results of group interaction in Chapters 5, 6, and 7, this fact was implicit all the way through. In those chapters we saw that a more or less well-defined structure is formed as a consequence of group interaction, even if such a structure is wanting initially. Formation of a group structure necessarily implies membership on the part of the individual. Membership implies *identification* with the group, and this subsequently reveals itself in ego-involved reactions when the group identification is situationally tapped in various relationships. When our group is insulted, for example, we feel personally insulted. We saw that relative positions emerge in group interactions, if they were lacking initially, and that we experience our positions in relation to such an established hierarchical scale. Our standards of achievement, our goals of attainment are determined accordingly. If the reader interested in ego-involvements glances through the group chapters with the main points of our account of ego-involvements in mind, he cannot help finding that group membership and relative position in the group are ego-involving situations.

In these findings—the formation of group structures, the emergence of relative roles for the members, and the rise of norms peculiar to the group—the work of sociologists and psychologists has been progressively converging. We utilized results of both psychologists and sociologists in our discussion of groups.

Informally organized groups are particularly adapted for singling out these facts, because we are able to trace the back-

306 An Outline of Social Psychology

ground of the individual members, the motives that bring them together, the progressive course of interaction, the formation of the group (clique, gang), and the rise of social norms (codes) which, in turn, come to determine and regulate the goals and behavior of the individual members. In the work of Thrasher and of Whyte we find some fine examples of such informal group formations.[28] The picture, roughly, is this (of course we have telescoped the peculiar individual features of particular groups): A group of boys lacking stable anchorages in society at large (which itself lacks integration in its organization) and in many cases suffering deprivations of their basic needs, gravitate toward each other to interact in informal situations on the street. As a consequence of group interaction (in play, in common enterprises, in conflict with other groups), a somewhat well-defined group formation emerges, with definite but by no means static roles, with a set of norms peculiar to the group that prescribes the behavior of the individual members in relation to each other and to outsiders.

In the impressive series of case studies by Clifford Shaw, we find the effects of group membership and group norms presented in terms of the experience and behavior of single individuals longitudinally and intensively traced.[29] Once a member, the identification, loyalty, and responsibility *that really count* for the individual are with the group. His knowledge that he is a member of a certain family, that he is a pupil in a school and a member of a church, and the exhortations all of them, do not really matter to him, unless he is ego-involved with them. The mere knowledge of prescriptions of groups in which we are not psychologically involved simply does not move us. Our ego-attitudes, and hence our concern over status and goals to be attained, are derived from the group to which we relate ourselves (our reference group). Any changes of attitude that really affect our experience and behavior can be brought about effectively only if we "settle down" and join other groups—a transformation which punishments and jail sentences, not to

28 F. M. Thrasher, *The Gang*, Chicago: University of Chicago Press, 1927; W. F. Whyte, *Street Corner Society*, Chicago: University of Chicago Press, 1943.
29 C. R. Shaw, *The Jack-Roller*, Chicago: University of Chicago Press, 1930; C. R. Shaw, *The Natural History of a Delinquent Career*, Chicago: University of Chicago Press, 1931; C. R. Shaw (ed.), *Brothers in Crime*, Chicago: University of Chicago Press, 1938.

mention exhortations, fails to produce. In the detailed case histories of Stanley and the Martin brothers, we have brilliant illustrations of the point. So, too, adolescents may pay not a bit of attention to the opinions and pleadings of their parents, but may follow with precision the dictums of their clique. This and other aspects of adolescence will be our concern in the following chapter.

Mass Media of Communication and Ego-Involvements

Mass media of communication have become such an important means of social stimulation, replacing to a great extent face-to-face relations and producing consequent participation of various sorts on the part of individuals, that a section on the topic is in order.[30]

The mass media (radio, movies, newspapers, magazines, and books) are products of the revolutionary technological development of modern times. The far-reaching effects of mass media on human relationships cannot be understood apart from the other products of technology, viz., the means of production and transportation (see Chapter 15). The same technological products (i.e., means of production, transportation, and communication) that brought about the concentration of wealth, the rise of great cities like New York and Chicago, also brought about the staggering proportions that mass media have acquired today. Great newspapers with a circulation of about a million copies a day are published in the big cities. Perhaps it is not too fantastic to say that the great newspapers are replicas in miniature of the highly differentiated lives of the great cities with all their integrating and conflicting values, loyalties, and affiliations.

It is not a mere coincidence that the owners of the mass media are usually, at the same time, owners of the big business enterprises which have direct or indirect control over production processes. William Allen White, in the report of the Commission on Freedom of the Press, says: "Too often the publisher of an American newspaper has made his money in some other calling than journalism. He is a rich man seeking power and prestige.

[30] The material presented in this section is taken, with some modifications, from M. Sherif and S. S. Sargent, Ego-involvement and the mass media, *J. Soc. Issues*, 1947, 3, 8–16.

He has the country club complex. The business manager of this absentee owner quickly is afflicted with the country club point of view."³¹ We are including these sociological generalizations to emphasize the fact that the "analysis of content" on a psychological level is mere discrete abstraction unless these causal factors are first brought into the picture. The content of radio broadcasts or newspaper columns is not chosen (out of the welter of countless other possible items) solely on the basis of its news value or its intrinsic significance. It is chosen *selectively* as determined by the personal involvements of publishers and editors and their friends. Therefore, an adequate psychology of mass media should start first with the personal involvements of the publishers themselves. Only on that basis do the direction and content of mass media, and their effects on people who are exposed to them become really intelligible. Recently Merton, among others, called attention to the necessity of this procedure (of taking the context into account) in his social psychology of mass persuasion. Until recently, only the selectivity of the readers or listeners (their prejudices, attitudes, ego-involvements) were emphasized in the studies dealing with the effects of mass media. An adequate social psychology should relate functionally the selectivity of the reader with the selectivity of the initiator of the stimuli pouring out of the mass media in increasing volume. The two act and react on each other. Unless the one-sided emphasis on the reader or listener is balanced by similar emphasis on the initiator of the stimuli, the social psychology of mass media is doomed to remain on a purely "academic" level.

The reach of the modern media of communication is so broad, especially since the advent of the movies, radio, and television, that hardly any corner of the world is free of them. However, we cannot here give an account of the staggering proportions that the mass media have reached in recent times.³²

The two features of the modern mass media of communication that are of particular significance for social psychology are: (1) They have replaced to a considerable extent *face-to-face* con-

³¹ Commission on Freedom of the Press, *A Free and Responsible Press*, Chicago: University of Chicago Press, 1947, pp. 59–60.

³² A concise summary is given in the report of the Commission on Freedom of the Press, *op. cit.*, chap. 3, pp. 30–51.

tacts in shaping attitudes, identifications (ego-involvements), and the subsequent "public opinion." Only a small fraction of the people exposed to the mass media ever come into face-to-face contact with their originators. (2) They reach millions of people, at times simultaneously.

These two features are already forcing us to revise our provincial views of social psychology based on social stimulation mediated solely through the actual presence of other individuals. To be sure, the presentations of the mass media are prepared by other individuals. Yet the radio, the movie, the newspaper, the book are or become institutions and have particular prestige halos as such. The printed word, the broadcast announcement, the image on the screen, appearing with the stamp of these crystallized institutions of prestige, have different effects than when they are transmitted in personal contact. Many a man must have discovered new qualities in the neighborhood girl when he saw her on the screen. A pronouncement of the propagandist acquires new proportions when it is disseminated through a high-powered medium of mass communication.

It is certainly true that the richness of the nuances of face-to-face contacts is lost in various degrees in presentations through the mass media of communication. On the other hand, a compellingness, a halo is usually bestowed in the impersonal presentation of radio, newspapers, magazines, etc. Many an author, movie star, or broadcaster has lost his magic grip when he mingled—with the same charms, the same wisdom—among his admirers.

The ability to reach millions of people through the mass media (especially through the radio and movies) is producing profound effects of not only national but also international proportions. This, together with the effects of other products of technology, is breaking down long-established patterns of culture. For example, millions of adolescents all over the world are coming into conflict with their own environments because of the dream world and the identifications engendered by the films (mostly of the Hollywood type).

The radio made it almost impossible during World War II for a nation to keep secret the fall or capture of a place for any considerable length of time. This certainly had a great effect on the propaganda tactics of different nations. The radio knows no boundaries. It is reported that their radio sets became symbols of freedom to many Frenchmen during the Fascist occupation. The radio set became a focal point, a preciously guarded personal friend, in the depressing atmosphere of oppression and confusion. And those who are concerned over the loss of individual nuances in mass media will do well to remember that the Gestapo in Hitler Germany threatened death to those who listened to foreign stations.

Now we come to one feature of ego psychology which is most relevant to the effects of mass media. Once the ego is formed, there is a tendency not to feel "left out" as a person from any situation of which we are a part. Let us start with the simplest illustration. In a group situation consisting of friends, we tend invariably to make a point of showing that we understood the joke, that we caught the drift of the subtle conversation (especially if there are persons present whose opinion is important to us). We laugh or smile with other people whether we understood the joke or followed the drift of the conversation or not. *It is a frustrating experience to feel "left out" in a situation in which we are participating or a situation in which we are led to participate psychologically.* For a group of movie fans, it is almost a personal disgrace not to be able to participate in a discussion of the latest movie and to advance remarks "of our own" about it. The lady in Middletown tries to keep up with the latest book recommended by a book club; she feels that she must be able to remark on the fine points of, say, *The Egg and I* at the next meeting of her club. Likewise, certain people feel that they are back numbers if they are not *au courant* with the latest Paris fashions.

With their staggering power of reaching millions of people at the same time or within a short period of time, the modern mass media are creating "atmospheres" into which the people who are constantly exposed to them are almost compelled to "fit." This "fitting in" is, psychologically speaking, becoming ego-involved. A "band wagon" effect is created which tends to attract people in ever-increasing numbers. Once ego-involved in the "atmosphere," or "on the band wagon," effective attitudes are molded or old attitudes played upon to lead people to act (e.g., vote, make a contribution) in the desired direction. Once enmeshed in the psychological situation created by mass media presentations (or by face-to-face relationships), people are bound to become personally involved in actual or announced situations of danger, crisis, action, and the like. "Get *your* copy and become one of the great company of ——— readers to-day," "A ——— car in every garage" are examples of the point.

Recently Merton made a detailed analysis of striking cases of ego-involvement (identification) and subsequent action brought about through the medium of radio.[33] Many people remember the Kate Smith "Marathon" bond drives over the radio. "September 21, 1943, was War Bond Day for the Columbia Broadcasting System. During the span of eighteen hours—from eight o'clock that morning until two the next morning—a radio star named Kate Smith spoke for a minute or two at repeated intervals. Stardom implies a mammoth audience: it was estimated that in 1943 some 23,000,000 Americans listened to Smith's daytime programs in a week and some 21,000,000 to her weekly evening program" (p. 2). The result was that she got "thirty-nine million dollars of bond pledges in the course of one day" (p. 3). Among the appeals she used throughout the Marathon drive, those that got her listeners personally involved were (it is safe to say) the most effective. The content analysis presented by Merton shows that "sacrifice themes" (arousing people to do their share) and "participation themes" (appealing for direct personal involvement) constituted about 70% of the appeals presented. A concrete illustration of the "sacrifice theme" demanding direct personal involvement and action is as follows: "Could you say to Mrs. Viola Buckley—*Mrs. Viola Buckley whose son Donald was killed in action*—that you are doing everything you can to shorten the war . . . that you are backing up her son to the limit of your abilities?"

Such group atmosphere-creating appeals, of course *against the stirring background of the war situation*, produced effective ego-involvement and action on the part of a great many people, as the huge sum pledged that day indicates. These ego-involve-

[33] R. K. Merton, *Mass Persuasion, The Social Psychology of a War Bond Drive*, New York: Harper, 1946.

ments on the part of the listeners are typified by the following reactions of two contributors:

"Well, Dad, we *did* something. I was part of the show" (p. 56).

"We felt that others had been impressed and bought a bond. And the fact that so many people felt the same way made me feel right—that I was in the right channel" (p. 56).

We cannot take space here to give examples of such ego-involving effects of each of the mass media. But we will note one attempt at creating a "band wagon" effect through the press. This particular illustration is of special interest because it was presented as one of the regular research reports of a "public opinion poll"—which itself is an institution with considerable prestige for a good many Americans, including some psychologists. The report is chosen at random from the recent publications in the daily papers. The title of the feature, "What People Are Thinking," is followed by the name of an established poll-taker. Under this compelling heading we find the following headline: "Public Support for Marshall Plan Seen." [34] Perhaps this is as far as a good many readers got. But it is worth our time to see what the investigator of "public opinion" considers sufficient evidence for this sweeping and compelling statement. We find, first of all, that the most recent concrete data presented were collected in "1945, just after V-E day." The Marshall Plan was, of course, promulgated in the middle of 1947. A nation-wide survey of this sort should not require much more than a couple of weeks; but apparently an up-to-date survey on this subject did not seem important, even though it does occupy a good deal of space in this "research" report.

Let us look then at the somewhat dated results which are presented among the speculations of the investigator. In 1943, the poll found that 72.8 per cent of the "public" thought "we should plan to help other nations on their feet by sending them money and materials." In 1945, just after V-E Day, the following question was asked: "Would you want your Congressman to vote for or against continuing the present rate of taxes after the war for the purpose of helping countries that have been

[34] Elmo Roper, "What People Are Thinking," *New York Herald Tribune*, July 17, 1947, p. 17.

freed from Germany get back on their feet?" The result was that 43.3 per cent of the cross section answered "yes," and 41.7 per cent answered "no." In view of the known errors inherent in cross-sectional surveys, a difference of 1.6 per cent would not seem to warrant the conclusion made.

This is all of the concrete evidence presented to show "Public Support for Marshall Plan," except a reference to "a survey made last March." The survey referred to was discussed in either of two earlier columns on the subject. One, headed "Survey Finds Public Backs Mid-East Policy," was based on results obtained by Gallup's American Institute of Public Opinion. The results here showed 56 per cent favoring the bill asking aid for Greece and 49 per cent favoring aid to Turkey. One response was clearly contrary to the "Mid-East Policy": Fifty-six per cent of the "public" thought the problem "should have been turned over to the United Nations." [35] A few weeks later, Roper headed his column "Truman Doctrine Stirs Doubts." Although no concrete over-all figures are given in this column, it does indicate that a majority of Americans are finding something about Truman's proposals that they do not like. [36]

There have been those who have argued long and loudly that the "band wagon" effect in the case of "public opinion" polls is non-existent. Perhaps this is why they are not somewhat more cautious in summing up their statistical results, or perhaps they may have other motives. Judging from the evidence, experimental and otherwise, a good many social scientists could demonstrate the "band wagon" effect by utilizing the cross-sectional survey technique.

[35] Elmo Roper, "What People Are Thinking," *New York Herald Tribune*, April 24, 1947, p. 25.

[36] Elmo Roper, "What People Are Thinking," *New York Herald Tribune*, April 24, 1947, p. 25.

13.

Adolescent Attitudes and Identifications

A CONSIDERATION OF ADOLESCENT ATTITUDES AND IDENTIFICA
tions will help pull together certain concepts stressed throughout this work. Particularly in the highly differentiated bourgeois
societies of our times, with their rapid tempo of transition and
contradictory (not infrequently conflicting) values and treatment from grownups, the youngster faces special problems
during the important phase in his physiological maturation
when he is on his way to the status of full-fledged man or
woman. These problems usually induce in him various degrees
of conflict with adults, including his own parents.

Conflicts with adults necessarily lead toward successful or
unsuccessful moves for emancipation from grown-up authority
and the world of unintegrated grown-up values to which the
adolescent is exposed. Of course, the degree of such strivings
is subject to individual variations because of (1) the adolescent's particular social circumstances and (2) his own individual characteristics.

As emphasized in the preceding chapters, once the ego
is formed with some degree of stability, the tendency is to keep
it anchored with stable links. But the adolescent, caught between his newly rising sex desires and his strivings to become a
fullfledged adult on the one hand, and the restrictive and
frequently contradictory grown-up values and treatment on
the other, finds many of his childhood attitudes burdens to be
thrown overboard. His ego-attitudes and, in fact, his very
identity become shaky. This situation is responsible in a major
way for adolescent crises in various degrees—feelings of facing
an adverse world, feelings of aloneness, the rise of doubts concerning the worth of things and, in extreme cases, of life itself,

314

etc. This instability or breakdown of established anchorings in the world around us is painful, at times unbearable.

In his efforts to re-establish himself now as a person in his own right, the adolescent resorts to various devices. These devices may be manifested in individual or group fantasies, in the tendency to withdraw into himself or to indulge in heightened social and other activities, in the appearance of socially approved or not-approved attitudes and interests, in intensified efforts of various sorts *to prove himself* to a world which may be adverse in his eyes, etc.

Among the adolescent's efforts toward establishing himself as a full-fledged man (or woman) in his own right, crushes, identification with some person or group with real or fancied achievement and prestige, and, especially, membership in more or less closed clique formations (with their own norms, loyalties, etc.) are of particular interest to the social psychologist. For they show dramatically that when the fairly well-established ego-attitudes are rendered unstable or critical because of motivational stresses—primarily sex in this case—and external (social) circumstances, especially at the height of organic maturation, intense efforts are made to re-establish one's self anew. These efforts may imply a change in certain established attitudes, now considered "childish" and hence to be left behind; they may imply adoption of new attitudes and identifications. Whether or not these attitudes and identifications last into adulthood depends upon the social and individual circumstances of the adolescent.

Adolescent Problems and the Social Setting

By the time the boy or girl approaches puberty, the major delineation of his identity is usually established with some degree of stability. He has reached the level at which he has learned the typical attitudes of his family, his social class, his school, etc. However, he has usually not yet achieved the status of a full-fledged man or woman with all the expectations, practices, rights, and responsibilities of the adult member of the group in question. The achievement of adult status comes ordinarily after the advent of puberty, which completes in a major way the process of bodily maturation. This spectacular phase of maturation, the "adolescent spurt," with its primary and secondary changes, has remarkable reverberations on the psychology of the youngster. We shall briefly present some psychological consequences of this bodily change a little later in this chapter.

The psychological effects of attaining adolescence were so dramatic in the culture studied by G. Stanley Hall, who at the turn of the century set the style of adolescent studies, that adolescence almost came to be known as a universal period of "storm and stress," marked with rather prolonged crises, religious conversions, etc.[1]

With the accumulation of comparable studies of different cultures and of different historical periods of the same society, it is becoming evident that the smoothness or turbulence of the transition to adulthood, and the length of the period in which "adolescent" reactions are manifested, vary as determined by the culture and the times. Here we can present only a few typical examples.

On the basis of his investigation of 250 people whom he studied intensively, the psychiatrist Sullivan explains why the American people have become so preoccupied with the problems of sex.

The data of these patients, in so far as they have been of American and Western European stock, certainly emphasize the significance of experience—remote and recent—connected with genital (sexual) behavior and the emotion of lust. I have to add a word of caution here, for there are those among us psychiatrists who make of sex a nuclear explanatory concept of personality, or at least of personality disorder. This is an error from insufficiency of data. The highly civilized Chinese of the pre-Christian era were not bowled over by sex. A number of the primitive peoples who have been studied by anthropologists are found to take sex rather in their stride. Even the American Negro crashes through adolescence with relative impunity—if he is of the lower classes.

The lurid twilight which invests sex in our culture is primarily a function of two factors. We still try to discourage premarital sexual performance; hold that abstinence is the moral course before marriage.

[1] G. S. Hall, *Adolescence, Its Psychology and Its Relations to Physiology, Anthropology, Sociology, Sex, Crime, Religion and Education*, New York: Appleton, 1904.

And we discourage early marriage; in fact progressively widen the gap between the adolescent awakening of lust and the proper circumstances for marriage. These two factors work through many cultural conventions to make us the most sex-ridden people of whom I have any knowledge.[2]

In contrast to the prolonged, and in some cases never-ending, adolescence period found in more complex societies whose values are, as a rule, "casually patterned" and conflicting, the transition to adulthood in many simpler cultures is achieved almost overnight through more or less laborious initiation ceremonies.[3] After such ceremonies, the adolescent acquires rapidly the economic, sexual, civil, etc., attitudes of the adult member of his society. In modern societies too, adolescent boys or girls who have to share the economic burdens of their family present a somewhat similar picture in terms of the duration of adolescence. Faced with the grim responsibilities of day-to-day work, these youngsters have little energy for the usual adolescent whims.

These ceremonies indicate the "passing of an individual from the position of an economic liability to that of an economic and social asset." [4] As pointed out by Radin, the character of these ceremonies and rites, and the subsequent adult attitudes defining the adolescent's new rights and responsibilities, are largely determined by the economic role of the youngsters prescribed by the particular social setting. In the primitive cultures in which the economic responsibility lies chiefly with men, the initiation ceremonies are centered on the adolescent boys. But in a society in which woman's economic role becomes important, such as the Ashanti of West Africa, puberty rites are centered on the adolescent girls.

In Mead's series of adolescent studies, we find some striking

[2] H. S. Sullivan, *Conceptions of Modern Psychiatry*, Washington, D. C.: William Alanson White Psychiatric Foundation, 1947, pp. 28–29.

[3] In the surveys of Van Gennep, Mead, Radin, and Webster, for example, we find concrete cases of rather sharp transition to adulthood achieved within a relatively short time. See A. Van Gennep, *Les Rites de passage*, Paris: 1909; M. Mead, *From the South Seas, Studies of Adolescence and Sex in Primitive Societies*, New York: Morrow, 1939; P. Radin, *Primitive Religion, Its Nature and Origin*, New York: Viking, 1937; H. Webster, *Taboo, A Sociological Study*, Stanford: Stanford University Press, 1942.

[4] Radin, *op. cit.*, p. 79.

variations in adolescent problems because of variations in social organization and prevailing norms.[5] Among the Samoans, where socially demanded conformity is predominantly in the direction of a collective type of behavior, the lot of the adolescent girl is rather an easy one. Certain social norms in Samoa enable youngsters to have premarital sexual gratification. Similarly, among the rather unaggressive Arapesh of New Guinea, adolescence is not a period of serious problems. The Arapesh consider "that all human beings, male and female, are naturally unaggressive, self-denying, lightly sexed, comfortably domestic, concerned with growing food to feed growing children" (p. xix). Comparatively speaking, the rites and experiences of adolescence are not turbulent.

On the other hand: "The Tchambuli attempt to standardize the personality of the sexes in contrasting ways—they expect men to be responsive, interested in the arts, women to be bold, initiating, economically more responsible" (p. xx). The problems are aggravated by the "patriarchal forms combined with personalities more appropriate to matriarchy. . . . Such mixed and badly co-ordinated elements cause a good deal of confusion and functional maladjustment, especially in the young men" (p. xxi).

The plight of the adolescents of the Manus of the Admiralty Islands is fraught with harsh problems in sharp contrast to their blissful childhood days free from any real responsibilities. The conflicting efforts of the Manus youngsters are summarized by Mead. The Manus are "driven by a harsh competitive system, hard working and with little tolerance for pleasure or art; each man worked for himself and for his own household; the future economic security of one's children was a principal goal. But the children had no part in this adult world of money values and hard work; they were left free to play all day in a pleasant co-operative world where there was no property and no possessiveness. . . . And yet, when they passed adolescence, the generous gay co-operative Manus children turned into grasping competitive Manus adults" (p. xii).

The picture of the adolescent period among the Mundugumors is no less trying. "They assume that all children, male and

<hr />

[5] Mead, *op. cit.*

female, are naturally aggressive and hostile" (p. xx). Consequently, "Pre-adolescent Mundugumor children have an appearance of harsh maturity and, aside from sex-experience, are
virtually assimilated to the individualistic patterns of their
society by the time they are twelve or thirteen. Initiation comes
to girls as somewhat of a privilege granted to them in proportion as they are aggressive and demanding, to boys as a penalty
they cannot escape . . ." (p. 212).

These examples of adolescent conflicts will suffice to show
that they are determined by cultural variations. But one does
not have to go to distant cultures to find variations in adolescent
problems, or in any other area of social behavior for that matter.
We invariably find variations in the same culture if we trace
facts in the same area of study with an historical perspective.
The pioneer in the field of adolescence studies, G. Stanley Hall,
reported over four decades ago that religious preoccupation
and conversions were among the universal solutions of adolescent crises. A glance at the current literature on the subject is
sufficient to make one realize that the realm of supernatural
values is hardly one of the main areas to which adolescents in
the same society turn for relief today.[6]

The changing character of human relationships today and
the mere juxtaposition of new values of modern life beside the
old complicate the problems of adolescents. This picture of
confusion is brilliantly described by the Lynds:

> Today, in the presence of such rigorous tenacity to the " old, tried
> ways " by part of the population, the range of sanctioned choices con-
> fronting Middletown youth is wider, the definition of the one " right
> way " less clear. That this is the normal situation in the process we
> call " social change " does not lessen the confusion it entails. . . . If the
> child up to high-school age associates, by reason of the assignment of
> each child to a grade school on the basis of residential propinquity,
> with other children from somewhat similar subcultural backgrounds,
> this homogeneity of sorts is lost when the children pour from all
> quarters into Central High School. Here the whole range of cultural
> tolerances and intolerances grind against each other; the child of
> parents who think it "cute" and "attractive" for a daughter to enamel
> her nails, use rouge, have a crisp " permanent," and " learn to handle

[6] See, for example, H. E. Jones, *Development in Adolescence*, New York: Appleton-
Century, 1943, p. 108.

boys" sits next to the daughter of a family in which the parents are engaged in a quiet but determined campaign to circumvent the influence of the movies and to keep their daughter "simple," "unaffected," and "healthy-minded." This widening of contacts with unevenly sanctioned choices, supported not by out-law individuals but by groups, means under these circumstances for both parents and children uncertainty and tension.[7]

The situation of conflict that the American adolescent faces today is concisely summarized by Kingsley Davis:[8] "In our society, even apart from the family, the adolescent finds an absence of definitely recognized, consistent patterns of authority. Because of the compartmentalization of the culture he is defined at times as an adult, at other times as a child" (p. 13). Davis shows how the individual adolescent may find sets of values which are in harmony at different stages of his development. He concludes: "The Soviet system suggests that to make the school an integral part of the political and economic structure, and to give youth a productive role, central planning of the whole economy is necessary" (p. 15). In a society in which different groups are integrated to function positively toward the same goals, the values that people face at different periods of their genetic development may constitute harmonious gradations rather than sharp and conflicting breaks.

Of course, we have to consider adolescents in their specific social classes and other significant settings if we are really to understand the particular problems of the particular adolescent. For example, the members of a group which is discriminated against in the general social setting face special problems with significant psychological consequences. Thus, in a revealing study of social status and physical appearance among Negro adolescents, Hill states:

These Negro youth live at an extremely high level of emotional tension by reason of the inconsistency between the democratic ideology and the reality of their inferior and immobile status in the caste-like social pattern. The basic need for security within this group remains unsatisfied so long as the racial status quo is maintained in

[7] R. S. Lynd and H. M. Lynd, *Middletown in Transition*, New York: Harcourt, Brace, 1937, p. 175.

[8] K. Davis, Adolescence and the social structure, *Ann. Amer. Acad. Polit. and Soc. Science*, 1944, 236, 8–16.

the democratic social order. A significant ramification of this unsatisfied need for security involves the circumscribed space in which Negro adolescents are permitted to move. To mention a few limitations: they are segregated on common carriers and in numerous establishments which cater to the "public"; sex contacts with whites are rigidly proscribed; the barrier between the races is at its height in regard to such intimate matters as dining and sleeping, extending to residential segregation; and finally the pattern of conduct of these adolescents toward whites is set by a definite racial etiquette.

As a result of the tension engendered by the lack of free space for movement, Negro youth become inhibited and frustrated. This frustration many times leads to overt aggression toward whites, but more safely, Negro youth develop overt aggression, defense mechanisms, states of apathy and inferior feelings within their own group. Moreover, and not infrequently so, adolescent Negroes attempt to "escape" the frustrating situations, physically, psychologically, and socially.

Still another fact of the tension felt by Negro adolescents may be found in the denial to the Negro social approval as a group. Even where a Negro is "lionized," he is, as it were, lifted out of his race and given a sort of quasi honorary white status because he, a Negro, has accomplished something assumed to be beyond the capability of the Negro. From that time forward he is never "just another Negro" as the implication of that expression is generally understood. Rather, he occupies a marginal position which deprives him of full acceptance in either racial group.[9]

With these social variations in adolescents' reactions clearly in mind, we can turn to the implications of adolescent attitudes and identifications for social psychology.

The "Adolescent Spurt" and Its Psychological Consequences

The spectacular period of adolescence, with its glandular and other physiological changes, their determination of bodily development (in height, weight, etc.) epitomized by the expression "adolescent spurt," their inevitable psychological correlates, necessarily produces far-reaching effects in the psychology of the boy or girl. These physiological changes have at their base changes in the endocrine processes. Different endocrine glands (the pituitary, thyroid, adrenal cortex, gonads, etc.) all contribute their share in the maturation process of this period. Under the regulation of these glands, the rate of growth in

[9] M. C. Hill, Social status and physical appearance among Negro adolescents, *Social Forces*, 1944, 22, 446–447.

height and weight, ossification, and development in other respects is accelerated as a forerunner of pubescence. As a consequence, the boy or girl approaches the adult male or female proportions. These changes are accompanied by the appearance of the secondary sex characteristics—pubic hair, change of voice and growth of hair in the boys, growth of breasts in girls, etc. The sex organs mature into full functioning with the advent of a system of changes resulting in mature spermatozoa in boys and menstruation in girls. All these changes are accompanied by changes in the vital functions of the organism (e.g., basal metabolic rate).[10] One of the important differences in the development of boys and girls at this time is the fact that girls mature, on the average, more than a year earlier than boys. As a result, girls mature earlier socially and can teach boys of their own age a few things.

Aside from any social consequences, these physiological changes themselves certainly produce significant motivational and emotional effects which are reflected in the whole psychological functioning of the youngster, in the changing selectivity of his perceptions and discriminations—in short, in his whole outlook.

The motivational and emotional tones centered around developing sexual maturity, the overflowing vitality of the adolescent, do not function in a vacuum. Hence psychological correlates are not restricted to the inevitable accompaniments of physiological changes in feeling and experience. For these changes impose demands in relation to other persons in general and to the members of the opposite sex in particular. Aware of his new powers and desires, especially as provoked by his surroundings, the adolescent recasts his whole established constellation of "childish" relationships. He gets ideas of the activities (sexual and otherwise) of the full-fledged man and woman in his setting. He has to fulfill them.

[10] The details of organic changes during the adolescent period can be obtained, for example, in the following sources: B. T. Baldwin, *The Physical Growth of Children from Birth to Maturity*, University of Iowa Stud. in Child Welfare, vol. 1, no. 1; N. Bayley, The adolescent growth study: III. Skeletal X-rays as indicators of maturity, *J. Consult. Psychol.*, 1940, 4, 69–73; N. Bayley and R. Tuddenham, "Adolescent changes in body build," *43rd Yearbook, Nat. Soc. Study of Educ.*, 1944, 33–55; R. G. Hoskins, *The Tides of Life*, New York: Norton, 1933; H. E. Jones, *op. cit.*; C. B. Zachry, *Emotion and Conduct in Adolescence*, New York: Appleton-Century, 1940.

On the other hand, the parents, other grownups, the social organization and its norms have their ready-made prescriptions as to how the transition to adulthood should be achieved; hence there are complications in the adolescent period which vary from culture to culture.

In many relatively simple societies, the young man or woman usually "settles down" after the onset of puberty, taking a definite adult role (as husband or wife, with prescribed economic and other status). Of course, he may still have his own individual problems. In cultures such as that in the United States, where adolescents receive contradictory treatment (at times still as children and at times as grownups), where it usually takes many years to settle down as a husband or wife and to become an economic and social unit, a prolonged adolescence is the general rule. The highly differentiated nature of the social organization, its "dilemmas of status," and its conflicting values do not make the transition to settled adulthood easy, to say the least. The social problems thus created, their effects on the ego-attitudes of the young boy or girl, are topics of primary concern to the social psychologist. Here we can present only a brief outline of these topics.

"*Changing Body and Changing Self.*" This terse expression of Zachry's epitomizes a part of adolescent psychology. The adolescent, now more keenly aware of his body and its parts, centers almost the whole ego on them; the body becomes "symbolic of the self." [11] Especially in a society where birthdays are very much in the foreground, any divergence from the prevailing standards for the body, and even for parts of it, becomes a great concern to the adolescent. Deviations in bodily development in relation to his age-mates and to socially established standards of development may cause him considerable maladjustment. The investigators of adolescence all present evidence to this effect. For example, Peter Blos reports the case of a girl to whom a mole on her cheek became a source of continued worry and "the focus of her self-consciousness." [12]

In his intensive longitudinal study of John Sanders, Jones

[11] Zachry, *op. cit.*, pp. 30 ff.

[12] P. Blos, *The Adolescent Personality, A Study of Individual Behavior*, New York: Appleton-Century, 1941, p. 93.

presents a detailed account of the far-reaching effects of a discrepancy in the timing of the "adolescent spurt" and the divergence in bodily proportions from those of the usual run of his age-mates.[13] John was an average boy in terms of various social characteristics until just prior to the pubescence period

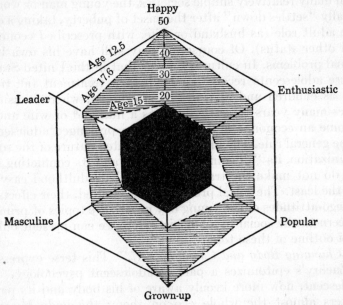

FIG. 27. Profiles of social characteristics for John Sanders.

The diagram represents John's relative standing in various social characteristics at different ages as expressed by his age-mates. It shows the effects of his retarded development during adolescence. The group mean for each characteristic is 50; 20 represents the lower end of the distribution. The standard deviation of the group is 10. (Reprinted from *Development in Adolescence* by Harold E. Jones. Copyright, 1943, by D. Appleton-Century Company, Inc.)

of most of his age-mates. His pubescence was retarded a whole year. As a consequence, "during his junior-high-school years John became markedly shorter, lighter and punier *in relation to classmates*" (p. 155, italics mine). When he was 15, in all sorts of ways John became a back number—in popularity, initiative, good-naturedness, etc. He exhibited unmistakable signs of "anxiety, show-off behavior, and affectation" (p. 155). But

---

[13] Jones, *op. cit.*

a little over two years after puberty, he regained his average position in the group. (See Fig. 27.)

In Jones' penetrating analysis of the case, we find the explanation which is applicable to all such cases. Out-of-phase development, like any out-of-phase steps in relation to the scale in one's group, is one of the main causes of one's status, hence, ego problems. In Jones' words: "... delayed [or premature] maturing may lead not only to loss of status with others, but also to the anxiety expressed in the question, 'Am I normal?' When the biological innovations of adolescence are at last clearly avowed, a turning point may be reached not merely in physiological development, but also in social recognition and in feelings of personal security. The interpretation followed above stresses the social significance of adolescent changes, and implies that the psychological effect of these changes rests upon the degree to which an individual is sensitive to the norms and values of his social environment" (p. 156).

The adolescent's concern to prove himself as a person approaching adult level is not limited to the desire to attain the body proportions expected in his group. He has to prove that he *feels*, *acts*, and participates in activities like the usual adult male (or female) of his group. From the prevailing norms and practices of masculinity or feminity, he derives his impression of the typical masculine or feminine roles, values, and preoccupations of his society. As pointed out by the Lynds [14] and others, his very conception of masculine or feminine "human nature" is formed on the basis of norms and practices that flourish in his setting. Some of the concrete features of this derivation are summarized by the California investigators who worked with Harold Jones:

Psychologically also the girl feels a necessity of proving to herself and to the world that she is essentially feminine; the boy needs to demonstrate that he has those masculine qualities which require others to recognize him as a man. This characteristic accounts for the girls spending a large part of their leisure time in shopping and in personal adornment. This is the secret of the manicured nails, painted red to match vivid lips. This is why they must wave and curl their hair, and, having perfected the process, must pin into it ribbon bows,

[14] See Lynd and Lynd, *op. cit.*, pp. 176 ff.

bits of lace, or flowers. This is the reason for the boy's urge to learn to drive a car and for his willingness to move heaven and earth to borrow or own one. Along with this development, also, we are told by our group that a girl to be popular must be modishly pretty, keep herself clean and neat, be a good mixer. A boy, on the other hand, must be aggressive and must excel at sports. He must have the ability to dance and to talk easily with girls, and in addition he must show that he can compete readily with other boys; that he can achieve and master. [15]

This dichotomous picture of male and female natures which was historically based on the economic roles of the sexes is not universal today. But only in a few social groups are the norms regulating masculine and feminine roles based on the facts of biology and not on the survival heritage that has come down from distant centuries.

Adolescent Instability and Crises. The frustrated desires (especially sexual during this period), the resistance to the adolescent's strivings to establish himself as an adult with the values, identifications, and activities that go with adult status, and the "marginality" experienced between the positions of child and grownup lead to feelings of inadequacy, aloneness, and instability. The result is a fluid state of ego-attitudes. In adverse social settings, there may be serious instability reaching the proportions of crises. These unstable ego-attitudes are manifested in various degrees of strivings by the adolescent for emancipation from the established authority of grownups and the prevailing practices imposed on him. This is characterized by Hollingworth as "psychological weaning." [16] (Of course the intensity of the strivings for emancipation or "psychological weaning" varies from society to society and is subject to variations determined by individual differences and the case history of the particular adolescent.) One of the best ways of gauging such adolescent instability and crises is by the manifestations of the adult-youth conflict.

The Conflict of Generations. The facts of parent-youth conflict, so colorfully portrayed in works on adolescence, have meaning only in relation to the conflict between the adoles-

---

[15] H. R. Stolz, M. C. Jones, and J. Chaffey, The junior high school age, *Univ. High School J.*, 1937, 15, 6 ff.

[16] L. Hollingworth, *The Psychology of the Adolescent*, New York: Appleton, 1928.

cent's overflowing desires and his strivings to establish himself
as a person in his own right on one hand, and adult authority
and values on the other. It is, therefore, safe to generalize that
the degree of parent-youth conflict in any society at a given historical period is proportional to the discrepancy between the
desires and values of the adolescents and of the established generation. Hence the conflict of generations can become meaningful only if we start with the sociology of parent-youth conflict.
The sociologist Kingsley Davis proposed the following as factors aggravating the conflict: "(1) the rate of social change;
(2) the extent of complexity in the social structure; (3) the
degree of integration in the culture; and (4) the velocity of
movement (e.g. vertical mobility) within the structure and
its relation to the cultural values." [17]

Today almost all the societies in the world are to some degree
in a state of transition. The contradictions and conflicts of old
and new values in contemporary American life have been forcibly brought to light by sociologists. The manifestations of the
conflict of generations are epitomized in one of the investigations
at the University of California "based upon an intensive study
of one hundred boys and one hundred girls which has been
carried on during the three-year period that they were enrolled
in junior high school." In the words of the authors:

Adult approval or disapproval meant almost nothing to these
adolescents except as it might affect the attainment of their goal. In
fact there was a noticeable resistance, not so much to authority, as
our rules seldom got in their way, but simply to adults as such. Those
girls, and boys who were in the throes of establishing themselves
socially were the most antagonistic toward adults. They manifested
this attitude chiefly by shunning adults and acting as if their presence
were a hindrance. Six months later these same pupils were likely to be
the ones who hung around and talked to adults as if, being quite
grown up now, they needed to talk and associate with other grown
persons. [18]

In a country undergoing a rapid transition, in which feudal
Oriental values of authority and the unreal world of Hollywood

---

[17] K. Davis, The sociology of parent-youth conflict, *Amer. Sociol. Rev.*, 1940, 5,
p. 535.

[18] Stolz, Jones, and Chaffey, *op. cit.*, p. 3.

exist side by side, the conflict of generations acquires still greater proportions. This was the case in Turkey, as shown in our studies of adolescence during 1937–1945. Among other material collected were the questionnaire results for over 3,000 boys and girls.[19] A special effort was made in designing these questionnaires to get reactions concerning the conflict of generations. The two following adolescent reactions chosen from this study reveal the conflict in a typical way. "The grown-ups cannot understand me, because they are people of the last century whereas I belong to this century. Things which do not please them are very pleasing to me." And: "We do not think grown-ups understand us. As there is a great difference between the periods in which we have grown up they misunderstand us and frictions come out as a consequence."

These reactions reveal typically the adult-youth conflict in urban areas—which are in a greater flux, with more contradictory values than rural. In rural areas the problem is not so intense because of the greater homogeniety of values, early marriage, and the change of economic status required of youngsters.

According to a journalist's recent report, a similar state of affairs exists in present-day Egypt.[20] As a result of the "social ferment" since the first World War and accelerated by the second, the youth of Cairo and Alexandria are overtly at odds with the adult generation. In rural areas of Egypt, life retains some of its homogeneity. But in the cities, some young men denounce their fathers as "reprobates" and even "robbers." Many a Moslem city girl defies her family by adopting all the Hollywood modes and manners within her means. As one girl, speaking of her family's disapproval of her unconventional behavior, said: "But I tell them I don't want to be like them. I want to be a new woman and nothing else. . . . It is so much fun to be free, and, anyway, I am earning my own living, and my family cannot stop me."

Special momentous events, such as war and depression, complicate things further. For example, Komarovsky reports on

[19] Some of these data are incorporated in a thesis by Nilufer Mizanoglu, on file in the Library, University of Ankara, Turkey.

[20] M. Hindus, "Spirit of Youth Stirs Egypt," *New York Herald Tribune*, August 14, 1947, p. 22.

families during the depression in which parental authority suffered heavily owing to the loss of employment and inadequate fulfillment of family responsibility.[21] We are all familiar with the effects of the recent war caused by youngsters', particularly young women's, participation in and retirement from war-time factory and military jobs.

Direct and Substitutive Reactions of the Adolescent in Satisfying and Establishing Himself Anew

The adolescent is motivated to satisfy the new desires which come to him crowned with a halo of dramatic proportions. And he is motivated to satisfy them in the approved ways of his group. He is now in the throes of establishing himself anew, with greater frenzy than in childhood. He is motivated to find appropriate channels for the tensions of his new, overflowing energy. Necessarily, he develops and adopts new interests, new attitudes, and new identifications. He devises new types of direct or substitutive activities. For example, meeting resistances in his surroundings, he may turn inward to a self-imposed isolation in a world of fantasy and reverie, to diary-writing, to the worship of real or imaginary idols, heroes of his own creation. It is interesting that in social settings which do not afford ample chances for overt activities such as dancing, sports, etc., keeping a diary and indulging in fantasies are more prevalent. In the extreme cases of introversion, substitutive reactions may result in abnormalities. Suicide may be thought of or attempted.

In other cases (especially in societies which encourage overt activities, competition, and perfection in work) school, social activities, or some other field may be seized upon as an outlet. Even though it makes fascinating reading, we shall not take the space to describe discrete items concerning adolescent interests, attitudes, and identifications.

Effects of Reference Idols and Groups in Determining Adolescent Attitudes and Identifications. It seems that the major adolescent attitudes and identifications can be encompassed within a functional scheme of reference idols and reference groups.

[21] M. Komarovsky, *The Unemployed Man and His Family*, New York: Dryden, 1940.

For the adolescent—driven by newly developed sexual desires, tossing around in instability and, at times, in crisis caused by conflicting situations, his ego caught in the most spectacular stage of transition—strives to re-anchor himself. Lack of stable anchorings, we repeat, is painful. This instability and crisis in ego-links, in turn, reacts on his sex desires, which initially may have been responsible for raising such acute ego issues. Any mate will not do; sex also must be satisfied within a framework of adolescent belongingness. As Tryon observed: "Boys, to be successful with girls, must be admired by boys. . . ." [22] This fact complicated the plight of John Sanders, whose case was reported by Harold Jones. Because he was considered a back number in his social setting around the age of 15, no girl with any self-respect would go out with him. If she did, she would lose her chances with the lionized boys.

Psychologically driven to a "self-imposed isolation" by the force of contradictory values at a time when they are super-sensitive, adolescents look toward each other to find a setting of security and recognition that actually counts for them. Usually the only confidants who really can be trusted are their age-mates. Age-mates can truly appreciate and share the significance of things that are important to them. Some of the by-products of these associations are the host of distinctive adolescent styles (blue jeans, etc.), standardized symbolisms, meaningful catch words, standardized conceptions of achievement and status, collectively lionized heroes (Frank Sinatra, Van Johnson, Clark Gable, etc.), exaggerated individual or collective hero worship. Such by-products and standardized status relationships, with their (of course, fluid) hierarchy of significant things and persons, are so widespread that Harold Jones refers to them as "adolescent culture," Peter Blos as "peer-culture."

Of course, adolescents know the values that grownups try desperately to implant in them. They are usually exposed to them and bored by them. A 16-year-old boy from Wilmington, Delaware, put his "gripes" and "peeves" against his parents

---

[22] C. M. Tryon, Evaluations of adolescent by adolescents, in R. G. Barker, J. S. Kounin, and H. F. Wright (eds.), *Child Behavior and Development*, New York: McGraw-Hill, 1943, p. 565.

in the following words: "Being called in the morning more than twice. Having them tell me what to eat. Being yelled at in the bathroom in the morning. Being asked questions about home-work. Being 'called down' about my school marks. Having to tell them where I've been on dates, where I'm going and who I'm going with. Always being nagged about the length of time I use the phone, the light I read in, and the radio programs I hear."

A high school girl in California, "peeved" by the interference of her parents in her activities with her age-mate group, re-marked: "I am afraid my friends will think I have no control over my parents." [23]

The adolescent's sense of belongingness is, to an important degree, with his group. Hence his allegiance, his conformity, his idiosyncrasies, make real sense in relation to his age-mate group and its values. To this effect Zachry writes: "In the struggle to establish himself as a person in his own right, inde-pendent of adults, the adolescent measures his success against that of those whose status is similar to his." [24]

Blos substantiates this generalization. "Group opinion serves, then, as a selective influence for desirable and undesirable be-havior, and the approval or disapproval of peers becomes pro-gressively the most influential force in motivating adolescent conduct. . . . This belongingness to the group, which becomes progressively important for the adolescent, replaces family ties to some extent and thus prepares him for new conformities and identifications implicit in the group life of adults." [25]

Similarly, Stolz, M. C. Jones, and Chaffey concluded:

As we look back over this three-year period during which we have measured, questioned, watched these youngsters in the early stages of adolescent development, certain changes in interests, attitudes, and activities seem to have accompanied the physical changes and to be more or less typical of the group. One of the outstanding facts that we have noticed about these children as they grow into adolescence is their preoccupation with social activities. There is an overwhelming desire among these typical junior high school children to be with other children, to understand themselves in their relations to others in their

---

[23] Stolz, Jones, and Chaffee, *op. cit.*, p. 4.
[24] Zachry, *op. cit.*, p. 369.
[25] Blos, *op. cit.*, pp. 249–250.

age group. . . . There are several characteristics of this phase of social awareness which distinguish it from the play of younger children and from the social contacts of adults. One of the most potent drives behind this urge for social activity is derived from the youngsters' desire for group approval. To achieve this approval they must adapt themselves to the ways of the group, substituting its standards for those of the home and the school.[26]

Clique Formations. Such terms as "peer-culture" give only a general picture of adolescent age-mate effects. We must now be more specific. As psychologists, we deal in terms of demonstrable group belongingness and its effects in forming tastes, attitudes, identifications, etc. Such adolescent reference groups are the cliques and gangs which are almost universally found in any social milieu which gives rise to motivational conflicts and renders the developing ego unstable.

Under the strain of adolescence one's stability is shaken with crisis, insecurity, and frustration in various degrees. Caught in this situation, adolescents gravitate toward each other. They try to find comfort in their own intimate relationships. They share secrets. They develop common tastes in movies, books, dancing, adventure, in relation to persons, groups, etc. With all of these common ties they form a group, a *clique* or *gang* of two, three, or more with the unmistakable properties of an informal group structure (see the discussion of the properties of groups, pp. 100–106).

Once the group is formed, even if it lasts for only a short period, the status experienced by the member is derived from his membership in it. His feelings of security are dependent to a large extent on his clique ties. The binding loyalties and goals for him are related to his clique or his gang. His attitudes and identifications are shaped or altered by the group norms and prestige idols that prevail in the clique. He goes a long way to defend or uphold the group members or persons high in the prestige hierarchy of the group—at times with a considerable degree of sacrifice to himself.

In return, the clique or gang provides him with a feeling of "security" in group belongingness and in collective responsibility at a time when he is abandoning childhood relationships

---

[26] Stolz, Jones, and Chaffey, *op. cit.*, p. 2.

and "reorienting himself in terms of mature goals. In response to the pressures of peer culture, his family patterns of relationship, identification, and feeling life are gradually modified in the direction of group norms." [27]

The strength of the solidarity that prevails in the adolescent cliques or gangs is concisely conveyed by Goodenough: "Not only does the adolescent, as a rule, begin to show a new interest in the opposite sex, but a new element appears in his relationships with persons of his own sex. This is the formation of clubs or gangs. It is, of course, true that long before the age of adolescence children play together in groups and form special friendships that give these groups something of a lasting character. But in most cases the social groups formed by young children lack the solidarity and the feeling of group-consciousness that characterize the adolescent gang or club." [28]

Very much in harmony with the significant finding of the experimental psychologists to the effect that one's goals and aspirations are determined by one's reference group, Zachry observed that the standards of the clique or gang become the adolescent's own standards: "It is significant also that in his compliance with gang standards he is taking a step toward self-determination in conduct, since this group is made up not of those who are much larger and stronger than he but of those who are like him in appearance, capacities, and interests. Thus these standards are *more nearly his own* than were those which he acquired so early that he does not remember how this came about, and some of which he is now relinquishing for the time being at least." [29]

As in any group, whether formally or spontaneously organized, adolescent cliques or gangs exert their own correctives in cases of deviation from their standardized norms. Cameron, who studied groupings among 200 junior high school pupils, vividly described an aspect of group correctives at work: "Let anyone get conceited about his status, or ride too high on a wave of popularity, and without warning a torrent of invectives will be let loose. With merciless directness and intolerance the

---

[27] Blos, *op. cit.*, p. 254.

[28] F. L. Goodenough, *Developmental Psychology*, New York: Appleton-Century, 2nd ed., 1945, p. 491.

[29] Zachry, *op. cit.*, p. 163 f. (italics mine).

offending person's prestige is battered into shreds and he is left to fend for himself in getting back into the group." [30] (p. 22)

In proportion to the *consequences* of deviation from the code of the group, correctives become more and more severe. As pointed out by Thrasher, in delinquent gangs squealing, which is considered the worst evidence of a rotten character, may be punished by ostracism, beating, and "in extreme cases . . . death." [31]

Before closing this brief discussion, we should call attention to the finding that adolescent school-girls around the age of 15 show a greater tendency to form cliques than boys at the same age level. On the basis of the results of a "best friends" item on a reputation test administered to boys and girls in an Oakland public school, Campbell constructed sociograms indicating reciprocal friendships. From these results, Campbell concludes: "Association into cliques of two, three, or more individuals seems to be fairly descriptive of the girls. In general, the cliques are rather closely knit together with few lines of relationship between members of one clique and members of another." [32] (See Fig. 28.) It is rather risky factually to interpret these interesting results in terms of a greater tendency for girls to form group structures. We should say that 15-year-old girls have reached a year or so earlier than boys of the same age the "psychological weaning" from parental authority and, in their efforts at emancipation, gravitated to each other to form somewhat closely knit groups. Under different conditions of the American setting, under the tough conditions of the slums of a large city, it is the frustrated and deprived boys who form cliques, at an even younger age. In short, we shall advance the hypothesis that states of insecurity or deprivation cause individuals (male or female) to gravitate toward each other to form temporary or lasting group structures. For we derive our status links and feelings of security, as well as our goals, from the

[30] W. J. Cameron, A study of social development in adolescence, unpublished, University of California Inst. Child Welfare.

[31] F. M. Thrasher, *The Gang*, Chicago: University of Chicago Press, 1927, p. 291.

[32] H. M. Campbell, Sex differences obtained by the "Guess Who" technique in reputation assessments given and received by adolescent boys and girls, Thesis on file in the Library of the University of California, 1941, p. 138.

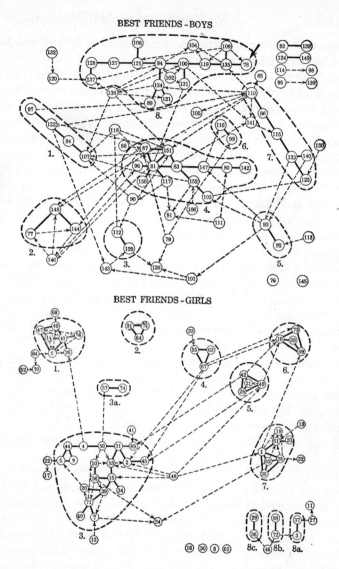

FIG. 28. Sociograms showing age-mate friendships in a class of adolescent boys and girls.

Note the well-knit friendship clusters (cliques) among the girls. Circle 78 in the upper right corner (see arrow) indicates the peripheral social position of John Sanders. (Reprinted from *Development in Adolescence* by Harold E. Jones. Copyright, 1943, by D. Appleton-Century Company, Inc.)

groups that we belong to. The experience of lack of group belongingness disrupts them all.

Adolescent Idols and Heroes. It would be incorrect to claim that all adolescent attitudes and identifications can be encompassed in relation to group formations. Belongingness and its derivatives need not have group references. They may be represented in crushes and love ties. For if the sexual factor goes beyond itself to embrace one's cherished ego components— this is characteristic of any love situation—we have a perfect case of identification with the constellation of attitudes that goes with it. Such identification need not be in relation to someone with whom we are in actual contact. The person may be a movie star or even a character in a play or a novel. Steinbeck describes a poor snack-room waitress, Norma, who, in her moments alone, tries to make herself in her own mind what Clark Gable would like. She speaks to him as if he were actually present. Hollingworth, in her work on adolescence, reports the delightful case of a 14-year-old boy who began to appear everywhere, in the lecture room, dining hall, etc., with his hat on. He would not take it off in spite of the warnings of his teachers and parents, who were aghast at this queer behavior. This idiosyncrasy, which certainly was part and parcel of other behavior manifestations produced by the same factor, was perfectly understandable in terms of the boy's reference idol. "He would not remove his hat, because William Penn (his model for the moment) had refused to take his hat off in assemblies!" [33]

Adolescents in the Established Social Setting

Lest the mistaken impression be given that adolescent reference groups and idols are lasting affairs, we should say a few words on the ultimate definitive effect of the established society. Some individuals may go through life or part of it without really reaching a psychologically settled state. And they may exhibit adolescent attachments, idiosyncrasies, and other manifestations of their unsettledness even in their old age—as evident especially in old maids and bachelors. Their adolescent affairs and adventures impel them to fantasies and actual monologue-like conversations.

[33] Hollingworth, *op. cit.*, p. 179.

But the majority do get settled down. Getting settled down means being established in a family, work, profession, club, or any other organized group with definite hierarchies of statuses and rather rigidly established codes of conduct that require conformity. Once enmeshed in the organized web of such groups, the former adolescent wants to and has to adopt the values of his established setting and to regulate his behavior accordingly. Through such conformities to his new reference groups, he becomes a respectable member of the group and attains a status more or less proportional to his zeal in assimilating and actively upholding the values and goals of the group. (Of course this group is not necessarily one whose values are in harmony with those of the larger social setting. However, most group values are.)

It is safe to generalize that the assimilation of the contradictory, rigid values of the established group is not due to mere knowledge or mechanical practice. The individual was exposed to adult values as an adolescent, and even before. Their effective assimilation is derived from accepted membership in established groups. As a result, these established groups become his *reference groups* in the psychological sense, and the abandonment of his adolescent loyalties and enthusiasms follows as a consequence. The studies on attitude change point in this direction. Just to cite one outstanding illustration, the Bennington study showed us that the change of attitude or, on the other hand, the resistance to change, was a function of (a) *the degree of assimilation in the new group and* (b) *the degree of adherence to previous groups of which the individual was a member.*

It is not the warnings, advice, and punishments of the parents, teachers, probation or reform school authorities which are really effective in eradicating gangs and the gang spirit. The effective factor is the feeling of becoming a member, of belonging (in the psychological sense) to other groups.

Once settled in the respectability of the established society, with aspirations to better his position in the hierarchical arrangements thus faced, the former adolescent may consider the associations, values, and feats which once seemed very urgent, as crazy recklessness. This is vividly portrayed in Steinbeck's artistic cross-section analysis of contemporary social relationships:

At bottom, and originally, Mr. Pritchard was not like this. He had once voted for Eugene Debs, but that had been a long time ago. *It was just that the people in his group watched one another. Any variation from a code of conduct was first noted, then discussed. A man who varied was not a sound man, and if he persisted no one would do business with him.* Protective coloring was truly protective. But there was no double life in Mr. Pritchard. He had given up his freedom and then had forgotten what it was like. He thought of it now as youthful folly. He put his vote for Eugene Debs alongside his visit to a parlor house when he was twenty. Both were things to be expected of growing boys. He even occasionally mentioned at a club luncheon his vote for Debs, to prove that he had been a spirited young man and that such things were, like a kid's acne, a part of the process of adolescence. But although he excused and even enjoyed his prank in voting for Debs, he was definitely worried about the activities of his daughter Mildred.

She was playing around with dangerous companions in her college, professors and certain people considered Red. Before the war she had picketed a scrap-iron ship bound for Japan, and she had gathered money for medical supplies for what Mr. Pritchard called the Reds in the Spanish war. He did not discuss these things with Mildred. She didn't want to talk it out with him. And he had a strong feeling that if everyone was quiet and controlled she would get over it. A husband and a baby would resolve Mildred's political uneasiness. She would then, he said, find her true values.[34]

[34] J. Steinbeck, *The Wayward Bus*, New York: The Viking Press, Inc., 1947, pp. 41–42 (italics mine).

14.

Social Distance (Prejudice)

UNDOUBTEDLY BECAUSE OF THE CONSEQUENTIAL EFFECTS OF prejudice in human relationships—as revealed in discrimination, in the denial of opportunities of living and development, in exploitation, and even in grim cruelties—more work has been done in recent years on prejudice than on any other special topic. In this chapter, we shall touch upon a few major features of prejudice which are most relevant to social psychology. Our concern will be *group prejudice*—viz., prejudice manifested by members of one group toward other groups and, consequently, toward individual members thereof. Psychiatrists are daily handling the psychology and therapy of inter*personal* frictions, maladjustments, and their consequences.

Group prejudice may be characterized as the negative attitude of members of one group toward another group and its members. We have already discussed the psychology of attitudes (Chapters 9 and 10). The designation of the attitude of prejudice as *negative* is amply justified by the results of prejudice studies. The negative feature of prejudice has been demonstrated in terms of the social distance at which the members of a prejudiced group hold another group and its members in relation to themselves. With the use of the Bogardus social distance scale [1] and variations based on it,[2] the degree of prejudice of one social group against another is measured quite satisfactorily. The scale discloses the degree of proximity to which members of one group would admit members of various other groups. In the form used by Murphy and Likert, the subjects

[1] E. S. Bogardus, A social distance scale, *Sociology and Social Research*, 1933, p. 17.
[2] For example, see G. Murphy and R. Likert, *Public Opinion and the Individual*, New York: Harper, 1938; and E. Hartley, *Problems in Prejudice*, New York: Kings Crown Press, 1946.

339

were asked to express their willingness to accept various groups (Canadians, Chinese, English, Spanish, Turks, etc.) on the following scale of proximity in relation to themselves:

1. To close kinship by marriage.
2. To my club as personal chums.
3. To my street as neighbors.
4. To employment in my occupation in my country.
5. To citizenship in my country.
6. As visitors only to my country.
7. Would exclude from my country.

As we shall see briefly in the next section, a rather consistent scale of social distance has been exhibited in America over a period of a good many years. The social distance thus manifested may be expressed as *ego-distance* in terms of the single individual members. At least a majority of the members identify themselves so closely with the standardized values and prejudices of their group that they experience them as their own ego-attitudes. It is off the mark to treat the problem of group prejudice only in terms of dynamics of individual frictions, jealousies, and enmities. Group prejudice is a standardized product of the group and in dealing with prejudice we have to treat it as such. Otherwise, we shall be paying only lip service to the conclusive findings concerning the structural properties of group interaction and its products. The member of a group acquires his prejudices against other groups in exactly the same way that he acquires his identifications, values, loyalties, and responsibilities. In order to be a good member of the group, he has to share these prejudices as well as other values of his group—positive and negative. This being the fact, it is no wonder that no significant correlations have been obtained between freedom from prejudice and the degree of contact with the members of the group against which prejudice is directed,[3] or between information and freedom from prejudice.[4] Therefore, characterizations of group prejudice as an attitude based on lack of information, lack or abundance of contact with the

[3] See, for example, E. Horowitz, The development of attitudes toward the Negro, *Arch. Psychol.*, 1936, no. 194; and E. Horowitz, "Race Attitudes," in O. Klineberg (ed.), *Characteristics of the American Negro*, New York: Harper, 1944, Part IV.

[4] Murphy and Likert, *op. cit.*, pp. 131 f.

group in question, have no basis in reality. Ameliorative measures that are based on increased information and contact
have failed utterly. As we shall see later in this chapter, the
presence or absence of prejudice in an individual is predominantly a result of membership in his group and the degree of his
conformity to its standardized values (positive and negative).
The *average* individual member of a group exhibits the degree
of prejudice toward the member of another group prescribed
by the social distance scale of his group. Otherwise, no white
boy or girl would keep the Negro nurse who cared for him
"in her place" as a Negro after he or she grows up and acquires
the masculine or feminine attitudes of the social setting. It was
with these considerations in mind that we deliberately specified
in our characterization of prejudice that it is the negative attitude of the *members* of the group.

After this brief characterization, we shall glance at the picture of prejudice in one country and then analyze it.

A General Picture of Prejudice

We have now a quantified picture of the social distance at
which the American people hold various national and religious
groups living in America and elsewhere. But, it must be said,
prejudice, or keeping other groups (minority or otherwise) at
certain social distances, is not the monopoly of the American
scene. Even a superficial glance at historical and contemporary
national groups reveals that wherever economic, political, and
cultural interests and institutions clash, a set of negative
"traits" attributed by one group to another emerges and becomes standardized as a result of the conflict. Once such
"traits" become standardized, they tend to continue to be held
by the group even after the actual conflict between the two
groups has shifted or disappeared.

One illustration of this point is the attitude toward Turks,
who are put consistently in the remotest segment of the social
distance scale in the United States. In reality, probably not one
American in a thousand has set eyes on a Turk—there being so
few Turks in America. The picture of the Turk held in the
United States certainly comes down all the way from the long
wars in the Middle Ages (the Crusades), the invasion of parts of

Europe by the Ottoman Empire which lasted until nearly the end of the nineteenth century, to the first World War. This fact, the implications of which have not been duly stressed in many social distance studies, is pointed out by Dollard: "It is probably also true that inherited patterns are records of ancient rivalries and exist as the detritus of former group conflicts. In the case of current American antagonism against the image of the 'Turk,' one has no difficulty in surmising that the historical conflicts between Mohammedanism and Christianity have given rise to this image, and that the threatening conception of the Turk has been still more recently reinforced by the war-time propaganda against Turkey." [5]

It is interesting to note that the prejudice against Turks is sharper in the United States than in the European countries that dealt more directly with them. This came out in our own observations in Europe in 1933 and 1936. It may be safe to posit the thesis that the more isolated a group is (which was the case with America until the recent technological and economic developments), the greater the tendency to perpetuate and even accentuate such features of the culture. Perhaps the archaic nature of the French used in Canada as compared with the French used in France may be accounted for on the basis of the same tendency.

On the other hand, it is not enough to emphasize this cultural lag. Certainly actual conflicts between groups contribute infinitely more effectively to the intensification of prejudice. As illustration of the point, we may cite the struggle of the Negroes in the South to achieve status as people, and the measures taken to keep them "in their place," chiefly by the monopolists in the economy (in both the South and the North).

In view of the recent attempts to account for prejudice in terms of frustrations of single individuals or in terms of knowledge or ignorance, it is necessary to keep in mind certain general facts which can be easily substantiated. The scale or hierarchy of prejudice, in settled and stable times, flows from the politically, economically, and socially strong and eminent down to lower hierarchies of the established order. The time to look for the greatest and most impregnable hierarchies of social dis-

---

[5] J. Dollard, Hostility and fear in social life, *Social Forces*, 1938, 17, 15–25.

tance is in the mightiest periods of the empires. A glance at the
Greek, Roman, Turkish, British, or French empire, for example,
shows convincingly that the periods of highly observed social
distances and their psychological correlates were the "golden
ages" of those empires. The caste system in India, which is
disintegrating now, was not the idea of the ignorant and
frustrated "untouchables." It was the philosophical Brahmins
and the British masters of the local Indian princes and rulers
who were interested in keeping these delineations intact. The
psychological correlates of these delineations in the form of
alleged inherent capacities and "traits" corresponding to the
politico-economic scales have certainly been effective at times
in keeping various groups "in their place," sometimes of their
own volition. Such a standardized product is the "white man's
burden" closely associated with the mighty days of the British
Empire. A standardized norm of this sort justifies the ruler's
feats and exploits in his own eyes. Its acceptance by the native
peoples (which was not lacking until recently) makes their
lot seem inevitable even to themselves. Consequently, as is the
case in America today, groups low in the hierarchical scale try
to approximate the position of the ones at the top and accept
the rest of the hierarchy intact. This has been the fate of peoples
low in the scale in powerful empires. Downtrodden people in
stable times received their honors and positions from the group
at the top or from their real or fancied approaches to the top.
It would make a fascinating psychological study to trace individuals as they move upward in their tireless efforts to be
"accepted"—in colleges, clubs, neighborhoods, and other environments of social distinction.

The most elaborate "race" superiority doctrines are products
of already existing organizations of superiority-inferiority relationships and exploitations. The superiority doctrines have
been the deliberate or unconscious standardizations of the
powerful and prosperous groups at the top and not the ideas
of the frustrated and deprived majority at the bottom. Once
established, such superiority doctrines find deft supporters in
the social setting—scholars and philosophers who give them
an air of respectability by impressive-appearing formulations.
As Winspear points out, Plato's social philosophy is such an

edifice; its origins lay in the social conditions of Greece at the time.[6]

Apologies for superiority are formulated in the philosophical, literary, scientific vernacular of the times.[7] For example, Aristotle explained the superiority of the Greeks over other peoples on the basis of the uniqueness of the geography of Greece. We find similar accounts of their own superiority by Roman and Arab writers. Jean Bodin tried to support his unquestioning assumption of the superiority of the French in the sixteenth century on the basis of the particular effects of astrological forces on France. After the conquest of parts of America, Spanish writers like Sepulveda and Quevido wrote apologies for the bloody treatment meted out to the Indians which were based on the inherent superiority of the Spanish. We have already mentioned the myth of the "white man's burden" during the great expansion of and exploitation by the British Empire. Superiority doctrines reached their worst proportions in the "Aryan" master-race cult of Hitler's Germany. The myth of the biologically non-existent "Aryan" race became the means by which the quest for world domination was justified by men in politics, economics, philosophy, and even biology, all of whom succumbed to the spell of the great plan, of course with social and economic advantages to themselves. The work of biologists (e.g., Huxley's *We Europeans*) indicates once and for all that doctrines of race superiority and race purity have no basis at all in biology or genetics.

The United States, in spite of its highly mixed racial and ethnic composition, has its standardized mythical superiority-inferiority scale. This has found outright expression in such works as Madison Grant's *The Passing of the Great Race* and *Conquest of a Continent*. The second-hand anthropological speculations advanced in such works fade away when viewed in the light of serious studies in the field.[8]

The above illustrations force upon us a general conclusion.

[6] A. D. Winspear, *The Genesis of Plato's Thought*, New York: Dryden Press, 1940.
[7] A brief survey of such superiority doctrines is given in O. Klineberg, *Race Differences*, Harper, 1935. The illustrations here are taken from Klineberg.
[8] See, for example, A. Hrdlicka, *The Old Americans*, Baltimore, Williams and Wilkins, 1925.

In societies in which inter- and intra-group relationships are based on political and economic power and are not integrated and planned, there necessarily arises a scale of social distances which become incorporated in the individual members. The prejudice thus created becomes intricate and effective in proportion to the rising economic and political power of the group in question. In every instance above, the superiority doctrines appeared and became standardized at the peak of the development of the specific social organization. Perhaps this will continue to be the tendency until societies are integrated and based on the findings of science (biological and human).

The Usual Social Distance Scale in the United States

Of course an established scale of social distances from various groups is not unique to the United States. Every national group has its own. However, to date investigations of social distance have been more numerous and comprehensive in the United States than in other countries.

The general picture of social distance for various national and ethnic groups in the United States is remarkably consistent.[9] Near the top of the scale come Americans, Canadians, English. Then follow the French, Norwegians, Germans, Swedish, and other Northern Europeans. Lower come the Southern Europeans—the Italians, Spanish, Portuguese. Jews are still lower on the scale, and near the bottom are Negroes, Turks, Chinese, Hindus. Of course, the specific rank of one group on the scale may vary—some people may rank the Hindu higher than the Turk and some the Turk higher than the Hindu, but both are near the bottom of the scale, thus representing the greatest social distance. Support for this general finding comes from several studies over a period of years. For example, Guilford's analysis (by "paired comparison") of the social distance scales of college students from various parts of the country in 1928 gives this picture. The responses of students in such diverse parts of the country as Florida, New York, Illinois, Kansas, Nebraska, and Washington correlated

---

[9] This section is based in general upon the authoritative review of the literature up to 1944 by Dr. Eugene Hartley, and upon a summary personally communicated by him. See Horowitz, " 'Race' Attitudes," pp. 141–248.

highly, with coefficients ranging from .84 to .99.[10] Similar agreement is shown by students preparing for different professions. Thus, in Allport and Katz' extensive study (1931), it was found that "Whether we took engineering students, Liberal Arts students, Fine Arts students, or graduate students, men or women, fraternity members or neutrals, the relative aversion to these racial and group stereotypes was everywhere the same."[11]

Meltzer found correlations ranging from .842 to .945 for the social distance scales of children in low, middle, and high economic classes in St. Louis. The preferences of these school children were very similar to those of college students. The scale was found to be similar for Jewish, Catholic, and Protestant children; Negroes and Whites; rural and urban children.[12]

Zeligs and Hendrickson found that the group preference of Jewish and non-Jewish children correlated positively, with a Pearson coefficient of .87.[13] Hartley found very high correlation coefficients between the "patterns of preference" for 35 groups displayed by students in such different colleges as Bennington, Columbia, Howard (a Negro university), Princeton, and the City College of New York.[14] The scale of these college students in 1938 was found to be significantly correlated with that of students in 1928 as measured by Bogardus.

Similarly, the stereotypes related to 10 groups by Princeton students and Negro college students have been found to be closely similar.[15] Of course the scale of social distance is not identical for the majority groups and for the oppressed minorities. Meltzer, Zeligs and Hendrickson, and Hartley have

[10] J. P. Guilford, Racial preferences of a thousand American university students, *J. Soc. Psychol.*, 1931, 2, 179–204.

[11] F. H. Allport and D. Katz, *Students' Attitudes*, Syracuse: Craftsman Press, 1931, p. 349.

[12] H. Meltzer, Group differences in nationality and race preferences of children, *Sociometry*, 1939, 2, 86–105.

[13] R. Zeligs and G. Hendrickson, Racial attitudes of 200 sixth-grade children, *Sociol. & Soc. Res.*, 1933–34, 18, 26–36.

[14] Hartley, *op. cit.*

[15] See D. Katz and K. Braly, Racial stereotypes of one-hundred college students, *J. Abn. & Soc. Psychol.*, 1933, 28, 280–290; and J. A. Bayton, The racial stereotypes of Negro college students, *J. Abn. & Soc. Psychol.*, 1941, 36, 97–102.

found that there is a tendency for the minority group members to maintain the essential established scale, but to move their own group from its low position to a place at the top. This indicates that the scale is determined first by their ego-involvement as members of their own special group within the general picture of their country, and then as Americans.

This finding of a generally established scale of social distance at which various national and ethnic groups in the United States are held, is sufficient in itself to show that degrees of *contact* with members of the given groups has little to do with the established relative positions on the scale. Individuals in Florida, New York, Illinois, Washington, Vermont surely have very different opportunities for contact with Negroes, for example; yet the social distance scale is highly similar in those states, revealing an established scale for the United States. Katz and Braly found that students assigned "typical traits" to 10 ethnic groups with remarkable consistency even in the case of groups personally unknown to the students. Horowitz found that sheer amount of contact with Negroes had no observable effect on the amount of prejudice displayed toward Negroes. Children in an all-white school and in a mixed school in New York City, and in schools in urban Tennessee and urban and rural Georgia gave remarkably similar reactions toward Negroes.[16]

Likewise, there seems little general relationship between information and acceptance of the established social distance scale. Murphy and Likert found low positive correlations between scores on a general information test and attitude scores toward Negroes. However, further investigation showed that these correlations resulted from the "greater scholarliness" of the "radical" students, who tended to reject prejudices toward Negroes, rather than a cause and effect relation between information and freedom from prejudice.[17] Hartley demonstrated this fact neatly by including three non-existent groups (the Danireans, Pirenians, and Wallonians) of which the subjects could have had no knowledge, on the list of actual groups.

---

[16] Horowitz, The development of attitudes toward the Negro, *op. cit.*
[17] Murphy and Likert, *op. cit.*, pp. 131–132.

The result was correlations from .78 to .85 between the average social distance for these groups and the average social distance for the actual groups.[18]

It would seem too that favorable contact with or information about individual members of a group held at considerable social distance produces little effect on the position of that group on the scale. Rather such individuals are considered "exceptions" to the generally accepted stereotypes concerning their group. This came out in Horowitz' early study on the development of attitudes toward Negroes. When members of a minority group accept the general frame of the majority concerning their group, they may consider themselves or their particular group as exceptions. This is evidenced in Meenes' study of the stereotypes of Negro students. The stereotypes assigned to their own group (Negro) were generally unfavorable (e.g., superstitious, happy-go-lucky, loud, lazy). But when asked whether they had in mind Negroes like themselves when they assigned the stereotypes, they "all said they had described 'Negroes in general.'"[19] Once a general frame is accepted, there is a tendency to evaluate specific items in terms of it. And those which do not fit easily into the frame (in this case one's self) are considered exceptions to the general rule.

Nor does similarity in taste among members of socially distant groups have much effect in eliminating social distance. We observed a scene during World War II which illustrates this point. The Turkish government, as a neutral, was doing its best to entertain impartially the legations of the United Nations and the Axis powers. One evening, the British and German embassies had been given corresponding boxes on the opposite sides of the auditorium at a concert. As the artist played Beethoven's "Moonlight Sonata," two attractive girls, one in the German box and one in the British, listened with bowed heads and closed eyes in communion with the music. But the harmony of this uplifting experience certainly had no effect on their activities the following day as active units in the embassies of two hostile countries. This point is further

[18] Hartley, *op. cit.*, p. 27.
[19] M. Meenes, A comparison of racial stereotypes of 1935 and 1942, *J. Soc. Psychol. SPSSI Bull.*, 1943, 17, 327–336.

illustrated by the intense hostility between the Chinese and Japanese in spite of similarities in cultural tastes.

Murphy and Likert found that the general level of social distance at which other national and ethnic groups are held is " strikingly correlated " with radicalism, and further related to a general dissatisfaction with " the whole social scene." [20] It was the " dissenters " who tended to reject the established social distances. Similarly, in Horowitz' study of attitudes toward Negroes referred to above, the one group of children who showed " no apparent prejudice against the Negro " was a group whose parents were Communist and who participated in a recreational program under the auspices of Communists—a group which has rejected the established social distance scales.

Slight regional differences in the scale of social distance in the United States are found—today, for instance, Japanese may be ranked lower on the West coast than in the East. In general, however, the pattern tends to be highly similar with somewhat different sets of beliefs and value judgments concerning the specific groups in different regions. While Negroes are low in the scale in all parts of the United States, the ascribed characteristics or beliefs relating to " their place " differ in the South and the North. [21] These views are often accepted by the members of the oppressed groups. Kay found considerable disagreement between different groups of Jews and non-Jews as to what constituted anti-Semitism. The question she posed illustrates this problem nicely: " Is it pro-Semitic (or pro-Negro) to remove barriers of economic discrimination but ' allow ' the group to ' protect ' its cultural differences by approving social segregation? Some Jews, and Negroes, and ' intercultural educators ' would say yes. To others that is basically a modified ' anti ' point of view and the real test of being ' pro ' is willingness to completely assimilate the minority groups." [22] It seems safe to generalize that as long as the social distance scale is kept intact, the particular set of beliefs and

[20] Murphy and Likert, op. cit.

[21] See, for example, R. Merton, Fact and factitiousness in ethnic opinionnaires, Amer. Sociol. Rev., 1940, 1, 13–28.

[22] L. W. Kay, Frame of reference in "pro" and "anti" evaluations of test items, J. Soc. Psychol., 1947, 25, 63–68.

stereotypes concerning the out-group and their station in life will largely reflect the norms of the in-group in question, which in some degree keep the out-group "in its place."

Quite different social distance scales are found in other countries. For example, Lapiere found very little prejudice against Negroes among the French (especially the middle and lower classes).[23] Striking differences from the scale in the United States have been observed in South American countries, e.g., Brazil. Apparently the social distance scale in Italy differs from that of the United States—at least the "majority" of Negro troops stationed there in 1947 dreaded to leave for the United States because they had not been discriminated against by the Italians.[24] To bring the point home, let us examine the picture of Americans prevalent today in England, a country comparatively close to the United States in terms of language and culture. In reporting the results of a survey,[25] Mass-Observation concluded: "A great many people have fundamentally the same idea of what the American is like" (p. 96). The central conception in the British picture is "the American who does *not grow up*." This stereotype may be favorable or unfavorable. If the person likes Americans, he ascribes the pleasant qualities of youth and childhood to them. But "unfavorable views of the Americans have steadily increased over the past year" (p. 98). These views emphasize the "less pleasant features of adolescence." Although one might expect the G.I.'s in Britain during the war to have modified these views, "in fact, the American soldier appears to have had relatively little effect on them" (p. 97). In closing, Mass-Observation notes that attitudes toward the G.I. "were often close to those shown toward Jews by anti-Semites, who will specifically excuse from their antagonisms Jews they know (and like) *as individuals*" (p. 98).

As the above survey indicates, social distance scales are not rigidly static. They do change, and under some conditions they break down entirely. An authority on the caste system

[23] R. T. Lapiere, Race prejudice: France and England, *Soc. Forces*, 1928, 7, 102–111.
[24] Reported in the *New York Herald Tribune*, July 9, 1947.
[25] Mass-Observation, Portrait of an American? *Inter. J. Opin. & Attit. Rev.*, 1947, 1, 96–98.

in India has found that there "caste distinctions ... invariably break down under the leveling influences of city and factory life." [26] There seems to be no indication of a breakdown of the established social distances in America; however, there are changes and shifts in the scale with the impact of events. Meenes secured the stereotypes of Negro college students for 10 ethnic groups in 1935 and again in 1942. The basic stereotypes were in significant agreement for all groups except the German, Japanese, and Chinese.[27] Since the groups of subjects were similar in both studies, we may assume that the changes were chiefly the result of the war with the Axis powers. "The 1942 stereotype of the Germans was much like that of 1935 except for the appearance of revengeful, cruel, and treacherous, in the 1942 picture" (p. 336). The most striking change was evident for the Japanese, who were well thought of in 1935, whereas in 1942, the picture was exceedingly uncomplimentary. The stereotype of Chinese, on the other hand, became increasingly favorable. Whether or not these shifts are temporary, the result of the momentous events of the war, or are of a lasting nature remains to be seen. A follow-up of such shifts would be interesting for social psychology.

The Individual and the Social Distance Scale

In order to handle the problems of social distance psychologically we must inquire into the origins of the individual's scale of social distance. From the foregoing material it becomes obvious that the scale is learned. Equally obvious is the fact that individuals do not form a social distance scale primarily on the basis of contact with the groups in question. As Horowitz concluded in his study of the development of attitudes toward the Negro, "attitudes toward Negroes are now chiefly determined not by contact with Negroes, but by contact with the prevalent attitude toward Negroes" (p. 35).

As we have seen, the child is born into a society in which social norms already exist as the result of previous interactions of the group in its distinct set of historical circumstances.

---

[26] B. Ambedkar, quoted in *Newsweek*, May 12, 1947, p. 40.

[27] Meenes, *op. cit.*

All aspects of the child's development—his total dependence on adults for the satisfaction of his needs, his gradual maturation in a specific social setting—lead to the necessity of following the mandates of the established group, whatever it may be.

Both Lasker's early study and the quantitative investigation by Horowitz reveal the early appearance of discriminations made on the basis of group membership.[28] Even the kindergarten children studied by Horowitz revealed a negative attitude toward Negroes. As Jersild has commented, such delineations may have their inception merely in the fact that the family with whom the whole well-being of the child is so closely bound makes it clear that they belong to such and such a group.[29] But surely more often the child forms his attitudes toward various groups from the statements of his grownups prescribing what a "nice" boy or girl is and does. This came out in the study of the development of attitudes by Horowitz and Horowitz.[30] Especially the children below the third grade freely acknowledged that the reason they chose white children to Negro children in social situations was because their parents told them to. As one child said: "Mamma tells me not to play with black children, keep away from them Mamma tells me, she told me not to play with them. Black (Why not?) Mother don't want me to " (p. 333).

Young children's attitudes toward various groups tend, however, to be rather unintegrated aspects of their psychological make-up. This is indicated by the low intercorrelations between tests of preference found by Meltzer,[31] and Horowitz' findings of lower intercorrelations between tests of attitude toward Negroes in younger children. As a result, children sometimes respond in an "inconsistent" way. The following observation related by a sociologist from Arkansas illustrates the point. A little girl was told by her mother to call older women "ladies." One day the little girl answered the door and then ran to her mother saying that a lady wanted to see her. Her mother went

[28] B. Lasker, *Race Attitudes in Children*, New York: Holt, 1929; Horowitz, The development of attitudes toward Negroes, *op. cit.*

[29] A. T. Jersild, *Child Psychology*, New York: Prentice-Hall, 1940.

[30] E. Horowitz and R. Horowitz, Development of social attitudes in children, *Sociometry*, 1937, 1, 301–338.

[31] Meltzer, *op. cit.*

to the door and when she returned she said, "That wasn't a
lady, dear. That was a Negro. You mustn't call Negroes
'ladies.'"

All of this is in line with what we have learned about the
development of the ego (pp. 252–262). The young child, having
as yet no clearly formed identity, reacts toward other groups
and people as he must in order to win praise and escape punishment from his parents. The Horowitzes found that the most
frequent cause of punishment in the community they studied
was for playing with Negro children. There seems to be every
reason for considering the development of attitudes of prejudice, formed chiefly in relation to the social norms prescribing
relative social distances, as one aspect of the development of
the ego. For the ego is simply a constellation of attitudes relating ourselves to the persons, objects, and groups around us.

This concept of the formation of attitudes toward one's own
and other groups "as in intrinsic aspect of ego development"
was clearly substantiated by Ruth Horowitz.[32] Pictures of
Negro and white children were presented to a group of pre-
school children (Negro and white). A child was asked to show
which child in the picture was himself. Horowitz found that
choices were made in terms of color by some of the children,
particularly the Negro children. For these Negro preschool
children, "the contrast there presented is a lesson well learned
and perceived immediately in terms of its pertinent elements."
However, the unintegrated nature of these youngsters' attitudes shows clearly in the reaction of the oldest white girl in
the group "who had expressed advanced and well crystallized
prejudice against Negroes." In one picture, she chose the Negro
girl "because the latter had curls and she, too, had curls which
were her glory and pride. Although accurately perceiving the
racial nature of all the other pictures, she denied that this one
was of a Negro child." [33]

Continuing this line of research with Negro children, K. B.
and M. K. Clark found increasing identification in terms of

[32] R. E. Horowitz, Racial aspects of self-identification in nursery school children,
J. Psychol., 1939, 7, 91–99.
[33] R. E. Horowitz, A pictorial method for study of self-identification in preschool
children, *J. Genet. Psychol.*, 1943, 62, 135–148.

color with age.[34] By observing the reactions of Negro children with different skin coloring (light, medium, dark), they found that an awareness of one's self as different from others on the basis of perceptible skin color comes first.[35] *These "concrete physical characteristics of perceived self" are modified by social definitions of differences between the Negro and white groups.* In the case of Negro children, such social definitions seem to affect the developing ego very early. The consequence of the conflict resulting from an unfavorable social definition of one's own characteristics is revealed in the Clarks' findings. Whereas the children increasingly made "correct" identifications with age, 67 per cent of the 3-year-olds said the brown child was *bad* and 58 per cent said the white child had a *nice* color. These results held true in both segregated schools in the South and mixed schools in the North.[36]

The formation of attitudes toward various groups as prescribed by social norms regulating their relative positions in the society is, then, one aspect of ego development. On the basis of what we have learned about ego formation and the relative inconsistency of a young child's behavior toward out-group members and symbols, it seems likely that these norms do not become an integrated part of his identity until he has grasped the reciprocity of interpersonal actions and can *psychologically* become a member of a group. This would seem to be the implication of the Horowitz' finding that the reasons given by young children for negative response toward Negroes were chiefly in terms of similarities and differences, whereas the older children (grades 3 and 4) acknowledged social pressures. Examples of correctives applied by the child's group are found in Zeligs and Hendrickson's study. As one child said: "If you even try to be sociable with Negroes the rest of the people lift up their eyebrows and say, 'Aw—that's awful.' I represent a room in safety council which has many Negroes. They say their safety laws to

---

[34] K. B. Clark and M. K. Clark, The development of consciousness of self and the emergence of racial identification in Negro preschool children, *J. Soc. Psychol.*, 1939, 10, 591–599.

[35] K. B. Clark and M. K. Clark, Skin color as a factor in racial identification of Negro preschool children, *J. Soc. Psychol.*, 1940, 11, 159–169.

[36] An unpublished study kindly made available by the Clarks.

me. When I meet them in the hall I say hello to them. All the other children look at me like it would be a crime to be sociable with them." [37]

When the children become participating members of their group, when their identities are formed to the level of grasping reciprocal interaction, the social norms become their own norms of behavior. Then, as Katz and Braly, and Horowitz point out, they forget the role of their parents and other agents in transmitting the norms, and claim them as their own. Then the norms of social distances become ego-distances in the psychology of the individual.

And of course, other groups of the community have this role in transmitting norms of social distance. An incident which occurred in Maine illustrates how such groups may crystallize prejudice even against people unknown to the children. In the summer of 1930, a Turkish university student spent his vacation in a small New England town. He became acquainted with a group of small boys who eagerly sought occasions to play with him and liked him so much that they called him "uncle." One Sunday, a revivalist preached in their Sunday School to raise some money and painted a dreadful picture of the "barbarity of the treacherous, heathen Turk" from the Crusades to the present. Afterward the boys came to their friend and told him about the sermon with enthusiasm and zeal. "Oh, boy, Uncle ——," they said. "We'll just kill those Turks. We'll just kick them down."

Once a part of the ego constellation, attitudes of prejudice are factors that regulate behavior in situations related to socially distant groups or individual members thereof. In some situations, other factors—e.g., the desire to make money, the urgent pressure of hunger or sexual deprivation, loyalty to other values—may take precedence in determining the reaction. To understand the specific individual's reaction in a prejudice-related situation, we must know something of his various ego-attitudes and identifications, and their organization in his psychological make-up.

[37] R. Zeligs and G. Hendrickson, Checking the social distance technique through the personal interview, Sociol. & Soc. Res., 1933–34, 18, 420–430.

Psychological Leads Suggested by the Foregoing Material

The findings concerning the social distance (prejudice) scale and its genetic development in the individual give us crucial leads for conceptualization. It is safe to assume that every society has its own standardized scale of social distances, and that a social distance scale reflects, in its major features, the hierarchical arrangements of the socio-economic organization. Thus in the United States, we find a more or less well-established scale of social distance which is standardized for the country, except for some variations here and there. This scale is certainly the historical product of the socio-economic structure. Once such a scale of human relationships and corresponding attitudes comes into existence, it cuts across objective class lines, social standing, and occupational standing. Even groups discriminated against, as we have seen, reflect the established scale of prejudice with displacement of their own particular group. This means that they reject discrimination only in the case of their own group, but keep intact the rest of the scale of prejudice. In other words, all conforming groups in the United States, the majority and minority (stemming from different ethnic, religious, and racial backgrounds), reveal a similar scale of prejudice with minor displacements. This fact, substantiated by concrete genetic studies, suggests that a social distance scale is built on the basis of prevailing values in the society and not on the basis of the experiences of the individuals themselves with the groups in question. In short, this generally established social distance scale seems to be an American institution almost like Thanksgiving. All the *respectable* members of society, all the *conforming* Americans seem to abide by the scale. Specific contacts and information concerning the groups in question are minor factors in determining the social distance scale of the *conforming* individual. On the other hand, those who are dissatisfied with things as they are (the socio-economic setup and the existing social norms)—in short, the radicals (the dissenters)—do not accept the prevailing prejudice scale. They exhibit the least prejudice, perhaps in proportion to the degree of their radicalism. We should say that personal reading habits, which seem to have an effect on the individual's prejudice scale, are not an isolated influence. It may be put as a hypothesis that the kind of reading material which is conducive to reducing prejudice is material of a non-conformist nature.

Linking together the conclusions reached concerning the products of group interaction and their subsequent effects on the individual, the genetic development and functioning of the ego, and the major line of findings on social distance, we may find substantial truth in the following summary formulation of the psychology of prejudice. A "we" and "they" delineation is one of the main products of group formation—with positive values becoming invested within the "we" formation, the "we" including the members of the group (small or large). The "we" thus circumscribed has real or fancied qualities and values to be upheld and cherished dearly. Any offenses from without and deviations from within are reacted to with appropriate corrective, defensive and at times offensive measures. "They," from the point of view of the group with all its survival values, are invested with a set of values, "traits" (favorable, unfavorable, or various combinations thereof). The favorable or unfavorable properties or "traits" attributed to "they" groups, and, inevitably, to their individual members in a rather absolutistic way, are determined by the nature of positive or negative relations between the groups in question. If the interests, direction, and goals of the intergroup relations are integrated or in harmony the features attributed to "they" groups are favorable. If the activities and views clash while the interacting groups pursue their peculiar interests and goals, the features attributed are negative. We see in the cooperating or conflicting intergroup relationships of small gang formations the manifestations in miniature of the rise of "we" and "they" delineations and the positive and negative attitudes that go with them (pp. 125–138). For example, if a gang happens to operate in the territory considered "ours" by another gang, the result is a clash and the application of unflattering adjectives to the first group and its members. Such an invasion is "indecent" and against the code. Even in these spontaneously formed little groups, feuds and corresponding negative attitudes arise which in time tend to become standardized, if the gangs last. This appeared in the experimental study by Lewin and his associates (pp. 119–120). Once groups of boys were more or less delineated in their "democratic" and "*laissez-faire*" atmospheres, *without any integration of the groups*, insulting words were hurled spontaneously at members of the opposite group and fights broke out. The members of the "democratic" group did not stop to resolve the friction by democratic methods. Democratic procedure was something to be practiced among themselves (the in-group) in making masks.

Even these simple illustrations lead us to the generalization that positive or negative attitudes in intergroup relationships are the outcome of integration or lack of integration of the interests, goals, and the resulting views of the groups in question. Once "in-group" and "out-group" delineations take place, attitudes necessarily arise that define the reciprocal positions of the groups. If one group takes the stand that the other group is in its way, interferes with its goals and vital interests, or should be working for its interests, all sorts of "traits" are attributed as inherent qualities of the out-group to justify the stand taken, and the existing or contemplated actions. All racial superiority doctrines are, deliberately or unconsciously, justifications of this sort. The attributed inherent "traits" are labels standardized to perpetuate certain practices advantageous to the interests of the dominant group.

A great many members of the groups to whom are attributed certain "traits" to justify their low position come to accept, in time, stereotyped characterizations of themselves. This was evident in the acceptance by Negroes of at least some of the features attributed to them by the existing social organization. It also leads them to accept their position as inevitable, and to serve their masters willingly. Any comfort or status they may attain they expect to be bestowed by the gentlemen or ladies they serve.

Closely connected with this is the fact that once a certain social distance scale, with "traits" attributed to each group on it, becomes standardized, it tends to continue as a result of psychological inertia and the active efforts of the interested groups. We do not and cannot every so often manufacture anew our personal identity in relation to others and the stability of our groups. This inertia is necessarily strengthened by the fact that we want to stay good members of our group. A young lady who went back to Alabama in the summer of 1947 with more liberal views toward Negroes soon had to fall in line in her social contacts with old friends because of the various correctives that were applied. The politicians and liberals who during World War II really wanted to arouse a favorable attitude toward the Russian people among Americans, who had been consistently exposed to the picture of a Bolshevik as a man stained in blood and carrying a bomb, had to resort to the usual stereotypes of the American political scene—a church service on almost every corner attended by pious people, child kissing, etc.

The idea of social distance which people have and which defines their position in relation to other groups is not built up on the basis of factual experiences or objective knowledge. It is a necessary derivative of the individual's membership in his group. This result is best shown in the genetic studies of the Horowitzes and the Clarks (pp. 352–354). Their finding is concretely substantiated by the high degree of prejudice that conformist church members exhibit—church members who hear week in and week out that all men are equal in the eyes of God and that it is a great virtue to love your enemy. The manifestation of greater prejudice on the part of more regular church attendants is reported in the survey of relevant studies by Horowitz, and it appeared in G. W. Allport and Kramer's recent study on prejudice.[38] This line of findings, which is full of implications for collective psychology and the psychology of the personal identity of the individual members in "closed" social groups, was evident more recently in "a survey made in the American zone of Germany by the Information Control Division of the American Military Government." We quote from a newspaper report of this survey: "The study, based on interviews with 3,415 persons selected as a cross-section of the American zone and the American section of Berlin, showed the following: Women are 'markedly more biased' against Jews

[38] G. W. Allport and B. M. Kramer, Some roots of prejudice, *J. Psychol.*, 1946, **22**, 9–39.

than men. Small town people are more prejudiced than those of the large cities. Prejudice is greater among people with a lower status in society (those with the least education and those with unspecialized jobs). *Protestants tend to be more biased than Catholics. Those who attend church regularly are more prejudiced than those who attend irregularly.*" [39]

It seems that if a group standardizes a prejudice scale, putting itself at the top and establishing contemptuous prejudice patterns in relation to other groups and their allegedly inherent unfavorable qualities, this scale becomes a generalized attitude of prejudice toward any people that sound unfamiliar, even though absolutely nothing is known about them. Such a generalized pattern of prejudice seems to be at work in the United States today, for example. This came out concretely in Hartley's investigation. As we have seen, Hartley included three non-existent groups among those to be ordered by the subjects in terms of their social distance hierarchy. The striking result was that conservative groups (Howard and Princeton students in the study) who consistently showed a rather high degree of prejudice, put these non-existent groups low on their social distance scale. The progressive groups (Bennington and a liberal section at City College) accepted them in rather close proximity—on the average beyond the degree implied in the statement "To my school as classmates." [40] These findings led Hartley to advance the hypothesis "that such tolerance represents to a significant extent a function of the persons responding, rather than of the groups responded to." [41] This we take to mean that an in-group which definitely classifies out-groups along an unmistakable scale of social distance develops at the same time a general tendency of prejudice toward others even though they may have not a single item of information concerning them.

[39] *New York Herald Tribune*, Sunday, May 4, 1947 (italics mine).

[40] We know from Newcomb's extensive study of the attitudes of these Bennington students (see Chapter 6) that some of them clung to the conservatism of their backgrounds and regulated themselves accordingly, isolating themselves from the liberal college atmosphere. If the results obtained from these students were separated from the others, we think that their rating of the non-existent groups would have been low, as was the case with other conservative groups.

[41] Hartley, *op. cit.*, p. 26.

Prejudice studies, too, will gain meaning if they are related to the *substantive mode of mentality* still prevalent not only among the more backward peoples, but in the great mass of conforming respectability of what is called "Western Civilization." By substantive mode of mentality we mean the tendency to account for or describe events (social and otherwise) in terms of the "essence" of things instead of in terms of related processes. The great mass of bourgeois respectability shows a tendency to deal with human and social events in terms of an eternal "human nature," qualities inherent in this or that group. It is expressed in the form, "What can you expect from a man coming from such a family?" During a war, the enemy nation is denounced in terms of inherent, immutable characteristics. For example, we were told that the Japanese are tricky and sly by nature; the Italians are inherently an easy-going, talkative bunch who spend most of their time singing operas in the street. This unscientific substantive mentality is clearly indicated in the Middletown attitudes concerning masculine and feminine characteristics.[42] In spite of the fact that the feminine and masculine roles and statuses have actually undergone considerable changes in the United States since the Revolution, the prevailing conceptions of men and women are held to be *inherent*, immutable qualities of the sexes. Popular attitudes in the human and social fields have not gone beyond the prescientific stage on the whole, in spite of the wonderful advances in the physical sciences and technological fields which are almost universally accepted. For example, when something goes wrong with his car, the resident of Middletown really wants to learn the cause of the defect; this is a case of applying the "process mentality" of science as opposed to "substantive mentality." [43]

Possibly this substantive mentality will continue until societies come to accept the process mentality in human and social fields too. The remedy for the prescientific substantive outlook

---

[42] See R. Lynd and H. M. Lynd, *Middletown in Transition*, New York: Harcourt, Brace, 1937, pp. 176 f.

[43] A book on social psychology is not the place to trace the origins of this substantive mentality in certain aspects of Greek philosophy, in theism, and in various idealistic philosophies of the last century.

lies in the acceptance and *application* of the process analysis of the scientific approach. When this is done, such generally denounced phenomena as imperialism, aggression, war, prejudice will not be dismissed in a summary way on the basis of an immutable "human nature" blindly seeking for power and domination; or on the basis of the inherently aggressive nature of a group or, worse, of a few ambition-immersed leaders (like Hitler); or on the basis of the inherent "traits" of an ethnic group. They will be approached in terms of observable variables that contribute to produce a certain effect. In this connection, it is relevant to mention that the Soviet denunciations of Hitler's aggressions during World War II, when they were in the thick of a life-and-death struggle requiring almost superhuman sacrifice, were not directed against any inherent barbarism of the German people as such.

Central Factors That Need Focusing in Social Distance Studies

The generally standardized scale of social distance, as we have seen, seems to be common to the great majority of conforming Americans. If similar methods were used to measure prejudice in other countries, probably we would obtain other established prejudice scales in most of them. In the United States, those who free themselves of prejudices are, on the whole, the dissenters, the nonconformists in various degrees. The rich and the poor, the college students studying engineering or liberal arts, minority groups as well as majority groups share these prejudices as long as they do not feel dissatisfied with things as they are.

All this goes to show that once a superstructure of values, of which the social distance scale is a part, becomes standardized for a group, it tends to be accepted even by those who suffer and are discriminated against because of its existence. This fact is becoming an established generalization. It is also a fact, in harmony with substantiations from the laboratory and from everyday life, that once such a prejudice scale becomes a part of the ego of the individual, it renders his reactions to related stimuli highly selective and partial.

Yet these findings constitute only a part of the psychology of social distance. If the psychologist complacently stops at this point in his account, he will soon discover in the development of actual life situations that his psychology covers only a few variables of social distance. We should always make adequate note of the fact that the whole superstructure of established human relationships and social norms is a product of the interaction of groups of individuals with strong motivations. Being a product of human interaction, it is not an immutable entity. With the rise of new conditions and changed modes of interaction, it is subject to modifications—gradual or, at times, abrupt. No superstructure of prejudice or other norms remains intact for long when conditions are changing. Negro veterans who heard during the war that they were fighting for the Four Freedoms are showing increasing signs of dissatisfaction and restlessness with things as they are. The recent law in India giving full citizen's rights to the "untouchables" is striking evidence that the caste system is breaking down—the caste system that was utilized as a strong point of argument by those students who assigned equal weight to all observed facts and refused to single out the independent and dependent variables in the determination of human relationships.

The psychologist may find it outside the scope of controlled observation to trace historically the rise of a superstructure of prejudice, or some other set of norms, on the basis of interactions of dominant and subjected groups with unmistakable motivation (economic and political). But, if he wants to complete the picture, he cannot very well ignore the motivations of interested groups who are striving to change or perpetuate the existing standardized scheme of human relationships.

Closely connected with this is the possible role of the mass media of communication in perpetuating or changing scales of social distance. This raises, in turn, the question of the role of the owners of these media in determining the direction of attitude perpetuation or attitude change. These problems have not yet been systematically approached by the social psychologist. Serious studies dealing with these factors will further help us in formulating an adequate social psychology of prejudice.

PART THREE

Individuals and Social Change

Introduction

IN THE PRECEDING CHAPTERS, WE DISCUSSED THE EFFECTS OF social products (values, norms, etc.) on the individual. We traced briefly the place of social values in the formation of his ego-attitudes and their effects on his ego-involvements. But, we repeat, social values, norms, and other social products are not fixed entities. They are products of social interaction that takes place under certain definite conditions (see Introduction to Part II, and Chapter 7). Changing conditions (such as scientific discoveries, new technological developments, mass deprivations, changes in the cultural level of the population, etc.) enter as new factors in social interaction. These new factors require a new set of norms—norms appropriate to the new conditions. Consequently, they disturb the existing human relationships and the superstructure of established norms.

The old norms do not relinquish their place to the new overnight, even if the new ones formulate the new conditions objectively. What is established as normal, as respectable, as sacred, is defended by groups of established respectability. Marked deviations from the norm are shocking at first to the rank and file of established society, even though the change may be to their benefit. The individual's very sense of stability and the continuity of this stability from day to day are derived psychologically from the existing set of values, whatever it may be in a given social setting (see Chapters 11 and 12). Besides, in times of social transition, there are always powerful groups who are the privileged beneficiaries of things as they are. They defend the established values to the last ditch. The American Tories during the Revolution and the aristocracy that clustered around the king during the French Revolution are examples of such groups.

Because of sheer inertia, or the conscious efforts of interested groups, there ensues friction of varying degrees between the established and the new. The survival of the established values in spite of the compelling onslaughts of new situations demanding the acceptance of their appropriate values is usually referred to as the "cultural lag" by the social scientists.

The study of social change as such is the concern of investigators in social sciences—the sociologist, political scientist, etc. As psychologists, our primary concern is the effect of change on the individual, and the effect of psychological factors (individual and group) in bringing about the change. The reciprocal effects of individual and social change cover a wide range of topics. Of this wide range of topics related to individual and social change, we shall briefly discuss only two which are surely among the most crucial: (1) the effects of technology and (2) the effects of mass deprivation. We shall not discuss such major related topics as the role of leadership and the effect of the intellectual-political level (e.g., class consciousness and intellectual movements).

15.

The Effects of Technology

WHEN THE ATOMIC BOMBS WERE DROPPED AT HIROSHIMA AND Nagasaki—killing tens of thousands, leaving untold devastation of human life and activities—the startled peoples of the world were forced to the realization of the inexorable trend of modern technology. Here is a weapon of war which in one stroke can eliminate a modern metropolis, for which no possibility of an adequate defense exists, and from which no peoples can count themselves safe. The scientists and technicians who developed the bomb envisaged its use by rockets traveling at such great height and speed that their source would be impossible to trace, from airplanes traveling faster than the speed of sound.

The United Nations, then in the process of formation, altered its plans for its first meetings to include discussion of the bomb. And in the United States, scientists who had traditionally pretended to keep away from political affairs met, organized, and used all the facilities available to convey the revolutionary significance of the development. As one eminent scientist said: "We who have lived for years in the shadow of the atomic bomb are well acquainted with fear." [1] Again and again they warned that "the devastating results . . . must be seen to be believed . . .;"[2] that the peoples of the world must revise their ways of thinking and acting in relation to each other in view of the bomb; that what these men's labor had produced, other men's labor could produce. One scientist, disturbed by the failure of politicians to grasp the significance of the atom bomb for their future actions, suggested that they be made to witness an atomic explosion.[3] Judging from Hersey's

[1] Dr. H. C. Urey, "Atomic Terror Tomorrow," *Colliers*, January 5, 1946, p. 1.
[2] Dr. J. R. Oppenheimer in the *New York Times*, October 18, 1945.
[3] L. Szilard, "We Turned the Switch," *Nation's* Supplement, Part II, December 22, 1945, pp. 718–719.

account of the survivors of Hiroshima, there are few individuals who can experience other than terror and awe after first-hand experience with the bomb.

It is unquestionably true that the major impact of atomic energy will be felt in the future. Perhaps too many people follow the lead of those who choose to ignore the considered counsel of the scientists and they treat the atomic bomb as a "secret" to be held in "sacred trust." But even if the peoples of the world are spared the tragedy of a war with atom bombs, rockets, and super-air power, they will inevitably face the problems created by the revolutionary potential of atomic energy. No less an authority than Dr. J. Robert Oppenheimer has estimated that it is entirely possible that an American city will be heated with atomic energy "in less than five years." [4] And this is merely one of many astounding developments which man's progressive understanding of nature holds for the future. Such developments will necessarily lead to a rearrangement of man's activities and social relationships, as other technological innovations and appliances have in recent centuries.

Even in a technologically developed country like the United States, the development and widespread use of such inventions as the automobile, airplane, radio, motion picture, have had far-reaching social and psychological effects. They have affected not only people's concepts of speed and time, but their whole life activities, their tastes, their dreams and aspirations. The peculiar psychological products arising in a great metropolis, like New York or Chicago, which has developed rapidly during the past century, exemplify the psychological effects of modern technology. The development and expansion of industry in all parts of the world are accompanied by the almost crushing impact of tools, arms, means of transportation and communication upon cultures which were heretofore relatively isolated; they are in a state of disequilibrium as they become increasingly functional parts of a world-wide industrial civilization. There was a time when we could speak appropriately of "patterns of culture" comparatively complete within themselves. But today, when the representatives of Samoa, Indo-

[4] Quoted by B. Pregel in "Power and Progress," *Nation's* Supplement, Part II, December 22, 1945, pp. 710–711.

nesia, Viet Nam, and Outer Mongolia come before the United Nations with similar social and political aspirations, it is hardly realistic to speak of closed culture patterns. A system or configuration is closed or self-sustaining only if the dominant interrelated factors are contributed by the system itself. If the functional interdependence of parts is violated in a major way by factors from the outside, one can no longer speak of a closed configuration. The stability is spoiled; the system is in a state of disequilibrium in which the inside forces tending to keep it intact are in sharp conflict with the outside forces tending to establish a new equilibrium.

The concern of ethnologists over problems of culture change and "acculturation" reflects this general trend toward a functionally interrelated world. This general concern is epitomized in the words of Malinowski:

The anthropologist is becoming increasingly aware that the study of culture change must become one of his main tasks in field work and theory. The figment of the "uncontaminated" Native has to be dropped from research in field and study. The cogent reason for this is that the "uncontaminated" Native does not exist anywhere. The man of science has to study what is, and not what might have been. When his main interest lies in the reconstruction of the tribal past, he still has to study the Native as he is now, affected by Western influences. . . .

The anthropologist could also usefully reflect on the fact that evolution and diffusion are processes not so different as they appear at first sight. Culture change in Africa does not differ profoundly from that which is at present transforming the rural and backward countries of Europe from peasant communities, living by indigenous age-long economic systems, by folklore and kinship organization, into a new type closely akin to the proletariat found in the industrial districts of the United States, England, or France. [5]

Our problem in this chapter is not that of culture change or technology-mentality relationships in all their various phases. Nor can we give even a partial account of the psychological effects of the automobile, airplane, radio, movies, or atomic bomb. Such effects are complicated problems of the first order.

[5] B. Malinowski, *The Dynamics of Social Change, An Inquiry into Race Relations in Africa*, New Haven: Yale University Press, 1945, pp. 2–3.

However, they may all be effectively considered as part of the problem of the effects of technology (or material culture) upon the psychology of individuals.

In stressing here the influence of material and technological conditions on individuals, we must bear in mind what we have already learned concerning one aspect of attitude psychology and the effects of the non-material culture—of concepts, values, norms. The material culture or technology seldom if ever affects the individual discretely. He is simultaneously affected by the many norms of his society, by the pressures of groups of individuals who are motivated to maintain the existing order of things or to mold his attitudes toward the technological product in a particular way. The existing superstructure of concepts, norms, and values (non-material culture) functions as an important factor in determining the speed or slowness with which technological developments are accepted and propagated, and human relationships brought into harmony with them. In the United States, for example, there was considerable resistance to automobiles, not only on the part of manufacturers of horse-drawn vehicles, but also on the part of many members of the older generation.

There are socially approved and disapproved ways of looking at things, approaching situations, and living everyday life. These social values, positive and negative, which in time become the individual's own attitudes, regulate and limit his whole outlook. Also, any deviation from these established ways on the part of the individual, even in the direction of an innovation which is destined to become "normal" in the years to come, is looked upon at first with almost invariable suspicion. In cases of deviation considered important by the group, and especially if "vested interests" are at stake, the deviator calls down upon himself the scorn and the wrath of "good people." Deviations even in the direction of innovations which have proved to be blessings have been risky. The resistance to innovations has been duly noted by those authorities who have most emphatically stressed the decisive effect of technological changes in shaping the mentality of man, and who, for this reason, have been criticized in a summary way for reducing everything to crude material determination. This resistance of the superstructure of established values is clearly stated by Engels in his frequently quoted passage:

According to the materialist conception of history the determining element in history is *ultimately* the production and reproduction in real life. . . . If therefore somebody twists this into the statement that the economic element is the *only* determining one, he transforms it into a meaningless, abstract and absurd phrase. The economic situation is the basis, but the various elements of the superstructure—political forms of the class struggle and its consequences, constitutions established by the victorious class after a successful battle, etc. —forms of law, and even the reflexes of all these actual struggles in the brains of the combatants: political, legal, philosophical theories, religious ideas and their further development into the systems of dogma—also exercise their influence upon the course of the historic struggles and in many cases preponderate in determining their *form*. There is an interaction of all these elements, in which, among all the endless *host* of accidents (i.e. of things and events whose interconnection is so remote or so impossible to prove that we can regard it as absent and can neglect it), the economic movement finally asserts itself as necessary. Otherwise the application of the theory to any period of history one chose would be easier than the solution of a simple equation of the first degree.[6]

As we have seen in earlier chapters, it has been demonstrated that when individuals face or use repeatedly in their daily work certain magnitudes, certain weights, certain proportions, a certain schedule of life, they cannot help forming appropriate psychological scales in relation to them, whether they are conscious of the fact or not. Subsequently when they face these stimuli or stimuli related to them, they react to them as regulated by the established scales. Thus regulated, they react to stimuli as normal or out of the ordinary, as too big, too small, too fast, too slow, too hard, too easy as the case may be. As we shall see presently, to a peasant from a primitive village whose travel speed is regulated by the fact that he must walk or ride on a donkey, a trip to the market town in a worn-out bus on a primitive dirt road is considered a rare luxury and a terrific speed. To him, an income of from three to four hundred dollars a year is great wealth. Such referential regulation of

---

[6] F. Engels, quoted from D. Guest, *Dialectical Materialism*, New York: International, 1939, pp. 61–62.

reactions according to definite established scales in the life circumstances surrounding the individual is not a psychological peculiarity of a poor Asiatic peasant. In an actual experiment, a college prefessor, when confronted with the task of judging a series of graded weights which had a range within well below a kilogram, *at first* gave a good many judgments of heavy, whereas a person dealing with relatively heavy weights in his daily job at first gave a good many judgments of *light* when confronted with the same task.[7] Of course the standards of income used by a poor worker and a rich industrialist in America are regulated by their respective established scales.

Definite important psychological products in the individual are determined by compelling material and technological conditions surrounding him. The urgency of these conditions corresponds psychologically to the compellingness of well-structured stimulus situations of the well-known perception experiments, in which the psychological frame and salient reference points correspond closely to those of the objective field of stimulation. Such evidence further shows that the changes in material and technological conditions are accompanied by similar, but by no means one-to-one, changes in mentality.

In presenting concrete illustrations of the effects of technology, we shall begin with relatively simple situations. In this way, we may single out some of the important variables involved. Groups of individuals who are somewhat isolated from the general run of modern industrial life are admirably suited for such study.

Contact with Modern Technology in Five Turkish Villages

In 1944, a study of the technology and mentality relationship was made in five Turkish villages with varying degrees of isolation from more developed centers and varying degrees of contact with modern technology. All these villages had some contact with the outside world and, along with the rest of the country, were in a stage of transition. But the contrast between the most and least isolated villages is sufficient to indi-

---

[7] Reported by M. E. Tresselt in The influence of amount of practice upon the formation of a scale of judgment, *J. Exper. Psychol.*, 1947, 37, 251–260.

cate the striking effects of the relative degree of contact with technology. The material was collected by students who came from the villages and hence were intimate with village life.

Two kinds of data were secured: (1) data concerning the material conditions and technological level of the village; (2) data concerning the mentality of the villagers.

Among the former were descriptions of the geographical situation; the general characteristics of the territory in which the village was situated; roads; the means of transportation and communication; the distribution of land; properties of the soil; the main means of livelihood (such as farming, animal-raising, dairy production); the tools used in production; trading and marketing within and outside the village; diverse occasions for outside contacts; the degree of mobility to towns and cities; schooling and the degree of literacy; etc.[8]

We limited the scope of the psychological data to a few basic phenomena dealing primarily with the units, precision, and scope of space, distance, and time perceptions, the scales and standards consciously or unconsciously regulating the villagers' conceptions of the alien or strange, and of wealth. These basic standards and scales and basic attitudes regulating in-group and out-group expectations are more than cognitive phenomena; they act in an important way to regulate the boundaries of the individual's activities and expectations, the scope and limits of his mobility in undertaking the vital concerns of his life.

Instead of presenting mere sketches of each of the five villages, we will obtain a more concrete impression of the study from summaries of the results for the relatively most isolated and least isolated villages—Karlik in the western interior of Turkey and Beşikdüzü on the Black Sea coast.

The Village of Karlik. Karlik is a village of 361 people situated in a rather mountainous region east of the Aegean coast. It is about 30 kilometers from the capital town of the province, Afyon, and about 5 kilometers from a larger village, Şuhut.

[8] The author gratefully acknowledges his debt to Dr. Behice Boran, assistant professor of sociology in Ankara University, for her effective cooperation in the preparation of this study.

Although there is a dirt road between the two villages, the villagers usually take the shorter path to Şuhut over the hills on foot or on donkey. The stream at the edge of the village is flooded most of the time during the winter. Since there is no bridge over it, all actual contact is cut off with the larger village while the stream is flooded. There is one telephone in Karlik for official governmental use.

There is occasional bus service to the more important towns from Şuhut. But the villagers cannot take advantage of this for trips to surrounding towns, because it is very expensive, almost a luxury for them. When they do use the bus for some urgent business, they describe it in superlatives. The railroad is 35 kilometers away.

The richest two or three families each owns about 200 *dönüm* (about 50 acres) of land.[9] Over 25% of the families own no land. They have to work on the farms of others to earn their living. The number of these landless peasants is increasing, since those who own a few acres of land are being forced to sell to those who already own larger tracts. The villagers who come between these two extremes own 15 to 20 *dönüm* (4–5 acres). Three-fourths of the people in the village have to work for larger land-owners to make ends meet. The villagers are dependent for their livelihood on the farming of grains. There are no animal herds of substantial economic value except the oxen, donkeys, horses, and cows kept for farm work, domestic use, and limited trading purposes. Only primitive tools are used in farming; no modern machinery is available. Some of the landless peasants who, in spite of their desperate efforts cannot make ends meet in Karlik go to work temporarily in the provinces along the Aegean. After making enough money to last for a few months, they usually return to the village, only to repeat the trip again when the money is gone. Between the planting season and harvest time, some of these poor villagers go to the capital town of the province (Afyon) to do construction work.

There are no stores in the village. Therefore the villagers have to go to Şuhut on market days to sell their goods and to buy their few necessities. Trips to and from the village on mar-

---

9 One acre equals approximately 4 dönüm.

ket days are made by donkey; on ordinary days, the trip is made on foot. A barber and a blacksmith come from a neighboring town every two weeks.

The village school was founded in 1938. The one teacher (a man who did not have the usual normal school training) has to teach all three classes and keep up school attendance, which is no mean task in itself because parents need their children to work on the farm, tend the few cows, and do other tasks.

This setting of Karlik, its mode of life and little contact with modern technology, produce definite psychological effects. As stated earlier, the psychological effects we will consider are confined to a few relatively simple though basic phenomena which tend to set the boundaries of the individual's world and activities.

Units of distance: The villagers express distances up to 3 or 4 kilometers by such expressions as: "Within a bullet's reach," "as far as my voice can go," "as far as (it takes) to smoke a cigarette," etc. Any more precisely standardized units of distance, such as kilometers or miles, are not used.

Long distances, for example 50 kilometers, are expressed as: "You start early in the morning and reach there by sunset," or "You reach there (by the time) you work on crops of one *dönüm* (of land)." The latter is, of course, based on the work done without the use of any modern agricultural tools. The guesses of distance in terms of time are always made in terms of the time a trip will take *on foot*. When the villagers figure out long distances involving travel by bus or train, they do it in terms of the number of days, nights, and fractions thereof (not in hours) spent on the bus or the train. They have no idea how far these distances really are. They cannot translate them into terms of walking time, their real psychological distance unit.

The greatest distances in their experience vary, in general, according to whether they are male or female and, among males, according to whether or not they have completed their compulsory military service. The farthest distance in the experience of men who have completed their military service is the place they were sent for that service. For women, the farthest distance is either the larger neighboring village (Şuhut, 5 kilometers away) or the capital town of the province

30 kilometers away. For males who have not yet left for their military service, the greatest distance is some place to which they have gone for the temporary work necessary to balance their annual budget. For older men who fought in World War I and the Turkish War for Independence, it is the distance to the places where they fought. Of other distant places or continents they have only vague notions.

In the experience of both older and younger men, the distances to places beyond their province are greatly distorted, the manner of distortion depending on whether their visit was made on foot or on the train. Far more distant places which were traveled to by train are guessed as closer than a shorter distance reached mainly on foot. For example, the town of Haymana in the neighboring province, to which one has to walk, is considered farther away than Istanbul, which by railroad is actually almost twice as far. The following illustration is still more striking: Older men who served in the army in World War I both in the province of Van, Turkey (near the Persian border), and in Galicia (now mainly in Poland at a distance several times that to Van) claim that Van is more distant than Galicia. They had to walk most of the way to Van; they went to Galicia on the train. In other words, before a conception of precise units of distance is grasped, the human effort spent to reach a place is a major factor in determining the experience of distance.[10]

Units of time: The following expressions, instead of hours, are generally used for the divisions of the day: "first rooster,"

---

[10] Hallowell found similar distortions among the Saulteaux owing to the fact that their psychological units of distance were expressed in terms of the number of nights spent en route to a place. In his words: "I do not believe that I ever succeeded in conveying to them any realistic notion of the distance I had travelled to reach their country. Matters were further complicated by the fact that my *rate* of travel in different kinds of conveyances was not the sort of knowledge that could be taken for granted. Consequently, my attempt to convert distance into concrete qualitative units intelligible to them (i.e., sleeps) made my home only twice the distance the mouth of the river lay from Lake Pekangikum, about 260 miles. Actually it was more than six times that distance. The difficulty lay in the fact that I spent the same number of nights on the train and the boat between Philadelphia and the mouth of the Berens River as I spent ascending the river. The differential factor, of course, was the speed of the train. This mode of conveyance was known to them only by hearsay." A. I. Hallowell, Some psychological aspects of measurement among the Saulteaux, *Amer. Anthropologist*, 1942, 44, 67.

dawn; "leaving of oxen" (for grazing), sunrise, mid-morning (*Kuşluk*), noon; "return of oxen," sunset, evening, and midnight (which covers two or three hours).

The day of the week that stands out from the others and in reference to which other days (ordinary weekdays) are regulated, is the market day of the nearest larger village (Şuhut). They refer to this village as simply "the Town" (*Gasaba*). The market day of this town, which happens to be Saturday and which regulates the periodicity of their shopping and other activities, is referred to as "Town Market" (*Gasaba Bazari*). Three other days of the week are known as market days for three important towns in the area and are so named. Thus for them the week starts on Saturday, called "Town Market," and runs as follows:

Saturday—Town Market (*Gasaba Bazari*)
Sunday—*Sandlıki* Market
Monday—*Garesar* Market
Tuesday—*Sali*
Wednesday—*Carşamba*
Thursday—*Çal* Market
Friday—*Cuma*

There are a few villagers who know the names of the days of the week and the calendar months. But on the whole the villagers do not express a day by the calendar date and month.

Divisions of the month are classified according to the appearance of the moon in the sky: "bright moon," "dark moon," and the dark moons are specified as coming during the first half and second half of the cycle.

Divisions of the year are expressed as summer, winter, spring, fall, and, in addition, such seasons as "haying" (*kağni çekimi*), "end of harvest" (*harman sonu*), sowing (*ekimler*), etc. These and several other divisions not mentioned here are named after their farming and animal-raising activities, and one or two after religious holidays.

Conceptions of the strange: All people who by their mode of life, clothing, speech, etc., are different from the villagers and government officials (*memur*), even though they may be known, are considered strangers. Anyone who comes from the outside and settles in the village is still considered a stranger in proportion to his deviations from the village norms in his living, appearance, and expression. Young men who return to the village from their military service make a point of coming home with a new suit. The usual reaction even to them is, at first: "Hey, *Memet*, you kind of look like a stranger. I didn't recognize you at first glance." This joking but tolerant attitude is maintained until the new suit wears out to the point where it is indistinguishable from other suits, and things picked up during the stay outside of the village disappear completely. Any deviations in speech are particularly singled out for teasing.

The villagers consider themselves in a somewhat strange place when they move 2 or 3 kilometers from their own village. Those men who happen to have stayed in comparatively prosperous and large cities and towns, with colorful surroundings and fertile soil, express a desire to go back and even to settle down in some such form as: "It is better to live in a place like that, even for one day, than living forty days in a place like this [referring to Karlik] on which the flies don't even like to make specks."

Standards of riches: Standards of riches vary, within limits, according to the economic standing of the villagers—according to the amount of land and the number of farm animals and horses they have and the size of the crops they raise. The few families who possess a relatively large piece of land are conceived of by the villagers as men whose farms exceed anything which is in their own power to attain.

Except for two or three men who own (to the villagers) disproportionately huge farms, the greatest sum of money one can actually conceive of is about $80 for women and around $800 for men; however, neither men nor women have succeeded in amassing such huge sums of money in spite of all their toil.

The following are some examples of what the villagers of Karlik consider waste and luxury: Buying a new suit when a man already has one, even though it may be full of patches (there are no everyday clothes and "Sunday best"); buying the shoes worn in towns and cities instead of simple leather sandals (*çarik*); wearing clothes made of the thin materials used in towns and cities. In short, anything other than the bare necessities of existence is considered a luxury.

The villages of Kalinagil, Zanapa, and Isabey represent in that order closer contact with modern technology and consequent gradations of these various concepts. For contrast with the findings in Karlik, let us examine a summary of the results obtained in the *least* isolated village, Beşikdüzü.

The Village of Beşikdüzü. Unlike Karlik, Beşikdüzü is a coastal village on the Black Sea. The consequent contacts afforded by sea communication and the scarcity of tillable land create conditions which, as we shall see, have far-reaching effects in the experience and behavior of the villagers. Beşikdüzü is about 4 kilometers from a somewhat larger village and about 51 kilometers from the capital city of the province of Trabzon, which is itself on the sea. At the time of the study, Beşikdüzü had a population of 842 people, of which 350 were males and 492 females. This disproportion arises because many men have to leave the village to make a living for their families in various kinds of work. (It is even more striking when one considers that 300 of the population were under the age of 13, the proportion of girls and boys being about equal.)

The main trade with the outside is carried on from port to port by boats and small motorboats. It is the businessmen of the village, not the producers themselves, who handle the shipping of produce, which consists mainly of hazelnuts. Since local means of transportation (both animals and vehicles) are scarce, goods are generally carried by the villagers to and from the loading places on their backs. Because of the scarcity of transportation inland, most trading is done by sea. Though there are occasional buses to the nearby town and city, the usual mode of travel inland is on foot. Some trading is done in the town 4 kilometers away where the villagers sell some hazelnuts, butter, and a small quantity of a few other agricultural products, and where they buy soap, salt, sugar, clothing, and other manufactured goods. In this area, as in many places along the Black Sea coast, the tillable farms are squeezed between the hills. The main means of livelihood consists of raising hazelnuts and corn, and fishing. About 80% of the villagers are unable to raise sufficient corn, the staple food, for their own use. During recent years, they had to import corn by sea from the outside. The money received from selling hazelnuts is not enough to give all the people a living; so many men have to look for other jobs.

In recent years many villagers have worked in the Zanguldak coal mines, the Karabük steel works, and the Divrik ore mines. Others work on boats, in fishing, in carrying small cargoes by rowboat or sailboat, or in small trades, e.g., carpentry.

Some of the men who go away to earn a living keep their roots in the village, but others have left the village with their families and settled in other places. During the last decade, 10 families moved away after selling everything they had.

There are about 10 stores, a few coffee houses, 5 shoemakers and repairmen, and 8 hazelnut traders in the village. All the coffee houses have radios. People are very much interested in listening, especially to news. There is an official telephone in the village. The villagers like political articles and the "funnies" in the newspapers.

Since 1909 there has been an elementary school in the village. Most of the young men are literate. A few are high-school graduates. The young men are aware of and discuss social, economic, and political problems, particularly those which have come to their attention as a consequence of their travel.

Units of distance: In expressing distance, the people of Beşikdüzü use the minutes, hours, and days it takes to make the trip. Distance by sea between the ports they express both in kilometers and in the hours' and days' travel required on ship. For example, they say "It takes — days to sail to Istanbul or Samsun or Rize," as the case may be. Some of the young people who want to impress their intellectual visitors use only kilometers.

Since inland trips are seldom made by motor or horse-drawn vehicles, but on foot, inland distances are usually expressed by the time that it will take to walk to the destination. Inland places which can be reached and returned from in one day are considered in the neighborhood. Points beyond this are considered distant.

Almost all parts of Turkey are known to the men, for many have gone to work in the various provinces. A few men had jobs in Poland and the Soviet Union when World War II started. Such men come back with concrete experiences of social and economic conditions in these places. They spontaneously compare conditions at home with those abroad. For example, they say, "In —— there are lots of crops, but they don't know what to do with them," or "It is better to be a lonely shepherd in —— than to be a farmer here."

To most of the women who have stayed at home while their husbands, brothers, or sons were away, these outside places are only names. The illiterate men who stick to the soil and who have not left the village to work are only slightly different from these women in many respects. The conception of faraway places varies in the case of literate men who have not been away themselves.

Units of time: Old people usually locate events which took place some decades previously in terms of past wars, the general emigration during the first World War, and other such memorable events. The activities most closely connected with their lives serve as reference periods for the subdivisions of time within the year, e.g., "the hazelnut-gathering period" (findik toplama), "the cutting of corn" (misir kesimi), etc. The most important period is the hazelnut-harvesting period. If the hazelnuts are abundant, it is an occasion of extraordinary rejoicing, of singing and dancing in the orchards. If the crop is poor, a general gloom prevails.

The days of the week used in the village are named for market days in the village and the vicinity, i.e., Beşikdüzü Market, Görele Market, Eynesil Market, etc. The market day of the village is especially important in regulating the activities of other weekdays. Time is generally designated in relation to the market day as, for example, a day or two days after market day.

About 80 people in the village regularly use a calendar and a watch or clock. People engaged exclusively in farming still use units based on natural phenomena (sunrise, sunset, etc.)

Conception of strangers: Since many of these villagers go to the markets in the neighboring villages and towns, and since many have worked in all sorts of places, their conception of strangers is rather broad. To them, unlike other villagers, the sight of city people and officials does not seem strange. They engage in long discussions with them. They are personally acquainted with many people from other coastal villages in the area.

On almost any seashore and in any place where there are hazelnut orchards, the people of Beşikdüzü do not seem to experience a feeling of strangeness. They have developed a capacity for making a rapid adaptation to new surroundings even in places with different characteristics. The poor and landless villagers tend to look for chances to work outside the village and to move away from it. This unmistakable impact of material and technological conditions (e.g., the scarcity of land and the travel by water) on the psychological mobility of these people is of particular importance. But the old folks react to this mobility unfavorably. In fact they resist it. It is psychologically painful for them to break the long-established ties with their land, neighbors, etc.

Standards of riches: Among the people, in general, the amount of hazelnuts one raises and hoards for trading purposes is usually used in gauging wealth. For the professional traders, the money accumulated is becoming a more important standard of wealth.

A person who owns 50 *dönüm* of hazelnut orchard and 25 *dönüm* of corn field, and raises 4000 to 5000 kilograms of hazelnuts and 2000 kilograms of corn is considered wealthy. The farmers consider the accumulation of about $2000 a fortune; but for the village traders it is a little over $5000.

Money spent on women, drink, and "luxury" items in clothing and furniture is considered wasted. But some villagers do indulge in them. A man who leaves the village in threadbare clothes and sandals and comes back in "city" clothes faces ridicule from the other villagers.

From this study of five Turkish villages, of which two have been summarized here, we may draw some definite conclusions concerning the effects of modern technology upon the psychology of individuals: [11]

(1) Before the individuals in a village reach the stage of development in which the internationally standardized units of distance, space, and time are used, certain units and anchorages do become standardized, chiefly (allowances being made for the influence of norms and values) as determined by (*a*) the periodicity of their economic and social activities (such

[11] This study is to be published in full.

as their market day); (*b*) the periodicity of certain natural events (such as the sunrise or cycles of the moon) and the compelling features of the surroundings (such as a mountain peak). But such standardized units and anchorages lack precision in varying degrees.

(2) As one passes from more isolated to less isolated, from technologically less-developed to more-developed villages, international units of distance, space, and time are used roughly in proportion to the degree of the impact of modern technology, and their use becomes correspondingly more precise.

(3) A scale of riches exists for every village, the limits of which are set by the financial levels of the rich and the poor in the village. The standard of riches of the individual varies according to his relative position on the scale.

(4) The radius of the world in which the individual lives his daily life widens in proportion to the degree of contact with the products and facilities of modern technology.

(5) Mobility (actual and psychological) is increased proportionate to the degree of these contacts and to economic scarcity and pressure. In other words, the greater the degree of contact and the greater the pressure of economic scarcity, the greater is the mobility toward towns and cities for trade and industry and the greater is the psychological mobility.

We must not lose sight of the effects and distortions brought about by the inertia and reaction of the existing superstructure of values or norms. Such effects, indeed, may roughly correspond to the degree of stability and rigidity of this existing superstructure. We have already discussed the effects of social norms. While keeping in mind all that we have learned concerning this important area of stimulation, we must examine further the effects of material and socio-economic conditions.

Substantiation from Similar Isolated Localities in America, Japan, South Africa, and Mexico

In ethnological and sociological literature, we find material which substantiates the hypotheses concerning technology-mentality relationships derived from this study of five villages. For the most part, of course, such material has been collected for the study of a variety of other problems. But some illustrations collected in different parts of the world are pertinent to these hypotheses. An even larger group of data, containing illustrations of more complicated psychological phenomena than we have considered thus far, makes possible further extension of the conclusions concerning the technology-mentality relationship.

Even in the United States, a country where modern technology has reached perhaps its highest and most widespread development at the present time, it has been possible in fairly recent years to find groups of people who have been virtually isolated from the impact of these developments. One such area in the Blue Ridge Mountains of Virginia was studied for two years by a staff of social scientists and psychologists and was reported by Sherman and Henry in their book, *Hollow Folk*.[12]

The communities studied are located in mountain pockets less than 100 miles from Washington, D. C. The ancestors of the present population, chiefly of English and Scotch-Irish origin, came to the area in the early 1800's. Their "peculiar language" retains many Elizabethan expressions.

The most isolated community is Colvin Hollow, a scattered collection of cabins with garden patches of about 2 acres each. There is no general system of communication between the cabins, and no road to the outside world. The garden plots furnish the main means of livelihood. No modern tools are available. There are "rudiments of a home industry"—basket weaving. About 3 miles away, over a high ridge and along a narrow path, is a summer resort where some of the men and women work sporadically at unskilled jobs in the summer. Only a part of the wages paid is cash. Some men occasionally work as farm hands in the valley, a difficult 8 miles away. Most of the little trading for the Hollow is done by one man who makes about four trips a week across the almost trailless mountains to the valley for supplies. No one in the Hollow can read or write.

The investigators note that in this isolated community:

Ability to make specific space and time differentiations also was quite undeveloped. When a boy nineteen years old was asked where the next family lived, he replied: "Over thar a piece."

[12] M. Sherman and T. R. Henry, *Hollow Folk*, New York: Crowell, 1933.

He didn't know what was meant when asked whether the distance was a mile or a hundred yards. Asked where another family lived, he again replied: " Over thar a piece."

One of these families lived a mile and the other about a quarter of a mile away. He could not differentiate distance in definite terms. The nearest any child came to making such a differentiation was that one family lived "not a far piece over the hill" and that the other lived " a good piece through the woods " (pp. 127–128).

Expressions of units of time were also vague. Only 3 children in the group, including boys and girls in their teens, could tell the days of the week. "Many Colvin children do not know the difference between Sunday and Wednesday or between morning and noon. It is not vital for them to have this information because their way of living does not take into account time or days. All days are practically alike in Colvin Hollow " (p. 135). Only 2 children could tell the year or the month. Three said they had heard of Christmas and Thanksgiving but they did not know what was done on these days. Only a few could give their birthdays.

Some idea of the radius of the world for these Hollow folk is given by the following:

"All the local government asks of the hollow folk is to stay hidden—and this is exactly what they themselves desire. So long as they remain in the mountain pocket the rest of the world is not concerned with their affairs, any more than they themselves are concerned in the affairs of county, state or nation. The Colvin Hollow children know only the name of the town at the foot of the mountains which is visited occasionally by their parents and where they have some relatives " (p. 210). Again: " All appeared satisfied with their environment. None wanted to live in a better house or to travel. They hardly knew that other places exist beyond the mountains " (p. 103). People from outside the Hollow are viewed with great suspicion.

The standard of living in Colvin Hollow is so uniformly low that "there is essentially no difference in the economic status of families " (p. 182). Every person strives only to subsist. As the authors put it, ". . . they measure success by the ability to ward off misfortune " (p. 200).

" In Colvin Hollow, due to limited contacts, the desires of the children are few " (p. 100). They hardly mentioned candy, since they had seen very little.

When asked, " What do you want to be when you grow up?" the children could not answer because they had never come in contact with a diversity of occupations. When the question was explained more fully the usual answer was: "I wants to be what I am " (p. 104).

Struggles for objects to satisfy basic needs and for status, thus, are also determined by the material-technological surroundings in which they occur.

Life in Colvin Hollow was so different from the general run of life in America that the men had little knowledge of regular or systematic work. In observing the rude construction work, the authors noted a lack of any system and even of "initiative" to do the work necessary for physical comfort. Work on garden patches comes closest to being regular; however, even in this case, regular work is done only at sowing and harvest time. Basket-weaving is so sporadic that even paid orders are likely to go unfilled. This slow tempo of life is reflected in the reactions of the children. On intelligence tests, they were found to be so slow and cautious in replying that speed requirements of the tests could not be fulfilled.

Needles Hollow has relatively more contacts with the outside world. It is situated on a trail which connects with the county road leading to the valley. The farms average about 5 acres apiece and almost every family has a pig and chickens. A few men are literate.

Here, " 'the poor and the rich' begin to appear . . . the wealthiest family . . . cultivates twenty-four acres and raises practically all the food it consumes. It also has a surplus of farm products for sale in the valley " (p. 182). Land is apparently the main standard of wealth. It is significant that " many of the farmers say [untruthfully] that they have twenty or thirty acres " (p. 6).

The change in the tempo of life upon leaving the Hollow is so great that comparatively few migrants remain outside. The former school teacher of Needles Hollow, one of the more progressive members of the community, sold all his belongings and moved to a small West Virginia town where he worked in a saw mill. A short time later he returned. When asked why he came back:

"'Wal,' he drawled, 'it's much better here. I gits up in the mornin' when I wants and I do what I wants. No gettin' up with a whistle and eating with a whistle here'" (p. 196).

Oakton Hollow is at the head of a difficult mountain road and "presents the third step upward in the scale." Here, agriculture is more organized. There is a surplus of apples and corn which is traded in the valley. The Hollow has a store and post office and nearly every home has a mail-order catalogue. Occasional trips are made to the valley even by the women.

The tempo of work reflects this increased contact with the outside. There is more specialization of work by sex; and the men are "more energetic" than in Needles Hollow. Further: "The work habits of Oakton Hollow men who seek employment outside the community are regular" (p. 185). The social and economic scales are clearer cut than in the more isolated hollows. Wealth is apparently based on having a surplus of goods or the outward signs of a surplus—clothes, the kind of house one can afford, etc.—much as in other parts of rural America.

But outside work is necessary for a good share of the population. Because of this economic pressure in Needles Hollow and because the people have easier access to the valleys, this Hollow and Rigby Hollow have lost more of their population by migration.

Rigby Hollow, a compact community connected with the valley by a country road, and Briarsville, the small farm and sawmill town in the valley, show a more complex social and economic life, increasingly similar to that in other rural towns in different parts of the country. In Briarsville, regular working hours are maintained.

The desires of these people are more numerous and varied than of the folk from more isolated hollows. "As the culture level rises wants increase. There is greater striving to satisfy additional desires . . ." (p. 100). "At each step upwards the wants of the children showed the influence of the general culture level and the amount of their information. *Wants develop only with experience, once elemental desires are attained*" (p. 102, italics mine).

Residents of Rigby Hollow and Briarsville originally came, for the most part, from the mountains; but now they consider themselves more like people outside the mountains. They are "more friendly to each other and to strangers"; and some families "are striving to 'pass over' from mountaineers to low-landers" (p. 7). In Briarsville, mountaineers are generally disliked. The authors note that the differences to be found between these two communities, particularly Rigby Hollow, and the more isolated hollows are not due to differences in the quality of land and natural resources, for in this respect, "all four communities are on an approximately equal plane. Yet because of the use of tools and equipment the output of Rigby yields incomes sufficiently large to maintain a standard of living far in excess of the three neighboring hollows" (p. 187). Thus, it is the impact of modern technology, in the authors' opinion, which is at the root of these great differences between the communities.

Since 1929, when the study of the Hollow folk was made, the area has become part of a national park. It would be interesting to return to the hollows today to see what changes the impact of the outside world has made on the lives and psychology of the people.

Turning now to a country in an entirely different part of the world, Japan in the period from 1917 to 1924, we find similar differences in behavior and experience in residents of communities with varying degrees of contact with industrial technology. Jones spent four summers among the relatively isolated "mountain folk of Japan" collecting data, by a carefully worked-out questionnaire, in 5 districts isolated in varying degrees from modern technology.[13] And these 5 areas show psychological differences in the conception of strangers, in standards of status, in the aspirations for professions, and in the authority of the family.

As in the Turkish villages and the Virginia mountains, we find the greatest suspicion of outsiders in the villages with least outside contact. The most isolated villagers "did not like"

[13] T. E. Jones, *Mountain Folk of Japan*, Doctoral Dissertation, on file in the Library of Columbia University, New York, 1926.

to call on government officials for help in managing their own affairs. Villagers "more engaged in commerce and in contact with the world outside" were more willing to bring their problems to government officials.

"Shame at having to earn one's living by working for wages instead of producing one's own crop was strongest in those communities little accustomed to the wage and money systems" (p. 48). On the other hand, in Maki, the district most in contact with urban centers, people are more eager to work for wages. Here is found the "greatest desire to become the wealthiest landlord."

As was observed among the Virginia mountaineers, foods, dress, and professions are desired "which have sufficiently entered into experience to appeal to one as possible to attain" (p. 41). Thus, in contrast to members of other communities, the villagers in areas where industry (lumber and silk) was recently introduced want to be merchants.

In the most isolated villages, Gokanoshi and Tatekoshi, the old feudal type of "Great Family" is found. Under this system, the individual has little choice in his behavior. The family council controls matters of discipline. "Where contact with the larger world had been made, its laws and sanctions became recognized in matters outside the immediate household and parents assumed more responsibility for preparing their children for the wider society. Together with the enlargement of the social unit came the growth of the concept of personal worth" (p. 110).

This difference in attitudes and behavior in relation to the family in Japan, as one goes from more to less isolated areas, represents a somewhat more complicated phenomenon than those mentioned earlier. However, there is ample evidence of such differences based on contacts with technology in other parts of the world. For example, Hunter reports them in her study of the effects of contact on the Pondo of South Africa.[14] She studied "three distinct sections of the Bantu community," those on reserves, those on European-owned farms, and those

[14] M. Hunter, *Reaction to Conquest, Effects of Contact with Europeans on the Pondo of South Africa*, London: Humphrey Mildford, Oxford University Press, 1936.

in towns. "The necessity of paying taxes, the desire to buy goods offered by the trader, and the growing land shortage which makes it impossible for the community while following old methods of agriculture to live on the land, drives men, and now also women, to work for Europeans" (p. 5).

As a result, "The co-operative economic unit, the *umzi*, is decreasing in size. . . . The decrease . . . entails change in attitude and behaviour towards kin" (pp. 546–547). On the reserves, where contact is chiefly through the European-owned trading posts, one important change is that "behaviour towards father's brothers and their children cannot approximate so nearly to behaviour towards own father and own brothers . . ." (p. 59). However, there is much visiting between relatives.

On the European-owned farms, where relatives are at some distance from each other but where there are occasional contacts with the towns, "kinship bonds with relatives . . . are weakened. . . . On the other hand, the ties binding neighbours who live on one farm, and work together are strong" (p. 523).

For the natives who work in towns as laborers, the *umzi* has broken down completely. The usual household group is that of man, wife, and their minor children. That this change is standardized is indicated by the fact that *the words used by these townsmen for relatives no longer differentiate between relatives of the father and of the mother.*

Many other changes have appeared in this latter group in particular. It is pertinent for us to note some of the developments resulting from this shift to an industrialized community. In the towns in South Africa, Hunter reports the rise of a class of industrial workers and gives an example of the consequent psychological changes in attitudes: "Here then is a Bantu Community living under what approximate to western economic conditions. We have the familiar picture of a large number of people dependent entirely upon their wage earnings, living in overcrowded insanitary slums. *The similar conditions breed similar attitudes.* I heard two Bantu men talking of the dangers of allowing women to enter industry and 'take men's jobs' and the advantages of a war in which 'all the unemployed would fight and be killed, and the rich men would have to put their hands in their pockets'" (p. 458, italics mine).

The comprehensive comparative study by Professor Redfield, *The Folk Culture of Yucatán*, is replete with material relevant to our problem of technology and mentality relationship.[15] This work brings together "the results of a comparative study of four communities chosen to represent points along this line of contrast: a village of tribal Indians, a peasant village, a town, and the city" (xv). The four communities are graded in the above order from more isolated to less isolated, from technologically less developed to more developed, from less mobile to more mobile.

The tribal village, Tusik, is in the Yucatán Peninsula of Mexico, and has a population of 106; it is at a distance of "three days' ride on a horse or mule" from Chan Kom, the peasant village. With only one exception, every man in the village is engaged in farming with primitive methods. There are no storekeepers, no masons, and no carpenters. "The Tusik people are not peasants but a people economically, politically, and socially independent of the towns" (p. 57).

Chan Kom, the peasant village, has a population of 250 people and is 30 kilometers south of Dzitas, the town that was studied. Chan Kom is at a distance of "a day's walk from the railroad, in the deep brush." The peasants of Chan Kom grow maize without the benefit of any modern tools. There are a few stores in the village, a mason who learned his trade in the city, and a few men who work as carpenters and barbers. But all of these men are farmers first.

Dzitas, the town, has a population of about 1,200 and is a railway junction for three other towns in that area. Most of the transportation from Dzitas is by rail. Dzitas is not altogether agricultural. There are some woodcutters and carters, and a few trackworkers, mechanics, and other artisans.

The city, Merida, with its rapidly increasing population of about 97,000, is the "unchallenged metropolis" of the peninsula in every respect. Merida almost monopolizes within its boundaries the industrial developments of Yucatán. It is the nerve center of Yucatán for both transportation and commu-

[15] R. Redfield, *The Folk Culture of Yucatán*, Chicago: University of Chicago Press, 1941.

nication. Hardly any of the inhabitants are farmers. Merida has a relatively high literacy rate.

With these graded variations in the degree of isolation and technological and economic development, we find, from the data presented by the author, a roughly corresponding gradation of mentality and behavior. Here we must limit ourselves to a few psychological indexes of this trend.

Concerning kinship ties and family relationships which entail various sorts of reciprocal expectations, rights, duties, and allegiances, Redfield concludes: "As one goes from Tusik toward Merida there is to be noted a reduction in the stability of the elementary family; a decline in the manifestation of patriarchal or matriarchal authority; a disappearance of institutions expressing cohesion in the great family; a reduction in the strength and importance of respect relationships, especially for elder brothers and for elder people generally; an increasing vagueness of the conventional outlines of appropriate behavior toward relatives; and a shrinkage in the applicability of kinship terms primarily denoting members of the elementary family toward more distant relatives or toward persons not relatives" (p. 211).

There is a marked change in the behavior of individuals in their commercial relationships. Ruling out the sharp contrasts between the extremes, i.e., the tribal village and the city, we find that the difference becomes marked even between the town and the city. "In Dzitas you may expect to bargain for most commodities sold in stores as well as by traveling merchants, but in Merida in recent years there has developed a conscious movement in favor of fixed prices. The movement is probably partly a direct reflection of foreign standards and partly a response to local conditions: stores have become so large in Merida that many clerks are employed and economic relations within them are as a result more impersonal" (p. 161).

The progressive differentiation of the social and economic functions that groups of individuals carry out is observed by Redfield too. "The differences as to division of labor that appear to the author when Tusik, Chan Kom, Dzitas, and Merida are compared seem to parallel changes which have occurred in the division of labor in the course of recent Western history" (p. 172).

Most of such gradations of psychological indexes and others are summarized in the following passage:

It is in the more isolated villages that the ways of living exhibit to the greatest degree an interrelation of parts and inner consistency. The mode of life of Tusik rather than of Chan Kom, and of Chan Kom rather than of Dzitas, can, therefore, be described as an organized body of conventional understandings. The reference here is not, essentially, to the fact that in the peripheral communities the habits of individual men conform most closely to the customs of the community. This is, of course, also true. In Tusik the outlook on life which one man has is very like that of any other, making allowances for temperamental differences. Even in Chan Kom this may still be said, in spite of the differing degree to which influences from the city have modified the ideas and practices of individuals. In Dzitas the heterogeneity of mental worlds and of corresponding overt behavior is much greater, while in Merida the range of interest, knowledge, belief, and general sophistication is so wide that in describing the life of the city it is necessary to deal with one social class or interest group at a time, and even then general statements as to thoughts and behavior of any one of these are more approximate than are corresponding statements for the entire subtribe in Quintana Roo (p. 110).

Effects of Technology at a More Complicated Level

In short, material and technological conditions play a part in determining not only relatively simple perceptual scales of time and distance, concepts of riches, and the radius of one's world, but also more complicated psychological phenomena. The tempo of life and work, the objects desired to satisfy basic needs, strivings for status (and other sociogenic motives), experience, and behavior toward relatives and friends are seen to be affected in a decisive way by the material surroundings of the individuals. As we have seen, social norms, either interiorized as ego-attitudes or imposed from the outside, are factors in regulating such experience and activity. But especially when the individual faces a concrete material situation with which the behavior regulated by the prevailing social norms conflicts or is at variance, inadequate, or inappropriate, the material stimulating conditions can and, in many cases, do determine the resulting reaction.

If we doubt in the least that material conditions may at times exert an influence more potent than the force of non-material stimuli—or ideas—we need only examine Lang's careful study of the changes in Chinese family life with the industrialization of that country.[16] Whereas it is true that the ideological influence of the West exerts its effect, Lang was forced to conclude: "The environment is mainly—if not exclusively—responsible for the changes among the peasants and workers. They have heard very little, if anything, of modern ideas; but those who live in industrial cities or in rural districts where innovations have taken place and especially those who work in modern factories have seen their family life and relations changed by industrialization" (p. 337).

Lang's surveys showed the reversal of authority in the Chinese family from that of the formerly all-powerful father to the now economically independent children. The once-honored old fathers, far from being the head of ¡the family, are frequently neglected by and are even forced to wait upon their children who have entered the modern industries in Shanghai. Even uneducated Chinese women, once kept busy at home with housework, now face the outside world in factories where they work alongside of men. Besides those who joined militant trade unions or the Red army, Lang found women, still in their old surroundings, assuming new attitudes toward their position and new behavior patterns. Wives who work in factories frequently become head of the family. "One woman explained: 'I have worked in the factory since I was very young and I know more of the world than my husband, who has never left his native village.' The roles of husband and wife were thus reversed. The wife's sphere of activity was the outside world and the husband's was the home" (p. 206).

Opler records an instance when, because of peculiar material conditions, the attitudes of parents toward their children changed radically. The Spanish frontiersmen introduced the horse to the Southern Ute of Colorado—a material innovation which became vital in the Ute's activities directed toward earning a living. They demanded a payment in meat and hides which was prohibitive to the Indians. So "during the period of early contact," the Ute hit upon another form of payment—

---

[16] O. Lang, *Chinese Family and Society*, New Haven: Yale University Press, 1946.

trading their children for horses. Such a practice "was not characteristic of the early family organization." [17]

It is a well-known fact that the number of children born in recent times has fallen off considerably with the coming of modern industrialization and the rise of great cities. An interesting ramification of this general fact is the finding that the birth rate in rural communities more recently mechanized and exposed to modern technology is now declining at a greater rate than that of the cities. A survey of farm populations made in 1931 showed a surprising change from the older rural attitude toward having a family. The large majority of people questioned advocated birth control.[18] Kolb and Brunner see this as directly related to the increasing mechanization of agriculture which makes the labor of children less valuable.

With the impact of modern technology and its products, prestige and status symbols change, and hence the ways and means of acquiring status. For example, a short time after modern goods and technological products were introduced among the Alkatcho Carrier of British Columbia, the possession and lavish display of these goods became "symbols of social prestige. For example, only one Indian at Alkatcho sleeps in a spring bed; but the possession of a spring bed as a display item is a *sine qua non* of social status. Phonographs, chairs, tables, and milled lumber serve the same purpose." [19] Similarly, while lavish giving was formerly the means of gaining status among the Muganda of Africa and the amount of land owned was not an essential reference point for judging status, in recent times, particularly with the introduction of a money economy, the ownership of land and a house with a corrugated iron roof and doors has become the goal of status striving.[20]

In their keen observation of America's Middletown in transition, the Lynds noted how the advance of technology creates status and hence ego problems for the individuals caught in

[17] M. K. Opler, " The Southern Ute of Colorado," in R. Linton (ed.), *Acculturation in Seven American Indian Tribes*, New York: Appleton-Century, 1940, chap. 3, p. 159.

[18] J. H. Kolb and E. de S. Brunner, *A Study of Rural Society, Its Organization and Change*, Boston: Houghton Mifflin, 1935.

[19] I. Goldman, " The Alkatcho Carrier of British Columbia," in R. Linton (ed.), *op. cit.*, chap. 6, p. 375.

[20] L. P. Mair, *An African People in the Twentieth Century*, London: G. Routledge and Sons, Ltd., 1934.

the trend. "Meanwhile, as technology adds more and more 'improved modern ways,' the distance between what different sections of Middletown's population do becomes wider. . . . In a world where everybody heated his house by stove and nobody had running hot and cold water, the lack of these things prompted no social differences, no sense of inadequacy of the family that could 'afford' nothing better, no caustic remarks by wife and children about the husband's meager wages. In such widening disparities in the performance of man's age-old tasks lies one of the most characteristic sources of minor tension in Middletown's culture." [21]

As we have seen in the studies of the Hollow folk and Japanese mountain people, technology may determine not only status strivings and aspirations and other sociogenic motives, but even the regulation and goals of the basic needs. Thus, the recent war brought unimagined work aspirations to the South Sea islanders and a "host of new wants," many related to a fuller satisfaction of man's basic needs.[22] The Ozark families transplanted to the modern industrial city of St. Louis come to prefer bakery sweets to their corn bread and hot biscuits.[23] And to the landowner among the Baganda of Africa who has had a taste of city life, country life and all of its ways seems dull, whereas the standards, ways, and goals of the city are all desirable.[24]

There is considerable evidence that some of the characteristic behavior patterns which psychologists have called "traits" and which are otherwise often considered just so much human nature are changed by material conditions in a society. Lewis' historical study of the effects of white contact on Blackfoot culture, for example, traces the effects of the introduction of the horse, gun, and fur trade upon the warfare of these Plains Indians.[25] The study makes clear that warfare changed, espe-

[21] R. S. Lynd and H. M. Lynd, *Middletown in Transition*, New York: Harcourt, Brace, 1937, p. 197.

[22] F. M. Keesing, *The South Seas in the Modern World*, New York: John Day, rev. ed., 1945.

[23] S. D. Queen and L. F. Thomas, *The City, A Study of Urbanism in the United States*, New York: McGraw-Hill, 1939.

[24] Mair, *op. cit.*

[25] O. Lewis, The effects of White contact upon Blackfoot culture, *Monogr. Amer. Ethnolog. Soc.*, 1942, vi.

cially with the coming of the fur trade, from concerted action of the tribe motivated chiefly by the desire to defend and expand tribal hunting grounds to frequent, small raiding parties carried out with secrecy and stealth for the purpose of securing the horses and guns which had become so vital to their pursuit of the fur trade. The Blackfoot had no "war complex" —the acquisition of their warlike aggressive attitudes can be traced in historic times. A similar change occurred among the Southern Ute of Colorado. Whereas war among the Ute had been "mere localized defense of one's kin," it became a means of enriching the entire band. "The mobility afforded the Ute band by the introduction of the horse led to a type of warfare motivated socially by a desire to loot." With this change, the qualifications for leadership changed. To be a camp leader now, a man had to prove his worth as a daring scout and wise organizer. The most popular camp leaders were those "who called out most often that tonight they danced and tomorrow they raided." [26]

Even within the lifetime of individuals, such changes in personal characteristics have occurred with changes in material conditions. Pointing out the difference between the "traits" of truck farmers with frequent contacts with the city and the Southern Highlander whose contacts with the "outside" are "few and far between," Kolb and Brunner cite the case of one farmer whose ideas changed in the space of ten years, chiefly because of the difficulties involved in the increasing tendency toward one-crop farming. "The farmer who declared in 1924, when asked to join a flourishing co-operative, 'I'll be blanked if anybody's going to tell me when to sell my berries,' was voicing the virile individualism that had characterized his forbears for three centuries in their struggle against the wilderness and the sea. The same man when he capitulated to the co-operative in 1934 had changed none of his innate, inherited characteristics. He was simply bowing to experience." [27]

Even the total conception of personal identity changes with changing material and technological conditions. One of the most penetrating analyses of the effect of the mode of produc-

[26] Opler, op. cit., pp. 164–166.
[27] Kolb and Brunner, op. cit., p. 263.

tion, ownership, and the appropriate social organization on personal identity is presented in Fromm's *Escape from Freedom*.[28] During the Middle Ages, dominated by a feudal system and the all-embracing Church, the majority of people in Europe, the serfs, were wretchedly poor and hardly able to maintain a subsistence level of living. They had no clear experience of themselves as distinct *individuals*. Yet in their role as part of the feudal organization and children of an all-embracing Church, they had psychologically the experience of *security* and *solidarity*. "Medieval society did not deprive the individual of his freedom, because the 'individual' did not yet exist; man was still related to the world by primary ties. He did not yet conceive of himself as an individual except through the medium of his social (which then was also his natural) role. He did not conceive of any other persons as 'individuals' either" (p. 43).

As the feudal system broke down, various religious formations independent of the Church arose (Protestantism) and national states were formed. As the industrial revolution, based on a private ownership system, created a newly propertied and strengthened bourgeois class, fundamental changes were brought about in the psychological picture. As a rising capitalist or *petit bourgeois* or worker whose labor became a property to be hired by the owning class, the individual came to experience his *individuality*. But in turn, owing to the highly competitive nature of the capitalist mode of ownership and the profound changes necessitated by it in social organization and human relationships, the new individuality was inevitably accompanied by the experience of *insecurity, insignificance*, and *aloneness*. "While competition was certainly not completely lacking in medieval society, the feudal economic system was based on the principle of co-operation and was regulated—or regimented—by rules which curbed competition. With the rise of capitalism these medieval principles gave way more and more to a principle of individualistic enterprise. Each individual must go ahead and try his luck. He had to swim or to sink. Others were not allied with him in a common enterprise, they became competitors, and often he was confronted with the choice of destroying them or being destroyed" (p. 61).

[28] E. Fromm, *Escape from Freedom*, New York: Rinehart, 1941.

16.

Men in Critical Situations

THE MAIN THEME OF THE COMPLICATED TOPIC OF THIS CHAPTER may be summarized in a few paragraphs. Critical situations, as represented by conditions of prolonged deprivation, insecurity, or some other kind of crisis, tend to break down, in varying degrees, the established attitudes and modes of social behavior regulated by them. It has been shown time and again that, under the impact of crisis, men become unusually susceptible to the acceptance of new formulations, whether or not these new formulations afford objective and lasting solutions. This fact is usually referred to as the increased suggestibility of the individual in critical situations. From Le Bon on, authors dealing with collective behavior have given detailed descriptions of the heightened "suggestibility and credulity of crowds." [1] Under such critical conditions, men are moved to behave in ways which deviate markedly from the customarily expected modes of reactions prescribed by the prevailing norms of the social setting in question. Out-of-the-ordinary behavior thus produced, exhibiting itself in extreme forms of, say, licentiousness, sadism, or, conversely, in self-sacrifice or heroism (on the battle field, for example), has been described in dramatic terms by various authors. There is danger, in our opinion, in stressing *only* the dramatic aspect of behavior in crisis situations. The analysis has to be extended longitudinally to include the consequences of the prolonged critical situations as well as the underlying conditions. If critical conditions, which may involve deprivations such as hunger, insecurity concerning one's status or one's very identity, etc., are prolonged and affect masses of people, the result in the long run is not

[1] See, for example, G. Le Bon, *The Crowd*, London: T. Fisher Unwin, 1914 edition, pp. 34 ff and 44 ff.

401

chaos or perpetual continuation of extreme modes of behavior, but the rise and standardization of new norms of human relationships and conduct. To toss around in the unstable fluidity of crisis is painful, especially after the initial stage of excitement has subsided. Man has to relate himself to his fellow men and to nature around him in some sort of established order. He tends to carry out the urgent business of living within the framework afforded by some relatively stable constellation of relationships. What we know from the psychology of ego development and ego functioning leads us to posit the hypothesis that man strives to anchor himself securely within a frame of human and natural relationships; that an established constellation of such relationships is the basis of his personal identity; that his feeling of security, his freedom from anxiety depend primarily on being stably placed and on his experience in such a constellation of relationships (Chapters 11 and 12).

The psychological aspect of the tendency of a crisis situation to stabilize is the standardization of a new set of values which, in time, come to be established as the regulators of the new order of things. A glance at any revolution, successful or not, will convince one that it is the end product of more or less widespread critical tension experienced and shared by at least a part of the population. In revolutionary situations, besides wholesale indictments of things opposed by the aroused group, there invariably arises a set of crystallizations embodied in appropriate slogans which express the cherished values of the proposed order. Of course, this does not mean that the values and norms embodied in the slogans of a social upheaval will always bring about lasting stability. They may be solutions or values arrived at by powerful demagogues, as in the case of a Mussolini or a Hitler. In such cases, of course, the crisis situations take new forms and even become intensified when viewed in a long-range perspective. Or, in terms of single individuals, such precarious solutions may reduce the individual to a mere automaton or to a regressed infantile level. For example, individuals under the stress of chaotic conditions and precarious day-to-day existence may seek the protection and security promised by an all-powerful leader like Hitler, thus reducing themselves to mere automatons. In such cases, existence **and** security are obtained at the cost of individual autonomy.[2] Henceforth, the values of the individual are handed down by the authoritarian leader. Security achieved through this kind of submission is not, as we have seen, conducive to the formation of an autonomous ego, which is achieved through the person's own experiences in interpersonal and group relationships (see pp. 258–259). A tragic case of striving to achieve some sort of security under extreme situations of frustration and oppression was reported recently by Bettelheim.[3] Prisoners in Nazi concentration camps, after the initial shock of their internment had subsided, resorted to various devices to preserve intact the identity of their normally established egos. But under the constant, systematic action of the guards to break them down through coercive measures and deprivations, the prisoners did eventually go to pieces, exhibiting individual differences in the rate of disintegration. They regressed to a childish level of behavior. Like children, the temporal and spatial scope of their psychological world became restricted to the immediate situation, with its momentary satisfactions and frustrations. But even at the regressed level of functioning, they did strive to achieve some security. They developed a "childlike dependence" on their guards. And as a corollary of this, the values of the guards and of the Gestapo became their values. They resented fellow prisoners who still tried to behave in terms of the values and relationships of the world outside. In this new atmosphere of childlike behavior, those who still resisted the breakdown of their former selves were accused of endangering the security of the group.

The great deprivations and frustrations experienced by masses of people, rendering them highly restless, excited, and determined to resolve the tension, the crystallization of organized leadership with the solutions and slogans it offers, and the subsequent uprisings, with various degrees of grim consequences and, at times, the overthrow of the old organization and values (as in the American, French, and Russian revolu-

---

[2] E. Fromm, *Escape from Freedom*, New York: Rinehart, 1941.
[3] B. Bettelheim, Individual and mass behavior in extreme situations, *J. Abn. & Soc. Psychol.*, 1943, 38, 417–452.

tions) afford illustrations *par excellence* of collective behavior of men in critical situations. But such great crises and upheavals are so complex, and conditions fluctuate through so many decades of time, that it will be safer to start with incidents which take place within a more easily specifiable and shorter time span.

Behavior in Critical Situations

Ours is a period of great mass deprivation and insecurity owing to prolonged unemployment, the most catastrophic of all wars in human history, economic and political unrest, etc. The bitter products are hunger, lack of shelter and fuel, and a prevailing sense of insecurity and anxiety in all nations throughout the world today. Of course, an adequate analysis of the situation itself goes far beyond the bounds of psychology. We can, as psychologists, deal only in terms of the effects on the individuals and their subsequent reactions to them. In short, these circumstances are changing men; and men, in turn, are changing the course of society. Even in less tempestuous times and societies human deprivation is an important factor in bringing about culture change. This is apparent in the recently accumulating accounts of ethnologists. For example, Linton concludes, on the basis of detailed study of various tribes in the process of transition: "Imperfections of cultural adaptations result in individual discomforts and dissatisfaction and these, in turn, provide the motives for culture change." [4]

In our day the crisis, in its various phases, is so sharp that one does not have to look in a longitudinal way to observe the unmistakable facts of collective unrest and collective action. The newspaper dispatches and on-the-spot radio broadcasts from various parts of the world almost constantly report some such conditions as: "The specter of hunger that stalks Europe has given rise to many 'food riots' from Germany to Italy and from France to the Balkans." [5] "Ruhr's 300,000 coal miners walk out with the slogan 'Fight the War Against Hunger,'"

[4] R. Linton, *Acculturation in Seven American Indian Tribes*, New York: Appleton-Century, 1940, p. 467.
[5] *New York Times Magazine*, May 25, 1947.

FIG. 29. Mass deprivations impel people to collective unrest.

Fig. 30. Mass movements cut across age levels.

while "German Youths Riot for Food." [6] Hundreds of similar cases could be cited.

The specter of hunger knows no boundaries. We see it in Austria where the strikers carry a huge self-explanatory poster. (Fig. 29.) The unrest and the inevitable collective protest strike all age levels as well as national boundaries. In Fig. 30 we see aged Parisian women demonstrating for more bread. In such times of frustration and disorder, the behavior of ordinarily civilized individuals regresses collectively to the uninhibited instinctual level. Several news correspondents accompanying the advancing American armies in early 1945 reported mass looting of fuel and food by the ordinarily well-disciplined German civilians.[7] When the German city of Essen fell in April, 1945, the troops "found the streets full of drunken civilians." [8] These are only samples. The collective unrest and action resulting from hunger and frustration, the widespread strikes of workers who cannot make ends meet with the wages they get, can be multiplied indefinitely.

In critical times of danger and suspense, as during the tense period of an approaching or actual war, or life under an enemy power, or defeat, feelings of security become so precarious, nerves so jumpy, that even relatively minor incidents (which might be taken for granted in more stable times) may be sufficient to create collective *panic* and disorder. Many incidents of collective panic are reported from present-day occupied Germany. We shall take our illustration from an altogether different part of the world.

In the tense and unsettled atmosphere of Japan today, a false radio announcement of the approach of a sea monster recently upset the people of Tokyo. "Tokyo was thrown into an uproar early tonight when a series of radio bulletins announced that a 20-foot-high sea monster was advancing into the center of the city. . . . Japanese police put out an alarm through all police boxes between here [Tokyo] and Yokohama. The number of Japanese telephoning for confirmation or denial was

[6] *New York Herald Tribune*, April 2 and 3, 1947.
[7] For example, see John Mecklin's reports to the newspaper *PM* during March and April, 1945.
[8] *New York Times*, April 12, 1945.

estimated in the thousands." [9] Such panic behavior is not the peculiarity of the Japanese psychology alone. During the tense days preceding World War II, thousands of people in the New York area were thrown into mass hysteria by Orson Welles' realistic radio presentation of H. G. Wells' play depicting an imaginary invasion by Martians. Right after the explosion of the atomic bomb in Hiroshima, some of the survivors tried to find refuge in a park. When it started to rain, a panic spread like wildfire: "The Americans are dropping gasoline. They're going to set fire to us!" [10] Similarly, the "flying disks" in the sky reported widely throughout the United States in the summer of 1947 coincided with the current intensification of war talk.

In considering the effect of prolonged deprivations and suspended anxieties in bringing about mass unrest and action, we as *social* psychologists must keep in mind the following significant facts that we have already encountered in our discussion of motivation and ego psychology:

1. A major implication for our present problem is the cyclical or periodic nature of basic needs. We are referring here, again, to the differential periodicity of the functioning of the biogenic needs. One has to breathe cyclically. One has to eat, drink, and sleep periodically. The periodicity of the different needs varies temporally. This may be seen by comparing the relatively short hunger circle with that of sex. The need cycles are, of course, subject within limits to cultural variations. But no culture can regulate eating, drinking, or sleeping so that they will take place, say, a week apart. As the daily papers are stressing nowadays, hunger cannot wait. Of course, we are aware that the whole organism may be gripped by whatever motive is suffering the greatest deprivation at the time.

2. Especially in modern differentiated societies, we are absolutely dependent on the smooth functioning of the services of other individuals and groups for the satisfaction of certain essential needs. Except for the air we breathe and, in rural areas, the water to drink, we are dependent on others for food, fuel, and shelter, especially in cities. Consequently, the

---

[9] Ralph Chapman, in the *New York Herald Tribune*, May 30, 1947.

[10] J. Hersey, *Hiroshima*, New York: Knopf, 1946, p. 52.

great social issues inherent in mass deprivation and its effects
appear in obtaining the goal objects (food, fuel, shelter, etc.) for
which we are dependent on social organization and collective
labor. It is the situations that bring about prolonged deprivation of food, fuel, shelter, and the like and that threaten masses
of people *simultaneously*, which are particularly conducive to
the emergence of direct mass action. And such mass action involves a crystallization of some sort of group structure embodying the leader-member relationship and supra-individual
properties peculiar to the group. (See the discussion of the
properties of groups in Chapter 5.)

Since a shortage of such essentials as food and fuel affects
people simultaneously, there tend to spring up collective
groupings of people with a common goal, impelled to meet
the situation in some way. Many concrete examples of this
result of simultaneous deprivation can be found in the present-
day world. At present, politicians seem fully to realize this
fact and its realistic implications. The same immediate need
for collective action cannot be posited for out-of-phase deprivations and frustrations suffered by single individuals in
the course of their life. However, these individually sustained
frustrations may drive people to be social dissidents or radicals
and thus, in their turn, eventually contribute their share in
effecting social change.

3. Another important area for special consideration by the
social psychologist is the situations of danger, the breakdown of
the established material and cultural moorings of the existing
society in which the individual is placed. Situations of mass unemployment such as the world at large faced in the 1930's, the
threat of invasion or air raids, the widespread suspense experienced by millions of people before a war, or a threat of loosing
firmly established interests and ways of life are illustrations of
the point. In all of these situations, thousands and even millions of people face the same fate *simultaneously*. Facing such
situations in common, people cannot help sharing their experience, and this sometimes leads them to collective action of
varying proportions. Of course, there are situations in which
individually we face real or fancied dangers. If these individual
cases are numerous, they eventually have an impact on the life

of the community. But as social psychologists, it is our concern to note the impact of danger and insecurity which descend upon masses of people simultaneously.

The illustrations of behavior in critical situations reported in the preceding pages and the statements made in connection with them were, on the whole, rather general. We need better-controlled observations and a more specific conceptualization of the topic, with a view to extracting a minimum of essential features common to behavior in all critical situations. Only after extending our observations to a more precise level can we find out if the essentials also operate in full-scale crisis situations as represented by social movements—of course always being sufficiently open-minded to recognize the wealth of special factors entering into each particular case.

Unfortunately, controlled observations of behavior in crisis situations are in their initial stages and are consequently scanty. Therefore, we shall have to derive our leads in large part from what we have already learned in the discussion of deprivations (pp. 75–90) and insecurities (pp. 124–132) and their effects on group behavior.

As was fully discussed earlier, the individual undergoing some deprivation tends to be preoccupied with securing the goal objects he is deprived of. His perceptions, memories, imagination, and, if circumstances permit, his actions are all colored accordingly. In cases in which positive action leading to the primary goals is barred by circumstances, a person usually indulges in individual or collective "substitutive activities" which may, at times, acquire pathological features. Resort, individually, to various kinds of fantasies or to fate-like resignation, and refuge, collectively, in bizarre cults, sects, or artistic ventures are examples. If the deprivation continues beyond certain limits, it so dominates the individual that the socially established level of attitude and behavior breaks down; that is, the experience and conduct regulated by moral values, observance of civilized codes, and etiquette are obliterated. For example, in the hungry, destitute Europe of today, the principles ordinarily observed in making a living no longer operate for large sections of the population. The only concern is to survive at any cost—"and there is no reason to be fussy about how you do it."[11] Semi-starved individuals have no qualms about licking the plates from which they ate their precious food, an act which would ordinarily shock people (pp. 75–82). Even such a fundamental psychological localization as the passage of time may be impaired.[12]

As we have stressed several times, the breakdown of established material and social moorings is painful for individuals whose psychological functioning on a higher cerebral level is not impaired to any extent. As several studies indicate, the tendency is to reestablish oneself with some degree of stability in a real or fancied way. Especially if individuals facing an unfortunate common lot are situated so that they can interact as a group, there invariably arises some sort of group structure determined by the peculiarities of the circumstances. Such group formations give the members a basis for an established identity, and a course of action directed toward relieving their deprivations and anxieties, as the case may be, within the framework of the newly emerging group. Spontaneous group formations embodying some form of status hierarchy and mutual loyalties and responsibilities among the down-trodden, wretched, and outcast demonstrate this fact, even though they may be precarious structures and may appear amorphous from outside.

The more usual and consequential outcome in chaotic times is that many people are compellingly attracted by the formulations or slogans of the *leaders* of organized groups. These are the times when wretched unstable people turn to the crystallizations of the pressure groups, even though at times their appeal may be merely demagogic. (This may give a clue to the myriad cults now flourishing.)

Unfortunately, direct evidence based on controlled observations is still wanting. However, some representative observations on individuals experiencing deprivation and insecurity concerning in-group and out-group delineations, and the attitudes that result from them, give substantial justification to our hypothesis.

---

[11] *This Week Magazine*, August 10, 1947, p. 17.

[12] P. Eisenberg and P. F. Lazarsfeld, The psychological effects of unemployment, *Psychol. Bull.*, 1938, 35, p. 360.

One telling line of evidence is the spontaneous formation of gangs consisting largely of youngsters who have been deprived of many essentials of life and of security because of broken or unsettled families and brought up in the interstitial areas of great cities. It has been found time and again that children who from early infancy are subjected to basic deprivations and do not succeed in establishing stable roots in established society gravitate toward each other, form more or less well-structured groups with a hierarchy of definite leadership-membership roles, and follow the dictates of group action, at times in the face of great hazards. It is from their membership in these groups as leaders or followers that they derive their sense of security and seek the satisfaction of their needs that is otherwise denied them. The frustrating conditions and unstable fluidity of the slum areas of great cities are conducive to such group formations and to action which occasionally leads to various kinds of riots. In an extensive survey of such group formations and activities in various cities, Shaw and McKay reached the conclusion that they are "products of the operation of general processes more or less common to American cities." [13]

The crisis situation that many adolescent boys (and girls) face as a consequence of being neither child nor adult and the, to them, hostile infringements of the adult world lead many of them to seek stability and satisfaction in the intimacy of groups spontaneously formed with kindred souls. As can be seen from so many newspaper reports, these youthful groups may turn to wildness.

The rise of strong in-group feelings and hostility towards others is well demonstrated in the controlled study of starvation reported earlier at some length (pp. 75–82). During the starvation period, in-group demarcations developed which excluded both non-starving friends and the laboratory personnel —in short, all those not on a restricted diet. The hostility toward outsiders is evident in this typical observation:

One man commented in a letter to a friend, "I'm so hungry I could eat anything, but I'd start on the fat staff first." The men were annoyed at seeing the staff eat their lunches, and were still more

[13] C. R. Shaw and H. D. McKay, *Juvenile Delinquency and Urban Areas*, Chicago: University of Chicago Press, 1942, p. 435.

annoyed when the staff tried to conceal the fact that they were eating—"There he sat, fat, hiding his lunch, while the aroma from his orange still permeated the air." [14]

A clear-cut illustration of in-group feelings aroused toward those who share a common experience and hostility toward others in a frustrating situation is reported by Sears, Hovland, and Miller.[15] These investigators observed the reactions of six university students to a variety of frustrating situations during the last 12 hours of a 24-hour period of sleep deprivation. The frustrating situations were as follows: At midnight, smoking by the subjects was prohibited, although the experimenters continued to smoke in their presence. An experimenter who was to have brought games and cards for their diversion at midnight appeared at 3 A.M. but had "forgotten" the games. An interesting discussion among the subjects was interrupted with a period of enforced silence. When the subjects requested food, they were told that a hot breakfast would be served at 5 A.M.; but the experimenter who went for the food failed to return.

These frustrating situations, endured collectively by the sleep-deprived subjects, encouraged the formation of an in-group from which the experimenters were excluded. Whereas there were only one or two instances of aggressive behavior within the group in the form of "socially acceptable jokes and wisecracks," the "aggression which all subjects showed was directed largely at the E's [experimenters]." "Aggression toward the E's was manifested by quite overt remarks, many of them in the form of accusatory questions asked in a hard, unfriendly tone" (p. 278). For example, toward the end of the experiment, the following remarks were recorded:

"*5:15* A.M. '*Are all psychologists mad?*' '*They're all queer. I've been watching 'em for a couple of hours.*' . . .

"*5:30* A.M. (One S addressed an E as '*Doctor*') '*Don't call him Doctor; you must be a freshman.*' (Mumbling agreement from other S's) " (p. 280).

One aggressive activity, carried out by the "most out-

[14] H. S. Guetzkow and P. H. Bowman, *Men and Hunger*, Elgin, Ill.: Brethren Publishing House, 1946, pp. 30, 28.

[15] R. R. Sears, C. I. Hovland, and N. E. Miller, Minor studies of aggression: I. Measurement of aggressive behavior, *J. Psychol.*, 1940, 9, 277–281.

spokenly aggressive" subject but shared by all, is the spontaneous drawing reproduced in Fig. 31. These sketches were passed around among the subjects who all laughed heartily at them. When the artist was asked what they represented, he replied: "*Psychologists.*"

If the experiment had been continued with no time limit, we believe that the in-group formation would have become even more clearly delineated, hostility toward those in authority would have increased—probably breaking down completely the established norms of respect regulating the professor-student relationship—and group action directed toward escaping from the frustrating situation would eventually have been taken.

Crystallization of New Values in Great Social Movements

Especially in our times, societies are far from being static patterns or closed systems. As a consequence of many factors— the introduction of new technological developments which sooner or later are reflected in new modes of human relationships; the contacts with and even onslaughts of other social systems and cultures which become inevitable whether culture purists like it or not; the inescapable cross diffusion of ideologies; and the catastrophic consequences of wars—societies are in the process of rapid change. In the preceding chapter we touched upon one aspect of the problem.

The periods of great social movements, like the rise of a propertied bourgeois class, the rise of modern industrialism, the Renaissance, the Reformation, various revolutions, are, it is safe to say, the periods of the greatest tempo of social change. It is at these times that new values appear, spread, and become crystallized to regulate the newly established order of human relationships.

An adequate account of the conditions that underlie the great social revolutions and the behavior of men in them holds the promise of revealing to us the major variables involved in the psychology of social change. This rather highly general statement has its basis, psychologically, in the results of recent controlled experiments. The verified findings of the studies in the past decade or so indicate that the acceptance of new ideas

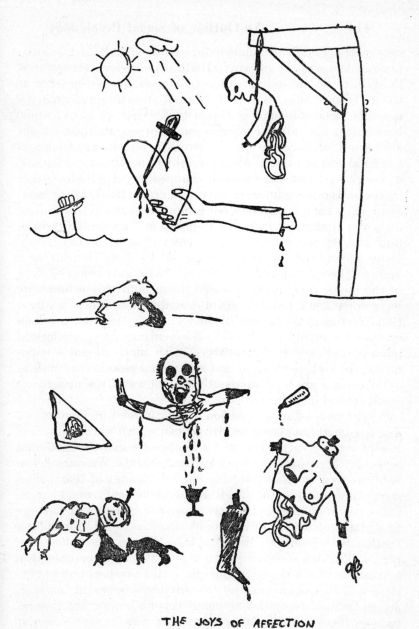

THE JOYS OF AFFECTION

FIG. 31. Spontaneous drawings revealing the hostility aroused in a deprivation situation. (From R. R. Sears, C. I. Hovland, and N. E. Miller, in *J. Psychol.*, 1940, 9, 275–295.)

and values is substantially enhanced by the instability, fluidity, and vagueness of the situations that the individuals face, and by the failure of the individuals' existing frames of reference to cover the new situation. This perceptual-attitudinal aspect is only one important part of the picture. What we have learned concerning the positive correlation between attitude change and group membership greatly broadens our understanding of the total picture. Social ideas are seldom accepted or rejected, and social attitudes are seldom changed or perpetuated solely on the basis of mere information or their objective truth or falseness. They are a function of our group membership—i.e., ideas, attitudes emanating from the in-group or "congenial" groups find a receptive ground; those emanating from out-groups (especially if the individual is hostile to them) encounter a highly deflecting medium. In the above recapitulation of some of the major conclusions stressed throughout this volume, we have not made a point of again describing the role of motivational factors in the process of change. Perception, attitude, and group membership are almost never mere cognitive, intellectual affairs; they are highly charged with motivational components. In fact, perceptual and attitudinal reactions as well as overt actions are used frequently as indexes of the underlying motivational factors.

After this brief recapitulation of certain relevant conclusions discussed earlier at some length, we can return to their implications for the greatly accelerated tempo of social change found especially in periods of great social movements. We cannot here venture even to enumerate the special features of the various social movements. But in all social movements which entail serious consequences in the experience and behavior of men, we find in a large section of the population discontent, unrest, and friction in relation to the established setup, its values and norms. The discontent, unrest, and friction may be caused in one case by the frustration inherent in the exasperating restrictions and checks imposed by the privileged governing class on an expanding, strengthening populace, or a large group thereof, to keep them in their place. In another case they may be due to oppression and tyranny experienced as such by the people who are subjected to them. In another, they may result from

serious curtailment of the means of livelihood or threats to the
security of life itself. In such cases, mass deprivation, insecurity,
and suffering reach compelling proportions. The existing setup
and its rules and values are no longer able to relieve the tension; in fact, they aggravate it. As a consequence, prevailing
values or norms begin to lose their hold on men. But the break
is not abrupt. People are not inclined to throw away their well-
established values as they discard an old pair of shoes. These
constitute the constellation of their subjective security and
the stable components of their very identity which contribute,
in a major way, to their continuity as *human* beings from day
to day. Men must find new moorings as members of a new
group with its appropriate values before they can get rid of
the old ones. Fundamental attitude shifts, especially if they are
ego-attitudes, are a function of new membership groups.

The people sharing the common lot of severe oppression,
exploitation, and deprivation eventually develop an in-group
belongingness and loyalty as distinguished especially from the
hostile out-group. Appropriate in-group feelings and values
arise or become strengthened. In conflicts with the governing
group, which naturally closes its ranks against the onslaught of
the new movement and resorts to various degrees of coercive
action to keep it in place, the in-group solidarity and its appropriate values are strengthened still further, and attitudes of
hostility toward adversaries become intensified in the same
degree. The direction and values of the discontented, restless
populace become crystallized in *slogans* which may be originated,
or at any rate are seized upon and widely circulated, by the
torch-bearers or leaders of the movement. In this tense and
critical atmosphere of conflict between the established order
and the rising movement, incidents which at ordinary times
might remain local may lead to great mass actions with eventful consequences. In time, the values embodied in the slogans,
which might be considered shocking or treasonable by people
of respectability at the time, become the source of the established values of the respectability of the new order.

It seems that the periods of momentous social change, as
exemplified by great revolutions, justify the formulation outlined above. The American Revolution, the French Revolu-

tion, the Paris Commune, and the Russian Revolution are the best testing grounds for any conceptualization of the psychology of social change. Since a book on social psychology is not the place for a detailed analysis of these momentous events, we shall restrict the discussion to the American and French Revolutions.[16]

The intensification of the spirit of self-government and liberty among the colonists in the decade or so preceding the outbreak of the American Revolution was the product of the characteristic imperial attitude and conduct toward colonies. This characteristic attitude of the British oligarchy of the time has been summarized by the Beards as "the almost universal belief in England that the colonies were subordinate socially and intellectually as they were politically and economically." [17] Hence, "the permanent subordination of the colonies to the interests of the British governing classes" was the generally accepted policy.

Whereas this attitude of the British ruling class did not meet active opposition in the politically, intellectually, and economically less-developed colonies at that time, it was opposed by the American colonists. Eighteenth-century Englishmen found these colonists "of a disposition haughty and insolent, impatient of rule, disdaining subjection." [18] They had achieved political maturity. They had managed their local affairs through their legislative assemblies to a large extent. They saw themselves politically on a par with their English brethren. This attitude was expressed by George Mason of Virginia: "We claim nothing but the liberty and privileges of Englishmen, in the same degree, as if we had still continued among our brethren in Great Britain." [19] Likewise, the American colonists were making rapid strides, on a domestic and international scale, in agriculture and commerce. "American business and agricul-

[16] The conceptual scheme in which the illustrations of great social movements are treated here is essentially the same as that presented by Sherif in The psychology of slogans, *J. Abn. & Soc. Psychol.*, 1937, 32, 450–461.

[17] C. A. and M. R. Beard, *A Basic History of the United States*, New York: The New Home Library, 1944, p. 87.

[18] Quoted by J. C. Miller, in *Origins of the American Revolution*, Boston: Little, Brown and Company, 1943, p. 3.

[19] *Ibid.*, p. 168.

tural enterprise was growing, swelling, and beating against the frontiers of English imperial control." [20]

On the other hand, the British mercantilists saw no reason for altering their established course in relation to the colonies—in fact, no "impropriety in consigning the Western Hemisphere to a position of perpetual economic inferiority." [21]

The bills curtailing colonial trade and the enactments of the British Parliament levying taxes caused serious discontent and resentment among different sections of the colonial population. The Royal Order of 1763 "reserving to the King the disposal of Western lands beyond a certain line" and the Sugar and Currency Acts of 1764 are among the curtailments imposed upon the colonists. These and other grievances were destined to find glowing expression in the Declaration of Independence.

Nor did the business depression following the war with the French which ended in 1763 and which was so costly to the American colonies help matters. "In the swift reaction that followed, inflated prices collapsed, business languished, workmen in the towns were thrown out of employment, farmers and planters, burdened by falling prices, found the difficulties of securing specie steadily growing." [22] The discontented urban laborers as well as the small farmers provided fertile soil for revolutionary ideas.[23]

The Stamp Act of 1765 "taxing numerous articles and transactions in America" solidified the in-group feelings of the colonists in their grievances against the mother country. For, unlike previous acts, this one hit everyone alike, "from the meanest peasant" to the "wealthy propertied class." [24] It started a chain of violent mass actions and inspired the convening of the Stamp Act Congress which signaled American solidarity.

Patrick Henry's fiery speech in the Virginia House of Burgesses denouncing the measure found almost universal response

---

[20] C. A. and M. R. Beard, *The Rise of American Civilization*, New York: Macmillan, 1930, Vol. I, p. 201.

[21] Miller, *op. cit.*, p. 5.

[22] C. A. and M. R. Beard, *The Rise of American Civilization*, p. 211.

[23] Miller, *op. cit.* p. 54.

[24] *Ibid.*, p. 129.

in the colonists' hearts. The slogan "No taxation without representation" became the expression of colonial unrest and defined the stand at the time. The British-appointed stamp masters were violently denounced and actually driven out or prevented from carrying out the duties of their office, especially by the Sons of Liberty who began to spring up in all parts of the colonies.[25] "Henry had in fact expressed what thousands of colonists were thinking but dared not speak. His resolves dispelled the indecision and doubt which had prevented effective resistance to the Stamp Act; where the Old Dominion trod, the other colonies did not fear to follow. The resolves gave 'the Signal for a general outcry over the Continent' and made certain that resistance would be based upon a denial of Parliament's right to tax the colonies. In this sense, they mark the beginning of the revolutionary movement in the American colonies." [26]

From that time on there was no end to the simmering of the colonial pot. The repeal of the Stamp Act, which soon followed, was hailed as a sign of the achievement of in-group solidarity and created self-confidence in the efficacy of collective action.

On the other side of the ocean, the British ministry and the Parliament were determined to keep their grip on the colonies. This determination was expressed in such acts as the Declaratory Act of 1766 "asserting the supremacy of the British Parliament in making laws for the colonies" and the Tea Act of 1767 "regulating importation of tea in British dominions in America in favor of the British East India Company." Such acts were not to be accepted any longer by the colonists, who were committed collectively to the principle of "no taxation without representation" and to defiance of laws not enacted by their own assemblies. The overwhelming attitude of defiance gave rise to a wave of collective outbursts, such as the Boston Tea Party, which spread like wildfire to other colonies. These actions were considered by them as being "of absolute moral and political necessity, and therefore exempt from even good laws." [27] Here

[25] A detailed account of these events may be found in Miller, *op cit.*, chap. 6, "The Stamp Act Crisis."

[26] *Ibid.*, p. 126.

[27] *Virginia Gazette*, March 3, 1774, quoted in *ibid.*, p. 349.

we see clear instances of the breakdown of the existing rules and norms when they are no longer the cherished property of an in-group in the process of formation. Conversely, here are revealed the spontaneous acceptance and observance of new norms when they are products of the interaction of the newly emerging in-group.

The coercive acts to which the British resorted to keep peace and order, as they conceived these qualities, precipitated new and more violent conflicts between the opposing parties, such as the Boston Massacre of March 5, 1770. As the intensity of the crisis grew, the contending groups became immersed in the self-righteousness of their own cause and deeds, and were prone to accept wholesale even the most exaggerated imputations concerning the other's conduct.

In this tense atmosphere, colonial solidarity and a possible course of action were focalized in the first Continental Congress, which brought together representatives of the aroused colonies. In the prevailing uncertainty and vacillation, the radical elements were veering in the direction of a clear-cut course for independence, at first without success. But the population, with the exception of some of the gentry, was so aroused that pursuit of the course advocated by the more radical elements in the Congress was inevitable. The fateful series of events which culminated in the Declaration of Independence was motivated by this "surge of revolutionary temper from below." As the Beards concisely summarized the situation: "Strictly speaking, the movement for the break with Great Britain was spreading upward from the colonies to the Continental Congress, rather than downward to the colonies from the Congress." [28] This spirit was expressed in Joseph Hawley's letter to Samuel Adams on April 1, 1776: "The People are now ahead of you, and the only way to prevent discord and dissension is to strike while the iron is hot. The People's blood is too hot to admit of delays—All will be in confusion if independence is not declared immediately." [29] This observation is an indication of the important functional relationship of *leadership-membership roles* in social movements. As we have already

---

[28] C. A. and M. R. Beard, *A Basic History of the United States*, p. 106.
[29] Quoted by Miller, *op. cit.*, p. 485.

said (pp. 101–106), *leadership* stands in a definite functional relationship within the given hierarchy of a movement. A movement may be initiated at the outset by a handful of determined leaders who know the discontent and restlessness of the people to whom they appeal. But once the movement starts to acquire a definite leader-and-membership structure and gets under way, the leader is no longer free to stop or alter the course of action as his whims dictate. If he does, he is cut off from the movement, loses his position, and, at times, attracts the wrath of the erstwhile admiring members. In short, the leader leads as long as he understands the basic objective of the movement, keeps pace with it, and has foresight in charting its direction.

The crisis in America had gone too far to be settled by ordinary methods of discussion within the limits of cold logic. The popular movement was too active to be retracted; it would subside only after positive gains. "During the winter of 1774–1775, the 'menaces of blood and slaughter' which reverberated through the New England countryside became increasingly ominous. New Englanders were clearly preparing to take full advantage of the approval placed upon a defensive war by the Continental Congress; and if the British troops ventured far from Boston they might well expect a warm reception from the Yankees." [30]

The outbreak of open revolution thus awaited a relatively minor incident. And on April 18 and 19, 1775, at Lexington and Concord, "the shot heard round the world" provided that incident, and the clash became open. It is psychologically noteworthy that the identity of the group which fired the first shot is still a source of controversy. In the tense atmosphere of crisis in the 1770's, the incident might well have occurred at another spot and on another day on the American coast wherever the aroused antagonists faced each other. People—stirred, moved, restless—cannot remain in the agony of suspense forever. One way or another, the tension has to be resolved.

In the clash of the two groups, the Americans emerged as a distinct sovereign group with its own structure and definite in-group and out-group delineation. Before this distinct group

[30] *Ibid.*, p. 398.

or national entity found formal expression in the statutes, it shaped itself psychologically in the hearts of the people. In the course of events, "the mother country began to appear in American eyes as a foreign, despotic and 'Papist' power." [31]

All of this found clear-cut crystallization in the resounding words of Tom Paine's *Common Sense* in January, 1776, and in the Declaration of Independence, which sums up the entire situation. In these documents, which were eagerly seized upon by the people as their own, the Americans found a glowing formulation of the thoughts and aspirations they were striving to express. These documents took the bull by the horns and removed the last vestige of doubt and vacillation. "Before *Common Sense*, Americans had professed to reverence the British Constitution and had declared that they were defending their own liberties and the rights of the King against the usurpation of Parliament. But Paine's attack upon the principle of monarchism struck at the very foundations of the British Constitution and largely destroyed its sanctity in the eyes of Americans. Its abuses and shortcomings were now laid bare in order to persuade the colonists of the necessity of independence; the beauties which Americans had once beheld in it withered under the blasts of Tom Paine and his fellow propagandists." [32]

The slogans that arose and became crystallized in the tense atmosphere of crisis, such as "Life, Liberty, and the Pursuit of Happiness," were destined to be the source of new established values which henceforth became the regulators of experience and conduct and, in time, solidified the cultural terrain of the new status quo and respectability.

The French Revolution which came into the open in 1789 constituted an epoch-making social transition and upheaval. The values that emerged as brilliant torches in the midst of crisis, violent collective action, bloodshed, and counterrevolution came to be the regulators of social relationships not only in France, but also eventually in many other countries. Here we can mention only the bare essentials.

[31] *Ibid.*, paraphrasing General Thomas Gage, p. 374.
[32] *Ibid.*, p. 469.

On one side, there was the growing influence of the propertied middle class which was acquiring a dominant position in industry, commerce, etc. On the other, there were the decadent privileged aristocracy and the remnants of feudalism, with their survival trimmings. The existing setup of rules and values did not express this social reality. There was no longer any connection between economic and social realities and the superstructure of norms and etiquette. The inevitable clash was long in the making. In the words of Mathiez, perhaps the greatest authority on the subject, the French Revolution "arose from the ever increasing divorce between reality and law, between institutions and men's way of living, between the letter and the spirit." [33]

Consequently, the prevailing values of the day, which were products of feudal times and the heyday of the rule of aristocracy, rapidly lost their hold on great masses of people. Even long-entrenched religious values "no longer had any attractions" (p. 13). On the intellectual side, the writings of Voltaire, Diderot, Rousseau, and others had been doing the spadework for a new revolt against the worn-out institutions and modes of human relationships. The innovators were destined to win the day (p. 3).

The living conditions which rendered life intolerable in the years just preceding 1789 brought the conflict to a head. A few concrete instances of these conditions, which become more meaningful against the general background of social relationships characterized briefly above, will make the picture of crisis more clear. For example:

At Abbéville there were 12,000 workmen unemployed, at Lyons, 20,000 and the numbers at other places were in proportion. At the beginning of the winter, which was a very hard one, it was necessary in the large cities to organize workshops supported by charity, especially as the price of bread was constantly rising. The harvest of 1788 had been much below normal. The shortage of forage had been so great that the farmers had been forced to sacrifice part of their cattle and to leave some of their lands uncultivated, or else sow it without previous manuring. The markets were short of supplies.

[33] A. Mathiez, *The French Revolution*, New York: Knopf, 1929, p. 1.

Not only was bread very dear, but there was a risk that it would run short. . . . The wretched people cast covetous glances upon the well-filled barns in which their lay and ecclesiastical lords stored up the proceeds of their tithes and their rents in kind.[34]

The counterpart of this critical situation in terms of single individuals is expressed by Taine in describing the plight of a peasant of the time:

I am miserable because they take too much from me. They take too much from me because they do not take enough from the privileged classes. Not only do the privileged classes make me pay in their stead but they levy upon me ecclesiastical and feudal dues. When from an income of a hundred francs, I have given fifty-three and more to the tax collector, I still have to give fourteen to my seignor and fourteen more for my tithe and out of the eighteen or nineteen francs I have left, I have yet to satisfy the excise-officer and the salt-tax-farmer. Poor wretch that I am, alone I pay for two governments the one obsolete, local, which is today remote, useless, inconvenient, humiliating, and makes itself felt through its restraints, its injustices, its taxes; the other new, centralized, ubiquitous, which alone takes charge of every service, has enormous needs and pounces upon my weak shoulders with all its enormous weight.[35]

The collective action as an inevitable consequence of the clash of interests and the widespread deprivation faced by masses of individuals simultaneously in this critical situation is exemplified in the outbreak in Nantes. It typifies similar outbreaks throughout France and indicates the direction of the revolution: "The rising was directed not only against those who were speculating in foodstuffs, against the old system of taxation, against internal tolls, and against feudalism, but against all those who exploit the populace and live upon its substance. It was closely connected with the political agitation. At Nantes the crowd besieged the Hotel de Ville with cries of '*Vive la Liberté.*' " [36]

The great slogans such as "Liberty, Equality, and Fraternity" which moved millions of people to feeling and action

[34] *Ibid.*, p. 34.
[35] L. R. Gottschalk, *The Era of the French Revolution, 1715–1815,* Boston: Houghton Mifflin, 1929, p. 39.
[36] *Ibid.*, p. 35.

during the eventful days of the revolution, and the declaration of the rights of man which crystallized the values of human relationships in the new era, remained as the established values for decades to come in spite of counterrevolutions and other events.

A fascinating study of the psychology of social change could be made, based on the great social movements and the critical conditions and events unrolling in our day. This would enable us to bring together all of the positive findings of social psychology concerning motivation, attitude change, group emergence and action.

PART FOUR

Individual Variations in Social Reactions

17.

Individual Differences in Social Reactions

THERE ARE FRENCHMEN AND FRENCHMEN; THERE ARE BRITISH-
ERS and Britishers, in spite of the common features that give
them their distinctive characteristics as Frenchmen or as
Britishers. Likewise, there are Catholics and Catholics, Mohammedans and Mohammedans. The same may be said of
radicals and conservatives. A certain individual will go all the
way for the values he stands for as a group member; another
will not go more than five miles for them; still a third will
break down in the first mile. One will express the views which
he has derived from his group and his loyalties toward it with
his characteristic zeal and enthusiasm; another with disin-
terested coolness. And there are all gradations between these
two extremes. In short, there are individual differences in the
reactions of people even to what constitutes their common
social bonds as members of the same group.

In dealing with various topics in the preceding chapters,
we restricted ourselves mainly to the treatment of general
principles and processes, merely calling attention here and
there to the fact of individual differences in the behavior in
question. Certainly, there are individual differences in hunger,
sex, or any other motive for that matter. There are individual
differences in group interaction—for example, in the time and
amount of interaction which are necessary before a given individual becomes a part of the group. Some individuals are
reticent and some are more forward. There are individual differences in the intensity and expression of prejudice and other
attitudes. Each topic dealt with in earlier chapters could have
been expanded by taking up the individual differences revealed
in its particular field. In fact, an adequate treatment of indi-

vidual differences would require greater space than each topic discussed in this volume, because representative samples of all the relevant individual differences (to which both heredity and environment contribute) would need so much space. We have reserved a brief general treatment of the subject for this chapter only to point out some major aspects of the vast, beguiling realm of individual differences—beguiling because a host of factors from heredity, lasting and momentary situations of the social setting, and vicissitudes of the life history of the individual come into the picture.

No New Principles Needed

In dealing with individual differences in social reactions, no new principles are necessary. In the same way that the principles valid in general psychology are valid in social psychology, so principles governing the individual differences in any field of psychology are valid in dealing with social differences. Whatever is found concerning individual differences in the course of research in genetics, child psychology, the psychology of perception, learning, motivation, affectivity, attitude formation and change, etc., can be extended to individual differences in social psychology. And the really established data of clinical psychologists and psychiatrists, whose concern necessarily is with the individual life history, are valid material for us. Here we can present only a scattering of relevant findings concerning individual differences.

Individual differences, as everybody knows, are due both to the biology of the individual and to his environment (physical, social, etc.). Although the general conclusion concerning the relative roles of heredity and environment belongs properly at the end of this section, it is interesting to note, in passing, that the problem of individual differences was basic to the adaptation and survival theory of Darwin, who more than any other one person was responsible for the rapid growth of interest in this field with all its ramifications. To this effect, he wrote:

The many slight differences which appear in the offspring from the same parents, or which may be presumed have thus arisen, from being observed in the individuals of the same species inhabiting the same confined locality, may be called individual differences. No one supposes that all the individuals of the same species are cast in the same actual mould. These individual differences are of the highest importance to us, for they are often inherited, as must be familiar to every one; and they thus afford materials for natural selection to act on and accumulate, in the same manner as man accumulates in any given direction individual differences in his domesticated productions.[1]

On the biological side, we realize the tremendous extent of possible variations in heredity when we consider the almost innumerable possible gene combinations in modern man. This fact renders every individual biologically *unique* at birth. This unique biological endowment of the individual can be summarized in the words of two distinguished biologists: "All we can tell is that mankind is capable of producing an almost infinitely greater collection of types than that which exists at present or existed in the past. The chance that any two human beings, now living or having lived, have identical sets of genes is practically zero, identical twins always excepted. The hereditary endowment which each of us has is strictly his own, not present in anybody else, unprecedented in the past, and almost certainly not repeatable in the future. A biologist must assert the absolute uniqueness of every human individual." [2]

Many of these unique biological characteristics, such as the individual's fingerprints or particular shade of eye color, may not interest us as psychologists. But we are certainly interested in such variations as those of body structure and glandular functioning. Without pushing the point to the extent that Kretchmer did, for example—he maintained that bodily types closely correspond to psychological types [3]—we cannot doubt that there is a relationship between "normal" or "abnormal" bodily development and functioning on the one hand, and psychological development and functioning on the other. To

---

[1] C. Darwin, *On the Origin of Species*, London: John Murray, 1902 ed., pp. 31-32.

[2] L. C. Dunn and T. Dobzhansky, *Heredity, Race, and Society*, New York: Pelican Books, 1946, pp. 45-46.

[3] In fact, on the basis of more recent research we have good reason to doubt the validity of the body type and mentality typology presented by Kretchmer. See, for example, O. Klineberg, S. E. Asch, and H. Block, An experimental study of constitutional types, *Genet. Psychol. Monogr.*, 1934, 16, 145-221.

illustrate the point with a crude example, a towering child or man or one who is a pigmy in his own group shows peculiarities due to his particular relative physical position. (Here, of course, we see one example of the merging of hereditary and environmental factors in the production of behavior.) The glandular functioning, the hyperactivity or hypoactivity of particular glands (pituitary, thyroid, adrenals, gonads, etc.), or the general balance or imbalance of glandular activity due chiefly to biological heredity is responsible, to a great extent, for the characteristics of the growth processes, sluggishness or vitality in reactions, moodiness and other manifestations of *temperament*, and their various disorders. We may cite a few concrete facts from an eminent authority in the field: "Severe grades of the [thyroid] deficit characteristically give rise to bodily and mental sluggishness which gives the superficial impression of placidity. In lesser grades of thyroid deficiency lack of ability for sustained endurance seems to be the outstanding characteristic." [4] The role of the pituitary in determining various sorts of bodily configuration, and the inevitable psychological consequences, is apparently well established. There also seems to be a fairly close relationship between temperament, which is so important in interpersonal and group relationships, and glandular functioning, especially gonadal factors. Early deprivation of the ovaries or castration in childhood causes the temperamental changes expected at the period of puberty to fail to appear.[5] The functional relationship between adrenal secretion and emotional states have been well demonstrated by Cannon and others. The main point for our present topic is that the bodily make-up and functioning, the glandular endowment, are subject to individual variations that have counterparts in psychological variations—of course with by no means one-to-one correspondence, because of the cultural and other factors which complicate the picture.

On the psychological side, capacities, intelligence, sensory processes, learning, memory, and other basic functions seem to vary according to a unimodal, usually normal, distribution

---

[4] R. G. Hoskins, *Endocrinology. The Glands and Their Functions*, Norton, 1941, p. 363.

[5] *Ibid.*, pp. 364, 225, 245, respectively.

curve for the population. The books on differential psychology contain detailed discussions of individual variations in many capacities and functions, the methods and techniques of determining the place of a particular individual in the population, and the results obtained to date. One interesting fact for our purposes in this connection is the increasing care devoted in the more recent studies to equating background (hereditary and cultural) factors of the individuals in the sample. Recent work has been careful to make explicit that claims of test validity are limited to the populations sampled. One outstanding illustration of this advance is the revised standardization of the Stanford tests. In this latest standardization, the authors make a special point of the fact that the test is valid only for the native-born white population of the United States.[6] This constitutes a great advance over the unqualified tests of previous decades—surely quite an advance over Galton and others who reached conclusions without giving due weight to background (cultural) factors. Certainly the work of social psychologists and ethnologists had a great deal to do with the attainment of this refinement in the field of individual and group differences.[7]

As we have pointed out before, individual variations in social reactions are embedded in the individual variations manifested in many other psychological functions. Examples may be taken from the fields of perception, learning, and maturation which, as we said at the outset, are basic in discussing social psychological phenomena.

Observation of differences in the ways individuals perceive the world around them has led to a good many schemes for classifying people according to perceptual "types." Some of these are fancy and some are simple. But whenever an attempt is made to sort out a large number of individuals into a few extreme perceptual types, the majority persistently fall somewhere in between. Most studies of individual variations

---

[6] L. M. Terman and M. A. Merrill, *Measuring Intelligence*, Boston: Houghton Mifflin, 1937.

[7] Among these studies, we may cite the work of O. Klineberg, *Negro Intelligence and Selective Migration*, New York: Columbia University Press, 1935; O. Klineberg, *Race Differences*, New York: Harper, 1935; S. D. Porteus, *The Psychology of a Primitive People, A Study of the Australian Aborigines*, New York, Longmans, Green, 1931.

in perception thus yield unimodal distribution curves, with only a few extreme cases.[8] Individual differences in perception persist, however. In piano lessons, one little boy tries and tries to "get the rhythm," whereas another "gets" and executes the most complicated kinds of rhythm. Schoolteachers have learned the importance of children's perceptual span in learning to read.[9] Such devices as sorting cards with different designs into appropriate pigeonholes have proved successful in selecting individuals best suited for tasks like inspecting shells.[10] Some people seem to perceive primarily color more or less consistently; to others, forms and shapes are most prominent. And to many people, either color or form may be prominent on different occasions.[11]

When internal factors come into fuller play, as in the perception of such unstructured stimuli as the Rorschach ink blots, particularly striking and colorful individual variations are found. Responses to the ink blots, for example, vary not only in content, but in the amount of form, color, or movement seen, and the relative emphasis upon parts or the whole of the figure. Studying large numbers of normal and abnormal individuals, Voth found that the extent and pattern of apparent movement in the autokinetic phenomenon vary widely for different individuals and are fairly constant for a given individual.[12]

In learning, individual variations are equally manifest. Illustrating the point on a relatively simple level of learning, we find individual differences exhibited in Pavlov's laboratory during his classic conditioning experiments. Like many an experimenter with human beings, Pavlov found that the individual peculiarities of his dogs led to practical difficulties. Perhaps partly for this reason, he classified his dogs on a scale

[8] M. D. Vernon, *Visual Perception*, Cambridge, England: Cambridge University Press, 1937, p. 190.

[9] H. E. Garrett and M. R. Schneck, *Psychological Tests, Methods, and Results*, New York: Harper, 1933, p. 69.

[10] *Ibid.*, p. 77.

[11] Vernon, *op. cit.*, p. 201.

[12] A. C. Voth, Individual differences in the autokinetic phenomenon, *J. Exper. Psychol.*, 1941, 29, 306–322; and An experimental study of mental patients through the autokinetic phenomenon, *Amer. J. Psychiatry*, 1947, 103, 793–805.

ranging from the excitable to the inhibitable.[13] According to Pavlov, only animals of extreme types developed experimental neuroses.[14] The relative ease of conditioning for dogs as well as for fish, rats, and men varies greatly from individual to individual. For us, it is significant to note that the distribution curves of ease of conditioning (number of trials) for animals and men agree, usually, in having a single mode. There is seldom multimodality; hence the rarity of valid types.[15]

Individual variations in the rate and pattern of growth and maturation from birth through adolescence are wide. In this day of extreme consciousness of developmental norms, many a mother must have wasted hours worrying because the babies in her book and the baby next door crawled and had teeth at an age at which her child merely sat and smiled at her in toothless glee. Gesell, who has given such intensive study to the process of growth and maturation, dispels the notion of uniformity of growth with one stroke: "The growth career of each individual infant assumes a distinctive pattern." [16] In this respect, even identical twins are not perfectly identical. Children vary not only in the age at which growth and coordinations occur, but also in the general interrelatedness of various motor performances. Five children observed extensively and analyzed from motion pictures at age one kept the same rank order in such discrete measures as general bodily control, manual dexterity, reach-grasp time, creeping speed, near-step, and one-step. From his observations, Gesell believes that every infant has a characteristic "motor habitude" which expresses itself in postural demeanor and modes of movement.[17] It has been discovered, of course, that modes of movement and posture are also influenced by cultural factors of the group in which a child develops.[18]

[13] E. R. Hilgard and D. G. Marquis, *Conditioning and Learning*, New York: Appleton-Century, 1940, pp. 299–301.

[14] *Ibid.*, p. 280.

[15] *Ibid.*, pp. 302–303.

[16] A. Gesell, "The Ontogenesis of Infant Behavior," in L. Carmichael (ed.), *Manual of Child Psychology*, New York: Wiley, 1946, chap. 6, p. 322.

[17] *Ibid.*, p. 324.

[18] D. Efron and J. P. Foley, Jr., Gestural behavior and social setting, *Zeitschrift für Sozialforschung*, 1937, 6, 151–159.

The differences in the age, rate, and growth and maturation of the body and sexual functions during adolescence are striking. The age of puberty for normal healthy girls may vary from as early as 9 to as late as 20 years.[19] As we saw in Chapter 13, such variations have their inevitable psychological consequences.

But the fact that individual differences are manifested in every conceivable psychological dimension does not invalidate the general principles governing the function in question— does not make each individual a law unto himself. For example, individual differences in auditory and visual thresholds or various kinds of color blindness do not work against the validity of general principles underlying vision and audition. Nor do the "peculiar channels" of perceptual patterns laid down in past experience and directed by the "particular innate affective and impulsive tendencies of the individual" violate the "configurational tendencies which appear in all individuals at all times" in the perceptual process.[20] The fact that some of Pavlov's dogs went to sleep during his conditioning experiments does not invalidate the principles of conditioning.

In approaching an understanding of individual differences in social reactions, we cannot be content merely to admire their almost infinite variety. The determination of the factors producing these individual variations is a problem of both psychological and social importance. A moment's thought is sufficient to indicate that there is not and could not possibly be a hard and fast line between the much discussed "hereditary" and "environmental" factors. As Woodworth stated, with justifiable certainty, in his survey of available material, "Heredity and environment are coacting factors in the development of any living individual and . . . both are absolutely essential. . . ."[21] We can, of course, inquire as to the relative weight of hereditary and environmental factors in determining individual differences. The air is cleared considerably when we

[19] W. Dennis, "The Adolescent," in L. Carmichael (ed.), *op. cit.*, p. 641.
[20] Vernon, *op. cit.*, p. 214.
[21] R. S. Woodworth, *Heredity and Environment, A Critical Survey of Recently Published Material on Twins and Foster Children*, Soc. Sci. Research Council, Bulletin no. 47, New York, 1941. p. 1.

realize at the outset that all the available evidence leads to the conclusion that there is no answer to this problem in general or in the abstract. As the biologists Dunn and Dobzhansky put it, we have to question the relative "importance" of hereditary and environmental factors separately in the study of each *physical* and *psychological* characteristic. The research of H. H. Newman, also a noted biologist, led him to the significant conclusion that heredity-environment is not one problem, but many. *It differs with respect to every human characteristic.* Consequently, there is no general solution for the heredity-environment problem as a whole.[22]

Here we cannot review the studies on the contribution of hereditary and environmental factors to variation in even one characteristic. We will, however, put the spotlight on a general trend that appears in the comprehensive reviews of such studies, for this trend is full of significant implications for us. In the determination of physical characteristics (height, weight, head shape, eye color, fingerprints, etc.), hereditary factors *as a rule* contribute heavily. As one ventures into the study of behavioral characteristics, the role of environmental factors requires more and more attention. Thus, motor ability as measured in studies of twins showed the effects of experience, training, and other environmental influences. Indeed, from the available evidence on the effects of technology and work tempo on behavior, we should expect this to be the case. But in the realm of social reactions environmental factors assume tremendous weight, so that behavior is extraordinarily modifiable. Measures of emotional stability (linked as it is with ego development as well as with biological variation) and of other relatively complex aspects of behavior are most affected by social setting.[23] This is, of course, a fact of profound importance for social psychologists. Whereas we must never lose sight of the biological factors inherent in all behavior, it follows that we must put the greatest emphasis upon the modifiability of the behavior with which as social psychologists we are chiefly concerned.

[22] H. H. Newman, *Multiple Human Births*, New York: Doubleday, Doran, 1940.
[23] See, for example, *ibid.*, and Dunn and Dobzhansky, *op. cit.*, p. 22.

Samples of Variations in Social Reactions

It follows from the foregoing discussion that the diversity to be found in the social behavior of individual humans is limited theoretically only by the size of the population. Individual variations in social reactions (being most influenced by environmental factors and hence the most modifiable area of behavior) are determined by a host of functionally interrelated factors, the identity of which must be studied for each characteristic or group of characteristics. Here we cannot illustrate the point comprehensively, partly indeed because of the paucity of clear-cut data but chiefly because such an undertaking would consume far more space than it merits. We shall merely glance at a few results of differential, clinical, and experimental psychology which reveal the major areas from which individual differences in social reactions spring, and provide some basis for the conclusions reached in the sections to follow.

Individual variations are found in infants' earliest reactions to social stimuli. Infants under a year vary widely in respect to the amount and frequency of smiling, laughing, and crying.[24] It is interesting to note that the consistency in the amount of crying of individual infants is greater in the second half-year of life, when social factors come to the fore with greater potency, than in the first half-year of life.[25] Individual variations in emotional susceptibility and irritability are observed in babies in the first two years of life.[26] Children of the same age vary in their responses to play material—in their enjoyment, handling, and constructiveness of various kinds of play—in the frequency with which they become engaged in fights with other children, in the amount and kind of sympathy displayed—in short, along almost any dimension.[27]

[24] R. W. Washburn, A study of smiling and laughing of infants in the first year of life, *Genet. Psychol. Monogr.*, 1929, 6, No. 6.

[25] N. Bayley, A study of the crying of infants during mental and physical tests, *J. Genet. Psychol.*, 1932, 11.

[26] M. M. Shirley, *The First Two Years of Life*, Minneapolis: University of Minnesota Press, 1933.

[27] See, for example, E. Lerner and L. B. Murphy (eds.), Methods for the Study of Personality in Young Children, *Monogr. Soc. Res. Child Develop.*, 1941, 6, no. 4; A. T. Jersild and F. V. Markey, Conflicts between Preschool Children, *Child Develop. Monogr.*, 1935, no. 21; L. B. Murphy, *Social Behavior and Child Personality*, New York: Columbia University Press, 1937.

Even though environmental factors necessarily receive emphasis in determining individual variations in social responses, hereditary factors are always present and may enter in a major way. A clear-cut example is the case of the child whose growth is in some way conspicuously unlike that of others in his group. He may resort to withdrawal from life around him or to aggressive attempts to excel in other respects. But such reactions are meaningful only in terms of the scale of values or norms of his group. A short boy like John Sanders (see pp. 323–325), growing up in California, feels his difference from the group, and his behavior is different as a result. But if the same boy grew up in Normandy where he would approach the norm for height he would not have this experience at all. Indeed it is difficult to view any individual variation apart from the social background in which it occurs.

McKinnon reports that poor health was associated with the predominance of *invasive* behavior (e.g., "infringement on the rights of others," "physical and verbal attacks," etc.) of the children she observed from nursery school into grade school. One child who was given a long-term rest program lost this aggressive trend in the course of time and became highly *conforming*.[28]

The case material of psychiatrists and clinical psychologists is rich with descriptions of the effects, on the development of individual variations, of circumstances, frustrations, conflicts, treatment (e.g., neglect or overattention on the part of grownups), etc., during the person's life history. A young child's lack of contact with the world around him because until the age of 4 he was kept in a stroller which prevented his feet from touching the ground and thus permitted little active contact with objects and persons around him, is a striking case in point.[29] Ellen Hill, a Negro adolescent studied by Davis and Dollard, changed from an agreeable, sweet, tractable girl to a belligerent, sly, and at last "definitely abnormal" one during her adolescent years. Her reversal was brought on by a series of intense economic and family difficulties which

---

[28] K. M. McKinnon, *Consistency and Change in Behavior Manifestations*, New York: Bureau of Publications, Teachers College, Columbia University, 1942.

[29] Reported by G. Murphy, *Personality*, New York: Harper, 1947, pp. 609–610.

snowballed to crush her own intense strivings for status.[30] Frustrations may lead to aggressive behavior, as extensive studies have shown.[31] In terms of constructiveness of activities in a definite play situation, a rather severe frustration may cause some children to regress and become aggressive; others go on playing as before; and still others show an improvement in performance following the frustration.[32]

Of course, satisfactory experiences in the life history also affect the individual development. A rather simple example is the consistently kind responses made to animals by a little boy who had lived on a farm and learned to like farm animals.[33] Continued success or failure in a group to which the individual relates himself may lead to characteristic aspirations and characteristic modes of behavior (e.g., confidence, caution, invasiveness, as the case may be) in social situations within the group.[34] Here again the individual characteristics must be viewed in the framework provided by the group.

Group factors or other aspects of the situation within which behavior occurs may lead to a change in the behavior of individuals and even to the appearance of hitherto undisplayed qualities. We have already seen how the group atmosphere created by an adult leader affects the aggressive behavior of boys (see pp. 116–118). L. B. Murphy showed how both the giving and receiving of sympathetic responses varied with the position of the child in the particular group (in terms of age, rank in the status hierarchy—which tends to be fluid for young children) as well as with the particular kind and frequency of distress situations in which the child becomes involved.[35] A

[30] A. Davis and J. Dollard, *Children of Bondage*, Washington, D. C.: American Council on Education, 1940.

[31] J. Dollard, N. E. Miller, L. W. Doob, O. H. Mowrer, and R. R. Sears, *Frustration and Aggression*, New Haven: Yale University Press, 1939.

[32] R. G. Barker, T. Dembo, and K. Lewin, *Frustration and Regression: An experiment with young children*, University of Iowa Studies in Child Welfare, 1941, 8, no. 1. In this study, 22 of the 30 children regressed in the constructiveness of play after frustration, 3 did not change, and the constructiveness of 5 increased.

[33] L. B. Murphy, *Social Behavior and Child Personality*, pp. 220–221.

[34] See, for example, P. S. Sears, Levels of aspiration in academically successful and unsuccessful children, *J. Abn. & Soc. Psychol.*, 1940, 35, 498–536; and K. M. McKinnon, *op. cit.*

[35] L. B. Murphy, *op. cit.*, pp. 158 ff., 242, 264.

situation in which a close friend in the group laughs at one's hurts may thus lead an habitually sympathetic child to sharp retaliation. Changes in self-confidence, fearfulness, emotionality, ascendance, and other characteristics have been experimentally produced in children when specific training is given or their status within the group is changed.[36]

Such research, revealing the importance of situational factors, is suggestive in relation to the transformations which sometimes occur during the lifetime of the individual. A study by Diamond of the relative change of radicals and conservatives along an introversion-extroversion dimension gives us some insight into these problems. The conservatives studied showed relatively stable characteristics, i.e., little change. The radicals, on the other hand, revealed the greatest change in introversion-extroversion. The distribution curve for the radicals in the sample was bimodal, some having become more introverted, some more extroverted. This bimodal distribution seems to result from the fact that some of the individuals were in earlier stages of radicalism, whereas others had gone on to active membership in radical groups. The latter showed the highest change toward extroversion. Diamond offers the hypothesis, substantiated by autobiographical material, that early phases of radicalism are often associated with introversion. The causes of both the non-conformity and the introversion seem to be stresses and strains suffered by the individual during his life (usually vocational difficulties). But after such an individual comes into contact with and accepts the views of radical groups, he loses his introversion through "active and confident participation in group activity." Even after this transformation, individual differences in extroversion still exist.[37]

---

[36] See, for example, L. M. Jack, "An Experimental Study of Ascendant Behavior in Preschool Children," in Jack, Manwell, Mengert, et al., Behavior of the Preschool Child, University of Iowa Studies in Child Welfare, 1934, 9, no. 3; M. L. Page, The Modification of Ascendant Behavior in Preschool Children, University of Iowa Studies in Child Welfare, 1936, 12, no. 3; F. B. Holmes, An experimental investigation of a method of overcoming children's fears, Child Develop., 1936, 7; M. E. Keister and R. Updegraff, A study of children's reactions to failure and an experimental attempt to modify them, Child Develop., 1937, 8, 241-248.

[37] S. Diamond, A study of the influence of political radicalism on personality development, Arch. Psychol., 1936, no. 203.

This problem of the differential acceptance of group norms and values is of major importance for adequate prediction in the social field. We have already seen experimental and sociological evidence showing how the individual's perception, judgment, memory, etc., are deflected, in a group situation in which he is ego-involved, in the direction of the group norms (Chapters 5, 6, 7). But not all individuals react identically to these norms. An especially dramatic case in point is that of the five Martin brothers, all delinquent boys studied by Clifford Shaw. According to the psychiatrist who examined them, the boys differed in physical characteristics, intelligence, and sociability, but all engaged in similar forms of delinquent conduct during the early periods of their careers because they were all members of similar neighborhood gangs. However, it was Carl, the least sociable, least friendly, least loyal of the brothers, who had the shortest delinquency career. Shaw suggests that this was directly related to his less desirable characteristics, which made him less of a social asset and complicated the process of adjustment to the delinquent group exactly as they would have with a non-delinquent group.[38] (We are reminded here of Bill Mauldin's observation during World War II that if a quiet fellow wanted to belong to the company or battalion as a regular fellow, he had to come out of his shell a bit.) Such factors are not, of course, the only ones influencing the differential effects of the group's norms on individual members. The responsible factors presumably are numerous and they vary from individual to individual.

A significant approach to this general problem in the perceptual process was made recently by Bovard using the autokinetic phenomenon.[39] As we have seen (pp. 161 and 228), the formation and effects of group norms or the norms imposed by an influential person upon the individual's perception have been studied in relation to this unstructured stimulus situation, as well as in more structured situations (pp. 235–238). All these studies have revealed individual differences in the rate and

[38] C. R. Shaw (ed.), *Brothers in Crime*, Chicago: University of Chicago Press, 1938, p. 313.

[39] E. W. Bovard, Jr., Social norms and the individual, to appear in *J. Abn. & Soc. Psychol.* The manuscript was kindly made available by the author.

degree of influence of the norm. Schonbar, studying reactions to situations with relatively higher objective structure, made a special point of this fact; she discovered that individuals with a higher variability (scatter) of judgments when they faced the situation *alone* tended to show greater convergence toward the group norm in a subsequent group situation than did individuals whose initial judgments were less variable.[40]

In light of these findings, Bovard set out to determine the differential effects of a group norm on individuals' perception in a group situation, and 28 days after they were subjected to its influence. The autokinetic technique was used (pp. 162–163). The subjects first made judgments of the apparent movement of the pinpoint of light alone, then with a "planted" subject with considerable prestige. They were told that the experiment would reveal a "personality characteristic." Twenty-eight days later each subject made his judgments alone.

The significant finding was that it was possible to predict the relative effect of the group norm on these subjects 28 days after they were subjected to it in terms of the change in the means and variability of judgments from the initial individual session to the group session. That is, by knowing the variability and means of the judgments in the first individual and group sessions, Bovard could predict the subjects' *rank* in terms of the influence of the norm after a 28-day interval.

The impact of the norm on the various subjects was highly differential. In general, subjects who showed a large shift in their mean of judgments and in the variability (standard deviation) of their individual judgments when in the group situation showed a corresponding tendency to retain this shift over a period of time.

These findings, of course, leave many questions unanswered. But as Bovard concluded, they do point to the means of measuring the differential effect of a social norm on the individual and a possible method of predicting in terms of performance who will and who will not remain under the influence of the norm.

As stated at the outset, we have given examples of indi-

[40] R. A. Schonbar, The interaction of observer-pairs in judging visual extent and movement: The formation of social norms in "structured" situations, *Arch. Psychol.*, 1945, no. 299.

vidual differences in social reactions with the intention of indicating the diversity and complexity of the factors that determine them. A more important task for the social psychologist, and one to which we now turn, is the attempt to discover the way in which such individual variations can be understood in terms of the major topics which we have discussed throughout this volume.

Individual Variations in Relation to Their Appropriate Reference Scales

The foregoing material, chosen almost at random, is sufficient to illustrate the fact that social reactions even of individuals of the same culture are subject to variations. It is evident that reactions of the individual will reveal his unique personal characteristics as well as the common characteristics of his group and culture. Individual variations, as we saw, are due to the combined effects of heredity and environment (both physical and cultural). As we proceed to more complex levels of psychological functioning, the modifiability of the organism by the environmental forces becomes more decisive. The level of behavior which is our main concern, i.e., the social level, is probably the most complex. Hence, in determining the individual's whole person, in his experience and behavior in diverse situations, environmental factors are most potent. No one is born a Protestant or a Catholic, a conservative or a radical, an individualist or a collectivist. He becomes one. To be sure, there may be potentialities in him which make him more or less susceptible to becoming a good or bad Protestant, radical, or individualist. But these potentialities are not sufficient *in themselves* to make the individual behave in this or that way and to this or that degree. These potentialities blossom or are transformed or deflected or blocked by the circumstances he goes through in a particular environmental setting. Many a man in the Middle Ages who lived and died with a sense of security—but hardly revealed individuality—might have developed into an ardent individualist, as his offspring did, had he lived after the industrial revolution in Europe. Today there are fully outgoing individuals heavily engaged in politics and engineering who are offspring of the Hindu whose philosophy of life is depicted as a complete introvert withdrawal from nature and life.[41]

These general remarks are made to emphasize the fact that the individual variations in social behavior acquire real meaning only when taken in relation to the social setting which contributes so decisively to their appearance. The necessity of relating items of individual behavior to the social setting in which they occur has become widely established in psychology in recent years, especially under the impact of the comparative material presented by social scientists. As psychologists, we must be more specific and carry the analysis further to the level of single individuals.

Individual variations taken in the abstract have little meaning in themselves. They make sense only in relation to the appropriate *reference scale*. This idea is not an academic novelty. People usually make their judgments and appraisals on the basis of an established range of relationships. To illustrate with a tangible example: When people see a man and a woman of the same height (say, 5 feet 9 inches) side by side and appraise their statures, they usually judge the man as medium and the woman as tall, even though both are of equal height. And they have good reason to do so. They do not take the absolute values of stature as the basis of their judgment. Whether they realize it or not, appropriate masculine or feminine scales of stature (between their averages there is a difference of four inches) form the basis of their appraisal.

As we go to different places, travel in different countries, sharp variations in behavior and expression come to our attention. We do not have to be psychologists to notice them. To an outsider, the New Yorker seems to be almost always in a *hurry*—in the midst of a thousand and one things he must catch up with. This may stand in contrast to the slower tempo of life in rural northern New York State, not to mention the "easygoing" South. But probably no two New Yorkers or no two Southerners are exactly alike in their respective tempos of living.

[41] Such a picture of ideal introversion is elaborated in C. G. Jung's *Psychological Types*, London: Kegan Paul, Trench, Trubner, 1923.

As we cross cultural boundaries, variations become even more striking. "As one takes the short, choppy trip from Dover to Calais, he moves almost from one world to another, from stolid, casual, pipe-smoking British tars and longshoremen to animated and confused bustle of excitable, irritable, nervously intent French sailors, baggagemen, and porters. The life of the whole city of Dover and of the whole city of Calais accentuates the contrast. . . . It is the nature of the British and Gallic character to be stolid and gay respectively, to be casual and excitable." [42]

But this does not mean that all Englishmen are stolid or casual in the same degree and the same manner. It does not mean that all Frenchmen are of the same mold. Some Englishmen are more stolid than other Englishmen. Some Frenchmen are gayer than other Frenchmen. If we should plot curves for these or other traits, the curve for the Englishmen and the curve for the Frenchmen would probably be normally distributed, with a great deal of overlapping between the two curves. But, in spite of this overlapping, it would be a serious error to compare an Englishman and a Frenchman on an axis with the same range and declare that this Frenchman is exactly so much more excitable than this Englishman. Probably the Frenchman who is of medium excitability in relation to his own group would be placed among the more excitable of the Englishmen.

Such illustrations will suffice to bring home the main point under discussion. In determining the functional significance and degree of individual differences in social reactions (or in any other respect for that matter), the particular place of the particular individual has meaning only in relation to the group of which he is a part. In many characteristics, groups have their modal area and deviate from it toward the extremes. And groups usually allow a certain range of deviations in particular respects. Beyond those points the individual is simply outside the group. There is a limit to the degree to which a person may be atypical or nonconformist as far as his group is concerned. If he is beyond the limits in a characteristic, he drops out of his group, at least in that respect. The groups may have larger or

[42] G. Murphy, *Personality*, New York: Harper, 1947, p. 763.

smaller permissible ranges at given times, and the range of similar characteristics may vary from group to group. For example, the range of colors from which men may ordinarily choose for a suit is somewhat limited, whereas women have many more colors to display their *individuality*. On the other hand, there are still many areas of activity, indulgence in which by women will be labeled *unladylike* but which will be taken for granted or at least viewed with tolerance for *gentlemen*. The particular range comprising the modal area and possible deviations to the extremes constitutes the *reference scale* of a particular group in that characteristic. The idea embodied in the notion of reference scale is now widespread. It is a more specific statement of the idea that behavior and variations thereof have meaning only in relation to the individual's particular setting or situation.

Not only in the ranges of the scales on which the individual members are scattered do groups differ; they may have their peculiar value scales which do not exist for other groups. Such distinctive scales are especially revealed in socio-economic and cultural realms. Even within the same social system, hitherto unknown scales of value for the whole group or a segment of it may appear. For example, a century ago it would have been meaningless to construct distribution curves for women along professional or political lines. It would have been unthinkable to try to find any wide individual variations in capacities used in modern industry or mercantilism in Japan, China, or India about two centuries ago.

The notion of reference scales enables us to see with the necessary perspective the bimodal or multimodal distributions, with their various degrees of overlapping, and the discontinuous distributions in certain cultures between which there is no overlapping at all. The notion of reference scales forces us, at the outset, to be concerned with whether scales of the values in question exist for the given culture or group, and if so, what the range is. Only on that basis can the more precise task of determining the place of individual variations on these scales serve a realistic scientific purpose. For example, it would be futile to study the drawing capacity of youngsters in a country where drawing is taboo, and make comparisons on the basis of the developmental norms obtained in a country in which such a taboo does not exist. Another concrete illustration may help to clarify this important point. We learned from the social scientist that the less differentiated, the less developed a social group is, the more homogeneous and more alike is the social behavior of the individual members. In such a group the range of individual variations will certainly be relatively narrow. But in a highly differentiated group, the range will be wide. The comparative study of individual variations on a conformity-individuality scale in the village of Chan Kom and the city of Merida, both of which are situated on the Yucatán peninsula, would really be a study of the social determination of individual variations in those two places. If this were the problem we wanted to study, we could have conveniently consulted the social scientist; a reading of Redfield's *Folk Culture of Yucatán* would have saved us all this effort (pp. 393–395). In fact, most of the results of comparisons of various psychological traits or processes in individuals belonging to different cultures proves, on finer analysis, to relate to the social value scales and practices prevailing in those social groups.[43] But this does not mean that all inhabitants of Chan Kom, where the range of individual variations is rather narrow, are alike. There are individual differences *within* the range of the village. These individual differences, we repeat, have meaning in relation to the particular limited reference scale that exists there. The individual differences within groups are recognized even by ethnologists.[44]

The point presented in the paragraphs above is stressed in various ways by many authors, of whom we shall mention just a few. Foley develops it in relation to variations in abnormal behavior in different cultures. After noting that different cultures have different norms for normality in various functions, he states: "Thus correlated with the difference in mores from

[43] The reader can find summaries of these facts in O. Klineberg's *Race Differences* (Part II) and also in *Negro Intelligence and Selective Migration*. The final chapter of Anne Anastasi's *Differential Psychology* presents a synthetic account of the conclusions reached.

[44] See, for example, E. Sapir, The emergence of the concept of personality in the study of culture, *J. Soc. Psychol.*, 1934, 5; and J. W. M. Whiting, *Becoming a Kwoma*, New Haven: Yale University Press, 1941.

group to group may be found various 'types' of abnormality, so classified because each shows a deviation from the norm or central tendency of the particular group in question; and the entire social structure of the group is devoted toward the further inculcation and development of behavior patterns which are 'normal' to that specific group." [45]

The multimodality and "discontinuity" of distributions in various functions resulting from the peculiar reference scales in various cultures is concisely expressed by Foley in relation to the normality-abnormality dimension (see Fig. 32).

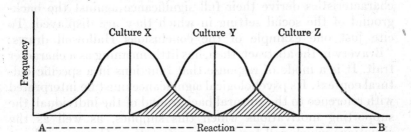

Fig. 32. Distribution of divergent cultures with respect to a given reaction, AB. (From J. P. Foley, in *J. Abn. & Soc. Psychol.*, 1935, 30, 287.)

For purposes of further elaboration, let us conceive of several cultural groups with widely differing "norms" with respect to a given behavior trait, three of which groups or distributions, presumably following the Gaussian curve of normal probability, are illustrated in Figure [32] with respect to the reaction AB. It will be seen that the central tendencies of these curves are far apart, although the distributions overlap at the extremes of the range. Such are the results usually obtained in investigations dealing with different racial or cultural groupings. Thus an individual who was "normal" or near the central tendency of culture X would be "abnormal" or widely aberrant in cultures Y and Z." [46]

To find diverse reference scales which encourage the development of certain reactions and discourage others, we do not have to turn to distant cultures. We have already mentioned the differing tempos of life in New York City as contrasted with

[45] J. P. Foley, The criterion of abnormality, *J. Abn. & Soc. Psychol.*, 1935, 30, 283.
[46] *Ibid.*, pp. 287–288.

rural areas. We could also contrast the reference scales for neighborliness in a rural Connecticut village and in a metropolis, where one may not know anyone who lives in his apartment house. Different scales may exist for different sections of the same country. "For example, certain types of religious fanaticism are normal in parts of the rural sections of southern states, while the same behavior may be the occasion for commitment to a hospital in a northern city." [47]

Taking his illustrations from bravery, stoicism, paranoia, and other characteristics, Hallowell shows concretely how these characteristics derive their full significance against the background of the social setting in which they are displayed. To cite just one example of the conclusions Hallowell draws: "Bravery in the abstract, then, has little meaning as a character trait. It is a mode of response that functions in a specific cultural context. Its psychological significance must be interpreted with reference to the cultural background of the individual, the supporting motivations which this supplies, as well as the situations which call forth its manifestation. Consequently, it may be assumed that bravery as a typical personality trait of individuals in particular societies is indissolubly linked with relevant culture patterns." [48]

Discontinuous reference scales produce more sharply delineated variations. In the present discussion we are forced to accentuate the decisive role of the scales of values or practices peculiar to various social groups, in producing wide variations in experience and behavior. These social scales are no mere artifacts, like scales of tones or odors conveniently chosen for laboratory experiments. They reflect standardized and lasting values and practices of given cultures. And they reflect socio-economic, political, professional, intellectual, aesthetic, religious, status, etc., cleavages and differentiations within the same society. Nowhere do individuals exist in a vacuum. They are members of a culture, a socio-economic class, a profession, a certain

[47] R. E. L. Faris and H. W. Dunham, *Mental Disorders in Urban Areas,* Chicago: University of Chicago Press, 1939, p. 155.

[48] A. I. Hallowell, "Introduction, Handbook of Psychological Leads for Ethnological Field Workers," mimeographed. This material was kindly made available to the author by Professor Hallowell.

status group, a club, a union, a college, a church, a fraternity, a gang, a family with a definite locus within the hierarchy of families, etc. These groups each have scales of values or practices, hierarchies of position, or roles peculiar to them. And the scales of values and practices of one group are, in some cases at least, far apart from the scales of other groups. Some scales that exist in a highly differentiated society do not exist in less differentiated, homogeneous groups. The individual variations in the observance of traffic regulations, or in movie going, or in newspaper reading, for example, will not be found in more primitive societies. On the other hand, individual variations in observing certain primitive ceremonials or rites will not exist in modern societies. Likewise, within the same modern society, certain scales peculiar to one socio-economic class or a certain profession, certain club, certain union do not exist for others. For example, individual variations displayed in the debuts of young girls of a certain class are not possible for the girls of another class.

Such cleavages or differentiations exist even within the relatively narrower bounds of the contemporary Middletown studied by the Lynds. As summarized by Murphy:

In their first study of Middletown, the Lynds found that people group themselves around fundamental discontinuous centers of activity which constitute nuclei for the life process. Almost everyone in Middletown worked either chiefly with his hands *or* chiefly with symbols. The two groups stood out in rather sharp psychological differentiation, despite the fact that some of the lower-paid members of the "symbol" group were on the same economic level as the higher-paid members of the "manual" group. When Middletown was studied later, in 1935, three fundamental constants or types had developed. The dominant clan, the "X" family, stood off from the common run of the business ("symbol") group, just as the latter did from the "manual" group. Other observers have made similar findings. Thus subcultural types, such as the French Canadians of the New England mill town, are sharply separated from the "Anglo-Saxons" on the one hand and the "Portuguese" on the other. Barriers of feeling are such that typing is extremely sharp.[49]

---

[49] G. Murphy, *Personality*, pp. 753-754.

An individual's activities and experience (the ones that really count for him) are necessarily bound by the scales and practices of the social group or groups in which he moves and has his being. We have designated these groups as his *reference groups* (see pp. 122–155). He makes a living, betters his position, shows his individuality, and excels within these bounds. In other words, the values and practices of his group become his personal values forming the basis of his major ego-attitudes (pp. 248–270). His personal aspirations are regulated by the scale of values and the hierarchy of positions in his group (pp. 296–313), and he mobilizes his unique personal capacities, his intelligence, etc., to make a place for himself within these bounds. The orientation of his activity and outlook with its highly selective nature is determined by the scales of value of his reference group. In his adjustment and strivings toward these goals he excels, or does poorly, or is in the medium range (like the majority of his fellow members) as determined by his personal endowment, training, and special life circumstances. *In short, the scope of his scales is socially set; his performance within them is his.* In his performance and experience in the process, all the unique traits of his person come into play. They come into play adverbially. As Woodworth and Marquis put it: "A moment's thought shows that these adjectives [designating trait names] are properly adverbs." [50]

Some workmen are faster and more efficient than others, and some executives are faster and more efficient than others. Some conservatives have more zeal than others and so do some radicals. Some Catholics are more devout than others, and so are some Protestants, Jews, and Mohammedans. Some totalitarians express their opinions more colorfully and dramatically than others, and so do some communists. Everyone in any group has his unique style of expression and way of doing things as determined by his personal traits.

The fact remains that the distribution of any one of these adverbial characteristics (traits) can be plotted on a unimodal curve, or at least on curves with a considerable degree of overlapping. Available data do not justify the classification of

[50] R. S. Woodworth and D. G. Marquis, *Psychology*, New York: Henry Holt, 5th ed., 1947, p. 88.

Individual Differences in Social Reactions   451

individuals into discontinuous types on the basis of such personal characteristics. After an exhaustive treatment of this and related topics, Murphy recently arrived at the following conclusion: "It must be conceded that the majority of these types as currently applied in psychology have not as yet been validated in terms of either empirical or rational definitions of points of cleavage. For example, with extroversion-introversion, or ascendance-submission, or superego vs. id orientation, or adjustment vs. maladjustment, or aggressiveness vs. shyness, the distribution curves are smooth—indeed, usually normal—with not even that suggestive trace of bimodality which might warrant the belief that a fundamental discontinuity has been smothered by accidental factors." [51]

Discontinuous distributions of variations appear with social and cultural cleavages and differentiations. These, in turn, are the basis of discontinuous reference scales. For our purposes, they express concisely cultural variations, class lines, and professional and religious demarcations. These lines of demarcation furnish the axis (abscissa) and the narrow or extended range on which the individual acquires a place in this or that respect. Really to comprehend the meaning of our data, our first concern should be an understanding of the nature and extent of socially existing reference scales. The frequency of individual cases can be plotted on the appropriate scale of the groups to which those individuals are related.

In studying discontinuous variations, our *first* task should be, therefore, to detect at least approximately the peculiar scales created by social cleavages and differentiations, so that the individual can be located on the appropriate axis. This means, plainly, placing him in his appropriate setting. We know from Hyman's work that the individual's own conception of standards of living is determined by the standards of his reference groups, which become his own. Here again we may call attention to the case of John Sanders (pp. 323–325). His growth was retarded at the time when other boys in his age group were going through the adolescent spurt. Consequently he was puny and unathletic in relation to his group. He could

[51] G. Murphy, *op. cit.*, p. 740.

not take part in dances and sports. He tried to make up for it by indulging in artistic activities. But art activity was ranked low by the group in its hierarchy of activities. As a result, he was relegated to a low position in popularity, social adjustment, etc., and was subjected to feelings of failure and other reverberations in his experience.

To sum up the point under discussion, social cleavages and differentiations are the basis of discontinuous distributions of behavior. These social cleavages and differentiations are reflected in the central identifications and ego-attitudes of the individual members. Hence, psychologically, these identifications and ego-attitudes, which the individuals acquire from their particular reference groups in the course of their socialization, constitute the basis of the major discontinuous variations.

At this point let us raise the inevitable objection. How about the individuals who change their group, who change their class, the individuals who become dissenters or rebels, the creative artists? The question is highly complex. Such people are, of course, real problems, especially in our time. In the above paragraphs we talked as though individuals were inexorable captives of their reference groups. Here we shall attempt to mention only a few points that come to mind in approaching the problem.

There have been numerous cases of individuals who start in life as, say, street vendors and break through social cleavages by dint of sheer ability. There have been and are cases of religious and ideological conversions. These things happen, on the whole, in societies with a rather high degree of differentiation and a high degree of mobility; they also occur in times of great social transition or change. In our account of individuals in social change we touched upon some aspects of the problem. Ethnologists hint that acculturation of the group seems to bring about maladjustment in its individuals.[52] Of course, not every individual reacts in the same way to social change. Some individuals, because of their circumstances of life, the strength with which they cling to the values of their egos as formed at the time, and no doubt their particular endowment,

---

[52] For example, see A. I. Hallowell, The Rorschach technique in the study of personality and culture, *Amer. Anthropologist*, 1945, 47, 208.

will remain relatively insulated from it or experience only minor conflicts. Others, because of particularly intense conflicts, frustrations, etc., that interact with their persons as endowed and formed, are particularly sensitive to new aspects of the world around them. The threshold for various kinds of psychological breakdowns, as we have seen in the case of ego-breakdowns (pp. 262–265), and for various forms of regression to lower levels of functioning is different in different individuals. (Such individual differences in regression were evident in the Barker, Dembo, and Lewin study reported above, p. 438.) No doubt intelligence, as well as temperamental factors, are important here, especially if they are in contact with non-conformist ideas and values, as was the case, in the studies on prejudice, with the dissidents whose reading lead them to adopt radical views (see pp. 356–357).

Having found their new groups, after considerable struggle and conflict before they broke away from their old bases, such individuals usually become meticulous, ardent conformists in their new group. M. Jourdain in *Le Bourgeois Gentilhomme*, the zeal of the new convert (e.g., St. Paul) typify the point. It may be safe to say that in societies which have little social mobility, little differentiation and great homogeneity, breaking away from the original group (unless sanctioned by existing norms) occurs very seldom.

We are not in a position yet to handle the puzzling case of the unique individuality with which the creative artist stands out from the rank of his contemporaries. It may be safe to say that sensitivity to his medium, intelligence, temperament, and talent are not alone in assuring his originality. We shall venture to guess that the frustrations and conflicts that he goes through, and their peculiar effects upon his temperamental make-up and ego formation, may also contribute to the emergence of the particular quality of originality he immortalizes in tones, colors, or words. In great creative artists like Beethoven and Van Gogh, we cannot help noticing an irrepressible freshness and non-conformist nature, like that of childhood. We find numerous concrete instances of the point as we read their biographies. Perhaps temperamental make-up and unfortunate life circumstances or experiences work together to make it impossible for creative artists to build up an ego that can conform to the established personal and group relationships of their times. Consequently, they look at things, hear things, react to their surroundings not with a stabilized ego, the constituents of which are derived from the values of the existing groups around them, but with a highly sensitized ego whose boundaries are in a fluid state because of the onslaughts of their unfortunate circumstances and the upsurge of their temperamental make-up. Not having stable and rigid ego formations in the image of give-and-take relationships of the established groups around them, they become highly susceptible to assimilating and reflecting the great human sufferings, conflicts, and strivings of their times. By this we do not mean that every sensitive person who does not establish a stable ego formation is bound to become a Beethoven or a Van Gogh. Individuals of lesser stature (and frankly the author does not know what accounts for this stature) are crushed under the powerful impact of the normal run of things.

Role of Individual and Social Factors in Determining a Trait at a Given Time

Before we close this chapter, a more specific treatment of various ways in which the individual and social factors interact to produce the particular manner in which a trait manifests itself at a given moment will clarify the problems involved. No potential capacity or trait of an individual operates in isolation. They function in interaction with the environment (physical and cultural) during the process of the individual's strivings to adapt himself successfully to the life conditions around him. Under the specific requirements of his environment, certain of his capacities and traits are sharpened to the fullest, certain others are barely called on to function, still others remain untapped. No one knows how many geniuses lived and died without being noticed outside their immediate group, because they had no chance to exercise their potentialities in channels leading to their full realization.

For the sake of brevity, we shall restrict our illustrations to a few traits. In different cultures and at different periods in the same culture, different traits are held at a premium. Naturally, such traits enjoy fuller blossoming as the individual members strive to achieve enviable statuses in their respective societies. Prussian discipline, American initiative, French sparkle, Balinese grace are examples. Even the expectations of outsiders who assume that people will display certain characteristic traits may lead them to behave accordingly.

Certain behavior characteristics necessarily are attributes closely connected with certain professions. A soldier is inextricably linked with being brave, disciplined, etc.; a professor, with being dignified and poised; a politician, with being quick and resourceful; an artist, with having a certain nonchalance and bohemian carelessness; etc. Individuals in given professions must develop the approved traits as fully as they can. Widely differing masculine and feminine traits have been assumed to inhere in men and women in different cultures and at different times, and the majority of both sexes do their best to display them. Otherwise, they themselves may feel that there is something wrong with them. And these desirable traits change with the times. An American lady of the Revolutionary period would be shocked if she saw the way her great-great-granddaughter argues, smokes, and travels around today.

Nor are such long-standing individual traits, which become distinctive characteristics of the individual in such quality and to such degree, displayed in the same manner and to the same extent on all occasions by the same individual. The poised man may be more poised in certain situations than in others. And, under exceptionally trying circumstances, his poise may break. The young lady with a certain degree of coyness may exhibit it to a greater degree in the company of the man she loves. The authoritative tone of a minor executive may lose this quality when he is talking to his superiors.

After this discursive citation of illustrations, we may profitably dwell briefly on a single characteristic. Because of the emphasis we placed, with good reason, on group interaction and formation, we select for consideration the special personal characteristic that determines the individual's place in leader-follower relationships—traditionally treated as a topic in personality traits.

We have seen that when individuals interact in a situation,

or participate in a common activity, they cannot help producing spontaneously (whether or not they are conscious of it at the initial stage) a group structure peculiar to them, with a hierarchy of positions. Individual members who fill places on the hierarchical scale of the group assume roles appropriate to the positions they occupy (chapters 6 and 12). Henceforth, the degree of responsibility, of loyalty, of initiative they exhibit in group activities depends on the role they have in the group. The higher the position that an individual member occupies in the group, the higher is the expectation for him to show great initiative and to live up to the decisions, interests, and code of the group. If he fails to do this, he loses his relative position. The leader is not a person who, from outside the hierarchy of the group, guides the members by his sheer power or capacity. He is an integral part of the group.

Spontaneously formed groups and the relative positions (or roles) within them afford an excellent opportunity to study individual differences in social relationships. The emergence of a group structure with relative positions for its members is a general phenomenon and a function of the interaction of individuals engaged in a common activity. But the relative role an individual member assumes within the group is determined by his personal capacities or the traits that differentiate him from other individuals. However (and this is the crucial point in our discussion), the role he achieves is determined not by his personal qualities in the abstract, but by his standing in relation to other members *in the special qualities* required by the particular group goal or situation. Recently Gibb contributed fresh theoretical and experimental substantiation to these findings.[53] As he observed, whatever the potentialities of the individual may be, no leadership or follower trait is exhibited in isolation. Such traits are relative to a specific social situation. The leader himself has to excel others in the qualities required by the situation or the goal of the particular group. But he cannot be too different from others. He has to be a part of the group; he must have membership character as must the other

---

[53] C. A. Gibb, The principles and traits of leadership, *J. Abn. & Soc. Psychol.*, 1947, 42, 267.

members. If he is too different, he cannot be part of the group in any capacity. Leadership is not a quality of which a person has a definite degree when he is not participating in a group situation. Different personal characteristics come into play and acquire new qualities to make a particular person a leader in a given group situation. "Leadership is both a function of the social situation and a function of personality, but it is a function of these two in interaction; no additive concept is adequate to explain the phenomenon. There is no justification for saying that personality qualities which make for leadership exist in latent form when not being exercised in a social situation." [54]

Let us take, as an example, twenty men, previously strangers to each other, who find themselves facing a common fate and are trying to reach safety after a shipwreck or some other accident. In their common efforts toward their goal, they weigh every frantic suggestion. An idea suggested by one of them will appear plausible. The group will focalize on that member. He emerges as the leader for the time being. In this case it is *intelligence* or *knowledge* that has pushed him to the top. In carrying out this plan, a different man may prove to be more *resourceful*, more *practical*, and he will lead. Consequently, the leadership shifts hands. In this case it is resourcefulness and practicality that weigh most heavily in determining leadership. In the last phase of executing the plan, *endurance* may be the greatest requirement. This will bring the man with the greatest degree of endurance to the foreground.

The principle was amply demonstrated, as Gibb reports, in the selection of military leaders and officers in the Australian army during World War II. The principle that leadership is not an abstract quality of which the individual has so much and of such a kind was borne out by the partial success in detecting it through psychiatric and psychological tests. "It soon became clear, however, that psychiatric and psychological assessment of the individual personality was not an adequate guide to leadership potential." [55] This result is in harmony with the converging reports of research workers on group dynamics,

[54] *Ibid.*, p. 268.
[55] *Ibid.*, p. 275.

that the individual in group interaction is not merely the individual in isolation plus the addition of new stimuli in the group situation.

It was found that an experimentally designed, leaderless group situation provided a more reliable way of singling out military leaders. The experimental device consisted of choosing a group of recruits among whom there was no established leader-follower relationship, then leaving it to its own devices in coping with a situation. Here we must note that the situation and the goals were designed by the investigators. Specifically, the situations were designed "to reproduce certain fundamental aspects of the officer's job, particularly those concerned with his personal interaction with other members of the group." (We mention this specially to point out that there are other situations which require different qualities and which propel other persons with these qualities to the foreground.)

In these leaderless groups, left to their own devices to cope with the experimental situation, leaders did emerge. The leaders certainly had personal qualities, relative to the situation, in which they surpassed others. The first of these traits was the relative standing in general *intelligence*. The nature of the civilian occupation was another factor that counted in these situations. The industrial and "white-collar" occupations were favorable, and rural occupations were unfavorable factors. On the basis of detailed results, Gibb concludes that "the characteristics which make for an individual's being propelled to leadership status in a group of which he is a member are any or all of his traits of personality, skill, and experience which enable him to make an interactional contribution toward the group's progress in the direction of its recognized goal." On the other hand, "in this military situation, there is no evidence that bearing, appearance, and speech play any part in determining leadership capacity." [56] In short, there is no leadership quality as such; it is relative to the situation. The member who excels others in the qualities required by the particular group situation makes his way to the top.

These significant findings are very much in line with the con-

[56] *Ibid.*, p. 283.

clusions reached by Jenkins after an extensive survey of studies on leadership: "Leadership is specific to the particular situation under investigation. Who becomes the leader of a given group engaging in a particular activity and what leadership characteristics are in a given case are a function of the specific situation including the measuring instruments. Related to this conclusion is the general finding of wide variations in the characteristics of individuals who become leaders in similar situations, and even greater divergence in leadership behavior in different situations." [57]

These conclusions fit well with their sociological counterparts, as we have seen on various occasions before. It may be well here to remind ourselves of a few concrete findings. In spontaneously formed gangs, which Thrasher and others studied, hierarchical roles emerge, with leadership at the top. Certainly personal qualities are decisive in determining what member will occupy what role. The qualities that are required for a leadership role vary from gang to gang. In one the leader may be the boy who excels in physical strength or athletic prowess; in another it may be gameness; in a third it may be firmness of decision; in a fourth it may be shrewdness. Different gangs specialize in different activities and have different objectives.[58]

In the gang which Whyte studied intensively, leadership changed hands when the emerging leader was beaten by a member lower in position (see pp. 125–131). The leader becomes conscious of the fact that he has to keep himself head and shoulders above his followers in order to maintain his leadership role. Accordingly, he discourages group activities in which he does not feel he can excel. So common is this that when members low in the hierarchy begin to show superiority, even in side-line activities which have nothing directly to do with the leadership functions, members at the top use all kinds of means, fair and foul, to keep them in their place.

The Martin brothers, studied intensively both longitudinally

[57] W. O. Jenkins, A review of leadership studies with particular reference to military problems, *Psychol. Bull.*, 1947, 44, 75.

[58] F. M. Thrasher, *The Gang*, Chicago: University of Chicago Press, 1927, p. 344.

and cross-sectionally by Clifford Shaw and his associates, give us a significant lead in this connection. Ordinarily a higher degree of sociability and outgoingness in the social milieu works toward shaping persons into the mold of higher respectability and conformity. Not so in the case of the Martin brothers. Their unfortunate life circumstances led all five brothers to join gangs which engaged in delinquent activities. The personal qualities which differentiated the brothers in terms of their length of membership in gangs have many implications for our problem. The more sociable of the brothers stayed longer in their gangs, and the less social ones belonged for a shorter period.[59]

Functional Relatedness of Different Phenomena

In this survey we have not raised as a special issue the all-important problem of the *initial* integratedness of the reactions of the organism, and of the progressive differentiation and integration of various processes during his development. We have not raised as a special issue the consistency (generality) or specificity of the individual's behavior in various situations in which he is reacting. These central issues necessarily entered into our discussions of the motivated state of the organism; into our various treatment of the ways the basic psychological

[59] It is evident that the above findings have direct implications for the whole theory of traits, but we cannot participate in the controversial problem. However, there is real weight in the following conclusion reached by Anastasi after a concise survey of the field: ". . . the diversity of trait concepts as well as the apparent factual inconsistencies in trait research result in large part from a predominantly factuo-descriptive approach. It is suggested that the greater consistency and ease of identification of traits in the intellectual as contrasted to the emotional aspects of behavior illustrate the greater cultural standardization of activities in the former category. The comparison of factor patterns among subjects differing in age, education, occupation, sex, cultural grouping, and species contributes toward an understanding of the conditions under which traits develop and presents a fruitful field for future research. A more direct approach is the experimental manipulation of behavior organization through the interpolation of relevant controlled activities. The problem of 'traits' is seen as but one illustration of the need for a more active search for the underlying behavior principles which unify the superficial divergencies of the descriptive approach." A. Anastasi, "The Nature of Psychological Traits," Presidential address to the Eastern Psychological Association, Atlantic City, New Jersey, April, 1947. (This passage is quoted by permission of the author.)

reaction to given situations—viz., perception—is cast and recast under the impact of changing internal and external factors at given times; and into the discussion of differential reactions of individuals under conditions of relative social stability and social change.

We saw that when the organism is strongly oriented toward a goal, a central motive state is generated which mobilizes all the perceptual, ideational, discriminative, and motor processes and capacities of the individual in the direction of the goal— thus rendering the individual highly selective in that direction, making him deaf and blind to other aspects of his surrounding stimulus world. We followed the implications of this almost possessed state for his remembering, rationalizing, behaving, etc. We tried to give a concise picture of its effects on his interpersonal relationships, and on group formation and disintegration. Taking perception as the paradigm of all other higher psychological functions, we saw how the perceptual process is organized, deflected, sharpened, rendered highly selective by positive and negative motivational and affective components coming from within the individual himself. All these reflect the unmistakable functional interrelatedness of various psychological processes in the individual. We are not prepared to take up these central problems with the degree of adequacy which they deserve, but in these paragraphs we shall point out a few facts closely related to them. We shall cite them rather discretely, because in the course of our discussions they kept getting in our way and, since we were unable to give them adequate treatment, we deliberately evaded them.

The functional interrelatedness of psychological processes is, of course, embedded in the biological interrelatedness and interdependence of the parts of the organism. We had one account of this in Sherrington's early authoritative treatment of the integrative function of the nervous system, of the way excitations and inhibitions are regulated under brain dominance. Biologists since his time—for example, Herrick and Child— carried the account further with emphasis on organismic principles. In the excellent theory of *homeostasis* presented by Cannon, based on the rich factual data he and his students discovered, we see an impressive picture of functional interrelatedness, with the potent role of humoral factors coming to the foreground. The more recent thoroughgoing organismic (holistic) approach of Goldstein leads us to the realization that no item of reaction (no matter how simple and elementary it may seem at first sight) is really discrete in the living organism, and that a seemingly simple reaction has a biologically adaptive significance which can be accounted for when studied in relation to the whole organism. Even the "patellar reflex," which is carried out primarily on the (involuntary) spinal level, is affected by what is going on in the other parts of the organism. "It varies, depending, among other things, on the position of the limb, on the behavior of the rest of the organism, and on whether or not attention is paid to it." [60]

Carrying the idea to a rather more complex psychological level, we know that the material we learn and memorize is affected by other things we learn and memorize, as seen in numerous studies dealing with transfer and interference effects. It is not only a question of the passage of time; the effect varies also with the nature of the material, with its similarity or dissimilarity to other material, etc. The brilliant work of Luria and others in detecting guilt or innocence was possible because of the underlying functional interrelatedness of various processes, even though interrelatedness in this case was through conflict. Because of this interrelatedness of the whole psychological make-up of the individual, considerable prediction of the whole person is possible through his perceptual reactions to the little patches of, in themselves meaningless, stimuli (ink blots, etc.) currently used widely in various projective techniques. (The reactions to these ambiguous stimuli sometimes reveal the momentary strains and stresses of the individual, rather than his whole person with all its background, but this is not the place to elaborate on this point.)

The functional interrelatedness becomes much more striking when we glance at the ontogenetic development of behavior. In connection with the early stage of development and maturation we cannot even talk of interrelatedness; we have to talk of total integration. The earliest reactions are the total inte-

---

[60] K. Goldstein, *The Organism*, New York: American Book Company, 1939, p. 69.

grated reactions of the whole organism. Development proceeds in the direction of individuation or differentiation of the functions of more specialized and distal organs, as Coghill and others have demonstrated in the case of lower animals. The course of this progressive differentiation becomes clearer when we note the concrete sequence of the integrated control of the specialized organs. In the words of Gesell, who for years studied ontogenetic development at the human level step by step:

> Just as neuromotor organization proceeds from head to foot in the direction of the longitudinal axis, so it tends to proceed from the central to peripheral segments. The fundamental axial muscles are among the first to react in a coordinated manner, as shown by the primitive body flexion of the fetus. There is a progressive advance of motor control from the larger, fundamental muscles to the smaller muscles which execute the more refined movements. This trend from fundamental or proximal to accessory and distal control is illustrated in the ontogenesis of postural attitudes, of prehensory approach, manipulation, and prone locomotion.[61]

M. D. Vernon brought together various studies dealing with progressive perceptual differentiation in children. At a more complicated psychological level with direct and explicit implications for social psychology, Piaget gave a detailed account of various phases of differentiated integration of development, starting with the initially "undifferentiated absolute" of infancy. Koffka, Lewin, and more recently Murphy have given us illuminating accounts of psychological differentiation in the course of development.

Differentiation certainly does not mean insulation of the higher processes either. They are functionally interrelated in various degrees as part processes occurring in the psychological make-up of the organism. Even though different psychological formations in the same individual may proceed seemingly independently of each other at times, sooner or later certain conditions arise under which their interrelatedness asserts itself—perhaps as a conflict. Sunday piety and Monday go-getting and greed cannot be kept apart indefinitely.

As we brought out in our discussion of ego formation and in-

---

[61] Gesell, op. cit., p. 301.

volvements, the identity of the person is not made over each day. There is ordinarily consistency from day to day, especially in the continuity of the central values of the ego. The values and items closely related to those central values likewise reveal corresponding consistency.

This fact came out clearly in a number of studies dealing with various ego-involvements during the last decade (pp. 284–305). The general fact that stands out in all these studies contributed to the solution of the long-standing controversy concerning the problem of generality or specificity of traits. Is the person who is honest or confident in one situation, honest or confident in all situations? Is honesty, for example, specific and changing in different situations? Both sides of the controversy reported results in their favor. The accumulating studies on ego-involvements convincingly point to the fact that confidence, honesty, or any other trait is, on the whole, general or specific depending on its place (centrality or peripherality) in the psychological make-up of the individual, and on whether or not it is drawn upon in a given situation along with a central ego-attitude. The concrete ego-involvement experiments furnished the principle of the synthesis of the whole issue. In Gordon Allport's words, "When there is ego-involvement there are general traits, when there is no ego-involvement there are no general traits." [62]

Thus it seems that with the functional interrelatedness or integration with central ego values the whole person "manifests greater consistency in behavior, reveals not specificity in conduct but generality and congruence." [63] Perhaps it will not be stretching the idea to a breaking point to say that if all the values and items (central and peripheral) that go into the psychological make-up of the individual were positively interrelated to or integrated with the major ego-attitudes, then we would have a harmoniously integrated person at peace with himself and consistent in various situations.

But, as we have seen before, this is not a feat that the individual can achieve by himself (see pp. 296–307)—even though

---

[62] G. W. Allport, The ego in contemporary psychology, *Psychol. Rev.*, 1943, 50, 461.
[63] *Ibid.*, p. 472.

some exceptional persons come close to achieving it, at the cost of putting themselves at great odds with their environment. For major ego values are necessarily derived from the reference groups to which the individual is related in so many capacities. The identity of our person consists of our being a member of an ethnic group, a social class, a church, a profession, a family, a club, etc. If the values derived from these groups conflict among themselves, we will be in conflict within our own ego and in the situations we face in actual life.

Being among the major components of one's ego, these values are functionally related to each other or become so as situations arise. But functional relatedness and integration are not one and the same thing. The functional interrelatedness becomes the cause of conflicts in the person when the component values contradict each other. There are many studies that give concrete instances of conflicts within the individual which result from conflicts in his various roles (as a member of a family, a profession, an ethnic group, ideology, etc.), and from conflicts over aspirations prompted by his various contradictory ego-attitudes. Particularly in the studies dealing with social marginality, adolescence in societies in transition, professional standing vs. feminine role, dilemmas created by contradictory statuses, the relation of the convert to a new religion or ideology and his past identity, with all that goes with it—in all these, there are conflicts between various ego components. All of them go to show that there are conflicts exclusively on the ego level as well as conflicts due to ego ("super-ego") and id polarity. Perhaps in more stable times and more stable societies the conflicts might have been chiefly restricted to the ego-id polarity.

With such considerations in mind we have been careful throughout not to use such terms as ego integration and ego structure. To be sure, various values that help to bring about the formation of the ego are functionally related, or become related as situations arise. But in numerous cases, this functional relatedness acts to produce conflict rather than integration. This is why we were not able to use functional relatedness and integration as interchangeable concepts. There are contradictory social cleavages and differentiations in modern life. The contradictory cleavages and differentiations are reflected in the conflicts taking place in the ego of the individual, which is formed on the basis of his different group memberships and roles. Various aspects of these conflicting states of the ego-attitudes of modern man, which tear him to pieces within himself, are well reflected in numerous sociological, psychological, and artistic works of our times.[64]

---

[64] For representative examples, see R. S. and H. M. Lynd, *Middletown in Transition*, New York: Harcourt, Brace, 1937; R. S. Lynd, *Knowledge For What? The Place of Social Science in American Culture*, Princeton: Princeton Univ. Press, 1939; E. V. Stonequist, *The Marginal Man*, New York: Scribner, 1937; E. C. Hughes, *Amer. J. Sociol.*, 1945, 50, 353–359; E. Fromm, *Escape from Freedom*, New York: Rinehart, 1941; K. Horney, *The Neurotic Personality of Our Time*, New York: Norton, 1937; R. E. Sherwood, *The Petrified Forest*, New York: Scribner, 1935; J. T. Farrell, *Studs Lonigan*, New York: Vanguard, 1935; J. Steinbeck, *The Wayward Bus*, New York: Viking, 1947.

Name Index

Adams, H. F., 163
Adams, S., 198
Adams, Samuel, 419
Adler, A., 20
Adrian, E. D., 218
Allen, E., 65
Allport, F. H., 6, 98, 204 f., 346
Allport, G. W., 223, 287, 359, 464
Alper, T., 287 ff.
Ambedkar, B., 351
Anastasi, A., 446, 460
Anderson, H. H., 300
Asch, S. E., 235 f., 240, 296, 429

Baldwin, B. T., 322
Barker, R. G., 116, 330, 438, 453
Bartlett, F. C., 45, 66, 187, 211, 223
Bayley, N., 322, 436
Bayton, J. A., 346
Bean, C. H., 198 f.
Beard, C. A., 416 f., 419
Beard, M. R., 416 f., 419
Beaumont, H., 54
Beaver, A. P., 259
Beck, S. J., 86 f.
Beebe-Center, J., 224
Beethoven, 848, 153, 154
Bender, J. F., 284
Benoit-Smullyan, E., 298 f.
Berne, E. V. C., 259 f.
Bettelheim, B., 403
Binet, A., 219
Bleuler, M., 226
Bleuler, R., 226
Block, H., 235, 240, 429
Blodgett, H. C., 62
Blos, P., 323, 330 f., 333
Bodin, J., 344
Bogardus, E. S., 339, 346
Bolles, M., 264
Bolton, E. B., 238
Boran, B., 375
Boring, E. G., 216

Bornemann, E., 244
Bovard, E. W., Jr., 440 f.
Bowman, P. H., 76, 79 f., 211, 411
Braly, K., 346 f., 355
Brandt, H. F., 300
Brian, C. R., 54
Bridges, K. M. B., 259
Brozek, J., 75 ff.
Bruner, J. S., 39, 66, 73 f., 227
Brunner, E. de S., 397, 399

Cameron, W. J., 333 f.
Campbell, H. M., 334
Cannon, W. B., 30, 44, 430, 461
Cantril, H., 159, 223, 254, 270
Carmichael, L., 197, 433, 434
Carroll, J. B., 198
Cartwright, D., 244 f.
Chaffey, J., 326 f., 331 f.
Chaplin, C., 110 f.
Chapman, D. W., 216, 224, 300 ff.
Chapman, R., 406
Chein, I., 39, 45, 69
Child, C. M., 461
Clark, K. B., 211, 260 f., 287, 353 f., 359
Clark, M. K., 260 f., 353 f., 359
Clemmer, D., 180 f.
Coghill, G. E., 463
Cohen, N. E., 224
Conant, J. B., 184, 191
Considine, R., 87, 179
Cottrell, L. S., Jr., 6
Cowles, J. T., 190
Crawford, M. P., 26

Dalton, M., 304
Darwin, C., 5, 19, 254 f., 428 f.
Davis, A., 437 f.
Davis, C. M., 59
Davis, J., 271
Davis, K., 320, 327
Dembo, T., 303, 438, 453
Dennis, W., 434

467

Subject Index